The Logic of Intersubjectivity

The Logic of Intersubjectivity

Brian McLaren's Philosophy of Christian Religion

DARREN M. SLADE

Foreword by Brian D. McLaren

WIPF & STOCK · Eugene, Oregon

THE LOGIC OF INTERSUBJECTIVITY
Brian McLaren's Philosophy of Christian Religion

Copyright © 2020 Darren M. Slade. All rights reserved. Except for brief quotations in critical publications or reviews, no part of this book may be reproduced in any manner without prior written permission from the publisher. Write: Permissions, Wipf and Stock Publishers, 199 W. 8th Ave., Suite 3, Eugene, OR 97401.

Wipf & Stock
An Imprint of Wipf and Stock Publishers
199 W. 8th Ave., Suite 3
Eugene, OR 97401

www.wipfandstock.com

PAPERBACK ISBN: 978-1-7252-6886-9
HARDCOVER ISBN: 978-1-7252-6884-5
EBOOK ISBN: 978-1-7252-6885-2

Manufactured in the U.S.A.   08/26/20

To my beautiful and brilliant daughter, Inara.

Nullis umquam verbis exprimi potest quantas gratias vobis propter auxilium vestrum in hoc somnio veridico facto debeam. Dilectione igitur obrutus sum erga vos ambas atque amore. Vos igitur mihi estis mundus et motus, fortitudo et spiritus.

Thank you to Brian McLaren for agreeing to review the final product and offer suggestions to ensure this study's accuracy.

Contents

Foreword by Brian D. McLaren   xi

Abbreviations   xv

1   Introduction   1
    1.0 Thesis   1
    1.1 Introductory Notes   3
    1.2 Purpose and Need of Study   3
    1.3 Definitions and Terms   13
    1.4 Problem Statement   14
    1.5 Locating Self as a Researcher   19
    1.6 Research Methodology   20
    1.7 Summary   23

2   McLaren the Man   26
    2.0 Introduction   26
    2.1 Experiential Knowledge and Belief Formation   27
    2.2 McLaren's Religious Odyssey   28
    2.3 McLaren's Resulting Temperament   37
    2.4 Conclusion   40

3   McLaren the Activist   41
    3.0 Introduction   41
    3.1 "Conflicted Religious Identity Syndrome" (CRIS)   42
    3.2 Americanized Culture-Religion   43
    3.3 Imperialized Suicide Machine   58
    3.4 McLaren's Resulting Disillusionment   63
    3.5 Conclusion   68

4   McLaren the Iconoclast   71
    4.0 Introduction   71
    4.1 Intransigent Neoconservatism   71

	4.2 Forestalling the Epochal Shift	73
	4.3 Modernization Effects on Christianity	84
	4.4 Postmodern Ethos for Christian Faith	89
	4.5 Conclusion	93
5	McLaren and Abduction	94
	5.0 Introduction	94
	5.1 Obligatory Self-Correction	95
	5.2 Abductive Logic	97
	5.3 McLaren's Postformal Abduction	100
	5.4 McLaren's Abductive Provocations	106
	5.5 Conclusion	112
6	McLaren and Christology	114
	6.0 Introduction	114
	6.1 McLaren's Christotelic *Prolegomenon*	114
	6.2 Christotelic Implications	125
	6.3 McLaren and *Star Trek* Eschatology	138
	6.4 Conclusion	140
7	McLaren's Deconstructive Rationale	141
	7.0 Introduction	141
	7.1 Deconstructing Institutional Christianity	141
	7.2 Deconstructing the Historical Jesus	148
	7.3 Scripture as Literary Art	152
	7.4 The Revolutionary Jesus	160
	7.5 Deconstructing the Cross	169
	7.6 Conclusion	173
8	McLaren's Existential Intersubjectivity	175
	8.0 Introduction	175
	8.1 Post-Ontotheology	176
	8.2 Existential Intersubjectivity	178
	8.3 Distinguishing Epistemologies	186
	8.4 Postcolonial Alterity	195
	8.5 Evaluative Criteria	205
	8.6 Conclusion	218
9	Conclusion	220
	9.0 Summary	220
	9.1 McLaren and *Semper Reformanda*	222
Appendix A: Extended Literature Review		225
Bibliography		235

Foreword

In 1980, I was an idealistic young graduate student studying philosophical literature. I had become intrigued with the interplay of literature, philosophy, and theology, especially in twentieth century writers like Franz Kafka, Jean-Paul Sartre, and Walker Percy.

I wrote a Masters thesis on Percy, Southern gentleman and author of novels like *The Moviegoer, The Last Gentleman, The Second Coming*, and *Love in the Ruins*, along with the seminal essay collection, *The Message in the Bottle*.

My thesis director, Dr. Lewis A. Lawson, was Percy's literary confidant, and he was kind enough to forward questions of mine to Dr. Percy and arrange a personal meeting. When I completed my research, Dr. Lawson sent my completed thesis to the novelist. To my surprise, Dr. Percy replied with a handwritten letter. He complimented my writing style, expressed hopes that I would continue writing ("rotten a profession though it may be"), and said it was the best thesis, masters or doctoral, that he had read on his work. He added six words that meant a great deal to me: "I don't recall your being wrong."

Although the ink has faded to near illegibility, that letter, now framed, is among my most prized possessions today, almost forty years later.

I now find myself writing a similar response to Darren M. Slade's new book on my body of work. As Dr. Percy did for me, I want to commend Darren for his writing style and urge him to forge ahead in the difficult professions of original research and writing in the zones of religion, philosophy, and culture.

I had the privilege of meeting and being interviewed by Darren during his research process, and he sent a few inquiries by email at various points along the way as well. He impressed me on many levels: the sincere curiosity behind his questions, the lack of a predetermined set of conclusions, the clarity of his writing, and the connection between his research and his own spiritual and intellectual growth. I gladly granted him permission to use these conversations and any other relevant material of mine in this book.

Darren decided to examine my work from the standpoint of philosophy of religion, and to that end, he examined my formally published work along with supplemental writings, sermons, lectures, interviews, blog posts, and more. He considered my thought in relation to both my biography and my literary and theological influences. Through the course of our conversations, he frequently asked me to alert him if I felt he had been factually inaccurate or unfair in any way.

I don't recall his being wrong.

Not only that, but I learned a lot about myself from Darren's book. I was surprised, for example, how early I expressed some ideas that I didn't think I articulated until much later. Even some of my most "radical" thoughts, it turns out, had actually been present from the beginning.

This insight has helped me better understand one of the ways religious communities, like other social groupings, resist change and suppress dissent. By putting older gatekeepers in charge as guardians of the tradition, certifying their power to marginalize and silence younger voices, communities teach younger voices to fear, to play it safe, and to distrust their own experience, discomfort, questions, and insight. As a result, by the time younger voices gain the courage to speak and the credibility to be listened to, they often have been domesticated, suppressing, rejecting, or forgetting much if not all of their own unique insight. If the Psalmist prayed, "Remember not the sins of my youth," religious communities often teach their adherents to pray, "Help me not remember the questions and insights of my youth." The social and spiritual architecture of religious communities is, in this way, perfectly designed to keep the old men in power and the young (both men and women) in compliance.

Reading this book helped me realize afresh how easily that could have happened to me, and it leaves me with a fresh sense of gratitude that, to some degree at least, it didn't.

I take pleasure in hoping that the current generation of young thinkers will find encouragement in Darren's book to respect the value of tradition while also respecting their own emerging instincts as the newest members of that tradition.

That pleasure is all the more intense knowing that Darren's religious background was similar to my own. The fact that a young scholar like Darren could undertake the research that led to this book while he was a graduate student at a fundamentalist university speaks to the foment of this moment in the Christian community.

When I wrote my thesis on Walker Percy back in my twenties, it was not simply an academic exercise for me. It was also personal, as I was grappling with whether and how a young man raised fundamentalist could hold on to Christian faith in a culture tipping from a modern into a postmodern paradigm. Percy's example of what might be called Christian existentialism provided me resources for a way forward, out of the framework of fundamentalism but not out of a framework of faith, meaning, and purpose.

FOREWORD

Similarly, I think you'll have the sense as you read this book that Darren's research was personal as well as academic, just as your reading of this book likely is.

Over these forty years, the dangers of fundamentalism have become more and more apparent across religious traditions. Readers of Darren's generation can't help but see how the world's largest religion, which is currently experiencing a global fundamentalist resurgence, can easily become either one the most destructive forces in the world, or one of the most creative and regenerative. Left to the powerful men of the older generation (and their loyalist sons), it almost certainly will become the former.

That's what makes voices like Darren's so important.

Every reader who engages with Darren's book wakes up each day in a world of acute challenges, from catastrophic climate change to a resurgence of vicious white supremacy and kleptocratic demagoguery, from obscene economic inequality to appalling religious corruption, from the proliferation of weapons (courtesy of the military industrial complex) to the proliferation of propaganda (courtesy of the corporate media complex).

In this world, the "old time religion" with its old-time version of good news makes less and less sense, especially in those religious sectors that have failed to face and learn from their history of complicity with slavery, colonialism, environmental plunder, greed, oppression, and corruption.

It is increasingly hard to deny that the old-time religion and theology in which both Dr. Slade and I were raised greased our civilizational slide into this existential predicament. I shudder to think that its worst days and deeds may still be in the future.

Some of us dare to hope that a creative new theological vision could help us find a path through and out of the mess we're in, especially with the help of a new generation of clear-thinking scholars and insightful writers like Darren Slade.

It is to them that I especially commend this book, along with a call (echoing Bob Dylan) to stay "forever young."

BRIAN D. MCLAREN
Marco Island, FL

Abbreviations

AIFA	Sweet, Leonard, Brian D. McLaren, and Jerry Haselmayer. *A is for Abductive: The Language of the Emerging Church*. Grand Rapids, MI: Zondervan, 2003.
AMP	McLaren, Brian D., and Tony Campolo. *Adventures in Missing the Point: How the Culture-Controlled Church Neutered the Gospel*. Pbk. ed. Grand Rapids, MI: Zondervan, 2003.
BMF	Burson, Scott R. *Brian McLaren in Focus: A New Kind of Apologetics*. Abilene, TX: Abilene Christian University Press, 2016.
CIEC	McLaren, Brian D. "The Method, the Message, and the Ongoing Story." In *The Church in Emerging Culture: Five Perspectives*, edited by Leonard Sweet, 191-230. Grand Rapids, MI: emergentYS Books, 2003.
COOS[1]	McLaren, Brian D. *The Church on the Other Side: Doing Ministry in the Postmodern Matrix*. Rev. ed. Grand Rapids, MI: Zondervan, 2000.
COOS[2]	McLaren, Brian D. *The Church on the Other Side: Exploring the Radical Future of the Local Congregation*. Rev. ed. Grand Rapids, MI: Zondervan, 2006.
CPA	McLaren, Brian D. "The Cross as Prophetic Action." In *Proclaiming the Scandal of the Cross: Contemporary Images of the Atonement*, edited by Mark D. Baker, 110-21. Grand Rapids, MI: Baker Academic, 2006.
CSS	McLaren, Brian D., and Gareth Higgins. *Cory and the Seventh Story*. N.p.: 2018.
CT	McLaren, Brian D. "Presence Means Everything." In *Cancer and Theology*, edited by Jake Bouma and Erik Ullestad, 19-22. Des Moines, IA: Elbow Co., 2013.

Abbreviations

EMC	McLaren, Brian D. *Everything Must Change: Jesus, Global Crises, and a Revolution of Hope*. Nashville, TN: Thomas Nelson, 2007.
FFR	McLaren, Brian D. *Finding Faith: A Search for What Is Real*. Grand Rapids, MI: Zondervan, 2007.
FFS	McLaren, Brian D. *Finding Faith: A Search for What Makes Sense*. Grand Rapids, MI: Zondervan, 2007.
FOWA	McLaren, Brian D. *Finding Our Way Again: The Return of the Ancient Practices*. The Ancient Practices Series. Nashville, TN: Thomas Nelson, 2008.
GDT	McLaren, Brian D. *The Girl with the Dove Tattoo*. Brentwood, TN: Creative Trust Digital, 2012. Kindle.
GI	McLaren, Brian D. *The Galápagos Islands: A Spiritual Journey*. Minneapolis, MN: Fortress Press, 2019.
GO	McLaren, Brian D. *A Generous Orthodoxy*. Grand Rapids, MI: Youth Specialties, 2004.
GSM	McLaren, Brian D. *The Great Spiritual Migration: How the World's Largest Religion Is Seeking a Better Way to Be Christian*. New York: Convergent Books, 2016.
JMBM	McLaren, Brian D. *Why Did Jesus, Moses, the Buddha, and Mohammed Cross the Road? Christian Identity in a Multi-Faith World*. Pbk. ed. New York: Jericho Books, 2012.
JP	McLaren, Brian D., Elisa Padilla, and Ashley Bunting Seeber, eds. *The Justice Project*. Grand Rapids, MI: Baker Books, 2009.
LWWAT	McLaren, Brian D. *The Last Word and the Word After That: A Tale of Faith, Doubt, and a New Kind of Christianity*. Book 3. San Francisco, CA: Jossey-Bass, 2005.
MRTYR	McLaren, Brian D. *More Ready Than You Realize: Evangelism as Dance in the Postmodern Matrix*. Grand Rapids, MI: Zondervan, 2002.
NKOC	McLaren, Brian D. *A New Kind of Christian: A Tale of Two Friends on a Spiritual Journey*. Pbk. ed. Book 1. San Francisco, CA: Jossey-Bass, 2001.
NKOCY	McLaren, Brian D. *A New Kind of Christianity: Ten Questions That Are Transforming the Faith*. Pbk. ed. New York: HarperCollins, 2011.
NS	McLaren, Brian D. *Naked Spirituality: A Life with God in 12 Simple Words*. New York: HarperOne, 2011.
PTP	McLaren, Brian D. "Preaching to Postmoderns." In *Preaching with Power: Dynamic Insights from Twenty Top Communicators*, edited by Michael Duduit, 115-30. Grand Rapids, MI: Baker Books, 2006.

RYC	McLaren, Brian D. *Reinventing Your Church*. Softcover ed. Grand Rapids, MI: ZondervanPublishingHouse, 1998.
SA	McLaren, Brian D. *Seeking Aliveness: Daily Reflections on a New Way to Experience and Practice the Christian Faith*. New York: Faith Words, 2017.
SMJ	McLaren, Brian D. *The Secret Message of Jesus: Uncovering the Truth that Could Change Everything*. Nashville, TN: Thomas Nelson, 2006.
SWFOI	McLaren, Brian D. *The Story We Find Ourselves In: Further Adventures of a New Kind of Christian*. Pbk. ed. Book 2. San Francisco, CA: Jossey-Bass, 2003.
TSS	McLaren, Brian D., and Gareth Higgins. *The Seventh Story: Us, Them, and the End of Violence*. N.p.: 2018.
TWLD	McLaren, Brian D. *The Word of the Lord to Democrats*. Brentwood, TN: Creative Trust Digital, 2012. Kindle.
TWLE	McLaren, Brian D. *The Word of the Lord to Evangelicals*. Brentwood, TN: Creative Trust Digital, 2012. Kindle.
TWLR	McLaren, Brian D. *The Word of the Lord to Republicans: A Tale for an Election Year*. Brentwood, TN: Creative Trust Digital, 2012. Kindle.
VA	McLaren, Brian D. *(The Voice of Acts) The Dust Off Their Feet: Lessons from the First Church*. The Voice: A Scripture Project to Rediscover the Story of the Bible. Nashville, TN: Thomas Nelson, 2006.
VL	McLaren, Brian D. *The Voice of Luke: Not Even Sandals*. The Voice: A Scripture Project to Rediscover the Story of the Bible. Nashville, TN: Thomas Nelson, 2007.
WMRBW	McLaren, Brian D. *We Make the Road by Walking: A Year-Long Quest for Spiritual Formation, Reorientation, and Activation*. New York: Jericho Books, 2014.
WP	McLaren, Brian D. "Walker Percy: The Point of View for His Work as an Author." Master's thesis, University of Maryland, 1980.

1

Introduction

1.0 THESIS

To survey harsh criticisms against Brian Douglas McLaren (1956–), readers gain the inaccurate impression that he is a heretical relativist who denies objective truth and logic.[1] While McLaren's inflammatory and provocative writing style is partly to blame, this study also suspects that his critics base much of their analyses on only small portions of his overall corpus. The result becomes a caricature of McLaren's actual philosophy of religion. The thesis of this book is simple: McLaren is, in fact, a rationalist and empiricist, who utilizes irony, humor, generalization, and ridicule to disturb those expressions of faith common to mainstream, Western institutional Christianity (i.e., "conventional Christian paradigms"). The difference is that McLaren is an *abductive* rationalist and a *phenomenological* empiricist, who objects to the Enlightenment's over emphasis on analytical rationalism because it overlooks ethereal elements such as intuition, mysticism, and personal experience. This "analytic" approach to religion has since created "notional" Christians who focus almost entirely on cerebral and abstract elements of faith while ignoring its real-world impact on daily living (cf. *GO* §13, 205; *SMJ* §4, 34). This study will show that what appear to be the musings of an unlearned and unnuanced writer are actually the tactics of a skilled rhetorician trying to expose

---

1. See for example, Johnson, "You Can't Handle the Truth," 219-45; Dixon, "Whatever Happened to Heresy?," 219; Blount, "A New Kind of Interpretation," 125; and the accusations of Albert Mohler, D.A. Carson, John Frame, and Michael Wittmer referenced in Burson, "Apologetics and the New Kind of Christian," 151.

the limitations (and even impropriety) of an overly analytic approach to faith. Indeed, McLaren's goal is to establish a robust paradigm through which believers can acquire more than just knowledge; they can live in solidarity with creation and Creator, as well. There will be three main divisions to support this thesis.

1.0.1 Outline of the Study

In the first division, this study will catalog several socio-historical influences that were vital to McLaren's philosophical development. For example, chapter 2 will detail different biographical experiences, chapter 3 will describe his moral identity crisis, and chapter 4 will trace his intellectual disillusionment with conventional Christianity. The second division will then explain McLaren's abductive reasoning processes (chapter 5), which he uses to expound upon the implications of the incarnation (chapter 6). Finally, the third division will explore the consequences of his logic: chapter 7 clarifies his deconstruction of conventional paradigms while chapter 8 systematizes his philosophy of religion.

In more detail, chapter 2 ("McLaren the Man") will reveal how McLaren's experiences with Christian fundamentalism encouraged him to pursue a new spiritual paradigm. Likewise, chapter 3 ("McLaren the Activist") will contend that his philosophy of religion is intricately tied to his observations of the Religious Right and dogmatic neoconservatism, which he believes turned Christianity into a tribalistic culture-religion. Chapter 4 ("McLaren the Iconoclast") will address his intellectual denial of Enlightenment-based paradigms that have caused both liberal and conservative Christians to become intransigent devotees to a bygone era. From these different socio-historical developments, McLaren subsequently established an idiosyncratic line of reasoning with which to approach Christian faith. Chapter 5 ("McLaren and Abduction") will argue that he employs logical inference-building to emphasize the pragmatic and aesthetic aspects of religiosity. Significantly, however, McLaren often masks his abductive reasoning through deliberate provocations and satirical writings. Chapter 6 ("McLaren and Christology") will then expose how he applies his abductive logic to the incarnation of Christ, suggesting that McLaren is distinctively attracted to Jesus as the paradoxical Divine Revealer. The result is a stress on divine mystery and the impression that Christianity is a faith-based, suprarational belief in God's loving solidarity with the universe.

Having concluded that conventional paradigms are ineffective at discipleship (chapters 2–4) and having, subsequently, inferred certain beliefs about the incarnation (chapters 5–6), McLaren formed a unique philosophy of religion that he believes can help alleviate many of the problems associated with Western spirituality. Chapter 7 ("McLaren's Deconstructive Rationale") will trace his exploration into the legitimacy of institutional Christianity and the church's articulation of Jesus' gospel message. He concludes that Neoplatonism and imperialism usurped Jesus' Jewish manifesto about God's kingdom, which has since caused Christians to misinterpret the essence of Christ's message. Chapter 8 ("McLaren's Existential Intersubjectivity") will demonstrate how McLaren seeks to overcome this foreign Greco-Roman framework, surmising that Christ's incarnation demands an existentially intersubjective relationship with (and obedience to) Jesus' kingdom ethics. Before discussing the significance of McLaren's religio-philosophy, however, a prefatory word is needed about referencing his many publications in this book.

1.1 INTRODUCTORY NOTES

Due to the large number of McLaren's writings, it has become standard practice to reference his book publications using parenthetical citations.[2] His less formal work (e.g., magazine articles, interviews, blog posts, YouTube videos, etc.) will appear in footnotes primarily because there is no standardization for referencing this material. However, researchers will quickly discover that some of McLaren's books have different page numbers depending on their edition and format (e.g., paperback or hardback). Thus, the page numbers cited in this study are solely those of the book editions listed in the abbreviations section. To help researchers locate material in their version of McLaren's work, this study will also include (where necessary) a section number (§) immediately following the book's abbreviation. For example, *EMC* §6, 45 references *Everything Must Change*, chapter 6, page forty-five.[3] This information will become useful as readers explore the purpose for studying McLaren's philosophy of religion.

1.2 PURPOSE AND NEED OF STUDY

Rudolph Bultmann once quoted Karl Barth as saying, "There is always the possibility that in one sense or another we may be in particular need of wholly unexpected voices, and that among them there may be voices which are at first entirely unwelcome."[4] By the late twentieth century, many Christians from diverse backgrounds began to recognize the need for a new approach to Christianity, one that accentuates human solidarity and interreligious collaboration. Carol Merritt remarks, "Writers like Brian McLaren put [this] longing into words."[5] Described as a "paradigm shifter" with a "kinder and gentler brand of religion," *Time* magazine included McLaren in its top

---

2. The abbreviations section for this book is an expansion and revision of those found in Burson, *Brian McLaren in Focus*, 9 and Reed, "Emerging Treason?," 66–85. Where needed, these modifications are meant to reflect a more precise, updated, and enumerated catalogue of McLaren's publications.

3. This citation practice should not be confused with this study's internal references to other sections of the book, such as the listing §7.4.1.2, which designates a particular subheading in chapter 7.

4. Quoted in Bultmann, "Introduction," ix.

5. Merritt, "The Church's New Foundation," 45.

twenty-five "most influential evangelicals in America."[6] To this day, he is considered the most controversial and influential representative of Emergence Christianity, particularly since "a whole sector of professing evangelicals gives considerable weight to his opinions."[7] According to D. A. Carson, McLaren is "probably the most articulate speaker in the emerging movement," further noting, "Most emergent leaders regard [him] as their preeminent thinker and writer."[8] Not surprisingly, then, McLaren has become the symbolic pastor for newer generations of believers and spiritual seekers.[9] The problem is that McLaren's line of reasoning and philosophical rationale are not apparent to much of his readership.

For example, Scot McKnight once commented, "I want to voice the frustration of many: McLaren's willingness to muddy the waters . . . goes only so far. Many of us would like to see greater clarity on a variety of questions he raises."[10] This book argues that there exists, in fact, a discernable logic behind McLaren's belief system, which spans the entirety of his writing career, albeit in an unstructured and veiled way. Nevertheless, his obscure writing style makes discerning this rationale difficult and, thus, is partly to blame for people's vexation. Therefore, since no resource systematizes McLaren's philosophy of religion, as expressed across his numerous publications, the purpose of this book is to arrange his line of reasoning into a coherent whole. The study's objective is to make McLaren's reasoning plain in order to help future readers decipher his veiled rationale. This book offers the first exhaustive examination of McLaren's entire writing career to date, which he himself has personally read, reviewed, and ratified prior to publication (see the foreword to this book). Here, the goal is to understand and articulate how McLaren perceives the current shifts within conventional Christianity.

---

6. Van Biema et al., "The 25 Most Influential Evangelicals in America," 34-45. In response to the *Time* magazine article, McLaren explained to Larry King Live, "I probably represent a lot of people who are not terribly comfortable with the direction that a lot of Christian discourse in relation to politics has been going in recent years" (McLaren, "America's Most Influential Evangelicals").

7. Burk, "Why Evangelicals Should Ignore Brian McLaren," 212. See also, MacArthur, "Perspicuity of Scripture," 143-44; King, "Emerging Issues for the Emerging Church," 34; and Sinitiere, "Embracing the Early Church," 27.

8. Carson, *Becoming Conversant with the Emerging Church*, 28, 157. See also, Mayhue, "The Emerging Church," 191.

9. Webber, *The Younger Evangelicals*, 92; Crouch, "The Emergent Mystique," 38; Taylor, "An Introduction to Postconservative Evangelicalism," 22-24.

10. McKnight, "McLaren Emerging," 62. R. Scott Smith concurs, "I also would love to see McLaren discuss the philosophical views that inform his own views. I think he owes his readers a candid discussion of them, as well as an assessment of where they might lead for the faith" (Smith, "Some Suggestions for Brian McLaren," 85). These annoyances are also echoed by Reed, "Emerging Treason?," 76-77 and, ironically, McLaren himself in McLaren, foreword to *The Holy No*, ix-x.

1.2.1 Christian Paradigm Shifts

Historical Jesus scholar, Dale Allison, writes, "It has been said that science progresses one funeral at a time, that a new theory does not always triumph by convincing its opponents but because the opponents die and a new generation, uncommitted to the past, comes along."[11] In 1962, theoretical physicist Thomas Kuhn published his groundbreaking research on the kinds of paradigms that supersede older scientific models. However, Kuhn observed that specialists tend to react negatively to newer models by dogmatically defending conventional wisdom. Rather than view science as the amassing of new data, Kuhn argued that theoretical advancements ("paradigm shifts") occur only after arousing conflict within the prevailing establishment.[12] Kuhn's work is, thus, representative of the shift presently occurring in Western Christianity and the religious establishment's reaction to emerging voices, such as Brian McLaren. According to Phyllis Tickle, these kinds of shifts in Christian faith occur about every 500 years.[13]

Part of the shift presently happening today is the realization that Christendom's control over Western culture has come to an end.[14] In fact, Ken Howard's demographic research on Christian growth trends reveals that institutional Christianity is in a state of total destabilization, having become more proficient at internal discord than actual discipleship (cf. *AIFA*, 21; *NKOCY* §1, 10).[15] With evangelicalism in particular, younger believers are either abandoning church entirely or are seeking to reform its expression of faith from within.[16] McLaren notes a pattern with regard to how Christians have historically reacted to these paradigm shifts. First, believers resist and denounce the changes, then they make small concessions before retreating into silence, and finally they eventually assent to the emerging paradigms (*NKOCY* §17, 177–78).

According to Barna Group's 2016 report, 48 percent of Americans are now "post-Christian," meaning they have no lasting involvement with Christianity or they have

---

11. Allison, "Jesus was an Apocalyptic Prophet," 19.

12. Kuhn, *The Structure of Scientific Revolutions*; cf. *NKOCY* §2, 14-19; *SWFOI* §31, 229-30.

13. See Tickle, *The Great Emergence*, esp. 13-40. For McLaren, these negative reactions are reminiscent of the Catholic Church's rejection of Nicolaus Copernicus (1473–1543) or Protestantism's resistance against the abolition movement. For him, Christians are still following their predecessors by staunchly defending outdated paradigms (*FOWA* §14, 133).

14. Smith, "The Work of the Holy Spirit," 20-31. See also, Jenkins, *The Next Christendom*, esp. 79-105 and McLaren, "Brian McLaren on How to Build the NSP," 67-68.

15. Howard, "The Religion Singularity," 77-93. McLaren appears to recognize this same trend, "The existence of thousands of denominations today is in part the fruit of this Protestant dividing frenzy" (*GO* §7, 125). See also, Smith, *Christian America?*, 88 and McLaren, "Interview: Brian McLaren on Anglicans."

16. Brow, "Evangelical Megashift," 12-14; Neff, "Has God Been Held Hostage by Philosophy?," 30-34; Streett, "An Interview with Brian McLaren," 10; Tomlinson, *The Post Evangelical*, 69-84; Stewart, *In Search of Ancient Roots*, 12-13.

abandoned faith altogether.[17] Gallup research from 2017 reveals that nearly three-in-four Americans believe religion is losing its influence. Likewise, almost half of Americans are not members of a church, the majority of people rarely attend services, roughly two-in-five Americans do not believe religion can help solve today's problems, and one-in-five have no religious affiliation whatsoever. In 2018, three-in-five Americans have little to no confidence in Christianity, and 43 percent of Americans are dissatisfied with how religion has affected the culture.[18] In total, there exists a growing disdain for how conventional paradigms have conditioned believers to behave in society (cf. *BMF*, 293; *SWFOI* §34, 258–59).[19] McLaren observes that despite the growth of church plants, religious entertainment, and religious publications, Christianity is still losing its cultural influence. For him, the answer is not more churches: the answer is adapting to the church's natural evolution through different stages of faith.[20]

1.2.1.1 *Stages of Faith*

In essence, Western Christianity has experienced what James Fowler labels the six "stages of faith," only on a wider social scale. In the first stage ("intuitive-projective faith"), believers view their religion in magical terms and use it to explain life's mysteries. In stage two ("mythic-literal faith"), people uncritically accept folklore as literal truths. With stage three ("synthetic-conventional faith"), believers focus on what feels right and comfortable over what is intellectually sound. In the fourth stage ("individual-reflective faith"), believers question conventional paradigms, relying on their own experiences to develop a personalized belief system. Stage five ("conjunctive faith") is a synthesis of affective and rational elements where people simply accept the existence of divine mystery. Finally, the sixth stage ("universalizing faith") focuses almost exclusively on universal principles of love, justice, and compassion as religion's defining goal.[21] Significantly, McLaren delineates four parallel stages: 1) the "simplicity" phase is dichotomistic and naïve; 2) "complexity" then focuses on the pursuit for absolute truth; 3) "perplexity" is the disillusionment that results from this pursuit; and 4) "maturity" is accepting epistemic humility and divine mystery (*AMP* §16, 249). For McLaren, Western Christianity's current paradigm shift is the natural growth toward

---

17. *The State of the Church 2016* (Barna Group).

18. *Religion* (Gallup, 2018). Cf. Kohut et al., *Some Social Conservative Disillusionment*, 35. As one 2009 *Newsweek* article explained, the percentage of people who believe religion benefits humanity is at an historic low of just under half the population (Meacham and Gray, "The End of Christian America," 34–38).

19. See Bass, *Christianity After Religion*, esp. 11–99. For McLaren's perspective on this disdain, see McLaren, "Beyond Business-as-Usual Christianity."

20. McLaren, "Brian McLaren on Outreach," 122–23; "Church Emerging," 149.

21. Fowler, *Stages of Faith*, 117–213. As Kathleen Berger explains, "If Fowler is correct, faith, like other aspects of cognition, progresses from a simple, self-centered, one-sided perspective to a more complex, altruistic (unselfish), and many-sided view" (Berger, *The Developing Person*, 531).

a more universalizing religion that seeks to reverse the ossification of earlier stages of faith (cf. *FFR* §9, 172, 183).[22]

1.2.1.2 Reversing Christian Ossification

In his pursuit of a "mature" faith (*NKOCY* §1, 6), McLaren asks several questions: "What kind of God do we believe exists? What kind of life should we live in response? How does our view of God affect the way we see and treat other people?" (*LWWAT* §Intro, xii). For him, what has most atrophied the church is its repeated suppression of paradigm shifts (*FFS* §1, 41–46). For centuries, Bible-appealing Christians had endorsed patently wrong ideas, such as white supremacy, Ptolemaic geocentrism, slavery, and apartheid, which has caused McLaren to question if there are other sacredly-held beliefs that are also false (*GSM*, 41). He reasons that if Christians today can engage in (or tolerate) torture, war, and sexual abuse, then something must be wrong with conventional Christianity (*COOS1* §2, 29). "*A message purporting to be the best news in the world should be doing better than this.* The religion's results are not commensurate with the bold claims it makes. Truly good news . . . would confront systemic injustice, target significant global dysfunctions, and provide hope and resources for making a better world—along with helping individuals experience a full life" (*EMC* §5, 34; italics in original).[23] McLaren's solution is that believers ought to reinvest the church with interpretations that are socially relevant and reflect a more mature understanding of God (cf. *CIEC*, 208–9).

Here, McLaren highlights the evolutionary nature of Christian beliefs over time (*COOS1* §5, 65–71), insisting that the church is, in fact, a complex *organism* of interdependent relationships (*AIFA*, 272–74, 277; *GO* §12, 191–93). Hence, as a "living tradition" (*LWWAT* §15, 93; cf. *NKOC* §4, 49), Christianity ought to appropriate new insights and new moral sensibilities (*GO* §12, 191–92). "To be a living tradition, a living way, [Christianity] must forever open itself forward and forever remain unfinished—even as it forever cherishes and learns from the growing treasury of its past" (*WMRBW*, xii). He clarifies further,

---

22. McLaren details some of this maturation process, "First they lose faith in the 6-day creationist god, then in the bible-dictation god, then in the male-supremacy god, then in the European-supremacy/western-civilization/colonialist god, then in the anti-gay god, then in the pro-war god, then in the American-exceptionalism/manifest-destiny god . . ." (McLaren, "Ask Brian McLaren. . .").

23. McLaren explains further, "Questioning widely held assumptions about God can be a dangerous venture indeed. But if our assumptions aren't sometimes questioned, belief in God becomes less and less plausible" (*WMRBW*, 29). Ron Sider concludes something similar: "Born-again Christians divorce at about the same rate as everyone else. Self-centered materialism is seducing evangelicals and rapidly destroying our earlier, slightly more generous giving. Only 6 percent of born-again Christians tithe. Born-again Christians justify and engage in sexual promiscuity (both premarital sex and adultery) at astonishing rates. Racism and perhaps physical abuse of wives seem to be worse in evangelical circles than elsewhere. This is scandalous behavior for people who claim to be born-again by the Holy Spirit" (Sider, *The Scandal of the Evangelical Conscience*, 27–28).

INTRODUCTION

> An important question today: if the Gospel of Jesus, a Jew, could be radically reinterpreted in the framework of Greek philosophy and Roman politics in the church's first five centuries, is it forever bound . . . to function within those exclusive parameters? Or is it free to enter and engage with new cultures and thought patterns, including our own—learning both positive and negative lessons from its earlier engagements?[24]

As an *organic* body, the church will either mature and grow or it will stagnate and regress (cf. *WMRBW*, xi). Labeling this growth as a "continuing conversion," McLaren concludes that without repeated change, believers will increasingly become arrogant, selfish, inflexible, and fraudulent in their claims to represent Christ (*GSM*, 13). The result is a loss of credibility with younger generations for being impractical and unrelatable (*SWFOI* §34, 258-59). "The point isn't to replace one mandated structure with another, but rather to realize that structures need to be created, adapted, outgrown, replaced, and reinvented as needed" (*AIFA*, 93). Hence, the significance of studying McLaren's philosophy of religion centers on correctly understanding how he wants to "change the framework" through which Christians approach their faith.[25] In so doing, readers can then comprehend and, perhaps, even empathize with how McLaren's new paradigm applies to the current socio-political destabilization of institutional Christianity.

1.2.2 Broader Socio-Political Context

In 2006, almost one-in-four Americans identified as white evangelical; but by 2016, that number dropped to less than one-in-five. Today, the religiously unaffiliated are seven percentage points higher than white evangelicals.[26] According to Gallup, in 1951, only 1 percent of Americans had no religious preference; by 2017, one-in-five Americans now list "none" as their affiliation, and 25 percent say religion is "not very important." However, the vast majority (87 percent) of Americans still believe in God, and the top two reasons why people seldom attend church is because they prefer to worship in private or because they dislike institutional religion.[27] Rather than being

---

24. McLaren, "Q and R: Hints of Kierkegaard."

25. McLaren, "Brian McLaren Reflects on 'Seizing An Alternative' Conference," 01:12-02:00. After all, McLaren asserts, this rethinking of old paradigms is the essence of Jesus' command to "repent" (*WMRBW*, 88).

26. See Jones and Cox, *America's Changing Religious Identity*. As McLaren explains, droves of Christians are leaving the church in order to *improve* their spiritual lives (McLaren, foreword to *The Way of Jesus*, xi).

27. *Religion* (Gallup, 2018). As McLaren comments, "For a variety of reasons, organized religion, including Christianity, seemed to have lost its power to satisfy us in the late old world. It seemed ingrown, tired, petty, crotchety, and out of touch" (*COOS1* §Intro, 14). In fact, McLaren is writing for those "who love God or want to love God or are seeking for a God to love but have been repulsed by ugly, unworthy images of a cruel, capricious, merciless, tyrannical deity" (*LWWAT* §Dedication, vii).

anti-God, the reality is that a sizable portion of the population simply favors the label "spiritual" instead of "religious."[28] Thus, it is no surprise that McLaren describes his audience as "the seeking mind" (*COOS1* §6, 79), who are "*spiritual questioners*" and "*spiritual seekers*" (*AMP* §6, 105; *MRTYR* §4, 48; italics original to both). He writes, "If you're like a lot of people I meet, you might describe yourself as 'more spiritual than religious.' You're seeking meaning and depth in your life . . . but you don't feel that traditional 'organized religion' helps very much" (*NS* §Intro., 1).[29] McLaren's goal is to help people embrace Christ without swearing allegiance to obsolete paradigms. "I'm especially hopeful that [I] will be helpful to people who consider themselves spiritual but not religious, or interested in Jesus but not Christianity" (*SMJ* §Intro, xvii).

Not surprisingly, Christian disillusionment has only been exacerbated because of America's polarized political environment. "We feel as if our founder [Jesus] has been kidnapped and held hostage by extremists. . . .he often comes across as antipoor, antienvironment, antigay, anti-intellectual, anti-immigrant, and antiscience (not to mention protorture, pro-inequality, proviolence, pro-death penalty, and prowar). That's not the Jesus we met in the Gospels!" (*GSM*, 6).[30] Here, McLaren's earlier warnings about right-wing authoritarianism have now manifested in what he labels the "Trumpcult," an uncritical allegiance to President Donald J. Trump, where conservatives now proclaim, "We have no king but Caesar."[31] The question is then raised, How could conservatives, the "moral majority" advocating for "family values" (cf. *COOS1* §11, 147), so easily embrace someone who boastfully flaunts his sexual immorality, misogyny, bigotry, corruption, and cruelty toward others? As Mark Labberton writes,

> The ease with which some on the right could affirm an evangelical faith connected to campaign rhetoric that was racist, sexist, and nationalist was disorienting to an extreme. It left many evangelical people of color gasping in despair and disorientation that so many white brothers and sisters in Christ could vote for someone whose words and actions were so overtly inconsistent with their common faith in Christ.[32]

---

28. See Lipka and Gecewicz, *More Americans Now Say They're Spiritual*; Wright, *Christians Are Hate-Filled Hypocrites*, 43; and Luntz, *What Americans Really Want*, 158.

29. According to McLaren, being "spiritual" is just another way for people to say they are "seeking aliveness" (*WMRBW*, xv). See also, McLaren, "Brian McLaren Rebuilds Spirituality" and his foreword to *The Emerging Church*, 9–10.

30. Jerry Falwell Jr.'s call for Liberty University students to shoot and "end those Muslims" who come on campus is a case in point. McLaren writes to Falwell, "How would you feel if you saw the president, faculty, and students in a radicalized Muslim university somewhere applauding and laughing about killing Christians and 'teaching them a lesson?' Do you see how you are helping your students become the mirror image of such a scene?" (McLaren, "An Open Letter to Jerry Falwell").

31. McLaren, "Q and R: Belief VERSUS Practice."

32. Labberton, "Introduction," 9. This "Trumpcult" becomes evident as one supporter stated during a CNN interview, "If Jesus Christ gets down off the cross and told me Trump is [colluding] with Russia, I would tell him, hold on a second, I need to check with the president if it is true" ("Trump Supporter Admits He Believes Trump"). Jerry Falwell Jr. echoed this sentiment when he declared that

Introduction

The disillusionment continues as McLaren cites Robert Cunningham, whose article on the evangelical "love" for Trump actually reflects their love for wealth and political dominance, fueled by paranoia and American nationalism (*GSM*, 240n16).[33] Regardless of how evangelicals rationalize their initial endorsement of President Trump, the fact that "Trumpism" continues unhindered indicates that many churches are causing irreparable damage to Christian identity.[34] As R. Albert Mohler, president of Southern Baptist Theological Seminary, once remarked,

> I hope every *one* of evangelical Christians in America thinks about what it's going to mean to vote for someone, much less to publicly support someone, that we would not allow our children to be around. . . . Can we put up with someone and can we offer them our vote and support when we know that that person [is] . . . a sexual predator? This is so far over the line that I think we have to recognize we wouldn't want this man as our next-door neighbor, much less as the inhabitant of 1600 Pennsylvania Avenue. And long term, I'm afraid people are going to remember evangelicals in this election for supporting the unsupportable and defending the absolutely indefensible.[35]

Russell Moore, president of the Ethics and Religious Liberty Commission, has also rebuked evangelicals for endorsing what psychiatrists are labeling malignant narcissism:[36]

> To back Mr. Trump, these voters must repudiate everything they believe. . . . His personal morality is clear, not because of tabloid exposés but because of his own boasts. His attitude toward women is that of a Bronze Age warlord. . . .

---

nothing could make him forgo his support for Mr. Trump, claiming it "may be immoral" for evangelicals to refuse offering the same type of support (Heim, "Jerry Falwell Jr. Can't Imagine").

33. See Cunningham, "In Love with Donald Trump." McLaren's fictional character, Old Skunk, captures the fear-based rhetoric of the 2016 Trump Presidential campaign, "When people are worried or afraid . . . you just have to give them somebody different to blame for their problems. If they call somebody else dirty or bad, they will feel clean and good. If they hurt somebody who won't hurt them back, they will feel very powerful, important, and safe. It works every time" (*CSS*, 13; cf. *TSS*, 20).

34. According to Baylor University, "Trumpism" is a type of anti-government nationalism that combines pro-Christian rhetoric with overt xenophobia, misogyny, and a tribalistic fear of diversity. Those upholding Trumpism describe themselves as "very religious," are typically white evangelical, believe the United States is a Christian nation, and believe God is an authoritative and judgmental deity. They believe Muslims are a threat to national security, men should run the government and earn more than women, working women are defective mothers, and the LGBTQ community should not have equal rights. See Froese et al., *American Values*, 7–27.

35. Mohler, "Mohler, Jr. Discusses Evangelical Support for Trump," 00:29–01:21; emphasis in original. Roger Olson parallels these sentiments, "My fellow evangelicals who continue to support and even defend Trump in spite of everything he has said about the weak and vulnerable people of the world: It is time to admit you have been wrong and stop defending the indefensible" (Olson, "An Open Letter").

36. For details on Mr. Trump's mental instability, immoral behavior, corrupt practices, and connection to multiple crime syndicates, see Lee, *The Dangerous Case of Donald Trump*; Woodward, *Fear*; and Brockenbrough, *Unpresidented*.

In the 1990s, some of these social conservatives argued that "If Bill Clinton's wife can't trust him, neither can we." If character matters, character matters. Today's evangelicals should ask, "Whatever happened to our commitment to 'traditional family values'?." . . .Mr. Trump incites division, with slurs against Hispanic immigrants and with protectionist jargon that preys on turning economic insecurity into ugly "us versus them" identity politics. When evangelicals should be leading the way on racial reconciliation . . . are we really ready to trade unity with our black and brown brothers and sisters for this angry politician?[37]

Eventually, even the evangelical magazine, *Christianity Today*, officially announced that President Trump ought to be removed from office out of "loyalty to the Creator of the Ten Commandments." Mark Galli, the editorial's author, explains further, "President Trump has abused his authority for personal gain and betrayed his constitutional oath. . . . None of the president's positives can balance the moral and political danger we face under a leader of such grossly immoral character."[38] *Christianity Today* then offered a sobering warning to evangelicals supporting President Trump:

> Remember who you are and whom you serve. Consider how your justification of Mr. Trump influences your witness to your Lord and Savior. Consider what an unbelieving world will say if you continue to brush off Mr. Trump's immoral words and behavior in the cause of political expediency. If we don't reverse course now, will anyone take anything we say about justice and righteousness with any seriousness for decades to come? Can we say with a straight face that abortion is a great evil that cannot be tolerated and, with the same straight face, say that the bent and broken character of our nation's leader doesn't really matter in the end?[39]

Sadly, this warning was quickly rejected within days as *The Christian Post* had nearly 200 evangelical leaders openly denounce *Christianity Today* for their editorial, self-righteously claiming that their continued support of Mr. Trump is in keeping with Jesus' own behavior in the first century (while never once explaining how their Christian witness remains unspoiled by defending a man who, in Galli's words, "is morally lost and confused").[40] As McLaren would say in response, "[Jesus] was very compas-

---

37. Moore, "Have Evangelicals Who Support Trump Lost Their Values?" Interestingly, McLaren notes that President Trump's mother was, in fact, an impoverished migrant to America who tried to escape economic hardship, the very kind of people that Mr. Trump has vociferously vilified during his campaign and presidency (McLaren, foreword to *Poacher's Pilgrimage*, xvii–xxii).

38. Galli, "Trump Should Be Removed from Office."

39. Galli, "Trump Should Be Removed from Office."

40. Barnhart, "Nearly 200 Evangelical Leaders." What is interesting, though not surprising, is just how Christian leaders on both sides will appeal to Jesus' communion with sinners in the first century to support certain theological beliefs. See for example, McLaren, foreword to *Love is an Orientation*, 9–11.

sionate toward many groups of people, but there is one group he had an absolute and uncompromising commitment to confront and expose, and it was those who dishonor themselves and others as humans made in the image of God."[41] This cult-like devotion to President Trump then prompted the international research institute and academic society, Global Center for Religious Research (GCRR), to respond with an open letter of its own (of which McLaren signed):

> It is with great sadness that we, the undersigned faith leaders, biblical scholars, philosophers, and other academics, many of whom began our walks of faith in the evangelical tradition, hereby call on all American evangelical Christians of moral conscience who recognize and regret the corrupting and corrosive influence of Donald J. Trump, to join us in repudiating those evangelical leaders and institutions that have politically entangled themselves with him. We believe this action to be an urgent moral imperative because these leaders and institutions, which have unfortunately become the dominant voice of modern American evangelicalism, have shown themselves to be obstinately bound to the control of influences overtly opposed to the gospel of Jesus Christ and have resisted repeated pleas to disentangle themselves.[42]

The point here is that there exists a deep sense of betrayal among many who believe evangelicals have sold out their faith to anti-Christ personalities (cf. *TWLE*). The impression is that these Christians will overlook or minimize any politician's egregious immorality, but only so long as they are Republican.[43] With these criticisms in mind, McLaren's activist role against political and social cruelty has increased as "Trumpianity" further replaces Christian identity (cf. *GDT*):

> Watching Trumpism's near total takeover of white American Evangelicalism . . . I think it's time for all white Evangelicals of conscience to consider withholding their consent from churches that aren't vocally and actively resisting, and then re-invest their time, intelligence, money, and energy where they will benefit the common good rather than the narrow, conservative, patriarchal, right-wing agenda of Evangelical whiteness and religious supremacy. . . .Evangelical leadership is [simply] too compromised.[44]

---

41. McLaren, foreword to *Love is an Orientation*, 10-11.

42. Global Center for Religious Research, "An Open Letter to Evangelicals."

43. For instance, in an open letter dated September 1998, James Dobson demanded that Christians abandon support for President William J. Clinton for his consensual affair with a White House intern. Most of Dobson's remarks would apply directly to President Trump today, but Dobson has remained steadfast in his support for Mr. Trump regardless and has not demanded Christians abandon their support (see Dobson, "Dedicated to the Preservation of the Home"; italics in original). As McLaren writes, "The things we are against often define us, so we are easily manipulated in this way. Consider some of the conservative political pundits who have never espoused any inclination toward Christianity. They gain millions of Christian followers by opposing the political enemies of conservative Christians" (*VA*, 106).

44. McLaren, "Q and R: When Do I Leave." McLaren writes elsewhere, "The ugliness of this

INTRODUCTION

In order to understand this socio-political context further, several key terms require delineation.

1.3 DEFINITIONS AND TERMS

evangelical/evangelicalism (lowercase 'e'): a transdenominational confederation of Protestant and free-church Christians, who share three essential axioms: 1) an emphasis on Christ's atoning death on the cross; 2) *sola gratia* and *sola fide* as the necessary channels for salvation; and 3) s*ola scriptura* as the singular source of religious authority.[45]

Existential/Existentialism: as used in this book, an "existential" lifestyle denotes the resolute and personally meaningful embodiment of Christian faith while reflecting on its pragmatic relevance for daily living and real-world dilemmas. Existentialism here parallels McLaren's other term, "aliveness" (*WMRBW*, xv), which aligns with Kierkegaardian and Percyean existentialism, as opposed to Tillichian or Sartrean existentialism (see §8.2.2).

Fundamentalism (Christian): George Marsden defines Christian fundamentalism as "a loose, diverse, and changing federation of cobelligerents united by their fierce opposition to modernist attempts to bring Christianity into line with modern thought."[46] Militancy, sectarianism, and dogmatic absolutism are its most distinctive characteristics (*AIFA*, 131; *FFS §3, 92*).[47]

Institutional Christianity: organized religion or "belief-system Christianity" that is often reluctant to change the status quo (*FOWA* §6, 52-53; *GSM*, 3, 13, 180). Institutionalism is a form of faith that has a highly developed sense of doctrinal standardization, particularly within each denomination's *ministerium* hierarchy, doctrinal or creedal adherence, sanctioned cultic practices, and prescribed social mores.[48]

---

ungenerous pseudo-orthodoxy is driving young people away from faith in unprecedented numbers, and it threatens to leave major sectors of organized religion a bastion of regressive and reactionary angry old men, along with the women and young people who defer to them" (McLaren, foreword to *Generous Orthodoxies*, xvi).

45. See Henry, "Who are the Evangelicals," 69-94; Bebbington, *Evangelicalism in Modern Britain*, esp. 2-17; Noll, *The Rise of Evangelicalism*, 1:13-18; and Sweeney, *The American Evangelical Story*, 17-25.

46. Marsden, *Fundamentalism and American Culture*, 4.

47. McCune, "The Self-Identity of Fundamentalism," 9-34; Balmer, "Critical Junctures in American Evangelicalism," 55-66; Blythe, "Missouri Synod," 31-51. Cf. McLaren, "A Brief History of the 21st Century," 16.

48. Cf. Rodes, "Last Days of Erastianism," 301-48; McMullen, "Institutional Church as House Church," 1-18; Schmitz, "The Authority of Institutions," 6-24; and MacCulloch, *Christianity*, 112-54. According to McLaren, this "organizationalism" is the mechanistic process of making believers mere cogs in a larger assembly line of commercialization. Promoting Christianity as an "organized religion" becomes the *bête noire* for those who simply want to join a "spiritual community" (*COOS1* §12c, 196).

INTRODUCTION

Intersubjectivity: empathic communication; the sharing of subjective experiences, thoughts, and emotions among people within a group, which works to co-create the group's perception of objective events and ontological reality (see §8.2.1).

Neoconservatism: Whereas classical conservatism intends to curb impulsive societal changes, dogmatic conservatism adds an unhealthy veneration for previous eras, most notably when white heterosexual males dominated the economy, government, and culture. Neoconservatism is the renewal of this dogmatic strain in the form of obstructionist policies, inflexible absolutism, refusal to compromise with opposing viewpoints, and a goal to revert society back to antiquated power structures (*GSM*, 41-42; *LWWAT* §2, 14).[49]

Neo-Evangelical/Neo-Evangelicalism (capital 'E'): popularly labeled "fundegelicals"; in this book, "neo-Evangelicalism" is the continuation of fundamentalist militancy, sectarianism, and absolutism with the addition of neoconservative political activism (*GSM*, xi).[50] Neo-Evangelicals are often hostile toward notions of social action and divergent viewpoints, becoming overly judgmental in the process (*GO* §6, 119). This offshoot of evangelical faith is synonymous with unquestioning sycophants of the Republican Party and the Religious Right (cf. *TWLE*).[51]

1.4 PROBLEM STATEMENT

With these definitions in mind, it becomes evident that McLaren believes the existentially intersubjective nature of Christianity (as defined above) has yielded to the fundamentalist tactics of neoconservatism and neo-Evangelicalism. Thus, McLaren endeavors to introduce a new paradigm through which people can approach faith in Christ. The problem, however, is that mainly conservative Christians either do not attempt to understand the socio-political rationale for his philosophy of religion or they misjudge it completely, resulting in vitriolic *ad hominem* attacks. This gap in understanding is exasperated when realizing that while very few writings give only passing reference to McLaren's internal logic, the volumes of reactionary critiques

---

49. Huntington, "Robust Nationalism," 31-40; Aronowitz, "Considerations on the Origins of Neoconservatism," 56-70.

50. What is deemed neo-Evangelical in this study is often identified merely as "Evangelical" (capital 'E'), the "Religious Right," or "fundamentalist" throughout McLaren's corpus. Significantly, McLaren still identifies as an "evangelical" (lowercase 'e') in the sense of being committed to the canonical Jesus' preaching of the *evangelium* (cf. §7.4.2). "I am happy and honored to consider myself an evangelical ... the more modest 'small e' evangelical" (*GO* §6, 116). For him, if other "evangelicals" behave in ways contrary to the good news of Jesus Christ, they become "betrayers" of the gospel (*AMP* §Intro, 12). See also, McLaren, "Between Mixed Martial Arts."

51. See Marsden, "Fundamentalism and American Evangelicalism," 22-35; Olson, *Reformed and Always Reforming*, 15-26; Catherwood, *The Evangelicals*, 91-144; Collins, *Power, Politics and the Fragmentation of Evangelicalism*, 54-86; Quebedeaux, *The Young Evangelicals*, 5-17; Fitch, *The End of Evangelicalism?*, 48-122; and Balmer, "Critical Junctures in American Evangelicalism," 67-75.

against him are not fully accurate in their assessments. Oftentimes, they have failed to appreciate the nuances of McLaren's actual belief system. This book will correct this gap in knowledge by answering two simple questions: if systematized, how does Brian McLaren hope to reform people's approach to Christian faith and how did he come to this conclusion? Consequently, what is not widely recognized (and what this book will demonstrate) is fivefold:

1. McLaren adopts post-objective intersubjectivity (*not* subjectivity);
2. he expands upon Kierkegaardian existentialism (*not* fideism);
3. he emphasizes a constructivist epistemology (*not* relativism);
4. he integrates multivocal alterity (*not* philosophical pluralism);
5. and he cherishes Jamesian pragmatism (*not* nihilism).

1.4.1 Attacks on McLaren

McLaren once commented, "I've been shocked by the venom and unfairness of many responses. Often, it's clear that they have not even read my books, or else they have only read them seeking to find fault, not really trying to understand what I'm saying."[52] Gerald Gauthier further comments, "His books have triggered a wave of criticism from fundamentalist Christians who view him and his work as a threat to the foundations of their faith. He's been labelled a heretic and a son of Satan."[53] In many cases, these critics argue that McLaren has no allegiance to Christ (cf. *GO* §17, 260, 264).[54] Many conservatives have dismissed him as a diabolical nonbeliever, a heretical liar, or a manipulative pagan trying to destroy the true gospel.[55] Denny Burk remarks "[McLaren] has more in common with the spirit of antichrist than with the spirit of Jesus (1 John 4:3)."[56] One North Carolina church even held a public book burning of McLaren's literature.[57] Tony Jones explains, "Entire Web sites [*sic*] are devoted to

---

52. Streett, "An Interview with Brian McLaren," 8.

53. McLaren, "Making Waves," 29. As McLaren remarks, "[Evangelical] activists may use the word 'love' to justify their behavior, but those who disagree with them are seldom treated with love. Many of us have already faced the scorn of the activists who promote this chosen lifestyle and defend it as legitimate and even godly. For doing so, we have received hate mail peppered with a wide range of threats and abusive speech" (*NKOCY* §17, 174).

54. Cf. Pettegrew, "Evangelicalism," 175; Woodbridge, "Evaluating the Changing Face," 185-205; Horton, *Christless Christianity*, 64; and Rhodes, "The Maze of Mysticism," 7.

55. See for example, Geisler and Howe, "A Postmodern View of Scripture," 92-108; Gray, "The Emergence of The Emerging Church," 27-62; and Johnson, "You Can't Handle the Truth," 219-45; Dixon, "Whatever Happened to Heresy?," 219-20.

56. Burk, "Editorial," 3. Cf. Wells, *The Courage to Be Protestant*, 86-87.

57. Winner, "Houses of Worship." Significantly, McLaren does disclose to his readers that he intends to create controversy in order to challenge the semiotic paradigms of conventional Christianity (*COOS1* §Pref., 8; *GO* §Intro., 22-23).

listing his heresies. Recently, Brian has been disinvited from several conferences at which he was scheduled to speak, usually after nasty letter-writing and blogging campaigns by his critics."[58] Intriguingly, however, McLaren concludes that these criticisms are an indication he is on the right path:

> What did I expect when I wrote about 'a new kind of Christian' or 'a new kind of Christianity' or 'a generous orthodoxy'—a standing ovation?.... Of course they would see anyone issuing such a call as a traitor, a threat, an outsider, a compromiser, an apostate, a revisionist, a heretic, and an infidel. Of course they would do all they could to marginalize, bypass, reject, discredit, and defund anyone advocating such radical change. Of course!.... If I were driven by the need to be right—or to be *thought* right by others—I would show how little I had experienced the liberation to which I was calling others! (*GSM*, 188–89; emphasis in original)

What is argued here in this book is that the biggest failure of these reactionary critiques is a lack of understanding McLaren's actual religio-philosophy (cf. *GO* §8, 138; *WMRBW*, 102). While people may continue to disagree with his conclusions, it is still possible to respect the reasoning process by which he approaches faith.[59] Thus, to understand these vitriolic attacks, it is necessary to elaborate briefly on McLaren's more controversial adherence to *semper reformanda*.

1.4.2 Introducing *Semper Reformanda*

McLaren recalls an incident when protestors distributed hundreds of flyers declaring him "dangerous" and "unbiblical." He subsequently asked himself, "How did a mild-mannered guy like me get into so much trouble?" (*NKOCY* §1, 2–3).[60] The answer is simple: McLaren's version of *semper reformanda*, which is his provoking belief that Christianity should continually change how it manifests within society (*GO* §12, 193).[61] For instance, McLaren states, "We must never again preach Christianity or promote Christianity. Instead, we must seek to see, learn, and live [God's] ways, which can never be owned or contained by any human label or organization."[62] Elsewhere, he remarks, "You have permission to redefine what it means to be a Christian. Other people might

---

58. Jones, *The New Christians*, 51. See also, *Christian Century*, McLaren Talk Canceled, 15.

59. Cf. McLaren, "Seeking to Do One Thing Well, 121–40 and "An Interview with Brian McLaren," interview by Rachel Held Evans.

60. McLaren writes elsewhere, "I'm not by nature a controversialist, so I didn't look forward to a hornet's nest being stirred up" (McLaren, "Brian McLaren's Post").

61. Mohler even complains, "This author's purpose is transparent and consistent. Following the worldview of the postmodern age, he embraces relativism at the cost of clarity in matters of truth and intends to redefine Christianity for this new age, largely in terms of an eccentric mixture of elements he would take from virtually every theological position and variant" (Mohler, *The Disappearance of God*, 99). See also, Hagerty, "Jesus, Reconsidered" and Murphy, "Evangelical Author."

62. McLaren, "Instead of Ruling," 228.

put the definition on you—you [have to] believe this, hate this—but you can say, 'Well, you can call me whatever you want, but I'd like to become a more compassionate person'" (cf. *NKOCY* §Book Two, 159-60).[63] Accordingly, the specific problem that this book addresses is the identification of McLaren's rationale behind his *semper reformanda*, particularly since he notes that it is this concept that causes him so many problems:

> What's gotten me into trouble, though, is my suspicion that a person can be a follower of the way of Jesus without affiliating with the Christian religion, and my simultaneous lament that a person can be accepted and even celebrated as a card-carrying member of the Christian club but not actually be a follower of the way of Jesus. And even worse, I've proposed that I would rather be a follower of the way of Jesus and not be affiliated with the Christian religion than the reverse. (*FOWA* §4, 33)

Nevertheless, because of the large amount of writings by McLaren and in response to his work, it is important to set limitations on the scope of this investigation.

1.4.3 Research Limitations

McLaren has an extensive writing career and presence online, most notably through his blog posts and other social media platforms (cf. *AIFA*, 155-56; *COOS1* §7, 89), which have generated a surplus of interactions with his work.[64] Consequently, this study will consult McLaren's many informal sources; yet, it will only prioritize his *published* work over other mediums with the assumption that his official publications reflect his most thought-out concepts. All other online material will be cited only if they introduce new content or help clarify McLaren's overall philosophy of religion. As an academic study, however, this book does not intend to be an apologetic defense of or polemical attack against McLaren's approach to faith. Instead, the investigation is merely a clarification of his philosophy of religion. Therefore, this study will address issues pertaining specifically to the academic study of the philosophy of religion, such as spiritual experiences, morality, metaphysics, and epistemology. More generally, the task of the philosophy of religion here is to provide a synoptic view of McLaren's approach to Christian religion in a systematic fashion. Hence, this book will not provide an in-depth engagement with his theological inferences nor the assertions of his critics. However, a brief literature review is still needed to understand how others have interpreted McLaren's ideas.

---

63. McLaren and Schaeffer, "Brian McLaren Talks with Frank Schaeffer," 00:14:14-00:14:28.

64. McLaren writes, "Originally, as an author, I used social media as a way to communicate between books and about my books. Gradually, as I began to see my role as a 'public theologian,' I sometimes felt that my social media work was as important as or more important than my published work. Now I feel that much of my work is movement building, and for this, social media is paramount" (McLaren, "Public Theology," 290). As Robert Webber explains, "The new postmodern shape of communications. . . .is knowledge gained through personal participation in a community" (Webber, *Ancient-Future Faith*, 24). See further, McLaren, foreword to *The Hidden Power of Electronic Culture*, 9-11.

INTRODUCTION

1.4.4 Literature Review

Since his earliest writings, numerous book reviews, editorials, magazine articles, conference papers, interviews, newspaper headlines, peer-reviewed journals, academic theses, dissertations, book chapters, and book publications have been written on McLaren and his affiliations.[65] The following is a selective list of writings that typify the lack of attention to McLaren's philosophy of religion and the reactionary attacks that have ensued.[66] For instance, in the *Master's Seminary Journal*, and later in the book, *The Truth War*, John MacArthur describes McLaren as a self-righteous hypocrite masquerading as a believer, declaring that anyone following him will not inherit eternal life because they must hate God and God's truth (*§8.3.1*).[67] In Spring 2008, the *Christian Apologetics Journal* devoted an entire issue to attacking leaders of Emergence Christianity. In one article, Thomas Howe offers an overtly hostile review of McLaren's work, scoffing at the notion of him being orthodox, biblical, and evangelical (*§6.1.1*). Howe ends his review by accusing McLaren of being a liar and then deliberately insults anyone who disagrees with his review.[68] Howe later co-authored an article with Norman Geisler, becoming a chapter entry in *Evangelicals Engaging Emergent*, where they both charge McLaren with being dishonest (§2.3), manipulative (§5.4), relativistic (§8.3.3), and sacrilegious (§6.2). For them, true Christianity must entail absolutism, foundationalism, propositionalism, and infallibilism; otherwise, it is not orthodox Christianity (§8.2).[69]

In late 2011, Mark Christy completed his dissertation on what he labels McLaren's "neoorthopraxy," meaning McLaren undermines orthodox Christianity and replaces it with a call for social action. Christy contends that McLaren rejects the exclusivity of salvation through Christ (§8.4.1.1) and maintains a heretical Christology (§6.1.1). Christy describes McLaren's belief that orthodoxy (right beliefs) is inseparably related to orthopraxy (right practices). The issue for Christy is that McLaren engages in relativistic syncretism with the postmodern culture (§8.3.3). McLaren denies Scripture as an objective source of divine authority (§7.3.1), making him both dangerous and misguided.[70] Likewise, a 2013 dissertation by Joe Stewart explores the influence of Lesslie Newbigin on McLaren's missiology. Labeling McLaren a "revisionist," Stewart distinguishes McLaren's ambiguous and provocative writing style

---

65. Cf. Swanson, "Bibliography of Works," 223–29.

66. Section numbers (§) *to other portions of the book are also included in this literature review to identify those portions of the study that directly relate to or address the contentions of these interactions with McLaren's writings.* For an extended literature review, see Appendix A at the end of the study.

67. See MacArthur, *The Truth War*, esp. x, 18-19, 34-40, 139, 144-45, 169 and "Perspicuity of Scripture," 141-58.

68. Howe, "A Review of *A Generous Orthodoxy*," 81–102. Howe ends his article by stating, "Some may disagree with my review, but if they do, that just means they are Postmodern, unthinking, wishy-washy, McLarenites" (p. 102).

69. Geisler and Howe, "A Postmodern View of Scripture," 63–79; "A Postmodern View of Scripture," in *Evangelicals Engaging Emergent*, 92–108.

70. Christy, "Neoorthopraxy and Brian D. McLaren."

from Newbigin's work, claiming McLaren prevents readers from comprehending his line of reasoning (§5.4).[71]

In a 2015 dissertation by Gary Blackwell on McLaren's spirituality, Blackwell investigated whether McLaren's piety is authentic to the practices of the ancient church (§6.2.2.3). He concludes that McLaren is a religious deconstructionist (§6.1), who incorrectly uses Medieval mysticism to combat modernistic forms of Christianity (§4.2.3.1). His spirituality is a creative "bricolage" of various source material and religious beliefs that combine together, without regard for consistency or accuracy, to produce a mosaic of culturally acceptable attitudes and practices (§8.4).[72] In the same year, John Hatch analyzed McLaren's bibliology, explaining that his hermeneutic is an innovative approach that views the Bible as an inspired library of divergent voices (§7.3) dialoguing over important social issues (§8.4.1). Using the insights of Mikhail Bakhtin's "centrifugal-centripetal dialectic," Hatch describes McLaren's hermeneutic as emphasizing Scripture's "heteroglossia," the appearance of multiple viewpoints, which he views as an embrace of competing voices ("polyphony") in order to stimulate conversation (§8.4.1.2).[73]

To date, the most extensive treatment of McLaren's work originally appeared in a 2014 dissertation by Scott Burson, which later became a book in 2016. Aiming to provide a critical examination of McLaren's postmodern apologetic method, Burson details McLaren's antagonism for the foundationalist-derived theology of Calvinism (§4.2.2). Using John Wesley's quadrilateral, Burson evaluates McLaren's defense of Christianity with a special emphasis on his use of moral intuition (§5.2). He ultimately agrees with McLaren's concern that analytic Christianity has deviated from its original social and moral obligations, though he does not embrace all of McLaren's ideas. Instead, Burson believes the solution to modernity is, in fact, an Arminian theology.[74] From this review, it is evident that McLaren elicits both outrage and praise from his readers, something the author of this book has observed in various contexts.

1.5 LOCATING SELF AS A RESEARCHER

I was first exposed to Brian McLaren's writings in the Fall of 2014 when I took a doctoral class on Emergence Christianity. It did not take long before a polarization occurred among the students. Those who openly advocated for tolerance toward divergent political and religious perspectives had also appreciated the aims of McLaren and the Emergent Church.[75] Those students who vociferously protested McLaren's

---

71. See Stewart, "The Influence of Newbigin's Missiology," esp. 25–27, 86–111, 225–26, 238, 255.
72. Blackwell, "Return or Rereading."
73. Hatch, "Hearing God Amid Many Voices," 23–47.
74. Burson, "Apologetics and the New Kind of Christian."
75. For a history and schematization of Emergent Christianity, see Clawson, "A Brief History of the Emerging Church," 17–44; "Emerging from What?"; and Burson, *Brian McLaren in Focus*, 273–83.

work tended to be older, opposed to diversity, and ultraconservative (politically and religiously). Despite being younger in age, I was originally intolerant of McLaren and other so-called "liberal" agendas. Soon, however, my religious prejudice diminished once professional and personal experiences forced me to confront what I perceived to be an increasingly radicalized and abusive evangelical culture. Unexpectedly, I found myself being able to discern the rationale behind McLaren's work while many other students simply refused to entertain his insights or contentions.[76] I likewise observed that the students who disavowed McLaren's beliefs were also hostile to his work's underlying principle. That is to say, instead of attempting to be intellectually incorrigible, McLaren believes it is spiritually and morally superior to withhold absolute judgment, maintain epistemic humility, and cultivate a willingness to doubt religious beliefs. Hence, those who are less troubled by McLaren, including myself, tend not to possess the same "uncertainty-phobia" (*EMC* §6, 44) as exhibited among his harshest critics. Consequently, I developed a research method that sought to answer one question as I read through his publications: If systematized, what would be the logical precursor or rationale for each of McLaren's religious contentions?

1.6 RESEARCH METHODOLOGY

The research methodology for this book is exploratory, meaning it examines the basis for McLaren's philosophy of religion and then organizes the results into a coherent system.[77] The methodology does recognize, however, that McLaren's reflexive reasoning processes likely did not occur in the same logical order of discovery as presented in this study. Historiographically, the book will appropriate an "integral-developmental" model, which will attempt an exposition of current philosophical developments leading to Christianity's present paradigm shift. As an approach to religious history, it will chronicle the dominant theo-political issues affecting McLaren by recognizing the interchange between his socio-political experiences and missiological concerns.[78] Likewise, the study will capitalize on Brian McLaren's agreement to review the final product so as to ensure the study accurately portrays his religio-philosophy.[79] In this sense, the book is a type of historical theology, with a "history of Christian theology" approach, that examines the interconnecting beliefs of a particular theologian and

---

76. As Tony Jones amusingly quips, "Evangelical pastors have to read [McLaren's] *A New Kind of Christian* wrapped in a *Playboy* cover" (Jones, *The New Christians*, 51).

77. Gibbs and Bolger, *Emerging Churches*, 329.

78. Bradley and Muller, *Church History*, 29–31.

79. Brian D. McLaren, email to author, January 24, 2018. As an informal consultant, McLaren was able to provide guidance and further insights into his thought processes. However, this book's assertions and judgments (in their final form) are solely mine and, thus, any errors or misrepresentations of McLaren's work are solely those of this author and not of anyone else.

his relationship to the surrounding milieu.[80] Nevertheless, taking an exploratory approach requires several nuances for the study of the philosophy of religion.

1.6.1 The Philosophy of Religion

The most basic assumption of this study is that McLaren is, in fact, a philosopher of religion.[81] Being different from an academic study of theology, the philosophy of religion systematizes the logical and philosophical rationale underlying a belief system's basic ideas, as well as the criteria used to evaluate those beliefs.[82] In the West, this undertaking has traditionally employed logical formulas to justify religious assumptions.[83] However, with McLaren's philosophy of *Christian* religion (often termed a "religio-philosophy" in this book), an academic survey of his beliefs must specifically investigate how McLaren approaches his Christian faith, the rationale for why, and the evaluative criteria he uses to assess Christian paradigms. The assumption here is that McLaren's belief system actually resembles a "body politic" where his beliefs and practices unite him to a particular subculture within American Christianity, being the overarching ideology that permeates his perceptions and interpretations of reality.[84]

Underlying this method is what Howard Kee refers to as social interior-exterior dimensions: "(1) the interior dimensions of social groups, by which groups form, merge, evolve, and by which leadership and group goals emerge and change; and (2) exterior aspects by which group identity develops in relation to the wider culture."[85] From these dimensions, this investigation will utilize social-scientific data (where appropriate) to identify the evolutionary development of McLaren's religiosity.[86] Nonetheless, because of its academic nature, the study will remain theologically impartial regarding his beliefs in order to focus on discovering, simplifying, and systematizing his reasoning processes within their socio-historical context.[87] As expected, however, any discussion of McLaren's work must also address his fictional novels.

---

80. Clark, *To Know and Love God*, 172-73.

81. This assumption is not unjustified since McLaren seeks to "discuss questions like what faith is, how faith and knowledge are related, whether God exists, and how thinking people can explore and evaluate various ideas about God" (*FFS* §Intro, 25). As Scott Burson remarks, "In 1974, [McLaren] enrolled at the University of Maryland originally as a philosophy major, but soon shifted to English while maintaining an interest in the aesthetic dimensions of philosophy" (Burson, "Apologetics and the New Kind of Christian," 272).

82. Peterson et al., *Reason and Religious Belief*, 10; Rowe, *Philosophy of Religion*, 1-2; Clark, *To Know and Love God*, 297.

83. See for example, Aldwinckle, "Is There a Christian Philosophy?," 233-42.

84. Fitch, *The End of Evangelicalism?*, 8-9.

85. Kee, *Christian Origins in Sociological Perspective*, 26.

86. Cf. Gleason, "How St. Mary's College," 257-60; Turcotte, "Sociologie et historie des religions," 43-73; and Marti and Ganiel, *The Deconstructed Church*, 197-208.

87. Unlike most other interactions with McLaren's work, this study recognizes that a simple scrutiny of his theological deductions is inadequate without consideration of the cultural and practical

1.6.2 McLaren's Fictional Writings

By acknowledging that his writing style is closely aligned with Søren Kierkegaard (cf. *MRTYR* §1, 27-28; *PTP*, 125), McLaren makes an explicit distinction between his nonfictional material ("signed" discourses) and his fictional "dialogs." This book views McLaren's novels as an indirect method for challenging the status quo of American religiosity by disturbing its culture-religion and exposing readers to the strengths and weaknesses of divergent approaches to faith.[88] The trouble is with how to identify McLaren's actual viewpoints from the fictional interactions of his characters. Mimicking Kierkegaard, McLaren states in one novel, "Please don't assume that any of these characters can be fully identified with the 'I' who wrote this Introduction" (*NKOC* §Intro., xxvi).[89] In a separate novel, however, McLaren explains, "Nearly all [the book's] conversations were drawn from the many real-life conversations I have participated in over recent years" (*SWFOI* §Pref., xiv).[90] Therefore, applying the "principle of coherence" derived from historical Jesus research, this study will presume McLaren agrees with a fictional character's contention if it coheres to one of his signed discourses.[91]

Underlying this method is a distinction between the historical (or "empirical") author and the aesthetic ("implied") persona of McLaren's veiled arguments. Narrative literary critics often argue that the "implied author" of a story can never truly be identical to the "empirical author" because the book's narrator, as well as the varied fictional characters, embody different cultural and emotional dimensions. The implied author becomes the voice behind the story, who regulates which information to consider, which questions to ask, and which value judgments to accept concerning particular plot points and ethical decisions. Stated differently, McLaren reasonably expects his audience to allow the embedded persona of his novels to guide readers

---

contexts within which McLaren must live out his religious beliefs. In other words, religion is ultimately a lived experience that must work in reality apart from the theoretical musings of the intellectual mind; and since McLaren does not endorse an analytic approach to religiosity anyway, investigations into his beliefs would be incomplete without relating his philosophy to the sociocultural, historical, and practical contexts of everyday life. See Cottingham, *Philosophy of Religion*, 1-24. For an elaboration on socio-historical investigations, see Slade, "What is the Socio-Historical Method," 1-15.

88. As Kierkegaard once wrote, "A pseudonym is excellent for accentuating a point, a stance, a position. He is a poetic person. Therefore, it is not as if I personally said: This is what I am fighting for" (Hong and Hong, *Søren Kierkegaard's Journals and Papers*, 6:6421). Cf. Clowney, "A Critical Estimate," 32-33; Vardy, *The SPCK Introduction to Kierkegaard*, 49; Roberts, *Emerging Prophet*, 10n21.

89. Kierkegaard wrote something similar: "Thus in the pseudonymous books there is not a single word by me. . . .if it should occur to anyone to want to quote a particular passage from the books, it is my wish, my prayer, that he will do me the kindness of citing the respective pseudonymous author's name, not mine" (Kierkegaard, *Concluding Unscientific Postscript*, 1:626-27).

90. Likewise, in the introduction to *A New Kind of Christian*, McLaren admits that his fictitious story incorporates numerous aspects from his personal life (*NKOC* §Intro., xvi-xviii). Thus, these books are semi-autobiographical without McLaren explicitly claiming ownership of the viewpoints expressed therein (see "Becoming Convergent").

91. Cf. Bohannon, "Preaching and the Emerging Church," 61n1.

toward self-reflection over their own beliefs. This tactic allows readers to appreciate the ethical-religious world of the plot's narrative and to understand the perspective of its characters, even if the reader does not ultimately agree with the book's conclusions.[92]

1.7 SUMMARY

Ultimately, McLaren contends that there exists an incongruity between what Christians *profess* to be true and what Christians *demonstrate* to be true in their personal lives. For him, conventional paradigms have capitulated to modernity, which has tarnished the way believers express their faith in both word and deed. Here, conventional paradigms have prioritized arguments *about* God so much that believers now cognitively *declare* their religion "true" but live as though their faith is not *real* enough to transform them personally. As McLaren explains,

> What many experience in religious communities on a popular level seems closer to the opposite of love. Religion as they experience it promotes conflict and selfishness rather than generosity and otherliness. It teaches them to prioritize their own personal salvation and religiosity over the well-being of others. It teaches practices and beliefs that make some fear, dehumanize, and judge others. (*NS* §2, 15)

In this sense, Christianity has become more of a culture-religion than an embodied relationship with the divine. Thus, the thesis of this book is that McLaren is an abductive rationalist and phenomenological empiricist, who deliberately creates controversy through rhetoric and satirical provocations to stimulate the rethinking of conventional paradigms, such as when he questions whether God himself is an atheist (*GI*, 200). Here, McLaren is not *anti*-conventionalism; he is simply *post*-conventionalism, meaning he wants to retain what is good in older paradigms while jettisoning what is bad.

Significantly, both conservative and postmodern Christians alike object to McLaren's ideas *and* his provocative writing style. The problem for many is that McLaren is deliberately ambiguous and controversial in his writings, which often leads to distortions about his actual beliefs, such as when McLaren writes, "As I get older, I confess that talking about God is getting increasingly uncomfortable, even painful at times" (*GI*, 178). Moreover, he purposely complicates his philosophy in order to be scandalous, capitalizing on inflammatory rhetoric in order to capture his readers' attention. One problem is that many of his critics do not realize he is intentionally engaging in generalizations, irony, and humor when critiquing conventional Western

---

92. For detailed explorations of the difference between the "empirical author" and the "implied author" within narrative literature, see Foucault, *Archaeology of Knowledge*; "What Is an Author?," 141–60; Suleiman, *The Reader in the Text*, Booth, *Critical Understanding*; *The Rhetoric of Fiction*; *The Company We Keep*; and Rimmon-Kenan, *Narrative Fiction*.

Christianity. Thus, his critics often complain that he merely reflects an increasingly hostile culture without the proper nuance of actual scholarship.

In short, what is argued here is that McLaren's philosophy of religion suggests a faith-based intersubjective relationship with the divine ought to result in an existential appropriation of Christ's religio-ethical teachings. When subjectively internalized, this appropriation will lead to the assimilation of Jesus' kingdom priorities, thereby transforming the believer's identity into one that actualizes Jesus' kingdom ideals.[93] To accomplish this new paradigm, McLaren enlarges empirical categories to include mysticism and divergent theological perspectives. In other words, numinous experiences become a type of "empirical" evidence for McLaren because they involve sensory data. Since many derive their religious beliefs from these sensory encounters, McLaren seeks to utilize both his own intuition and experiences, as well as the intuition and experiences of others, in developing a new philosophy of Christian religion.

In axiomatic structure, which will be elaborated and clarified in the following chapters, McLaren's religio-philosophy is divisible into two main sections:

A. An authentically beautiful and plausible Christian belief system that is both objectively true and subjectively meaningful will derive from the faith-based paradoxy of the incarnation, signifying that

   i. Jesus Christ is the ineffable embodiment of transcendent Truth,
      a. who stimulates divergent theological perspectives to correct the myopia of human dogmatism, thereby compelling
      b. an intersubjective relationship with the Creator and his creation
      c. in pursuit of existentially embodying Christ's kingdom values,
   ii. which reprioritizes Christianity from a system of doctrinal esoterica to a suprarational organism that
      a. evolves over time as people's experiential intimacy with Christ deepens their spiritual knowledge of the divine.

B. To evaluate whether a Christian belief system is beautiful and plausible, its proponents ought to attain

   i. firsthand corroboration,
   ii. a transformative internalization,
   iii. and an emulative actualization of Christ's incarnation,
      a. with the goal of creating human solidarity in defiance of an unjust and unequal status quo.

---

93. Though McLaren does not argue that his beliefs are self-evident or incorrigible, he does conclude that his philosophy is not self-referentially incoherent, either, especially because of its pragmatic worth for Christian faith (cf. *AMP* §18, 278; *FOWA* §1, 4; *SMJ* §9, 72–89).

The hope is that by tracing McLaren's philosophy of Christian religion, future researchers will not only be able to comprehend (and perhaps empathize with) McLaren's line of reasoning, but they will also possess a more nuanced discernment of where they agree and disagree with his overall rationale. To accomplish this objective, researchers must first understand the socio-historical context that influenced McLaren's personality and religious temperament.

2

McLaren the Man

2.0 INTRODUCTION

Discussing the novelist Michael Crichton, Brian McLaren remarks, "Crichton's books incarnate the spirit of the day. And instead of offering a view from the outside, they serve to put readers into the postmodern world so we can see the rest of the world, including the modern world, from its perspective" (*COOS1* §12a, 161). The same is true for McLaren, who attempts to "incarnate the spirit" of his own socio-historical context. Born in 1956, McLaren attended a Plymouth Brethren church during the 1950s and 1960s before having "a powerful conversion" experience through the Jesus Movement of the 1970s.[1] His faith journey began in dispensationalism as a boy, then Calvinism as an adolescent, only to transfer again into "charismaticism" as a young adult, and finally settling within mainstream evangelicalism as a pastor (*NKOC* §Intro, xx, xxiv). Eventually, however, McLaren concluded that none of these approaches provided the vigorous spirituality that he craved (*FOWA* §1, 4; *SMJ* §, xiii-xv, 5-6). The thesis of this chapter is that McLaren's natural temperament and personal history have combined together to create a public theologian whose personal, educational, vocational, and spiritual experiences are the basis for his philosophy of religion.[2]

---

1. McLaren, "Everything Old Is New Again," 23.

2. While a brief biography is standard in other studies, they seldom make an overt connection between McLaren's life experiences and his theological inferences. Thus, the purpose of this chapter is to present only those biographical details that directly contributed to McLaren's religio-philosophy (cf. Christy, "Neoorthopraxy and Brian D. McLaren," 3-10 and Blackwell, "Return or Rereading," 15-19). For a detailed and comprehensive biographical sketch of McLaren and his career, see Burson, *Brian*

Three sections will support this thesis: 1) the effects of experiential knowledge on religious belief; 2) McLaren's religious journey away from fundamentalism; and 3) his resultant spiritual disposition. It is first necessary to discuss how life experiences shape a person's religious sensibilities.

2.1 EXPERIENTIAL KNOWLEDGE AND BELIEF FORMATION

According to the behavioral sciences, human information-processing typically involves two trajectories (a "dual-systems" approach). The first system is intuitive (nonreflective), which displays an involuntary emotional response to stimuli, while the second is reflective, which is slower and more deliberate. Oftentimes, intuition is the default system that informs cognitive-based reflective reasoning; and unless there are sufficient reasons to dismiss it, information-processing will largely depend upon a person's emotions.[3] Consequently, experiential knowledge will almost always receive priority over indirect, propositional knowledge, meaning people are unlikely to believe something contrary to their personal experiences. Labeled the "affect-as-information model," people rely on emotion and, thus, rarely change their established beliefs despite the potential wrong-headedness of their convictions.[4] This means that experiential-affective knowledge is essential to the formation and strengthening of religious beliefs.[5]

Significantly, McLaren describes his estrangement from Christian fundamentalism as the result of "cognitive dissonance," a theory originating in 1957 by Leon Festinger. "I was in a sense losing the faith that my parents and church had tried to give me. But this was necessary, because I had to find a faith with my own name on it, not just theirs. I guess psychologists would call this cognitive dissonance—that I had two conflicting value systems at work in my mind" (*FFR* §9, 181). According to cognitive dissonance theory, information that is inconsistent or contradictory to people's religious beliefs will propel them to alleviate the resultant negative emotional state ("dissonance").[6] People often engage in a deliberate suppression of the conflicting data, which can then manifest in the form of irrationally rejecting counterevidence, restricting interactions only to those who have the same beliefs, attempting apologetic defenses of the religion's validity, and *ad hoc* rationalizing to explain away the discordant information.[7]

McLaren in Focus, 10-12, 31-66.

3. See Sperber, "Intuitive and Reflective Beliefs," 67-83; Kahneman, "A Perspective on Judgment and Choice," 697-720; and Stanovich and West, "Individual Differences in Reasoning," 645-65.

4. Schwarz and Clore, "Mood, Misattribution, and Judgments of Well-Being," 513-23; "How Do I Feel About It?," 44-62; Clore and Gasper, "Feeling is Believing," 24-25.

5. Frijda et al., "The Influence of Emotions on Beliefs," 1-9.

6. Festinger, *A Theory of Cognitive Dissonance*. Cf. Festinger et al., "When Prophecy Fails," 258-69.

7. See esp., Eller, "Agnomancy," 150-80 and McLaren, *Why Don't They Get It?* In one study, for example, it was revealed that those who accept the divinity of Christ, when presented with disconfirming

Once these reactions reach a sufficient level of discomfort, however, people frequently abandon their original beliefs. Although cognitive dissonance can produce maladaptive behavior, forcing some to avoid important data altogether, others simply change their beliefs in various ways. For McLaren, his cognitive dissonance culminated in retaining an affection for Jesus, who he insists is still the answer to life's great problems (*SMJ* §1, 5), while also abandoning Christian fundamentalism. As he explains, this separation was the only way for him to maintain faith in Christ (cf. *EMC* §5, 35; *JMBM* §2, 13-24; §23, 211n8).[8] With cognitive dissonance in mind, readers are able to appreciate the psychological consequences of McLaren's life experiences.

2.2 MCLAREN'S RELIGIOUS ODYSSEY

As the Rector of an Episcopalian church once told McLaren, "Scratch the paint off a liberal . . . and you'll find an alienated fundamentalist underneath." It is in this sense that McLaren admits to being on a similar spiritual quest as theological liberals (*GO* §1, 59), using his writings as a medium for confessing his spiritual struggles (*JMBM* §2, 13-24; *NKOCY* §Preface, xii). In fact, there exist several elements from McLaren's chronosystem (i.e., historical context) to suggest that his experiential knowledge is the strongest determiner of his philosophy of religion.[9] Hence, readers should not attempt separating the man from his literature, especially for someone who has placed so much of himself into his own writings.[10] "I am a Christian, and all I write flows from my experience in that rich tradition" (*NS* §Preface, vii). Ultimately, for McLaren, following Jesus is, at its core, an existential journey rather than an academic chore (cf. *GI*, x):

> I don't just aspire to believe in God or think correctly about God. I want to love God and worship God and serve and experience God. If my view of God changes, well, that changes everything for me. This [spiritual] quest stirs up all kinds of psychological issues for me too, because my theology and my biography are deeply integrated in my 'be-ology'—my sense of who I am and what I want to be as a human being. (*NKOCY* §Book Two, 159-60)

Not surprisingly, then, McLaren's "be-ology" began with his fundamentalist upbringing.

---

information, paradoxically intensified their conviction in Jesus' divinity once they also accepted the truthfulness of the dissonant information (Batson, "Rational Processing or Rationalization?," 176-84). See also the numerous studies cited in Harmon-Jones, "A Cognitive Dissonance Theory," 192.

8. Cf. Aronson, *The Social Animal*, 185 and Harmon-Jones, "A Cognitive Dissonance Theory," 185-211.

9. McLaren comments, "Show me a person who has rejected faith, and nine times in ten I will show you a person or group nearby who turned him or her sour with their example of bad faith." He also remarks in the same book, "The search for a faith that makes sense has been the most challenging and life-changing quest of my life" (*FFS* §Intro, 18; §1, 46). As Roger Olson explains, theologies do not develop spontaneously. All arise from the experiential challenges to the church as perceived and felt by particular theologians (Olson, *The Story of Christian Theology*, 15).

10. See for example, Garff, *Søren Kierkegaard*, xvii-xxi.

2.2.1 Formative Personal Experiences

McLaren attended a highly conservative church that he admits had sincere followers of Christ, but his childhood experiences with the Plymouth Brethren exemplified some of the worst parts of Christian fundamentalism, particularly its widespread anti-intellectualism (*GO* §12, 187; *GSM*, x). For example, people often told McLaren that evolution was a lie and that God created the earth in six literal days (cf. *GI*, 147-67).[11] They also told him that only those within his denomination were saved, everyone else was going to hell, the world's end was imminent, and academics are conspiring against Christianity, thereby making the study of science and philosophy immoral.[12]

There were socio-political tensions, as well. McLaren remembers at the age of eight, during the Civil Rights Movement, when his Sunday School teacher warned the class that marrying someone of a different race would be an affront to God (*GSM*, 85-86). There was also a deep prejudice against "liberals," where the term became a pejorative to foster hatred for other Christians (*GO* §1, 59; §8, 131). Likewise, his church wholeheartedly supported the Vietnam War, "which made no sense to me—even if communism was as bad as everyone said, were people better off bombed and napalmed to death?" (*GO* §1, 44). Soon, McLaren developed a suspicion of the "pro-war, anti-hippie churchy role models" (*NS* §1, 7), who seemed to oppose any and all social reform. From these personal experiences, McLaren started having real doubts about the sustainability and legitimacy of fundamentalist Christianity (cf. *WMRBW*, 94).[13]

McLaren reports that he had his first "faith crisis" at the age of twelve when he was told to choose between God and science (*FFS* §Intro, 17), making his passion for science increasingly incompatible with fundamentalism (*COOS1* §6, 75-76).[14] He eventually rebelled by growing long hair and joining a rock band (*FFR* §9, 180-81), despite having learned that "rock 'n' roll was really of the devil" (*GO* §1, 44). "By my

---

11. Accordingly, as McLaren developed an interest in science, he grew weary of hearing anti-evolution rhetoric (*NS* §1, 7). He recounts, "When I was 13 my Sunday school teacher said: 'You can either believe in God or evolution', and I remember thinking: 'Evolution makes a lot of sense to me'" (McLaren, "Changing Faith, Staying Faithful," 14). Elsewhere, he comments that evolution "seemed elegant, patient, logical, and actually quite wonderful to me, more wonderful even than a literal six-day creation blitz" (*GO* §1, 44).

12. McLaren describes this period as "a full-dose, hard-core" style of fundamentalism that compelled its congregants to attend numerous church services, revivals, prayer meetings, youth programs, Bible studies, and devotionals. For more details on his personal life journey, see Brian D. McLaren, "How I Got Here," *Progressing Spirit* (blog), April 11, 2019, https://progressingspirit.com/2019/04/11/how-i-got-here/; *AMP* §16, 245; *FFR* §9, 180-81; *FFS* §3, 87; *MRTYR* §Intro, 11; and *NS* §1, 5-6. Elsewhere, however, McLaren labels the Plymouth Brethren as only "mildly fundamentalist" (*FOWA* §6, 56).

13. McLaren explains, "To a teenager in the early 1970s, church culture seemed like a throwback to the 1950s—or the 1850s, or the 1750s, take your pick" (*NS* §1, 7). Developmentally, it is common for teenagers to question the religious beliefs of their chronosystem, especially as their cognition expands to include more analytical discernments. See King and Roeser, "Religion and Spirituality in Adolescent Development," 435-78.

14. Cf. Jones and Gerard, *Foundations of Social Psychology*, 191.

teenage years, it was clear that I simply didn't fit in the rigid Brethren box. My love for philosophy, evolution, and rock and roll were three spiritual strikes that counted me out" (*GSM*, x). By his twenties, McLaren befriended non-fundamentalist believers, including mainline Protestants and Catholics (*NKOCY* §Preface, xii), which were two groups that the Brethren considered enemies of true Christianity (cf. *COOS1* §4, 53-54; *GO* §8, 131). He eventually joined an Episcopalian church where the conservative Rector exposed him to theological liberalism, which helped him to value Christ's love, justice, and sense of compassion. Then, his later encounters with Pentecostalism helped him to retain belief in Jesus' active presence in the world (*GO* §1, 51; §1, 59-60; §12, 186-88).[15] However, while McLaren remained attracted to Christ (*SMJ* §1, 5), he also knew he needed a more unrestrained spirituality.[16]

2.2.1.1 *The Pursuit of a Liberating Spirituality*

It is apparent that McLaren's early writings are a response to his negative experiences with fundamentalism. "My own upbringing was way out on the end of one of the most conservative twigs of one of the most conservative branches of one of the most conservative limbs of Christianity, and I am far harder on conservative Protestant Christians who share that heritage than I am on anyone else" (*GO* §0, 35). While admitting he overgeneralizes, McLaren's experience fits the growing cultural perception of conservative Christians as being pompous, egotistical, and intolerant of diversity (*FFR* §8, 166).[17] Thus, he ended up wanting a liberating type of faith that beckons and unfetters people to join ever-expanding possibilities, not confine and limit them to old patterns.[18] Not surprisingly, then, McLaren's work resonates predominantly with those who have had similar experiences, and it explains why McLaren felt he gained a sense of spiritual freedom when joining the Jesus Movement (*GSM*, x). Here, McLaren's faith in Jesus was revitalized as he became engrossed in the movement's emphasis on "simplicity, a childlikeness, a naïveté, and a corresponding purity of motive that I have seldom seen since" (*GO* §1, 45).[19] McLaren would later model a high school

---

15. See also, McLaren, foreword to *Generous Orthodoxies*, xiv.

16. Like McLaren, few adolescents actually reject the religion of their childhood, particularly if they have a good relationship with their parents. See Kim-Spoon et al., "Parent-Adolescent Relationship," 1576-87.

17. See the multiple polling data in Kinnaman and Lyons, *Unchristian*, 26-30 and Wright, *Christians Are Hate-Filled Hypocrites*, 14-15, 186-90, 200-202.

18. McLaren, preface to *Blue Ocean Faith*, xiv.

19. McLaren states, "I became a committed Christian during the Jesus Movement in the early seventies, a context in which being a Christian felt more like following a leader than accepting a code or creed" (*COOS1* §13, 207). He describes the experience elsewhere, "It was a movement known for being hip, not ancient; contemporary, not contemplative; and oriented around evangelistic practicalities, not spiritual practices" (McLaren, "Everything Old Is New Again," 23). For a history of the Jesus Movement, see Hubery, "Jesus Movement," 212-14 and Lyra, "Rise and Development of the Jesus Movement," 40-61.

youth group, "the Fellowship," after these experiences with the Movement by welcoming ostracized students into the club (cf. *MRTYR* §16, 121-23).[20] Eventually, however, McLaren felt the Jesus Movement had been "co-opted" by the Religious Right and "the religious marketing machine," forcing him to doubt his faith once again (*GO* §1, 45). It was at this point that McLaren developed a lifelong cynicism for conventional paradigms (*JMBM* §2, 13n1), which would subsequently manifest in his educational, vocational, and spiritual growth toward a new paradigm.

2.2.2 Formative Educational Experiences

McLaren describes his higher education as one of "liberation" from spiritual myopia, which helped him to question the status quo of conventional religion (*JMBM* §9, 74). He obtained a Master of Arts in English literature from the University of Maryland where he was particularly fond of Romantic poets, medieval dramas, and philosophical writings (*FOWA* §Author, 215; *NKOC* §Author, 251). It is significant to note how he describes the Romantic poets, commenting, "They are of special interest to people doing postmodern ministry because romanticism was a recurring protest movement in the modern era representing a dissatisfaction with modern rationalism. In some ways romanticism anticipated postmodernism" (*AIFA*, 39).

What had influenced McLaren the most in college, however, was his graduate studies in deconstructionism and literary criticism, which he admits conditioned him to view religion differently (*COOS1* §12b, 187).[21] These studies made conventional paradigms feel inadequate and outdated, appealing only to society's most unsophisticated religionists. Luckily, McLaren recounts, he had patient friends who expressed empathy toward his latest spiritual doubts (cf. *AMP* §16, 245), though he would continue to struggle with religion for most of graduate school (*COOS1* §12b, 187-88; *FFS* §3, 89-92).[22] During this time, it was two literary figures in particular who would ultimately have a major impact on McLaren's philosophy of religion.

2.2.2.1 *The Study of Walker Percy and Søren Kierkegaard*

Remarkably, McLaren never intended to be a pastor, believing he could better serve God apart from the "religious bureaucracy and politics" of ministry; yet, his master's thesis on the Catholic novelist and existentialist philosopher, Walker Percy (1916-1990),

---

20. Cf. McLaren, foreword to *A New Kind of Youth Ministry*, 6-8.

21. For McLaren, his exposure to deconstructionism was not an accident. Instead, much like the prophet Moses, whose Egyptian education prepared him for revolution, McLaren believes God had directed his graduate studies in order to prepare him for ministry during Christianity's epochal shift (*COOS1* §12b, 187-88).

22. Developmentally, young adults will often attend religious services less but, paradoxically, also develop more religious convictions throughout college. See Barry et al., "The Role of Mothers," 66-78.

who wrote substantially on semiotics and modernization, made pursuing a vibrant faith plausible for McLaren again (*FFS* §3, 92). Describing it as the "highlight of my higher education," his Percyean research also introduced him to the existentialism of Søren Kierkegaard (1813-1855), who was a major influence on Percy's philosophy of religion (*COOS1* §7, 91). For McLaren, Percy's writings reflected the same anguish he had experienced with conventional Christianity.[23]

In terms of scholastic inspiration, McLaren is indebted to Walter Brueggemann, N. T. Wright, Francis Schaeffer, C. S. Lewis, Dallas Willard, John Caputo, Stanley Grenz, John Franke, Leonard Sweet, René Girard, and (most influential) Leslie Newbigin.[24] Nonetheless, in terms of a religio-philosophy, both Percy and Kierkegaard are the most instrumental (and least recognized) of McLaren's mentors. In fact, many are unaware of the philosophical parallels between McLaren and the existentialism of these two authors (§8.2.2). "My research led me to study Søren Kierkegaard in some detail, and his work also left a lasting mark."[25] In *A New Kind of Christian*, McLaren laments the absence of a Christian innovator: "Is there no Saint Francis or Søren Kierkegaard or C. S. Lewis in the house with some fresh ideas and energy?" (*NKOC* §Intro, xviii). In *More Ready Than You Realize*, he praises a Kierkegaard publication as one of the most influential, captivating, and inspiring books on evangelism he has ever read (*MRTYR* §1, 27-28). McLaren even imitates Kierkegaard's "indirect communication" so as stimulate critical thought (*PTP*, 125). He also quotes Kierkegaard extensively to argue that an overly analytical faith is a hindrance to authentic worship (*SMJ* §, 215-16).[26] It is no surprise, then, that McLaren is reminded of Kierkegaard in relation to social justice issues, "I'm reminded that Soren Kierkegaard said, 'The essence of all true preaching is malice,' by which he meant that unless the preacher is

---

23. Streett, "An Interview with Brian McLaren," 6. McLaren comments that Percy's essays in *The Message in the Bottle* (1954) were especially influential to his theology (McLaren, "What I'm Reading," 21). Here, Percy helped McLaren dialogue to himself about sensitive and problematic issues of faith while recognizing the limitations of people's culturally embedded perspectives (*FFS* §3, 92-94; *GO* §1, 52-53).

24. See McLaren, "Becoming Convergent"; "Ruining Your Ministry for Good," 56; foreword to *What Would Jesus Deconstruct?*, 9-12; foreword to *Renewing the Center*, 7-14; foreword to *Manifold Witness*, xi-xiii; forward to *Life at the End of Us Versus Them*, xxi; "What I'm Reading," 21; and Streett, "An Interview with Brian McLaren," 6-7. For an exploration of Leslie Newbigin's influence, see Stewart, "The Influence of Newbigin's Missiology," 86-111 and McLaren, "Brian's Annotation." For Walter Brueggemann, see McLaren, "Brian McLaren on Walter Brueggemann."

25. Streett, "An Interview with Brian McLaren," 6. In fact, McLaren even credits Kierkegaard for his postmodern ethos (Christy, "Neoorthopraxy and Brian D. McLaren," 97-99).

26. This Percyean-Kierkegaardian influence is more evident as McLaren mimics both of their writing styles, tactics, and religio-ethical conclusions. In fact, the three iconoclasts often have similar syntax and vocabulary. McLaren especially imitates Kierkegaard's use of irony, humor, satire, hyperbole, and pseudonymous story-telling (cf. §5.4.1). As Carl Raschke remarks, "Postmodern thinkers have adopted Kierkegaard as their prime mentor" (Raschke, *The Next Reformation*, 163). Kyle Roberts also comments, "In many ways, the concerns that give rise to emergent Christianity parallel Kierkegaard's critique of Christendom in his own context" (Roberts, *Emerging Prophet*, 6). For more on Kierkegaard's influence on postmodern thought, see Best and Kellner, *The Postmodern Turn*, 38-78.

mad about something, he has no passion."²⁷ From here, it becomes evident just how Percy and Kierkegaard prepared McLaren for his later nonconventional ministry.

2.2.3 Formative Vocational-Ministerial Experiences

After graduate school, McLaren taught college English from 1978 to 1986. After marrying a Catholic woman, McLaren and his wife co-founded Cedar Ridge Community Church in Spencerville, Maryland, which began as a small fellowship in their home and quickly became a pronounced congregation in the community. McLaren became its full-time pastor in 1986 and remained there for over twenty years until 2006 when he resigned to become a full-time author and activist.²⁸ As a pastor, McLaren felt his basic job description was to disseminate correct doctrines to the congregants, even though he started to question the validity of some of those doctrines (*GSM*, 23). However, McLaren's church consisted predominantly of new believers who were transparent about their own doubts and routinely asked tough questions. McLaren ultimately realized that he shared just as many, if not more, of the same reservations as his own church.²⁹ "What does a pastor do when he questions the stock answers he's supposed to be convincing others of?" (*NKOC* §2, 17). Commenting that he entered ministry "with mountains of idealism," McLaren quickly learned that hard work, sincerity, and prayer were not enough to be a successful pastor in the postmodern era; he had to find an alternative method.³⁰

Then, a significant change occurred in San Antonio, Texas, around the turn of the century when McLaren, in a moment of divine clarity, believed he had finally comprehended the true nature of Christianity: faith is meant to be an intersubjective relationship with God and an existential appropriation of Jesus' kingdom teachings (§8.2). At this point, McLaren experienced a dramatic change away from the mentality that "faith" equated to the dogmas of a particular belief system. Though scared to admit his changing convictions, the seemingly divine character behind this insight made McLaren confident that God was directing these changes (*GSM*, 22-25; cf. *NKOC* §7, 84-85). "My theology sincerely attempted to be biblical, but it had become so enmeshed with modernity, American consumerism, modern western

---

27. Enns, "My Interview with Brian McLaren."

28. *FFS* §Intro, 20; *GSM*, 50; *NKOC* §Author, 251; *NKOCY* §Preface, xii.

29. *AMP* §16, 243; *EMC* §1, 3; §32, 275; *FFR* §Intro, 18; *LWWAT* §1, 6; *NKOC* §Intro, xix. McLaren describes pastoring to a congregation of doubters: "The very formulations that sound so good and familiar to the 'saved' sound downright weird or even wicked to the 'seekers' and the skeptics. These people come to me and ask questions, and I give my best answers, my best defenses, and by the time they leave my office, I have convinced myself that their questions are better than my answers" (*NKOC* §Intro, xix). Though he found a faith that sustains him, McLaren admits to wanting to give up several times because of doubts and other troubles (*FFS* §Intro, 17-18). See also, McLaren, "Emerging Values," 34-39.

30. McLaren, "5 Books for Ministry," 32; "Everything Old Is New Again," 23-24. McLaren once described his church as "a cross between Willow Creek, Vineyard, and an Episcopal service" (*PTP*, 128). See also, McLaren, "Fire Without Brimstone."

rationalism, and a host of other things, that it somehow was out of synch with Jesus Christ. Through Newbigin's writings, I realized I was a Christian who needed to be reached for Christ."[31] Over time, McLaren's church reflected his newfound convictions, explaining, "We aren't creating a 'you're in, you're out' mentality at our church. Our message is: The Kingdom of God is available to everybody, and now the ball is in your court."[32] He sought to create an environment that allowed for "adult integrity, clear intelligence, and open-eyed honesty," hoping for an inspirational spirituality that would foster a more meaningful faith (*FFS* §Intro, 23, 25). Becoming increasingly open about his new insights, McLaren soon began his writing career as a public theologian and iconoclast.

2.2.3.1 The Public Theology of Iconoclasm

One major irony is the fact that McLaren does not view himself as a religious authority but, rather, a public theologian (*WMRBW*, 282), meaning he seeks to overcome the privatization and compartmentalization of religious faith so as to reintroduce and, therefore, legitimize Christianity as a means for bettering the world (§3.4.1).[33] His goal is to transform Christianity from "*a religion organized for self-preservation and privilege to a religion organizing for the common good of all*" (*GSM*, 153; italics in original). Despite being proficient in church history, philosophy, theology, psychology, and ministry (*BMF*, 291-303), McLaren humorously regards himself as "an amateur pastor and a hack theologian" (*COOS1* §5, 71):[34]

> I myself will be considered by many to be completely unqualified to write such a book of theology, being neither a trained theologian nor even a legitimate pastor if legitimacy is defined by ordination qualifications in a bona fide denomination. Rather I am only a lowly English major who snuck into pastoral ministry accidentally through the back doors of the English department and church planting....In other words, I am a confessed amateur....[who lacks] "proper credentials." (*GO* §0, 34; §6, 115)[35]

---

31. McLaren, "Ruining Your Ministry for Good," 56.

32. McLaren, "Brian McLaren on Outreach," 122. To read a detailed explanation of how McLaren's vocational ministry changed, in which areas, and why, see McLaren, "Ruining Your Ministry for Good," 49-63.

33. See McLaren's book, *Everything Must Change*, for an expansive portrayal of his public theology. Cf. Marty, "Reinhold Niebuhr," 332-59; Cady, "A Model for a Public Theology," 193-212; and Rasmussen, "Reinhold Niebuhr," 198-210.

34. Cf. *FOWA* §Author, 215; *GSM*, x; *NKOC* §1, 9; §Author, 25; *NKOCY* §Preface, xii. See also, McKnight, "McLaren Emerging," 58-66.

35. This minimizing of his competency is especially noteworthy considering McLaren has received two honorary doctorates of divinity: one from Carey Theological Seminary in 2004 and one from Virginia Theological Seminary in 2010 (*FFS* §Intro, 20; *NKOC* §Author, 251). McLaren does hint elsewhere, however, that he is well-read on current scholarship but seldom cites other scholars to support his religious claims simply because it is provocative not to do so (*GO* §0, 34). Interestingly,

What McLaren's critics often misunderstand is that he deliberately tempers his credentials in order to assume the posture of a fellow seeker.[36] As he explains, "I remember getting a feeling . . . that something I was doing was counterproductive to really getting through to the more postmodern people who were coming through our doors" (*PTP*, 117). Emphasizing humility is not only concomitant with his overall approach to religion (§5.1), but it highlights McLaren's desire to enculturate Christianity for contemporary audiences (§4.4.2). Thus, McLaren's self-deprecating specifically appeals to a new generation of disillusioned and disenfranchised seekers, who no longer esteem analytic-style learning or magisterial authorities (§4.4).[37]

Interestingly, this self-deprecation partly derives from McLaren's distinction between "Nobodies" and "Somebodies." The latter seek to conserve the status quo for their own benefit, but it is the marginalized "Nobodies" who create everlasting change (*NKOC* §16, 214-15). McLaren, therefore, shrewdly remarks that he is not an ecclesial authority and does not ever want to be one (*AMP* §11, 180).[38] "I work as a pastor and write books on theological topics, yet have no formal training in theology" (*GO* §9, 156). Accordingly, McLaren labels himself "a practitioner, not an academic" (*COOS1* §Preface, 8) and a fellow pursuer of truth (cf. *FFR* §Intro, 19; *FFS* §Intro, 24; *NKOC* §7, 80-81). These statements allow McLaren to distance himself from "the religious establishment" in order to appeal to the nonreligious.[39] Hence, McLaren does not really feel it is beneficial to possess religious credentials (*NKOCY* §6, 55), especially when spiritual experiences can be much more instructive to Christian faith.

2.2.4 Formative Spiritual Experiences

By the age of sixteen, at the height of puberty, McLaren started having strong spiritual experiences, making him choose a lifelong pursuit for Christian vitality in the process. His encounters with other teenagers also had a major impact on his development. Seeing the dramatic change that Jesus had on the lives of others subdued McLaren's

---

Kierkegaard also strategically downplayed his ability to develop sophisticated theological systematizations (Come, *Kierkegaard as Theologian*, 3-4).

36. Cf. *FFR* §Intro, 19; *FFS* §Intro, 24; *WP*, 30-31, 41-42.

37. Thomas Howe remarks, "McLaren's discussions give evidence of his never having been very well versed in Christian doctrine," (Howe, "*A Review of A Generous Orthodoxy*," 83). Unfortunately, Howe's review fails to recognize that McLaren purposefully downplays doctrine in order to highlight the existential need for imitation and action (§8.2).

38. He writes, "I'm not an economist, politician, or certified expert on anything really" (*EMC* §1, 2), nor "a professional philosopher" (McLaren, foreword to *What Would Jesus Deconstruct?*, 9).

39. McLaren explains that unlike modernity, which dissents with ecclesiastical authorities, postmodernity dissents with the hierarchical bureaucracies of corporate and political power. Authority is increasingly residing among the amateur, self-taught masses while the professional elite no longer have the same social dominance as before (cf. *AIFA*, 177-78). McLaren labels this authority reversal as a "devolution revolution," where relationships, dialogues, and power become more localized and dispersed among the general populace (*AIFA*, 92-94).

instinct to escape his already "hyperreligious life" (*NS* §1, 6-7). Nevertheless, one experience in particular stands out as the pivotal moment that would end up guiding McLaren's religiosity for the rest of his life.[40]

One day at a youth retreat, McLaren prayed, "Before I die, please allow me to see the most beautiful sights in the world, and hear the most beautiful sounds in the world, and feel the most beautiful experiences in the world" (cf. §5.3.2). That night, while observing the majesty of the night sky, McLaren had an unforgettable, life-transforming experience of pure joy. He could feel the Creator of the universe watching him, causing an indescribable and uncontainable feeling of love that let him know God was paying attention. He began to laugh and then to cry until his stomach ached. Soon afterwards, McLaren heard other boys and girls on the retreat saying how much they loved each other. It was then that he realized God answered his prayer:

> I had seen the most beautiful thing on earth—the glory of God shining through creation . . . And I had heard the most beautiful thing in life—human beings telling other human beings that they love one another. And I had felt the most beautiful feeling in life—to be loved, really loved, by a God who knows me—my secrets, my faults, my doubts, my wrongs, my shame, along with my strengths and dreams and hopes and gifts—simply to be known and loved.
>
> The fact remains that it is twenty-five years later, and I am still on that same path, learning to open my heart in new ways, savoring the same beauty, desiring that same spirit (or Spirit) of joy and love to fill me. (*FFR* §9, 186-87)

The experience later deepened that night through a vision he had while praying of a pair of feet wearing sandals. McLaren felt himself transform into the water droplets of a woman weeping at Jesus' feet (cf. Luke 7:37–38). It was at this moment that McLaren dedicated his life to Christ. "From that night on, I was a wholehearted lover of the Creator, a person thirsty for the Holy Spirit, and a devoted follower of Jesus. That was my triune baptism into spirituality. . . .So everything I write about spirituality today has been tested in the crucible of my own experience during the nearly forty years since that night" (*NS* §1, 10; cf. *MRTYR* §14, 103-4). Indeed, his starry night experience continues to influence how he interprets Scripture and how he understands the person of God today (*GI*, 185).

McLaren does point out that this pivotal spiritual experience occurred at a Southern Baptist retreat in a context that would eventually form the Religious Right. Afterwards, his continued exposure to conservative Christianity gradually soured as arguments about ancillary issues overshadowed his encounters with the divine (*NS* §1, 10-11). The ensuing tribalism (§3.2.2) was enough for McLaren to realize that conservativism was not spiritually appropriate for him (*GO* §1, 50-51), as expected from psychological studies on numinous experiences.

---

40. For details of McLaren's dramatic spiritual experience, see *FFR* §9, 183-86; *FFS* §3, 88-89; *MRTYR* §14, 103-4; *NS* §1, 7-10; and McLaren, "Changing Faith, Staying Faithful," 14-15.

2.2.4.1 The Psychology of Spiritual Experiences

For many conversion experiences, the concept of an ideal religious fit is paramount to a person's overall decision to subscribe to a particular ideology. "What makes any voluntary conversion process possible is a complex confluence of the 'right' potential convert coming into contact, under proper circumstances at the proper time, with the 'right' advocate and religious option."[41] In McLaren's case, he notes that his pacifistic temperament (*GO* §1, 61; §12, 183) would eventually mean Christian tribalism could not work for him (*MRTYR* §5, 57-58). His developing philosophy would make characteristics such as "alive, genuine, purposeful, free, [and] kind" (*FFR* §9, 183) the leading distinctives of his newfound spirituality, indicating that an ideal religious fit would be one that aligns with what he learned from his spiritual experiences.[42]

Significantly, during adolescence, the reward center of teenage brains intensifies the neurotransmitters that respond to events, making a positive experience more memorable and intense.[43] A consequence of strong emotional occurrences is the attentional funneling that narrows people's focus onto "goal-relevant" information, meaning McLaren's desire for a vibrant spirituality actually heightened his emotional connection to these experiences. Here, his salient emotions now become empirical evidence in confirming his burgeoning religious beliefs by attributing his emotional high directly to his starry night prayer (the "feelings-as-evidence hypothesis").[44] Deriving in part from the strong emotions associated with his conversion, McLaren now approaches faith with an emphasis on beauty (§5.3.2), creation (§4.3.2), and love (§6.2.4). The psychological implications mean that McLaren's philosophy of religion derives from the experiential knowledge he obtained through mystical experiences (§6.2.2.3), ensuring that these factors would become the foundation of his overall spiritual temperament (cf. §8.5.1).

2.3 MCLAREN'S RESULTING TEMPERAMENT

The consequence was that McLaren's formative experiences developed into a more compassionate disposition. As is typical of college-age adults, McLaren appears to have developed an "individual-reflective" spirituality where he detached himself from the customs and mores of his upbringing in order to question the validity of his beliefs. Though this stage is intellectual, it is also existential in the sense that McLaren needed to develop a spirituality that was his own (*FFR* §9, 181). Here, McLaren quickly realized that his natural disposition was not that of a fundamentalist. "This kind of

---

41. Rambo, *Understanding Religious Conversion*, 87.

42. Cf. Richardson and Stewart, "Conversion Process Models," 819-38. McLaren also describes himself as naturally shy, which originates "from a temperamental preference for understating rather overstating" (*NKOCY* §20, 225).

43. Berger, *The Developing Person*, 418.

44. See Clore and Gasper, "Feeling is Believing," 10-44.

environment was impossible for a boy of my reflective temperament—there wasn't room there for a person like me" (*FFS* §3, 87).⁴⁵ Once, when asked how he developed a gentler temperament that is now more concerned with showing compassion, McLaren reflected on a number of experiences, both in adolescence and in ministry, which make him "cringe" at how many people he has hurt. He reflected on one incident in particular when one of McLaren's best friends "came out" as gay his senior year of high school. McLaren eventually perceived a mismatch between the homophobic rhetoric preached in fundamentalism and his own relationship with homosexuals (cf. *NKOCY* §17, 177). There were enough of these discordant experiences to make him realize that conservatism clashed with the kind of Christianity he wanted, namely a faith that cared more about people than dogmas.⁴⁶

Most notably for the study of McLaren's religio-philosophy is his resultant Hegelian-dialectical temperament toward faith. Having had a short but penetrating period of doubt (*SMJ* §1, 5), McLaren's early tension between his environment and his emerging self-identity resulted in a thought process that first manifests as a dichotomist mode of thinking ("Stage 1 dichotomy," *FFS* §3, 88; cf. "dualist faith," *NS* §3, 30). Here, McLaren initially believes there can be only two choices for a particular theological impasse (both choices of which McLaren loathes). Eventually, however, he realizes that the predicament is, in fact, a false dilemma, which propels him to find a third alternative (cf. *AIFA*, 286-87). In this way, McLaren's Hegelian thought process tries to learn the best parts of each option within Christian tradition so as to create a synthesis that also eliminates each of their shortcomings (§8.4.1.2).⁴⁷

McLaren's religious journey exemplifies this dichotomist pattern. He initially felt he had to decide either to deny his doubts and return to the Plymouth Brethren or embrace his doubts and deny his Christian faith. Eventually, a third option manifested when he encountered other believers who portrayed their religion as "an adventure

---

45. Cf. Fowler, *Stages of Faith*, 174-83 and *AMP* §16, 249. Intriguingly, McLaren says he thoroughly enjoys speaking with nonChristians because of their thoughtful discussions and critical questions (McLaren, foreword to *Reimagining Evangelism*, 7).

46. McLaren would later remark that he is ashamed to have pandered to the hypocrisy of the neoconservative Religious Right out of distress of losing congregants and their monetary donations (*NKOCY* §1, 7). See also, McLaren and Schaeffer, "Brian McLaren Talks with Frank Schaeffer," 00:45:17-00:47:52.

47. In fact, the entire book, *A Generous Orthodoxy*, is about McLaren's attempt to identify the best of all religious traditions while simultaneously learning from their mistakes. As McLaren explains, even the internal tension he experiences with his external experiences generally follow a cyclical pattern of "crisis management" where he first finds hope in God, then becomes disillusioned with his faith, then becomes elated once he finds an answer or formula to resolve the disillusionment, and then becomes depressed again when he discovers the answer is no longer satisfying (*FFS* §Intro, 17). This pattern helps explain why McLaren has had a "lateral conversion" multiple times, a phrase he uses to describe his perpetual movement from one Christian sect to another (*FOWA* §6, 58). As he writes elsewhere, "Back when I was a teenager faced with this unacceptable choice, I knew that I couldn't accept option A or B, but had to search for, or make if necessary, an option C" (*SWFOI* §Pbk. Preface, ix).

they were on with God . . . an adventure with joy and reality and purpose" (*FFR* §9, 182-83; ellipses in original). From these experiences, McLaren learned the necessity of creating communities focused on expressing love (*GSM*, 56). In essence, McLaren's exposure to fundamentalist believers provided a type of pro-social "deviancy training," whereby he learned how to dissent against the social norms of fundamentalism and to reorient himself toward the common good.[48]

What had captivated McLaren in his teenage years was the good news of Jesus Christ (*GO* §1, 48). His resultant temperament made him realize that the problem he experienced among fundamentalists was not because of Christianity or the Bible. The problem was what some fundamentalists had done with their religion (*AMP* §16, 245). By the end of high school, McLaren had read the philosophical and theological works of multiple intellectual Christians (e.g., C. S. Lewis and Francis Schaeffer), who helped him to realize that it was possible to be a reflective thinker and still remain a believer.[49] This exposure, coupled with several more powerful spiritual experiences, made it possible for McLaren to gain a better sense of a well-balanced approach to Christianity (*FFS* §3, 88-89). Still, even with a newfound appreciation for critical thinking, there was one final temperamental result that proves essential to understanding McLaren's philosophy of religion: his artistic personality.

2.3.1 An Artistic Disposition

As a child, McLaren developed a passionate love for nature and always felt he could experience God's presence through creation (*GSM*, xii-xiii; cf. *GO* §11, 177-78). For him, the artistic beauty of nature made doubting God's existence an absurdity. Not surprisingly, then, McLaren produced poetry about finding God in creation, commenting that he wrote song lyrics well before writing prose (*FFR* §7, 145-49). To this day, McLaren maintains a penchant for creativity, including an interest in art, songwriting, and music (*NKOC* §Author, 53).[50] Even in high school, McLaren was infatuated with the art of literature and decided he wanted to become an English teacher (*NKOCY* §1, 3). Hence, McLaren's starry night prayer to God emphasized a desire to see and experience *beauty*. "Obviously, 'beautiful' was an important word to this adolescent fledgling musician/hippie/spiritual seeker" (*FFR* §9, 184).

Readers and critics must not underemphasize McLaren's artistic propensity. Much of what he declares throughout his line of reasoning and religio-philosophy all contain elements of an "artistic disposition," defined here as a preference for unstructured and

---

48. Cf. Dishion et al., "Peer Group Dynamics," 79-92.

49. For the traits of a "reflective Christian," see Taylor, *The Myth of Certainty*, esp. 13-63.

50. For example, McLaren has a music album entitled *Songs for a Revolution of Hope*. McLaren even labels one of his fictional characters, an allusion to Christ, as the "poet" and "storyteller" (*TSS*, 30-36). Interestingly, those with open personality traits often have a higher IQ and oral articulacy. See Silvia and Sanders, "Why are Smart People Curious?," 242-45 and Berger, *The Developing Person*, 419, 634.

dynamic practices that accentuate self-expression, especially through artistic media. "What kept me on the religious path was not the fundamentalist God. . . .It was the holy and utterly loving presence I felt one night under a starry sky. . . .It was the creative spirit I felt when I composed music or poetry or opened myself to authentic art" (*GI*, 185). Thus, McLaren likely scores high on a psychological "openness" scale, meaning he is creative, inquisitive, imaginative, innovative, and open to new experiences. What is suggestive is that these artistic values developed early in life and are now what constitute his code of behavior as an adult. The experiential knowledge obtained during McLaren's psychological development transformed into a heightened sense of "passion for ideas and ideals, passion for beauty, passion to create music and art."[51]

2.4 CONCLUSION

What McLaren's biography reveals is that he has developed an iconoclastic approach to religion with a propensity for challenging the status quo of his particular strain of Christian tradition. Not only do the events in McLaren's life explain the shaping of his personality and temperament, but his life experiences also explain the more idiosyncratic elements of his religiosity that would, otherwise, seem eccentric to conventional theologians. They reveal why McLaren cherishes interreligious dialogue (§5.3.1), an allegiance to Christ but not to any Christian denomination (§6.1), a rejection of ontotheology (§8.1), a love for the marginalized "other" (§8.4), and an emphasis on the intersubjective and existential aspects of religious faith (§8.2). Nonetheless, it is important to remember that McLaren's perception of conservative Christians is a result of *his* personal upbringing. While it may not be everyone's experience, his writings do reflect an honest appraisal of his many encounters with fundamentalists. Consequently, since no person is detachable from their experiential knowledge, McLaren's biography explains why he would seek out an alternative Christian paradigm. In other words, McLaren naturally sought out an approach to faith that would cognitively, affectively, and socially align best with his experiential knowledge.[52] In this way, McLaren's sense of compassion and dialectical temperament forecasts his subsequent moral disillusionment with the Religious Right and their adoption of neoconservatism.

---

51. Dahl, "Adolescent Brain Development," 21.
52. Paloutzian et al., "Conversion, Deconversion, and Spiritual Transformation," 399–421.

3

McLaren the Activist

3.0 INTRODUCTION

Brian McLaren once wrote an open letter to the white evangelical community, "You don't have to follow the path being laid for you by Jerry Falwell Jr, Franklin Graham, Robert Jeffress, Pat Robertson, and others like them."[1] By 1994, McLaren became so disillusioned with the Religious Right's takeover of Christianity that he contemplated abandoning faith altogether (*FFS* §3, 72), arguing that the most outspoken "Christians" were also the least Christ-like (*NS* §3, 24). From his perspective, a predominant reason the Christian church is failing in the West is because of its representatives.[2] As David Kinnaman observes, "Most people I meet assume that *Christian* means very conservative, entrenched in their thinking, antigay, antichoice, angry, violent, illogical, empire builders . . . they generally cannot live peacefully with anyone who doesn't believe what they believe."[3] David Hempton concurs, "Nothing bred disenchantment faster than profound disillusionment with the lives, characters, behaviors, and opinions of fellow evangelicals. . . . people whose pious claims are not matched by the quality of their lives."[4]

---

1. McLaren, "Dear White Evangelical Christians . . ."
2. McLaren, "Conditions for the Great Religion Singularity," 40–49. McLaren explains elsewhere, "Too many of our most 'educated' Christians are some of the meanest. They may know the most information about the Bible but are the least Christ-like" (McLaren, "Informed, but Not Transformed").
3. Kinnaman and Lyons, *Unchristian*, 26; italics in original.
4. Hempton, *Evangelical Disenchantment*, 192.

The thesis of this chapter is that it is impossible to comprehend McLaren's philosophy of religion without also recognizing the disconnect he observed between the Right's religious proclamations and their behavior, which forced him to reconsider conventional paradigms (*SMJ* §Intro, xiv).[5] Three areas will support this thesis: 1) McLaren's moral identity crisis; 2) the grounds for this crisis; and 3) his resultant disillusionment with neo-Evangelicalism. To begin, readers must first understand how McLaren describes his religious identity crisis.

3.1 "CONFLICTED RELIGIOUS IDENTITY SYNDROME" (CRIS)

McLaren jokingly asks why the founders of the four great world religions (Jesus, Moses, the Buddha, and Mohammed) would cross a road together? To which McLaren comically responds, "To escape from a mob of their angry, hypercritical, and hypocritical followers" (*JMBM* §1, 5n7).[6] Part of McLaren's spiritual development was the realization that a "hyperorthodox" worldview had actually caused him to betray Christ (cf. *COOS1* §2, 33; *WMRBW*, 108), particularly with the hypocrisy, hatred, and neoconservative conformism being promoted. To him, the tolerant attitude of many nonbelievers has put Christians to shame, and the information he has learned from history, philosophy, and science do not always support conventional Christian teachings (*FFS* §Intro, 23). He labels this realization the "Conflicted Religious Identity Syndrome" (CRIS), a neologism meaning a person cherishes certain religious principles (e.g., loving others) but is convinced that his religion fails to embody those values. As a result, CRIS spawns the desire to initiate a spiritual reformation (see *JMBM* §2, 13-24).

At its core, CRIS stems from in-group/out-group attitudes that derive from assuming Christians must oppose all other worldviews, which itself originates from a fear of cultural syncretism (cf. *GDT*).[7] "In the Bible I read about love, love, love, but in various Christian subcultures . . . I keep encountering fear, superiority, and hostility. . . .[where] I can't belong to our *us* unless I am against our *them*" (*JMBM* §2, 14; italics in original). The result for McLaren was a felt need to separate himself from other antagonistic believers (*JMBM* §2, 17; *NKOC* §Intro, xvi), realizing that Christianity is now tainted specifically because of these attitudes (*BMF*, 293; *GO* §18, 267-68;

---

5. Cf. Niebuhr, *The Kingdom of God in America*. The significance of this chapter is that while many may presume McLaren has a *theological* or *epistemological* objection to neo-Evangelicalism, the chapter will demonstrate that these issues are actually peripheral in nature to his overall *moral* dissent from the wider neoconservative subculture. The aim here is not to corroborate or promote McLaren's socio-political sentiments; rather, the point is to systematize the tensions that caused McLaren to forsake what he believes is an increasingly immoral approach to faith.

6. According to McLaren, the label "Christian" has now become synonymous with animosity (*VA*, 15). His fictional character Dan utters an all-too-common experience, "I have never been treated as badly by a single non-Christian . . . as I have by dozens of zealous but angry Christians" (*NKOC* §11, 142).

7. Larson and Shady, "Love My (Religious) Neighbor," 134-48.

TWLE). He soon asked himself, "What's wrong with us?" (*EMC* §5, 32), eventually concluding that America's culture-religion is partly to blame.[8]

3.2 AMERICANIZED CULTURE-RELIGION

McLaren argues that Christianity has degraded into a culture-religion, creating "disciples" who facilitate American imperialism more than Christ's teachings. Branding it "the civil religion of the West," he characterizes American Christianity as maintaining the privileged standing of national, political, and social control with the promise of wealth, particularly for already-affluent, white suburbanites (*FFS* §1, 43; *GO* §12, 185; *NKOC* §9, 107). "Here in the United States we see large sectors of the Christian community associated with American hyperconfidence, white privilege, institutional racism, civil religion, neocolonialism, and nationalistic militarism—often fortified by a privatized faith in a privatized national/tribal god."[9] The term "culture-religion" suggests that both secular and religious institutions have, in fact, become indistinguishable. According to Leigh Jordahl, evangelicalism in America has adopted an anti-intellectual and anti-institutional mentality, emphasizing an individualized yet unyielding moralism that distrusts authorities while praising the "self-made man."[10]

Consequently, culture-religions become stagnant, apathetic, and preoccupied with their own dominance, being mere collaborators with corrupt power structures (cf. *EMC* §9, 72-73):

> One of my deepest concerns, because I do a lot of international work, is that here in America our churches have so identified themselves with American nationalism, and especially with a certain neoconservative ethos in the Republican Party. That kind of partisan alliance is dangerous, I believe. It puts us in the tradition of being a "civil religion" much like mainline Protestantism was in the first two-thirds of the twentieth century. Civil religions lose their prophetic voice. As a result, for many people—especially young people and highly educated people the word "Jesus" now means things it shouldn't mean: judgmental, angry, exclusive, unkind, lacking understanding, reactionary, violent, pro-war, anti-poor, and the like. (cf. *TWLR*)[11]

---

8. As McLaren clarifies, understanding his identity crisis explains why he writes books in the first place, "Much of my writing has been literary self-therapy for my own chronic case of CRIS" (*JMBM* §2, 21).

9. McLaren, "Church Emerging," 148. Not surprisingly, then, a "civil religion" to McLaren is often synonymous with white nationalism (McLaren, "The Secret Message of Jesus," 20).

10. Jordahl, "The American Evangelical," 188-93. See also, Noll, *The Scandal of the Evangelical Mind*.

11. Streett, "An Interview with Brian McLaren," 6. See also, McLaren, "Our Allergic Reactions." For more on evangelicalism's cosmopolitan alliance with the political, corporate, and Wall Street elite, see Lindsay, *Faith in the Halls of Power*.

The effect becomes a belief that people are responsible for their own fortunes and, therefore, should not blame institutionalized prejudices for their inability to attain upward economic or social mobility.[12] As Douglas Sharp explains, "This should not be surprising, given the enculturation of Christianity in this country and the way the Christian community in general tends to absorb and reflect the cultural values and attitudes at work in the surrounding milieu."[13] Naturally, then, a culture-religion tends toward the accumulation of political power.

3.2.1 Identity Politics and Bigotry

What distresses McLaren is the fanaticism and militancy of neoconservative Christians (*EMC* §16, 132-33), whose politicking seems overly preoccupied with power (*NKOC* §9, 103-4). For him, while outspoken leaders proclaim Jesus as "Lord," in actuality, they peddle his name like a cheap political slogan (*GO* §1, 70) where God-talk is used to excuse the morally unjustifiable and to elect the morally repugnant (*GI*, 178-79). The result is Christianity becoming "little more than a chaplaincy for other ideologies, offering its services to the highest bidder" (*GSM*, 6). He writes,

> Exposing this theological connection between white Christianity and white supremacy is especially urgent now because Donald Trump, his Republican Party, and their media (Fox, Breitbart, etc.) have forged alliances with both white Christian leaders (Evangelicals like Franklin Graham, Jerry Falwell Jr, Pat Robertson, Rick Joyner, and Robert Jeffress) and with alt-right white nationalist organizers and media outlets. They are building momentum for an American future that many of us feel is not merely conservative; it is radically regressive and downright evil, seeking to return to the ugly American past of Jim Crow and American apartheid.[14]

McLaren explains that conservatives felt socially alienated from the nonconformist culture of the 1960s. By the 1980s, however, conservatives regained social and political control in the nation (*GO* §8, 136; *NKOCY* §1, 10). It was then that McLaren became cynical of the Religious Right:

---

12. Accordingly, two-thirds of evangelicals do not believe the government has an obligation to help improve the lives of the black community and over one-third believe too much money has already been spent on the problem of racism. Nearly half simply believe African-Americans ought to overcome prejudice on their own and four-fifths believe blacks ought to "work their way up" in society without the backing of government policies. Likewise, over half of evangelicals believe blacks lack the motivation to pull themselves out of poverty and almost three-quarters do not think the impoverished plight of blacks is due to discrimination. See Sharp, "Evangelicals," 245-55.

13. Sharp, "Evangelicals," 238. Cf. Emerson and Smith, *Divided by Faith*, 21-22, 93-113. Bruce Fields also relates, "Because the issue of racism still exists in our society, it still exists in the church" (Fields, *Introducing Black Theology*, 53).

14. McLaren, "Why I'll Be in Charlottesville this Weekend." See also, McLaren, "Targeted Medicine."

> My disillusionment was intensified by what was happening in the Christian community in America during the 1980s and 1990s. A large number of both Protestant and Catholic leaders had aligned with a neoconservative political ideology, trumpeting what they called "conservative family values," but minimizing biblical community values. They supported wars of choice, defended torture, opposed environmental protection, and seemed to care more about protecting the rich from taxes than liberating the poor from poverty or minorities from racism. They spoke against big government as if big was bad, yet they seemed to see big military and big business as inherently good. They wanted to protect unborn human life inside the womb, but didn't seem to care about born human life in slums or prisons or nations they considered enemies. They loved to paint gay people as a threat to marriage, seeming to miss the irony that heterosexual people were damaging marriage at a furious pace without any help from gay couples. They consistently relegated females to second-class status, often while covering up for their fellow males when they fell into scandal or committed criminal abuse. They interpreted the Bible to favor the government of Israel and to marginalize Palestinians, and even before [9/11], I feared that through their influence Muslims were being cast as the new scapegoats, targets of a scary kind of religiously inspired bigotry. (NKOCY §1, 6-7)[15]

From his viewpoint, neoconservatism has intensified through "politically inflammatory rhetoric," which convinces good-natured Christians to engage in modern-day witch hunts (FFR §8, 163).[16] McLaren describes the situation, "Listeners/viewers are told of vast left-wing conspiracies to 'destroy the family' or 'stamp out religious freedom.' They are then begged to help fight against 'the homosexual agenda' or 'secular humanism' or 'postmodernism' or 'terrorism' or some other real or imagined bugaboo"

---

15. Cf. "On the Danger of a Single Story" and McLaren, "Conditions for the Great Religion Singularity," 40-49. One of McLaren's novels depicts the Biblical Evangelical Fellowship (BEF), a fictional organization devoted to lobbying for so-called "traditional" morals. As one lobbyist describes it, "We stand for biblical values, biblical absolutes, the biblical worldview, and we also are strong supporters of pro-life causes, states' rights, and free markets. Lately we're working very hard to oppose genetic engineering and to reduce the size and power of the federal government. And we're really trying to push for a constitutional amendment to protect the family from, you know, immoral forces." In response, a local community pastor thought to himself, "I couldn't help but notice that the BEF was against a stronger federal government yet wanted the federal government to be strong enough to 'protect the family,' but I didn't want to point out that irony" (LWWAT §26, 159).

16. He states, "Conservatives grew because their faith was self-centered and self-serving, compromised with the 'low-culture' of middle-class racism, greed, and apathy, pandering to the fears and prejudices of the masses" (GO §8, 137). Christian Smith writes, "Evangelicals . . . thrive on fear of impending catastrophe, accelerating decay, apocalyptic crises that demand immediate action (and maybe money). All of that can be energizing and mobilizing. The problem is, it also often distorts, misrepresents, or falsifies what actually happens to be true about reality. And to sacrifice what is actually true for the sake of immediate attention and action is plain wrong" (Smith, "Evangelicals Behaving Badly with Statistics," 11).

(*GO* §17, 245-46).[17] It was this mentality that led McLaren to recognize Christianity's syncretism with white supremacy and imperialism (cf. *AIFA*, 23-24; *COOS1* §12a, 167-68).[18] For him, neoconservatism is merely a front for racial and social bigotry.

What is not widely recognized is that conservative religious leaders initially entered politics to promote racial segregation. In the 1970s, district courts denied the tax-exempt status of Christian "segregation academies," such as Bob Jones University, because they discriminated against African-Americans. These rulings prompted the burgeoning Religious Right to seek changes in federal anti-segregation laws.[19] The basis of the movement, then, was not abortion or same-sex marriage. It was a belief that religious liberty should grant the freedom to discriminate against segments of the American population. In the aftermath of the Civil Rights, however, religious conservatives realized that overt racism was no longer acceptable outside of the South.[20] Thus, they hid their discriminatory agenda behind a number of emotionally-infused issues in order to galvanize, polarize, and distract religious voters.[21] Jerrold Packard explains,

> With few exceptions, Southern Protestants defended segregation as strongly in the mid-twentieth century as they had slavery in the mid-nineteenth. As it remained quiet about race riots, and as it did the same in questions of lynching, so, too, did the voice of the Southern church remain silent about the primal Christian command to love one's neighbor. . . . American Protestantism before the civil rights revolution stood foursquare, shoulder to shoulder, and homily to homily as a defender of white supremacy.[22]

The Republican Party, in turn, capitalized on the situation by politicizing Southern sentiments, masking their other political agenda in the process (e.g., tax cuts for the rich, elimination of environmental and free-market regulations, voter suppression of

---

17. For example, James Dobson writes, "The homosexual activist movement and related entities have been working to implement a master plan that has had as its centerpiece the utter destruction of the family. . . .[Their] goals include . . . overturning laws prohibiting pedophilia. . ." (Dobson, *Marriage Under Fire*, 19). Cf. Bivins, *Religion of Fear*.

18. McLaren, "12 Ounce Interview," 01:39-01:56. Cf. Quebedeaux, *The Young Evangelicals*, 115-17; Diamond, *Not by Politics Alone*; Berlet and Lyons, *Right-Wing Populism in America*, 265-86; and Sharp, "Evangelicals," 237-61.

19. Even Jerry Falwell Sr. advocated for racial segregation and Jim Crow laws in the South before it became expedient not to do so. In a 1958 speech, Falwell remarked, "The true Negro does not want integration. He realizes his potential is far better among his own race. . . . We see the Devil himself behind [integration]. It will destroy our race eventually" (quoted in "The Nation's Best Bible College," 43). See also, Harding, *The Book of Jerry Falwell*, 25-26.

20. For the political realignment of the South toward Republicans, see Fitzgerald, *The Evangelicals*, 319-36 and Micklethwait and Wooldridge, *The Right Nation*, 249-69.

21. On the Religious Right's historical involvement in politics, see Martin, *With God on Our Side*; Utter and Storey, *The Religious Right*, 1-76; and Labberton, "Introduction," 1-17.

22. Packard, *American Nightmare*, 159; emphasis in original.

minority groups, etc.). Prior to this time, Republicans had no stance on abortion and avoided religious talk altogether.[23]

McLaren comments, "I do think it's dangerous when Christians become unthinking devotees of any political party. 'The religious right' in practical terms means 'Republican Christians'—and in this case, the placement of modifier and noun is significant. Does being a Republican modify the way a person is a Christian, or should being a Christian modify the way a person is Republican?" (cf. *TWLD; TWLR*).[24] In one public statement, McLaren declares:

> We hope that those who would like to disassociate us from the term *evangelical* will be aware of the tendency of some in their ranks toward narrowing and politicizing the term so that it only applies to strict Calvinists, conservative Republicans, people with specific views on U.S. domestic, foreign, military, or economic policy. (cf. *TWLE*)[25]

From McLaren's view, while objecting to abortion and homosexuality are now hallmarks of the Republican base, the reality is that the Religious Right was originally animated by a cultural grievance against social equality.[26] McLaren believes things like abortion are mere "fringe issues upon which [Republicans] never planned to take action" in order to arouse religious voters.[27]

Eventually, a mutual co-opting occurred where the Republican Party exploited the fears of religious Southerners while the Religious Right exploited the Republican Party's willingness to endorse segregation.[28] Today, significant percentages of evangelicals continue to believe racism does not exist, believe blacks are inherently unintelligent and lazy, oppose laws that protect racial minorities, and object to having

---

23. See Kyle, *Evangelicalism*, 167-220; Wuthnow, *After the Baby Boomers*, 171; and Lewis, *The Rights Turn in Conservative Christian Politics*, esp. 1-28.

24. McLaren, "Religious Right or Wrong?," 10. McLaren recounts the time a group of fundamentalists began preaching on his college campus. It was not long before their preaching switched to promoting the Republican Party as though the gospel and Republicanism were the exact same (*COOS1* §12a, 167-68). "Everyone knows how much influence they have in our political system, and how one political party in particular panders for their votes. But look at the countries where this lifestyle runs rampant, and you'll get an idea what our nation will be like if some of us don't have the courage to stand up and speak up. Wherever this lifestyle spreads, a whole host of social problems inevitably follows" (*NKOCY* §17, 174).

25. Jones et al., "Response to Recent Criticisms"; italics in original.

26. For details, see Conway and Siegelman, *Holy Terror*; Diamond, *Spiritual Warfare*; Frank, *Less Than Conquerors*; Williams, *God's Own Party*; Raja, *The Religious Right*; and Micklethwait and Wooldridge, *The Right Nation*, 27-128.

27. McLaren, "A Brief History of the 21st Century," 16-18.

28. For instance, the Religious Right secured the Presidential election of Ronald Reagan whose administration, in turn, actively defended Bob Jones's discriminatory practices before the Supreme Court. See Balmer, "Critical Junctures in American Evangelicalism," 67-75. Cf. Ryden, "Evangelicals," 205-24.

neighbors of a different race.[29] Many religious leaders have even resorted to political sabotage and outright deception. For example, "[Jerry] Falwell's eagerness to discredit President Carter prompted him, just weeks before the election, to fabricate an unflattering story about homosexuals on the president's staff. The minister later confessed his lie."[30] In fact, sociological studies reveal that the more religious a person is, the less tolerant they are of opposing viewpoints.[31] McLaren describes the conservative temperament as a new "club" for modern-day Pharisees. Eerily similar to a cult of personality, they often close themselves off from dissenters and attempt to convert through massive money-marketing events, youth recruitments, and political subterfuge (*NKOCY* §1, 7; §17, 174-75).

He captures the sentiment of many who are mortified about how conservative Christians will spend money on buildings but ignore the poor. Their talk of morality appears to ignore the mistreatment of homosexuals and other minorities (*FFR* §4, 84-85), though Jesus condemned that kind of political and religious duplicity (*WMRBW*, 106-107). McLaren explains further,

> Republicans were gradually won over to a different moral agenda: oppose environmental protections . . ., oppose programs to help poor people . . ., promote programs to help rich families get and stay richer at a faster rate than anyone else . . ., oppose abortion, oppose gay marriage, and promote unlimited increase in weapon sales in personal and public life, deny racial injustice in the present and minimize it in the past, etc.[32]

Jim Wallis's evaluation of the situation helps to illuminate McLaren's own disillusionment:

> It is important to recognize what a historical aberration the Religious Right represents. For a biblical religion to be put at the service of the rich instead of the poor, the powerful instead of the oppressed, of war instead of peace, turns Christian teaching upside down. For evangelical religion to be used to fuel the engines of racial and class division, to block the progress of women, to undermine care for the creation, to fight the banning of assault weapons, to end public legal services to those who can't afford them, and actually encourage public policy that abandons our poorest children runs counter to Christian

---

29. See the statistics in Jones et al., *Who Sees Discrimination?*; Sider, *The Scandal of the Evangelical Conscience*, 24-26; Smith, *Christian America?*, 209-12, 221-22; Sharp, "Evangelicals," 240-45; and Emerson and Smith, *Divided by Faith*, esp. 69-91.

30. Utter and Storey, *The Religious Right*, 12. Sadly, Falwell had a penchant for distorting facts, as well as outright lying (see Harding, *The Book of Jerry Falwell*, esp. 25-28 and Martin, *With God on Our Side*, 191-220).

31. See Wilcox and Jelen, "Evangelicals and Political Tolerance," 25-46; Woodberry and Smith, "Fundamentalism et al," 25-56; Reimer and Park, "Tolerant (In)civility?," 735-45; and Gushee, *The Future of Faith in American Politics*, 141-74.

32. McLaren, "Q and R: Should I go." Significantly, McLaren believes Jesus resembles an Hispanic migrant worker more than a white suburbanite (*GSM*, vix-x).

> Scripture, tradition, and history. The Religious Right has accomplished an almost complete reversal of Christian teaching and all in the name of God.[33]

This aberration led Wallis to ask elsewhere, "How did tax cuts for the rich become a religious imperative?"[34] Accordingly, McLaren insists that Christians need to "wake up" to how their religion is being used in furtherance of injustice and inequality (*GSM*, 85).[35] The hope is that Christians will begin asking, "To what degree have political movements co-opted us? To what degree do political movements use our religious convictions for their own agendas?"[36] In his view, Republicans want sycophants, not Christ-followers (*WMRBW*, 216-21, 231-34):

> If I say "Jesus" to many. . . .They don't think of someone who had special good news for the poor; they think of people who want to give every possible advantage to the rich because they think the poor are to blame, largely, for their poverty. They don't think of someone who overturned the status quo, but of people who represent the status quo. They don't think of someone who talked about turning the other cheek, but of people who defend preemptive violence. So, I wish people would seek to understand the rising dissatisfaction surrounding how the Religious Right has "re-branded" Christianity.[37]

To McLaren, as Christian teachings are minimized, its re-branding morphs into nationalism.

3.2.1.1 American Exceptionalism

John Seel writes, "Many American evangelicals have been truly more American than Christian, more dependent on historical myths than spiritual realities, more shaped by the flag than the cross" (cf. *TWLE*).[38] According to McLaren, underlying this culture-religion is a misguided belief in American exceptionalism, which suggests the

---

33. Wallis, *Who Speaks for God?*, 17-18. It is interesting to note that Arizona Republican Senator, John McCain, once condemned both Pat Robertson and Jerry Falwell Sr. (by name) as "agents of intolerance" (Barstow, "McCain Denounces Political Tactics of Christian Right").

34. Wallis, *God's Politics*, 82. McLaren exhorts elsewhere, "To the degree that they have sold their spiritual birthright for a political ideology, they must repent; neither left nor right leads to the higher kingdom" (*GO* §8, 140).

35. See further, Turner, "Black Evangelicalism," 40-56; Heltzel, *Jesus and Justice*, 13-44; Rah, *The Next Evangelicalism*, 64-87, 127-40; and Putnam and Campbell, *American Grace*, 419-42.

36. McLaren, "Religious Right or Wrong?," 10. Cf. Diamond, *Spiritual Warfare*, 45-81. McLaren asks elsewhere, "Do the teachings of the gospel and the Bible in general form us into a truly unique community, or are we a religious echo of secular movements?" (McLaren, "A Postmodern View of Scripture," 10).

37. Streett, "An Interview with Brian McLaren," 13-14.

38. Seel, "Nostalgia for the Lost Empire," 66.

United States receives divine favor so long as it remains faithful to God.[39] As Christian Smith summarizes,

> Christian Right rhetoric contends: America was founded as a Christian nation and prospered under God's blessing. Having recently abandoned its commitment to God's unchanging truth and morality, however, America is now suffering social breakdown. Unless America repents and returns to "traditional" values and morals, America will suffer God's judgment. Turning America around from its anti-Christian moral drift will require the active struggle of Christians and supportive allies—the moral majority of Americans—against hostile forces.[40]

Arguing that this belief is simply a national form of white supremacy (*GSM*, 253n10), McLaren asks, "When was [America] a Christian nation? When we were killing, culturally imprisoning, and stealing the lands of millions of native peoples in a New World version of the holocaust? When we were importing and exploiting millions of slaves?" (*COOS1* §2, 33). Thus, McLaren forewarns Christian nationalists that they may, in fact, be supporting "Babylon" by refusing to challenge American atrocities (*AMP* §4, 71; cf. *TWLR*). "I feel surrounded by Christians who very much like the idea of an American God and a middle-class Republican Jesus, first and foremost concerned about Our National Security and Our Way of Life. 'The Lord is My Shepherd' becomes . . . 'The Lord is Our Secretary of Defense,' ready to sacrifice 10,000 lives of noncitizens elsewhere for the safety of U.S. citizens here" (*GO* §3, 82). He continues,

> My nation was founded on land theft and countless broken treaties, on the suppression exclusion, ethnic cleansing, and near eradication of the people who inhabited this land (Native Peoples). And having stole the land, my forefathers prospered on the subjugation and enslavement of another people (African slaves). Now, my country dominates the world and sees American self-interest as its "prime directive." Everything I know of God tells me that God was outraged by the atrocities of my European ancestors and brokenhearted for the victims, and that God remains outraged. (*GO* §10, 168)[41]

---

39. For more on American exceptionalism, see Lipset, *American Exceptionalism*; Madsen, *American Exceptionalism*; Sutton, *American Apocalypse*, 47-78, 263-92; Kruse, *One Nation under God*; and Micklethwait and Wooldridge, *The Right Nation*, 291-353.

40. Smith, *Christian America?*, 199. In 1996, 87 percent of evangelicals and 82 percent of fundamentalists believed America was founded as a Christian nation (pp. 201-2). As Falwell Sr. once wrote, "We are not a perfect nation, but we are still a free nation because we have the blessings of God upon us. We must continue to follow in a path that will ensure that blessing. We must not forget that it is God Almighty who has made and preserved us as a nation" (Falwell, *Listen, America!*, 20).

41. McLaren also recounts that American atrocities have continued with the creation of concentration camps, racial cleansings, mass incarcerations, and mass executions. He also argues it is important to recall that all of these brutalities occurred under the explicit support of many (if not most) "good" and "biblical" Christians (*GSM*, 80-85). Elsewhere, McLaren notes the irony that European colonists apparently did not believe God created Native Americans with the same unalienable rights as their white counterparts (*GSM*, 82). In fact, it was common for early settlers to compare Native Americans

For McLaren, only the promotion of justice and equality are worthy of the label "exceptional."[42] Unfortunately, American exceptionalism has led to a dehumanization and hatred of others.[43]

3.2.2 Christian Tribalism

The inevitable result of an Americanized culture-religion is Christian tribalism (*COOS1* §2, 33), which promotes an unjustified conviction that God favors one particular subculture, thereby categorizing all others as an enemy of "true" Christianity (*JMBM* §2, 13n1). As James Barr writes, "Conservatives have been on the whole a remarkably quarrelsome segment of Christendom," arguing that conflict and internal strife lie at the heart of the evangelical movement.[44] McLaren has personally witnessed churches embroil themselves in trivial squabbles, wasting energy on deciding who among them is truly born again and who really possesses gifts of the Spirit (cf. *MRTYR* §13, 101; §14, 103-4). All the while, the rest of the world endures violence, war, drugs, racism, and greed (*LWWAT* §25, 154).[45]

It was this "groupishness" that solidified McLaren's belief that tribal Christians praised "judgmentalism and anger as fruits of the Holy Spirit" (*GO* §6, 117). The problem is that religious hostility occasions more segregation and suspicion in the world (*JMBM* §1, 11n16; §2, 19-20; §7, 58-59), which can then foster violence toward others (cf. *AIFA*, 283-84). "To me, deep, theological conversations about the shape and purpose of the gospel, along with issues of justice—racial, environmental, and economic—are far more urgent and important than arguments about what goes on

---

to the biblical Canaanites in order to justify genocide (*JMBM* §9, 77). Consequently, the United States demonstrates just how unchristian America really is (cf. *COOS1* §10, 124), manifesting a deep insecurity in its delusional sense of superiority (McLaren, foreword to *Christian America*, xi-xii).

42. McLaren, "America the Exceptional," 17-19. Cf. Berlet and Lyons, *Right-Wing Populism in America*, 247-64. For McLaren, the result of not promoting global justice is a distorted image of Christ where Christians prize "the nuclear bomb-dropping America-first Jesus . . . the Native American-slaying genocidal Jesus, the homophobic 'God-hates-fags' Jesus . . . the anti-Muslim Crusader Jesus, and so on" (*NKOCY* §12, 122).

43. McLaren, "A Postmodern View of Scripture," 8; "America the Exceptional," 17-19. See also, Miller, "Brian McLaren."

44. Barr, *Fundamentalism*, 187. Cf. Johnson, *Evangelicals at an Impasse*, 1-8, 147. For McLaren, Protestants seem incapable of not protesting each other (*GO* §7, 125).

45. For instance, the so-called "moral" controversies of his youth involved headcoverings for women, long hair on men, the use of guitars and drums in worship, and women speaking in church. What was important in the past is now distracting and trifling today (*COOS1* §4, 60-61). According to McLaren, this in-group mentality demands that people "*believe right, think right, speak right, and act right, and we'll let you in*" (*MRTYR* §11, 84; italics in original). For him, the Apostle Peter's first encounter with the Gentile Cornelius (Acts 10) is instructive. Just as Peter could no longer label segments of the population as unclean, so too should Christians not malign people as "unsaved" or "lost." These labels are pretentious and distracting. In any case, tribalistic believers steadily become insalubrious, creepy, and uncharitable, failing to resemble a community truly filled with God's gentle Spirit (*GO* §1, 50-51; *MRTYR* §5, 57-58). See also, Bendroth, "The Search," 122-34.

in church services."⁴⁶ Consequently, Christians recklessly squander resources trying to identify and censor perceived threats to their clan more than they try to better the world (*JMBM* §7, 61). The ramification is a promotion of self-serving household deities and nationalistic tribal gods who support only one particular group of people (*GDT*).⁴⁷ "It's an old and tired game: quoting sacred texts to strengthen an us-versus-them mentality that, in today's world, could too easily lead to a last-tango, nuclear-biochemical kamikaze Crusade jihad" (*NKOCY* §7, 70). From this tribalism naturally develops a fear of diversity.

3.2.3 Heterophobia and Homophily

McLaren begins by describing "heterophobia" as the fear of those who differ morally, theologically, politically, or philosophically, which often concludes with threats of "God's violent wrath" (*NKOCY* §17, 173-75; cf. *LWWAT* §Comm., 183). He refers to this hypervigilant partisanship as a "mean world" syndrome where people are wary of new information, which impedes their ability to act on behalf of the poor and marginalized.⁴⁸ Their evangelistic mantra soon becomes "turn or burn" and "capitulate or we'll legislate" (*COOS1* §12b, 180), naïvely thinking they are the sole possessors of truth while everyone else needs to conform (*GO* §3, 85). The effect of heterophobia is a paralyzing "religious homophily," which prevents entire subcultures from exposure to different viewpoints (*VA*, 106).⁴⁹ As McLaren explains,

> One of the greatest enemies of evangelism is the church as fortress or social club; it sucks Christians out of their neighborhoods, clubs, workplaces, schools, and other social networks and isolates them in a religious ghetto. There it must entertain them (through various means, many of them masquerading as education) and hold them (through various means, many of them epitomized by

---

46. McLaren, "Overcoming Resistance," 19.

47. McLaren, "Risky Business," 18.

48. Csinos and McLaren, "Breaking the Bubble Wrap," 16-22. McLaren argues that the problem is exacerbated when certain "colorful Southern Baptists" regularly appear on television to spread animosity, "which doesn't seem to bother them at all" (*GO* §12, 200). Significantly, surveys do indicate that evangelicals are considerably more exclusivistic in their beliefs, resulting in them being more antagonistic toward other perspectives than the average American (Smith, *Christian America?*, 201-3). It is no surprise, therefore, that political and social conservatives are less questioning, resourceful, and open to new experiences, which happen to be the characteristics that define McLaren most (§2.3). See Gerber et al., "The Big Five Personality," 265-87.

49. The term "homophily" describes a psychological phenomenon where those with similar characteristics tend only to associate with one another (Lazarsfeld and Merton, "Friendship as a Social Process," 18-66). "Religious homophily," therefore, suggests people are inclined to associate almost exclusively with people who share their particular religious beliefs; but as McLaren remarks, "It would be kind of boring to only have friends who are exactly like you, don't you think?" (McLaren, foreword to *Branded Faith*, xiii). For more details, see Slade, "Religious Homophily and Biblicism," 13-28 and Emerson and Smith, *Divided by Faith*, 135-51.

the words *guilt* and *fear*). Thus Christians are warehoused as merchandise for heaven, kept safe in a protected space.[50]

The problem is that conservative churches tend to be substantially less open to alternative beliefs and potentially edifying viewpoints.[51] "We have long doctrinal statements about every little thing that people agree with—otherwise they can't belong—but then as a result we don't have much practice in diversity."[52] Consequently, as religious homophily increases, the ability for Christians to befriend others, especially nonbelievers, quickly diminishes.[53] This mentality only perpetuates the notion that dissenting tribes are actually enemies of truth in need of conquest (*JMBM* §7, 62-63). The result is the now infamous culture wars of the late twentieth century.

3.2.4 Moralistic Culture Wars

For McLaren, while proponents of the culture wars sought to recapture "traditional moral values," the result was actually a general opposition to civil rights in the form of racism, sexism, and homophobia.[54] From his standpoint, these moral "warriors" have repeatedly been on the wrong side of history (*EMC* §5, 33), opposing things that would later be declared good by the culture at large (*GO* §1, 44). McLaren offers a contemporary example:

> Fifteen or 20 years ago it was: "If you're gay, it's a choice, it's a sin, you should repent and change." Five or 10 years ago it was: "If you're gay, you have a psychological problem and you can be healed." Fewer and fewer evangelicals are saying that; they're saying: "If you're gay this is your sign that you should be celibate." I still don't think that's the only valid response, but it's interesting how those answers change.[55]

The transient nature of these so-called traditional morals results in Christians succumbing to a war-like stupor, forcing them to amplify their own righteousness while

---

50. McLaren and Litfin, "Emergent Evangelism," 43; italics in original. As one study indicates, religious characteristics are the most significant determiner of psychological homophily than any other grouping, including gender, age, ethnicity, and social class (Adida et al., "Religious Homophily in a Secular Country," 1187-1206).

51. Scheitle and Adamczyk, "It Takes Two," 24-27. Cf. Granovetter, "The Strength of Weak Ties," 1360-80; Coleman, "Social Capital," 95-120; Schwandel, "Individual, Congregational, and Denominational Effects," 159-71; and Stark, *What Americans Really Believe*, 34, 41.

52. McLaren, "Practicing and Loving Diversity," 35.

53. As sociologist Robert Wuthnow remarks, "Evangelicals are a more likely source of mobilized resistance against newcomers than any other religious group" (Wuthnow, *After the Baby Boomers*, 196). See also, Smith et al., *American Evangelicalism*, 89-119, 178-217 and Stark, *What Americans Really Believe*, 30-33, 43-44.

54. Cf. Lienesch, *Redeeming America*, 52-76; King, "Evangelical Confessions," 67-68; Micklethwait and Wooldridge, *The Right Nation*, 83; and Berlet and Lyons, *Right-Wing Populism in America*, 228-46.

55. McLaren, "Changing Faith," 16.

exaggerating the wickedness of others (*FOWA* §13, 127).[56] As a result, any change to the status quo is interpreted as an evil incursion by the enemies of God (*MRTYR* §2, 30).[57] For McLaren, the "real enemies" of humanity are invisible forces, such as nationalism, religious supremacy, self-indulgence, xenophobia, and selfish ambition (*WMRBW*, 240-42). Sadly, however, conservative churches in America ignored these other problems and became obsessed with fighting over just two issues, instead: abortion and homosexuality.[58]

3.2.4.1 Abortion and Homosexuality

From his outlook, topics such as abortion are really just a way to assess a person's political affiliation more than their moral disposition (cf. *AMP* §13, 211).[59] Although McLaren does not explicitly state his position ("pro-life" or "pro-choice"), his writings suggest a moderate stance that prefers abortion rates decrease while recognizing that some women reluctantly choose abortion as the lesser of two evils. However, as he explains, not even the most dedicated "pro-choicer" believes abortion is a societal "good." They merely believe abortion is an undesirable way to prevent even worse health, financial, or psycho-emotional suffering (cf. *EMC* §33, 286-89).[60] For McLaren, abortion is actually a *symptom* of things like greed, fear, poverty, and a lack of education; yet, too many focus on fixing the symptom and not the societal norms that create it.[61] "We presume to call ourselves pro-life, yet we are merchants of death—death by greed, death by fear, death by war, death by overconsumption, death

---

56. McLaren writes, "I fear that American Christians may be going into a kind of warrior trance, that perhaps we are being seduced by 'principalities and powers,' so that we keep saying, 'Lord! Lord!' but do the opposite of what the Lord says" (McLaren, "Practicing and Loving Diversity," 30).

57. It was these culture wars that made Christianity lose credibility among younger generations. Cf. McLaren, "Take Time to Breathe," 21-23; Mukan, "Some evangelicals"; Diamond, *Not by Politics Alone*, 131-72; King, "Evangelical Confessions," 60-72; and Harding, *The Book of Jerry Falwell*, 183-209. For details on the culture wars, see Hartman, *A War for the Soul of America* and Martin, *With God on Our Side*, 117-43.

58. McLaren, "Christian Conference."

59. Interestingly, McLaren lists abortion and homosexuality as "huge moral issues" that need addressing (*COOS1* §4, 61). Elsewhere, he remarks that the Religious Left do the same thing as the Religious Right when they tally support for same-sex marriage and opposition to war (to the neglect of abortion) as an assessment of a person's faith (see McLaren, "A Bridge Far Enough?," 16).

60. McLaren, "Can We Talk?," 13. Cf. Williams, "Prolifers of the Left," 200-20.

61. *GO* §12, 185; cf. *EMC* §33, 286-89; *NKOC* §11, 142-45. For example, many conservatives believe abstinence-only education prevents sexual behavior (*EMC* §4, 27), yet data indicates that white evangelical teenagers are more sexually active than Jews and mainline Protestants. Not surprisingly, these same evangelicals are less likely to use contraceptives, making them rank higher in teen pregnancy and sexually transmitted diseases (*NKOCY* §17, 187; 282n13). For more on how the culture wars prevent practical solutions to abortion, as well as distract believers away from other equally important "pro-life" issues, see Krattenmaker, *The Evangelicals You Don't Know*, 135-55 and Claiborne and Campolo, *Red Letter Revolution*, 85-95.

by hoarding, death by bombing."⁶² One of his biggest concerns is how debating this legally and morally complex issue has forced each side to demonize and dehumanize the other. The resultant polarization stymies compromise on other (sometime more urgent) work, such as climate change, gun violence, and inequality. For him, there are more than just "pro-life" and "pro-choice" options concerning abortion, and the goal of both positions ought to be to reduce the frequency of abortion while protecting vulnerable women.⁶³

Regardless, McLaren does perceive a glaring hypocrisy in any "pro-life" stance that is also pro-war and pro-economic policies that result in the suffering and exploitation of human life. He argues that being pro-*fetus* does not make a Christian pro-*life*. "They wanted to protect unborn human life inside the womb, but didn't seem to care about born human life in slums or prisons or nations they considered enemies" (*NKOCY* §1, 7). "Why do we need to have singular and firm opinions on the protection of the unborn, but not about how to help poor people and how to avoid killing people labeled *enemies* who are already born?" (*EMC* §1, 3; italics in original). "What of the abuse of Muslim children who are bombed with weapons our tax dollars build and drop . . . or children from same-gender parents or undocumented parents whose lives are harmed by our discrimination?"⁶⁴ Ron Sider echoes McLaren's position on abortion:

> We must be pro-life *and* pro-poor, pro-family *and* pro-creation care, pro-racial justice *and* pro-peacemaking. This "completely prolife" agenda is now the official stance of both the Catholic bishops and the National Association of Evangelicals. . . .life does not begin at conception and end at birth. When millions die of starvation or diseases we know how to prevent, when millions die prematurely from smoking, when terrorism and war destroy innocent persons, the sanctity of human life is violated. But that broader "completely pro-life" agenda does not mean we forget about abortion.⁶⁵

Notably, McLaren's views on abortion parallel his position on same-sex marriage, believing the issue is actually one of hypocrisy and bigotry. Labelling it "fundasexuality," McLaren describes neoconservatism's fixation with sexual sin as reactionary and belligerent, reflecting fear more than faith (*NKOCY* §17, 174-75).⁶⁶ This obses-

---

62. McLaren, "'Instead of Ruling'—Prayers," 226–27. Raja summarizes the position: "It is no surprise, then, that the states that profess one or other form of political conservatism are also the last in provision of healthcare, early childhood education, natal care, as well as care for the elderly and infirm" (Raja, *The Religious Right*, 104). See also, Monsma, "Evangelicals and Poverty," 41–55.

63. Carolan and McLaren, "It's Time to Change the Abortion Debate in America."

64. McLaren, "'Instead of Ruling'—Prayers," 227–28. For detailed essays on some of the politically motivated aspects of the pro-life movement, see Segers and Byrnes, *Abortion Politics in American States*.

65. Sider, "McCain or Obama?," 46, 48; italics in original.

66. McLaren writes, "Homosexuality has become . . . a line in the sand, turf upon which a political power struggle occurs, a symbol of the loss of cultural dominance, a kind of moral 'last straw'"

sion with homosexuals perplexes McLaren because evangelicals actually have higher rates of divorce and sexual promiscuity than the general public (*NKOC* §Intro, xx; cf. *NKOCY* §17, 187).[67] In fact, he argues, Christians ought to focus on how they stigmatize others (cf. *NKOCY* §17, 178) before they pronounce judgment over people's sex lives (*AMP* §13, 211).[68] Though he once believed accusations of immorality against homosexuals, McLaren's experiences with gay friends and family made him conclude that these narratives had to be ridiculous. For him, to side with outdated beliefs would require him to assume unconvincingly that his loving relationships with homosexuals were, in fact, a ploy by the gay community (*GSM*, 38-41; *NKOCY* §17, 177).[69]

Consequently, for McLaren, the real issue is a matter of civil rights. When conservatives failed to secure legislative approval in discriminating against African-Americans, the Religious Right turned their attention to denying equal rights to American homosexuals.[70] To illustrate how this part of the culture war resembled racist bigotry, readers need only to alter one word in statements about homosexuals. For example, Jerry Falwell Sr. once declared in 1977, "[*Black*] folks would just as soon kill you as look at you."[71] In 1981, he sent out a mailer that stated, "The [*negros*] are on the march in this country. . . . .And, many of them are after my children and

---

(*MRTYR* §2, 30). Thus, he asks, "Who killed Jesus, adulterers or Pharisees? I'm not trying to minimize adultery. . . .I'm just saying that our modern preoccupations don't seem very informed by the gospel" (*NKOC* §11, 141).

67. McLaren comments, "They loved to paint gay people as a threat to marriage, seeming to miss the irony that heterosexual people were damaging marriage at a furious pace without any help from gay couples" (*NKOCY* §1, 7). Cf. Sider, *The Scandal of the Evangelical Conscience*, 18-20. For a discussion on current perceptions of Christians as homophobic and anti-gay, see Kinnaman and Lyons, *Unchristian*, 91-120.

68. This caution toward attacking homosexuals is especially important considering gay teenagers are at a greater risk of suicide when they feel forced to hide their sexual orientation (see Saewyc, "Research on Adolescent Sexual Orientation," 256-72). McLaren recounts a time when a fundamentalist couple excommunicated their gay son, who later killed himself. For McLaren, an "uncritical loyalty to our ancestors" is simply not worth the cost of committing an "injustice against our descendants" (*JMBM* §6, 52-53). For the scientific and clinical evidence that indicates same-sex attraction is a genetic orientation and not a choice, see Cooke and Sheard, "Understanding Homosexuality," 7-14.

69. In 2014, McLaren publicly demanded that Florida recognize the legality of his son's same-sex marriage. As a pastor, McLaren had numerous encounters with gay congregants asking for spiritual guidance through the travails of stigmatization. For him, marriage is so important (legally, spiritually, economically, and relationally) that it would be unjust to allow only certain people to partake in it (McLaren, "Florida"). Cf. Woodbridge, "Understanding the Emerging Church Movement," 97-113.

70. Significantly, younger evangelicals are more likely to make the distinction between morality and civil liberties, meaning that while evangelicals may disagree with homosexual "behavior," they accept that homosexuals should still have civil liberties without interference from religious sensibilities (Wuthnow, *After the Baby Boomers*, 174-77). According to McLaren, the question of how Christianity will treat women, minorities, and homosexuals (i.e., people's friends and family) in the future is a very real concern and will be an important determiner in whether nonbelievers think religion has anything constructive to offer the new era (*MRTYR* §8, 71).

71. Quoted in Lancaster, *Sex Panic and the Punitive State*, 42.

your children."[72] The word "homosexuals" and "gay" in Falwell's original statements now read "negros" and "black" in order to illustrate that if Falwell had been speaking about skin color, his statements would be considered racist.[73] From McLaren's view, "They're still trying to defend immoral and outdated ways by treating homosexuals in the same unjust and uncompassionate ways they used to treat blacks and women and Jews" (*MRTYR* §2, 31). He further questions,

> If you take the 'conservative' position, assuming you are right, how do you believe homosexual people should be treated? Should they be constantly shamed? Made to live in secret or hiding? Deprived of basic human rights, equal pay, housing, and so on? Accepted, but on some second-class status that would treat them differently from other people? And if you cannot accept homosexual people in your midst, can you accept those who do, or must you reject (on some level) both homosexual people and those who accept them? (*LWWAT* §Comm., 184-85)

Elsewhere, McLaren wonders how the homosexual issue ought to be resolved, "By outlawing them? Jailing them? Shaming them?" (*AMP* §7, 122).[74] For him, the love of neighbor includes defending same-sex couples, and it also means loving without prejudice (*GSM*, 43).[75] However, it was not just how the culture wars victimized other Americans that caused McLaren to separate himself from the Religious Right. It was

---

72. Quoted in Eskridge, *Dishonorable Passions*, 215. It was comments like these that influenced McLaren to declare a "five-year moratorium" on pronouncing judgments on homosexuality so as to dialogue and discuss the issue without such hateful rhetoric (McLaren, "More Important Than Being Right?," 128). Cf. Burk, "Why Evangelicals Should Ignore Brian McLaren," 212-26.

73. Sadly, though advocating "pro-life" values, many Christians at this time began displaying bumper stickers that read, "Kill a Queer for Christ" (Agostinone-Wilson, *Marxism and Education*, 52). Significantly, McLaren is not the only evangelical ethicist who has changed his mind on LGBTQ issues (see McLaren, foreword to *Changing Our Mind*, xviii-xx). Whereas Falwell Sr. vilified homosexuals without recourse, his son (Falwell Jr.) has made Muslims the new target for hateful rhetoric. "Your father used antipathy towards gay people to rally his base, and now, you are doing the same with Muslims. You are being deeply faithful to a tradition that is deeply unfaithful to the life and teaching of Jesus" (McLaren, "An Open Letter to Jerry Falwell").

74. Interestingly, roughly one-half of evangelicals believe their strain of Christian moral sensibilities ought to be legislated despite the fact that not all Americans are Christian. Not surprisingly, three-quarters of Americans disagree. Approximately 70 percent of evangelicals also want the federal government to advance so-called traditional family values, but half of all Americans disagree. As a result, only two-fifths (40 percent) of evangelicals agree with laws designed to protect gays and lesbians while the majority do not (Smith, *Christian America?*, 201-3, 213-18).

75. See McLaren, "Florida." Of course, McLaren insists on the same principle for those who have a history of gay-bashing. When former National Association of Evangelicals president Ted Haggard had been caught in a sex scandal involving a male prostitute, McLaren refused to condemn, criticize, or self-righteously judge. In fact, McLaren defended Haggard as a human being in pain, reminding Christians about Scripture's command to show love and compassion to everyone (McLaren, "'Lord, Have Mercy,'" 7). For a socio-historical examination of both ancient and modern conceptions of sexuality and marriage, as well as how they differ significantly from the monogamous, heteronormative practices of today, see Coontz, *Marriage, A History*; Hubbard, *A Companion to Greek and Roman Sexualities*; and Skinner, *Sexuality in Greek and Roman Culture*.

also how Christianity had "baptized" America's imperialist policies, which have been known to cause suffering and death around the world.

3.3 IMPERIALIZED SUICIDE MACHINE

According to McLaren, "To a great degree, Christianity in America has become a civil religion. In many ways we've become the religious legitimizer of a lot of deeply held American myths."[76] Part of these myths include the idea that America is the savior and ethical leader of the world; yet, the reality is that the United States and its churches have now colluded with neo-colonialist and neo-imperialist agendas, placing American economic interests above the lives of other human beings globally.[77] Resembling old-time atrocities, such as the Crusades and the Holocaust, the American church today is complicit in these oppressive agendas (*FFR* §8, 163; *GO* §Intro, 15).[78] He explains there exists three interconnected global subsystems: 1) a "prosperity system" of industry and trade; 2) a "security system" of military infrastructure and border control; and 3) an "equity system" of judicial processes and regulations. These three systems can do real-world good. Nonetheless, their corruption has since created what McLaren calls the "suicide machine," a metaphor for the mechanistic influences of modernity (§4.2.2) that are now economically, socially, and politically out of control (*EMC* §7, 52-58).

What is significant is the relationship between religious identity and the suicide machine. Referring to it as a "spirituality crisis," McLaren became aware that his own religion enables (and even intensifies) this suicide machine (*EMC* §1, 5; §6, 50; *FOWA* §1, 4). The American church now promotes "the spirit of war, the spirit of racism, the spirit of hate, the spirit of militarism, the spirit of greed. . . .a spirit of patriarchy, a spirit of fear, a spirit of privilege, a spirit of whiteness."[79] Subsequently, too many Christians invoke the name of God to justify these colonialist elements, which has tarnished the name of Jesus around the world (*FFR* §8, 163). In many ways, the individual components of the suicide machine have become a sacred idol to which many Christians unquestioningly defend, particularly social apathy, capitalism, and war.[80]

---

76. McLaren, "*PW* Talks," 20-22.

77. McLaren, "Conversations," 342-43.

78. According to McLaren, many of the "unintended consequences" of institutionalized religion manifest in numerous ways, "from colonialism to environmental destruction, subordination of women to stigmatization of LGBT people, anti-Semitism to Islamophobia, clergy pedophilia to white privilege" (*GSM*, 2). For details on Christian atrocities throughout history, including evangelical and fundamentalist attacks on women, blacks, gays, immigrants, Jews, Muslims, and others, see Cannon et al., *Forgive Us* and Edward T. Babinski, *Leaving the Fold*, 34-60.

79. McLaren, "Q and R: Discernment of Spirits?" Cf. McLaren, "Go Deeper" and "'Instead of Ruling'—Prayers," 225.

80. For McLaren, this sanctifying of certain ideological, political, racial, and religious elements is then used to justify a "good guys" versus "bad guys" mentality (cf. *JMBM* §7, 58-59). See also, McLaren, "The Stories We Tell Ourselves," 16-24.

3.3.1 Social Apathy

Perhaps the most pervasive feature of the suicide machine is its social indifference. Simply stated, Christians have an abysmal record of addressing global problems, having failed in its mission to be "peace-makers and justice seekers" while cowardly allowing the status quo to remain unchallenged (*JMBM* §19, 169-70). Throughout his adolescence, McLaren routinely heard messages that endorsed the marginalization of certain people groups while insisting God cared only about the afterlife (*NS* §1, 11). "Sadly, we wish that religion, especially the Christian gospel, were truly a message of good news and liberation; but so often, the message has been twisted to become a kind of pacification, and co-opting, and domestication so that people just become... religious drones within an existing system that's terribly destructive."[81]

Believing social apathy is a harmful feature of "bad" religion, McLaren denounces how conservative churches focus more on battling each other over theological minutiae than they do on remedying global crises. The result is that conservatives excel at being opinionated but, in the end, do nothing to better humanity (*FFS* §1, 44-45). They adopt a naïve belief that individual Christians, not the government, should be the ones to help society. However, as Tony Campolo explains, "We must know that the church by itself lacks the financial resources to meet all the needs of those who are in desperate straits. There is not enough money in the offering plate to care for the needs of those who, in the race for the American dream, fall by the wayside."[82] McLaren concurs: "Love one another? [Churches] can't even get together to plant real geraniums" (*FFR* §4, 84). This apathy appears to derive from a Christian fixation on wealth.

3.3.2 Consumptive Theocapitalism

McLaren argues that the entire world is deteriorating from the "McDonaldization and Wal-Martization" of society (*GO* §17, 254).[83] For him, this increasingly consumeristic culture is simply the embodiment of what the Bible refers to as greed (*CIEC*, 95). He explains,

> The system disproportionally benefits the most powerful and privileged 1 percent of the human species, bestowing upon them unprecedented comfort, security, and luxury. To do so, it destabilizes the climate, plunders the planet, and kills off other forms of life...

---

81. McLaren, "Brian McLaren Reflects on 'Seizing An Alternative' Conference," 01:24-01:51.

82. Campolo, *Is Jesus a Republican or a Democrat?*, 5. Statistics reveal that only 56 percent of non-millennial evangelicals and only 65 percent of millennial evangelicals believe the government should do more to help the poor and those in need (Smidt, *American Evangelicals Today*, 131).

83. He references Alexis de Tocqueville (1805-1859) to support the belief that Americans have become so focused on earning money that they have almost completely abandoned the social and natural sciences, literature, art, and even religion (McLaren, "America the Exceptional," 17-18).

The rest, especially the poorest third at the bottom, gain little and lose much as this economic pyramid grows taller and taller. One of their greatest losses is democracy, as those at the top find clever ways to buy votes, turning elected governments into their puppets. . . .this is a formula for death, not a recipe for life." (*SA*, vii-viii)

McLaren is dismayed by how the United States, the most powerful economic and military nation on earth, actually fosters wealth inequality and antagonism between the social classes (*JP* §Intro, 19; *TWLD*, 46; cf. *SWFOI* §25, 187).[84] This greediness then transforms into a gluttony that devastates the environment to the privation of other people (*JMBM* §8, 65n2).[85] He clarifies that his concern is not with buying or selling products for profit (*CIEC*, 95; *TWLR*); instead, his concern is that the current economic system favors "the rich getting richer and more careless while the poor grow poorer and more desperate."[86] From his view, Jesus was clearly not a capitalist. In fact, as economic theorists illuminate, capitalism is based on greed, not altruism or love of neighbor (cf. *AMP* §7, 117-118; *SMJ* §15, 133).[87] McLaren briefly explains,

> [Capitalism] seeks the quickest return on investment without taking into account long-range social consequences; it empowers corporations that privatize profits for shareholders and externalize costs especially upon the poor and powerless; it turns governments into puppets that serve the interests of those corporations without regard for justice and the common good; and it even co-opts and corrupts authentic spirituality by commodifying it for a religious-industrial complex. (*JMBM* §8, 65n2; cf. *TWLD*, 47)

Thus, McLaren believes that unless wealth is used for the betterment of the world, capitalism inherently defies God's kingdom ethics (*EMC* §26, 221; *WMRBW*, 236).[88] He labels those who theologically rationalize this greed and invert Christ's teachings on wealth as "theocapitalists":

---

84. McLaren writes, "Worse, the richest and most powerful nation on earth seeks the right hand of God for more riches and power, so that this hand is now seen as being strong and generous on behalf of the strong and rich, and callous toward the vulnerable and marginalized" (McLaren, "Healing the Political Psyche," 36).

85. McLaren, "The Stories We Tell Ourselves," 18. He comments elsewhere, "The world of the 21st century will see a multiplication of extreme poverty and that's something people have to understand. Eventually the bubble of affluence will burst and we have to realize that a third of the people on the planet lives in ways that make it very hard for us to go on in comfort and luxury" (McLaren, "TPC Interviews," 13).

86. McLaren, "Religious Right or Wrong?," 10. See also, McLaren, "Making Waves." Of course, when criticizing something as "sacred" as capitalism, many critics assume McLaren is a communist, which he explicitly denies (cf. *EMC* §25, 214; *TWLR*).

87. See for example, Rand, *The Virtue of Selfishness*, esp. 125-46 and *Capitalism: The Unknown Ideal*.

88. McLaren, "The Stories We Tell Ourselves," 18. Cf. Reed, "Emerging Treason?," 74-75.

> Theocapitalists have tended to trust the rich, to believe that they deserve freedom and support, not accountability and oversight. They seek to bring the suffering rich "relief" from taxes, for example, and they speak of the "burden" of government regulations. If the rich profit more and more, they believe, benefits will trickle down to the poor. The best thing the rich can do for the poor, then, is make all the money they can, and the best thing the rest of us can do for the poor is to encourage the rich, to relieve them of their burdens so they can . . . mediate economic salvation to the world. (*EMC* §26, 220; cf *TWLE*)[89]

For McLaren, the church needs to hold the free market accountable, not be its unquestioning apologist (*EMC* §26, 223). Unfortunately, however, the "consumerization of Christianity" has led to "its bastardization" (*COOS1* §12c, 197).[90] Not surprisingly, then, this fixation on attaining wealth ends up contributing to the increase in violence and warfare around the world.

3.3.3 Warfare and Violence

McLaren once asked a critical question of himself, "Was the message of the kingdom of God intended to cause more religious wars, or was it actually a nonviolent alternative to war itself? Was it another violent movement or a movement against violence itself?" (*SMJ* §17, 154; cf. *JP* §Intro, 18). In one post-apocalyptic portrayal, McLaren describes the inevitable result of Christianity failing in its role as peace-makers (cf. *SMJ* §9, 78-79). "The Ruling Party also enlisted notable religious leaders to support the war effort, which many saw as a fulfillment of obscure biblical prophecies. Those who opposed the build-up to war . . . were labeled as 'peace-at-all-costs liberals,' 'unpatriotic cowards,' and 'naïve leftist idealists.'" In McLaren's futurist telling, the "war on terror" destroyed Christianity (and America), proving that Jesus was right when he said violence only begets violence (cf. *CSS*; *GDT*).[91] McLaren attributes this tendency toward violence to conservative Christianity's erroneous image of a violent God. He relates stories of actual seminary students advocating genocide simply because the Bible appears to sanction it (*GSM*, 71-74). "Put a trancelike, unreflective, God-is-on-our-side self-confidence together with the richest economy and the most dangerous weapons in the history of the world, and I can imagine two things: millions dead and

---

89. For more examples of theocapitalism, see Lienesch, *Redeeming America*, 94-138.

90. As Otis Moss explains, "The church is becoming a place where Christianity is nothing more than capitalism in drag" (Moss, *Blue Note Preaching*, 4). Cf. Barnett, "Enlightened Economics and Free Markets," 75-94; Hawtrey and Lunn, "The Emergent Church," 65-74; and Lienesch, *Redeeming America*, 107-23.

91. McLaren, "A Brief History of the 21st Century," 16-21. McLaren uses the "war on terror" as an example of one group retaliating against another group, who will in turn retaliate back, so on and so forth (*EMC* §20, 166-67). "We don't pray, 'Forgive us our sins and punish those who sin against us,' but rather, the [Lord's] prayer engenders in us the hope that we and our enemies will be treated mercifully" (*SMJ* §Prayer of the Kingdom, 213). See also, McLaren, "Beyond Fire and Brimstone," 19-20.

Christianity associated with the killings."⁹² He concludes that this image of an aggressive deity must change quickly: "For the world to migrate away from violence, our [concept of] God must migrate away from violence" (*GSM*, 94).

For McLaren, the religious establishment today is so unstable that it could actually cause a nuclear catastrophe (*FOWA* §1, 4-5). As proof, McLaren presents the following statistics:

> Is it ever justifiable to intentionally target innocent civilians in order to achieve political or military ends? Eighty, 81 and 86 percent of British, Canadian and American citizens say never. But only 46 percent of Iranians say never. A striking 24 percent of Iranians say attacks on civilians are often or sometimes justified, and 6 percent say such attacks are completely justified. The previous sentences are lies, dangerous lies. . . .
>
> The truth is that the scary figures I attributed above to Iranians actually apply to Americans, and the more civilized figures I attributed to Americans, Canadians and British citizens apply to the people of Iran, Bangladesh and Pakistan. In contrast to the 6 percent of Americans who say attacks on civilians are completely justified, only 2 percent of Iranians and Lebanese would agree, and only 4 percent of Saudis.⁹³

In his estimation, the tribalism of Christianity naturally inclines believers to dehumanize others, causing them to contemplate which "impure" people groups are also expendable (*SA*, 16; cf. *CSS*).⁹⁴ "After all, if *they* were good, they would ask to be admitted under *our* sacred canopy and they would join us in circling around *our* sacred center" (*JMBM* §7, 63; italics in original). Thus, McLaren is less worried about religion dying than he is about it killing others. "*In an age of religious violence like ours, people care much less about what you believe, and much more about whether you will kill for what you believe*" (*GSM*, 73; italics in original).⁹⁵

What particularly appalls McLaren is the fact that neo-Evangelicals today are more likely to endorse "state-sponsored torture" than their nonreligious counterparts (*JMBM* §2, 18n9; *NKOCY* §19, 215). "Churchgoers in the United States often seem to

---

92. McLaren, "A Postmodern View of Scripture," 10. McLaren cautions, "We can't use violent means to achieve peaceful ends; we can't use discordant means to achieve harmonious ends; we can't use dishonest means to achieve honest ends" (McLaren, "A Memo on the Arc of the Universe," 57). Only "nonviolent social change" will resolve violence and hate (*SA*, 171).

93. See the entire discussion in McLaren, review of *Who Speaks for Islam?*, 44-46. McLaren concludes, "The less aware Christians are of how dangerous Christianity has been, the more dangerous Christianity will be" (*GSM*, 71).

94. McLaren asks elsewhere, "Given the chance, would Christianity eradicate every vestige of the world's other religions?" (*GO* §17, 254).

95. McLaren identified some of this hypocrisy in one interview, "I had started a rewrite of *Onward, Christian Soldiers* lyrics awhile back. . . .But after watching one of the Republican presidential . . . debates and hearing several candidates in one breath speak of Christian faith and Jesus and in the next breath speak of carpet bombing and the like, I felt it was time to finish some alternative lyrics" (McLaren, "Brian McLaren").

be the first to support and the last to abandon wars of questionable morality" (*EMC* §19, 152). By giving theological justifications for warfare, believers no longer take account of the destruction and death that ensues (*JMBM* §7, 56n4; *NS* §Part I, 30).[96] According to McLaren, however, the kingdom of God never expands through war or violence (*SMJ* §17, 158; §Prayer of the Kingdom, 213). Christianity has simply devoted far too little time and resources to world peace (*GDT*; *JMBM* §2, 14).[97]

The problem is that there are very real ecological, economic, and political problems that could quite literally ruin the globe and, thus, destroy all life. In the case of religion, the "suicidal" theologies of the past, which conceived of a violent deity, need correction if humanity wants to survive (*GSM*, 101-4; *TSS*, 56-82). As an impromptu ode of his explains,

> We made a suicidal system. . . . It was a system of injustice, built on arrogance and greed. It was an empire for the powerful, and a hell for those in need. . . . we made a billion guns and more wars to utilize them. And we keep the poor in slums, to ignore them or despise them, and we broadcast shows and movies, to amuse and tranquilize them. . . . And we built a lot of churches, and we saved a lot of souls, but we destroyed a lot of good things, and our way of life was full of holes. (*GI*, 61-63)

Thus, for McLaren, it was the enablement of this suicide machine that forced McLaren's identity crisis to result in full on disillusionment with the church.

3.4 MCLAREN'S RESULTING DISILLUSIONMENT

Politically, McLaren describes himself as "purple," meaning he has elements of both red conservatism and blue liberalism (*TWLD*; *TWLR*). For example, his Christian faith informs both his displeasure with abortion *and* war, as well as his concern over sexual ethics *and* the environment, and his desire for family values *and* the sympathetic treatment of homosexuals. Conservatives are right that businesses are able to liberate people from poverty, but liberals are also right that businesses need oversight since they tend to exploit and oppress people.[98] Nonetheless, liberals and conserva-

---

96. Cf. McLaren, "A Brief History of the 21st Century," 16-21; Calo, "'The New Internationals': Human Rights and American Evangelicalism," 149-64; and Amstutz, *Evangelicals and American Foreign Policy*, 118-42.

97. He argues, "When young adults from churchgoing backgrounds lose confidence in this version of the Christian religion to address the pressing issues of our world, their faith becomes . . . diminished." McLaren also remarks, "When religions perpetually incite war, violence, and mutually assured destruction, to me it is less a wonder that people want to reject or marginalize religion than it is that anyone sticks with it" (*EMC* §5, 33-34; §19, 152-53). Cf. Gushee, *The Future of Faith in American Politics*, 199-213.

98. McLaren, "A Bridge Far Enough?," 17-19. See also, McLaren, "Red State, Purple Church," 26-29. McLaren explains, "There's a stereotype out there that I think has a lot of truth to it: liberals are concerned about issues of public and social morality (poverty, oppression, injustice) and conservatives

tives are both secularists who are more interested in following their "sacred" political ideologies than Jesus' own teachings.[99] Accordingly, to have faith in God ought to mean abandoning all other *-isms*, including conservatism and liberalism.[100]

Despite his objections to neoconservatism, McLaren actually faults both the conservatives and liberals for sustaining the suicide machine (*GSM*, 134-35, 250n9). He argues that the Left has been just as guilty of systemic injustice nowadays as the Right was in their "biblical" defense of slavery and genocide (*NKOC* §6, 73).[101] For him, American Christianity has simply become "a public civil religion that compromises with partisan politics (of either the right or the left)."[102] From these observations, McLaren concludes, "[There are] high percentages of the population claiming to be 'born again Christians,' but too few who exhibit Christ-likeness, which in turn results in social inoculation against the gospel being anything more than a privately held opinion with little social impact."[103] It is noteworthy that McLaren does not believe all conservatives practice a "bad" religion. Instead, he views the situation in devilish terms where the "spirit of racism, revenge, religious supremacy, nationalism, political partisanship, greed, [and] fear" has possessed otherwise virtuous communities (*WMRBW*, 241). Nonetheless, he believes that neoconservatives are using the Christian religion to acquire socio-political dominance while neglecting ideals of justice and social equality (*GO* §12, 185).

What these issues reveal is that McLaren's philosophy of religion appreciably stems from his experiences with what he sees as the Religious Right's moralistic façade, appearing to care less about global justice than about obstructing civil rights (cf. *NKOCY* §16, 165-66). "Their stridency and selectivity in choosing issues and priorities at first annoyed, then depressed, and then angered me. They had created a powerful, wealthy, and stealthy network dedicated to mobilizing fighters in their '"culture war'" (*NKOCY* §1, 7). He then recognized the association between Christianity and

---

are more concerned about issues of private and personal morality (sexual immorality, lack of personal integrity). I would hope that a full-bodied Christian would realize that the two while they may be distinguished, must never be disassociated" (McLaren, "Religious Right or Wrong?," 9).

99. Cf. McLaren, "A Bridge Far Enough?," 16-17; "A Postmodern View of Scripture," 9; and Suskind, "Without a Doubt," 44-106.

100. McLaren, "Found in Translation," 17. With McLaren, Democrats are "incompetent accomplices" to Republican vice (*TWLD*, 14). Cf. Wilson, "Practicing Church," 69-70.

101. Douglas Sharp summarizes, "Christianity in general and evangelicalism in particular . . . contributed willingly as a moral and social force to the legitimacy of slavery" (Sharp, "Evangelicals," 239). McLaren is aghast at how American Christianity, both in its liberal and conservative forms, has become tantamount to white privilege, affiliating itself with those in positions of power who ratify policies that ultimately afflict the already-marginalized and oppressed of American society (*GSM*, 71-88).

102. Streett, "An Interview with Brian McLaren," 11. He also remarks, "My biggest fear is about the conservatives. They are no less compromised with right-wing politics and culture. . . .[and can] lose their equilibrium and go into a kind of warrior trance" (McLaren, "A Postmodern View of Scripture," 9-10).

103. McLaren, "Conversations," 342.

American governance ("as go the churches, so goes the nation"). If churches focus on polarizing issues, perpetuate discrimination, and sanction inequality, then America's politicians will champion those same causes. In a sense, to view the state of American politics is to view the state of American Christianity (cf. *JP* §Intro, 19). He writes,

> Those of us with CRIS don't want to be held hostage . . . to a religion that is hostile toward science and learning, hostile toward honest questions and new ways of thinking, and above all, hostile toward other human beings—especially those of other religions (or other versions of our own religion). Something deep in our conscience tells us that hostility is part of the problem to be overcome in the world, not the means by which problems will be overcome. Hostility is a symptom of the disease, not part of the cure. (*JMBM* §2, 20)

His concern is that Christians no longer follow the same gospel that Jesus preached, having either misconstrued or deliberately twisted Christ's teachings so as to foster social complacency (*SMJ* §1, 3, 7).[104] "Maybe, by some absurd twist of history, we Christians have become the very kinds of religious people who would kill Jesus if he showed up today" (*COOS1* §2, 37; see also, *GDT* §). "These days, *Christian* often seems to apply more to the kinds of people who would push Jesus off a cliff than it does to his true followers" (*WMRBW*, 94; italics in original).

The main revelation McLaren had was that neo-Evangelicalism had become uncharitable and unempathetic. He reasons that where there is no compassion, Christ cannot be present (cf. *JMBM* §15, 143; *NKOCY* §11, 114; *TWLE*). As Gerald Gauthier remarks, "[McLaren] openly questions why so much Christian activism has been preoccupied with abortion and gay marriage, yet has paid scant attention to problems which pose far greater threats to humanity."[105] From this realization, McLaren concludes that the church needs to reprioritize its mission to the world.

3.4.1 Reprioritizing the Church's Mission

As McLaren sees it, current paradigms for both religion and politics merely exasperate the problems of the suicide machine (*SMJ* §19, 181; *WMRBW*, 123). The biggest effect that McLaren's identity crisis had on his philosophy of religion is the need to reprioritize the stated mission of the Christian church. Instead of political influence, he believes the church's mission ought to be the establishment of God's kingdom with a focus on eradicating systemic injustice throughout the world. "In the middle of the battle the church is realizing we were not placed on earth to fight about morality and

---

104. For McLaren, the American church has become a dangerous culture-religion that does not experience persecution but, instead, partakes in the persecution of others (cf. *AIFA*, 238).

105. McLaren, "Making Waves," 29. Cf. Sider, "Evangelicals and Social Justice," 128–33. Since McLaren's initial disillusionment, there have been major developments in making the evangelical engagement with politics more centrist, focusing not only on pro-family values but also on poverty, ecology, war, and human rights. See Gushee and Phillips, "Moral Formation and the Evangelical Voter," 23–60.

culture. We are here to bring the kingdom of God to earth. His kingdom will not come by means of legislation, but by the working of the Holy Spirit within the church" (*VA*, 106-7). He further explains that Christianity has become depressingly selective:

> When Christians in recent decades concerned themselves with contemporary issues, they focused primarily on personal and sexual matters, simultaneously neglecting larger societal and systemic injustices that caused unimagined suffering. And even in regard to their narrow range of "moral issues," they were consistently effective in generating heat and conflict but consistently less effective in making a lasting, constructive difference. In so doing, they created an image of the typical Christian believer as tense, judgmental, imbalanced, reactionary, negative, and hypocritical. (*EMC* §5, 33)[106]

For McLaren, fights between the Left and Right are merely "a smokescreen, a distraction, or camouflage under which a more dangerous battle of values is waged covertly" (*EMC* §33, 286). There are simply more important issues that ought to be prioritized in Christianity, such as (to name only a few) the unsustainability of the world's current resource depletion, environmental destruction, and poverty (cf. *AMP* §7, 122-24; *NKOCY* §7, 69).[107]

The problem with identity politics and the culture wars is that they become a distraction from actually curing human misery by diverting attention to ceaseless theological arguments. While polarized Christians continue to argue, the world's disadvantaged continue to suffer (*EMC* §2, 15-16).[108] In one *USA Today* article, McLaren explains, "At the height of lynching in the early 20th century, for example, most white American Christians were in an uproar — not about lynchings, but about the Scopes Monkey Trials and the teaching of evolution in public schools. When Native Americans were being forced on death marches and herded into death camps in the early 19th century, many white Christians began organizing . . . to make alcohol illegal."[109] He goes on to ask elsewhere, "Why are we so concerned about the legitimacy of homosexual marriage but not about the legitimacy of fossil fuels or the proliferation of weapons of mass destruction (and in particular, *our weapons* as opposed to *theirs*)? Or why are so many religious people arguing about the origin of species but so few concerned about the extinction of species?" (*EMC* §1, 3-4; italics in original). With McLaren, this misguided prioritization is especially evident in cases of same-sex

---

106. McLaren explains in one interview, "I am unhappy about the Religious Right's narrowing of the gospel's social impact to two or three issues, and I think the rhetorical strategy of the Religious Right has made evangelism harder here in America and around the world" (Streett, "An Interview with Brian McLaren," 8).

107. Cf. Reynolds and Offutt, "Global Poverty and Evangelical Action," 242-61; Monsma, "Evangelicals and Poverty," 41-55; and Quebedeaux, *The Young Evangelicals*, 124-28.

108. For details on evangelicals losing their compassion for society's vulnerable, see Gaebelein, "Evangelicals and Social Concern," 17-22.

109. Brian D. McLaren, "Is It Christian or Illegal to Aid Migrants?"; ellipses in original.

marriage. While hordes of Christians protest this one issue, they are oddly silent on issues of more pressing importance, like taking a stand "on behalf of the poor, or the mentally ill, or refugees, or other forgotten people."[110] When contrasted with "good religion," the Christianity that McLaren campaigns against is more interested in dividing people than uniting them toward the betterment of the world (*NS* §2, 14-15).[111]

McLaren points out that according to multiple international organizations, the world's biggest problems are both preventable and improvable, such as malnutrition, hunger, climate change, violence, contaminated water, communicable diseases, child mortality, and wealth inequality (*EMC* §6,46-47; §29, 252). Unfortunately, instead of uniting together to solve these crises, Christians remain polarized and paralyzed because they are "drunk on dogmatism" (*JMBM* §1, 6). For McLaren, the religiopolitical state of American Christianity resembles someone with bipolar disorder where extremes of mania and depression are preventing the public from thinking clearly. What McLaren wants to see is a balanced perspective that focuses on the more important mission of "cooperating with God in the making of a better world."[112]

Throughout the Hebrew Scriptures, prophets demanded that the government focus on one major topic: the protection and elevation of society's impoverished, marginalized, and subjugated.[113] Regrettably, Christians today continue to ally themselves with institutional oppressors rather than with the oppressed. Because of these moral failings, according to McLaren, Christianity has become just another failed religion (*GSM*, 85, 93). He remarks,

> From the Civil War in America to the Rwandan genocide, from illegitimacy in American churchgoing teens to the spread of AIDS among young African Christians, from televangelists' scandals to rising divorce rates among fundamentalists, Christianity doesn't seem to stop Christians from killing and enslaving and hating and fornicating any less than people of other religions or no faith. If Christianity can't solve poverty, racism, or family breakdown, does it really deserve the sacrifice of missionary endeavor? (*COOSI* §10, 124)

---

110. McLaren, "Conversations," 343. An example of what McLaren considers more deserving is the time he was arrested in Washington, DC for protesting budget cuts that unduly benefited the rich while taking money away from the poor (McLaren, "Everything Old Is New Again," 27). As Jim Wallis remarks, "In the debate over much-needed welfare reform, the Christian Coalition supports cutting support to single mothers and their children, despite the fact that these women and children are the modern-day equivalents of the 'widow and orphans' for whom the New Testament shows such special concern" (Wallis, *Who Speaks for God?*, 20). See also, Sider, *Rich Christians in an Age of Hunger*).

111. Remarkably, in a 2011 survey of global evangelical leaders, only 73 percent agreed that helping the poor and needy was obligatory while another 24 percent responded that helping the poor is important but not necessary to be a good Christian (Cooperman et al., *Global Survey of Evangelical Protestant Leaders*, 20).

112. McLaren, "Healing the Political Psyche," 37. See also, Brumley, "Moderate Churches," 13.

113. McLaren even uses biblical stories like the Tower of Babel and the calling of Abram as examples of God wanting to destabilize socio-economic structures where the few live in extravagance while the rest live in poverty (see *WMRBW*, 21-25). Cf. Amstutz, *Evangelicals and American Foreign Policy*, 95-117.

Christian Smith concurs: "It appears, then, that conservative Protestants as a whole... do not distinguish themselves as leading champions of the rights of the disadvantaged and vulnerable."[114] Hence, for McLaren, only an authentic community of believers who actually live and practice Jesus' gospel teachings can legitimize Christianity again (*COOS1* §12b, 183–84).[115]

From the Religious Right's engagement in culture wars came a motivation to censor, stigmatize, and ostracize segments of the American population, largely ignoring things like poverty, disease, and environmental catastrophes. McLaren asks his readers to imagine what would happen if the political influence of American Christians resulted in congressional budget-makers allocating money to address the underlying causes of conflict around the world, such as social inequality, rather than perpetuating the cycle of violence through more conflict (*SMJ* §17, 160).[116] He also asks, "What would happen, for example, if the energy directed against homosexuality could be directed toward the poor, toward building neighborly relationships with people of other races and religions, toward motivating their employers toward more just and equitable business practices?"[117] The result for him has been society's "revulsion to Christianity" since people now associate the church with "just another rigid belief system instead of a unique, joyful way of living, loving, and serving" (*MRTYR* §3, 41).[118]

3.5 CONCLUSION

McLaren summarizes his overall position: "I would probably differ from the religious right in my emphasis on the social dimensions of morality, without downplaying personal morality of course. As well, I would be more careful than the religious right about identifying the agenda of the Kingdom of God with the agenda of the United States of America."[119] Regarding his disillusionment with conventional paradigms, the antago-

---

114. Smith, *Christian America?*, 209.

115. In 2011, 87 percent of North American evangelical leaders believed that society should discourage the practice of homosexuality. Conflictingly, however, almost half (44 percent) of American evangelical leaders do not believe the government has an obligation to help those in extreme poverty despite 21 percent of evangelicals believing that the government should be Christian *and* that the Bible should be the law of the land (Cooperman et al., *Global Survey of Evangelical Protestant Leaders*, 12, 30–32, 82–83). Likewise, nearly one-half of conservative Protestants believe Christian conceptions of morality should be the law of the land despite the fact that not all Americans are Christian and roughly three-quarters of Americans reject this position (Smith, *Christian America?*, 201).

116. Cf. Ryden, "Introduction," 1–19. McLaren writes, "Faith should not be reduced to a tool of social control or political manipulation" (*GSM*, 30).

117. McLaren, "Religious Right or Wrong?," 10.

118. In one Barna poll, only 32 percent of nonChristians have a positive view of born-again Christians and only 22 percent have a positive view of evangelicals (Sider, *The Scandal of the Evangelical Conscience*, 28). For current perceptions of Christians as hypocritical and judgmental, see Kinnaman and Lyons, *Unchristian*, 41–66, 181–204.

119. McLaren, "Religious Right or Wrong?," 9. Elsewhere, McLaren explains, "I'm not at all against the idea of a personal relationship with God. I think that's where it all begins. And I think this is part

nistic and combative disposition of neoconservative Christians ultimately conflicted with his growing belief in the harmony of creation (*FOWA* §5, 41–42; *JMBM* §12, 104) and the need for religious cooperation for the betterment of the world (*AIFA*, 277; *JMBM* §26, 242).[120] The significance of these tensions is that his moral identity crisis not only aids readers in understanding the origins of McLaren's philosophy, but it also illuminates the cathartic nature of his own writings.[121]

He does recognize, however, that many believers are often politically conservative because it provides them with a strong faith identity (*JMBM* §2, 13; §5, 40–43). While he realizes that many in the Religious Right share his convictions on poverty, war, and the environment (cf. *NKOCY* §17, 174–75; *WMRBW*, 241), his contention is that Christianity today, precisely because of current paradigms, does not actualize its own religious convictions consistently. The consequence is that McLaren believes conventional religious paradigms are making people less Christ-like (*NKOCY* §16, 278n3). For him, the modern approach to Christian faith, particularly among Westerners, has transferred the promises of God's kingdom to the powerful and elite of society away from the marginalized and impoverished. American Christians especially appear more concerned with spreading panic and acquiring wealth than they are with Jesus' kingdom ideals of love, justice, and compassion (*SMJ* §9, 78–79).

In essence, McLaren's perception of the Americanized civil religion is that it has hardened into a "mythic-literal" and "synthetic-conventional" religiosity, which are simplistic approaches to religious faith that naïvely ignore the complexities of morality (*AMP* §16, 249). They favor an emotional attachment to the status quo more than introspection and critical thinking.[122] As McLaren explains, "People have some sense that the Christian faith has been co-opted by our societal machinery, and they're relieved to hear someone validate that suspicion. . . .it helps them get the Christian message back as a force for social transformation, rather than social control."[123] In essence, he believes Christians need to begin treating their neighbors and their enemies precisely as Jesus commanded.[124] Thus, he warns his own readers, "One of the worst things that could happen to you who read this book (and like it) would be to develop a critical and harsh attitude toward Christians who resist the other-side changes," confessing that for all he knows, God wants some conservative congregations to remain

---

of the beauty of the message of Jesus. Every individual is invited into a personal relationship with God. But personal is not private" (McLaren, "The Emerging Church, Part Two").

120. See Burson, *Brian McLaren in Focus*, 186–89, 192–95 and McLaren, "The Politics of Joy."

121. Mark Braverman explains, "Brian wants us to have an identity crisis [just like his]—to ask ourselves what it is about our group identities and the beliefs we profess that causes the addiction to chosenness, to uniqueness, to projecting our fears and insecurities on to the other" (Braverman, endorsement to *Why Did Jesus, Moses, the Buddha, and Mohammed Cross the Road*, iii).

122. See Fowler, *Stages of Faith*, 135–73.

123. McLaren prays, "We have sinned against you [God]—because we have sinned against others, not treating them as we would have been treated" (quoted in Riess, "Emerging Star," 52).

124. McLaren, "'Instead of Ruling'—Prayers," 225.

intact to serve his own purposes (*COOS1* §13, 204-5). Ultimately, McLaren insists that his readers must not become hypercritical of other Christians, conservative or liberal, but instead attempt to understand differing viewpoints with the hope that they spread empathy and compassion, not more hate (*JMBM* §5, 43). He wants believers and nonbelievers alike to recognize that no person and no ideology possess the absolute, incontrovertible truth, something McLaren eventually learned through his intellectual disillusionment with modernity.

4

McLaren the Iconoclast

4.0 INTRODUCTION

In addition to the experiential (chapter 2) and moral (chapter 3) influences on Brian McLaren, there was also an intellectual disillusionment relating to the current epochal shift away from modernity. For him, if Christians had become intolerant, bigoted, and partisan, then there must be something wrong with the way they intellectually perceive the world (cf. *NS* §3, 24). The thesis of this chapter is that McLaren's philosophy of religion also derives from a belief that liberals and conservatives are forestalling the much-needed transition into postmodernity.[1] Five areas will validate this argument: 1) McLaren's objection to intransigent conservatism; 2) his periodization of church history; 3) the modernization effects on Christianity; 4) the postmodern ethos; and 5) McLaren's rejection of propositional systematic theologies. To begin, readers must first consider McLaren's belief that neoconservatism inclines toward inflexibility.

4.1 INTRANSIGENT NEOCONSERVATISM

For the disheartened, the Republican Party has only one agenda: the maintenance of political power; and they are willing to beguile sincere Christians into equating

---

1. Like McLaren's socio-political formation, the purpose of this chapter is to systematize and clarify McLaren's *personal* understanding and articulation of postmodernity; it is not to authenticate his claims historically or philosophically.

Republicanism with spiritual piety (cf. *TWLR*).² McLaren identifies two stereotypes: liberals believe society will continue to improve and, therefore, are open to progress (cf. *AIFA*, 217-18), but conservatives believe society will continue to degrade and, therefore, revere previous eras. For McLaren, the Religious Right possessed a "utopianism about the 1950's (or some other mythical decade of the past)."³ While McLaren acknowledges Christianity's conservative relationship to tradition, what he has observed among believers today is not "conservative" in the classical sense. Rather, what he notices is an obstructionist mentality toward any and all progress (*GSM*, 41-42). This dogmatic neoconservatism is Elysian in nature, meaning it seeks to reclaim the so-called "God-fearing" sensibilities of a departed age, with the goal of regaining old power structures that once marginalized minorities.⁴ As Jack Rogers explains,

> "Conservative" is a good word. It marks continuity with the past. . . .There is another sense in which the word "conservative" is used. The dictionary defines "conservative" as: "tending to favor the preservation of the existing order and to regard proposals for change with distrust." Being conservative in that sense leads to conserv*atism*. . . .That is the sense of being conservative which confuses Christianity with our culture. Salvation is not found in the *status quo*. From apostolic times Christians have challenged the existing order.⁵

This nostalgia is worrisome when considering America's history, as McLaren's novel depicts:

> That famous white guy who always talks about saving America was on . . . He kept talking about how we need to go back, you know, back to when they had prayer in schools and all. Is he serious? Sure, let's go back—back to when my grandmother wasn't allowed in a white church, and when my grandfather got beat up for going into the white part of town, and when my parents were forced to attend a segregated school. Yeah, those were the good old days. [Commenting sarcastically] Prayer in the schools did a whole lot of good back then. Sure, let's go back to that" (*SWFOI* §35, 266).

---

2. Though Cal Thomas and Edward Dobson were co-founders of the Religious Right movement, they suggest the Religious Right has since lost its claim to moral superiority precisely because of its unquestioning allegiance to the Republican Party. See Thomas and Dobson, *Blinded by Might*, esp. 53-142.

3. McLaren, "Religious Right or Wrong?," 9. As he describes elsewhere, "When a culture needs wise spiritual guidance the most, all it gets from religious leaders is anxious condemnation and critique, along with a big dose of nostalgia for the lost golden age" (*GSM*, xi-xii).

4. For a distinction between classic and dogmatic conservatism, especially as applied to religiosity, see Huntington, "Robust Nationalism," 31-40 and Raja, *The Religious Right*, 43-44.

5. Rogers, *Confessions of a Conservative Evangelical*, 11; italics in original. Recognizing the desire to return to an alleged "idyllic" past, McLaren writes, "Maybe a hundred years from now, the descendants of my fellow evangelicals today will be like the Amish of tomorrow, but instead of maintaining 1850s German culture, they'll perpetuate 1950s American culture" (*NKOC* §11, 139).

Intransigent conservatives do not merely sustain the status quo; they actively seek to recover power structures that benefited only European white males, which makes the idea of a re-Christianized America completely foreign to post-conservatives (*SWFOI* §34, 258-59). This focus on the past has now conditioned the church to reject sound cultural progress.⁶ McLaren argues that the more dogmatically conservative a belief system is, the more repressive and dichotomistic it becomes, viewing ethics in black-and-white categories with no real desire (or ability) to comprehend the complexities of culture. Instead of progressing for the better, the church remains archaic and draconian (*AMP* §16, 249; *FFS* §1, 45-46; *WMRBW*, 211). Thus, as Leigh Jordahl explains, it is not that neoconservatism is the intellectual culture-religion of today; instead, it is the culture-religion of an obsolete era that tries to forestall the postmodern turn.⁷

4.2 FORESTALLING THE EPOCHAL SHIFT

Eventually, this rigid mentality resulted in McLaren questioning the intellectual "framework" through which conservatives approached their faith, realizing that Western civilization adheres to an untenable Enlightenment ontology (*NKOC* §2, 18; *SMJ* §7, 52; *SWFOI* §6, 38). Today, significant portions of the world are undergoing socio-political, epistemological, and philosophical changes. This "postmodern turn," or what McLaren sometimes labels a "transition zone" (cf. *COOS1* §12a, 168), is essential to comprehending the intellectual context of his philosophy of religion and the growing disillusionment among younger generations.⁸ At its crux, Western society is moving away from patriarchal, white European domination in both society and religion. There exists a feeling of tentativeness and insecurity during this transition due to sizeable demographic shifts and changing cultural values, which cause a backlash from older generations. However, there also exists a sense of empowerment among those who have felt marginalized under the old framework (e.g., racial minorities, women, etc.).⁹ As a result, younger generations are almost entirely removed from the thought processes of older generations (cf. *COOS1* §Intro, 12; §1, 19-21). To simplify

---

6. For example, dogmatic conservatives routinely fought to keep women unequal before the law and legally dependent on men for economic stability (Kyle, *Evangelicalism*, 191-94). Today, conservative Protestants are more likely to believe laws protecting women "go too far" and that there should be no laws elevating women out of societal vulnerability (Smith, *Christian America?*, 209-12). Their reasoning is that gender equality would be a precursor to embracing liberalism. See Grudem, *Evangelical Feminism*.

7. Jordahl, "The American Evangelical," 192; italics in original. For a detailed explanation of the socio-historical context involving traditional family values of gender hierarchy and other ideals, see Gallagher, *Evangelical Identity*, 3-62.

8. Crouch, "The Emergent Mystique," 36-41.

9. See Hoeveler, *The Postmodernist Turn*.

this epochal shift, McLaren divides church history into three periods: the precritical, critical, and postcritical eras.[10] He elaborates,

> We talk about pre-history, which is before people have the ability to write. Generally we put that about 2500 B.C. Then people talk about the ancient world, which was the world of a number of significant civilizations . . . that brings us from about 2500 B.C. to about 500 A.D. . . . Then there's the medieval period from about 500 A.D. to about 1500 A.D., and the modern period from 1500 to the present. For us, modern tends to just mean now, but if we think of it as a period, we realize that someday it is going to end and something else will take its place, if past history is any model. (*PTP*, 115)[11]

McLaren then offers a brief reconstruction of Western church history (see *FOWA* §1, 4-5; *FFR* §Intro, 15; §7, 152-53), first recounting that Christianity began as a faith-based, "premodern" sect of Judaism before transforming into the institutionalized culture-religion of Medieval Europe and early modernity. By the late-modern era, however, the prestige of organized religion collapsed and secularism slowly replaced religion in the West.[12] The current epochal shift reveals a general dissatisfaction with all three phases: premodern superstition, institutionalized religion, and modern secularism (cf. *AIFA*, 242; *AMP*, 278; *FOWA* §1, 4-5). In each era, Christians have had to address different challenges (*NKOC* §3, 35-36), which McLaren believes reflects the church's natural maturing process in understanding God (cf. *GO* §18, 282-83; *MRTYR* §5, 53).

His periodization also distinguishes between societal *change* and a *transitional* movement. While every epoch contains small cultural fluctuations, not every age has a total conversion from one worldview to another.[13] These transitions are also geographically relative, meaning they occur at different rates in different places around the globe. It is the West's current transition from modernity to postmodernity that dogmatic conservatives resist the most, becoming "a buffer to constructive change

---

10. McLaren also divides the precritical era into smaller segments: "prehistoric," "ancient," and "medieval" (cf. *COOS1* §Preface, 8; §Intro, 12; *NKOC* §5, 62). At other times, McLaren only considers the medieval portion of the "precritical" era (cf. *SWFOI* §6, 38). None of these epochs appeared spontaneously but, instead, took centuries of socio-political, cultural, and philosophical shifts before each one emerged (*AMP* §18, 276-77). It is important to note that *precritical* is not the same as being *uncritical* or *anticritical*; it simply denotes the time period before critical thinking was widely practiced among religious adherents.

11. See also, McLaren, "Dallas Morning News." Gary Blackwell implies that McLaren mislabels his sources as "ancient" when, in fact, they are medieval (Blackwell, "Return or Rereading," 196-97). However, as Mike Featherstone exemplifies, the term "ancient" is often a general designation for any premodern period before the Renaissance (Featherstone, "In Pursuit of the Postmodern," 197-98).

12. Cf. the "God is dead" cultural analysis of Friedrich Nietzsche (1844-1900) in Nash, "Nietzsche," 1-8.

13. McLaren likens these progressions to beating eggs with a fork in a process of slowly cooking an omelet. At some point, a major transition occurs when the eggs transform from a liquid to a solid, requiring the use of a new tool (e.g., the spatula) to preserve the integrity of the omelet (*NKOC* §5, 58).

rather than a catalyst for it" (*GSM*, xi-xii).[14] McLaren notes, however, that conservatives are not defending a precritical form of Christianity.

4.2.1 Precritical Christianity

McLaren first emphasizes that Jesus existed in the precritical age in order to highlight the disparity of modern Christians embracing a premodern belief system (cf. *MRTYR* §5, 52-53). He explains that Jesus' worldview did not divide the natural from the supernatural; instead, it was "more organic, less mechanistic" in terms of envisioning God's immanence.[15] In the precritical era, the divine permeated everything, "God was connected to the universe, present with it, and intimately involved in it. So the universe was less like a machine and more like a family" (*SMJ* §7, 52). In adopting a more scientific (but not naturalistic; *FFS* §4, 106-107) worldview, McLaren argues that God's presence in the world makes mysticism and miracles (as well as the mundane occurrences of everyday physics) completely *natural* (*SWFOI* §9, 70-71).

Of particular importance to premodern religion was Greek philosophical justifications.[16] During the Patristic era, a paradigm shift occurred when Gentile apologists appropriated Neoplatonic concepts to supplement their evolving (Gentile) theologies.[17] As these early apologists contended with pagans, they still operated in a cognitive environment that presumed the existence of the divine. The Middle Ages, likewise, accepted divinities, but the apologetic focus switched to a rivalry among Jewish, Christian, and Muslim truth-claims.[18] Noteworthy for McLaren is the medieval affinity for Ptolemaic cosmology, as well as its perpetual warfare and persistent exposure to plagues and diseases, arguing that these factors comprised the socio-historical context of medieval beliefs (*AMP* §18, 276). Rather than engage in leisurely critical thinking, premodern believers expected to receive "truth" from divinely-sanctioned

---

14. For some regions, a medieval version of Roman Catholicism is still culturally viable. For those provinces abandoning the precritical age, however, people will embrace Charismatic forms of Christianity because it is slightly more "up-to-date" (*NKOC* §5, 58-59, 62). Some would rather reverse course entirely and return to precritical beliefs, such as Roman Catholicism and Greek Orthodoxy (see Stewart, *In Search of Ancient Roots*, 13).

15. According to McLaren, the postmodern era embraces social-organic imagery more than mechanistic ones (*EMC* §7, 307n7), making Jesus the "first premodern postmodern" (*AIFA*, 170). McLaren also recognizes that it is tempting to think both the Bible and Christianity inherently possess a modern rational mindset, but attempting to make premodern Christianity fit with Enlightenment ideals merely results in a disillusionment with either the Christian religion or the paradigm through which people have approached their faith (*EMC* §9, 82; §11, 91).

16. Though the Apostle Paul denigrated pagan wisdom (1 Cor 1:20; 3:18-19), both he and John applied Greek concepts to proliferate the gospel message in order to give Christianity its needed believability. See Dulles, *A History of Apologetics*, 1-25 and Boa and Bowman, *Faith Has Its Reasons*, 10-12.

17. See for example, Dillon, "Logos and Trinity," 1-13; Gaston, "The Influence of Platonism," 573-80; Hödl, "Das scholastische Verständnis," 1-22; and Bastit, "Le Thomisme," 101-16.

18. Dulles, *A History of Apologetics*, 27-144.

authorities.[19] They were unquestioningly loyal to their prescribed beliefs (*GO* §8, 132; *MRTYR* §17, 128).[20]

Here, premodernity is represented by a man in his priestly vestments, epitomizing the priesthood's unchallenged power over others (*COOS1* §12a, 160). For the ancient world, reality was mostly a mystery with unexplainable phenomena. The precritical mind had a grim view of the chaotic world, which prompted a desire for an all-powerful deity (*SWFOI* §14, 102; §30, 224) who made Neoplatonic distinctions between spiritual virtue and carnal decadence.[21] While acknowledging its depth and wisdom, McLaren describes the premodern era as naïve in certain respects (*GO* §13, 206; §18, 269n136) and, therefore, does not view this phase of church history as normative for later eras (cf. *FFS* §1, 41). By the Renaissance, however, people began questioning ecclesial authorities (cf. *NKOC* §3, 32). "In the ancient world, people were aware that there was so much that they didn't know; they lived with a sense of swimming in mystery. But in the modern world we believe that mystery is going to be removed through rational processes" (*PTP*, 116-17). It was because of the development of medieval and Protestant scholasticism that discussions emerged about the proper interaction between faith and reason. Apart from appeals to divine revelation, Western rationality became the dominant heuristic model for apologetics.[22] Truth soon resided in abstract notions of logic, forcing people to rethink spiritual knowledge in terms of rational discovery through autonomous reason (*GO* §8, 132; *MRTYR* §17, 128). These changes ushered in the modern era of analytic Christian faith.

4.2.2 Analytical Christianity

According to McLaren, the Protestant Reformation was part of Western culture's intellectual movement away from the medieval mindset, which matured (in part) from the bloody aftermath of the Thirty Years War. People increasingly realized that religious authorities could be (and in fact were often) wrong about many subjects.

---

19. McLaren conveys the premodern mindset: "We know the truth because the authorities are given, by God, truth that they convey to us. Our job is to trust them because they are God's channels of truth" (*GO* §8, 132). Cf. Blount, "A New Kind of Interpretation," 109-28.

20. Much like today, precritical Christians do not question the source or accuracy of religious truth-claims, nor do they recognize the inconsistencies, biases, evolutionary development, or socio-historical parallels in their own belief system. However, being *pre*critical does not equate to being willfully *un*critical; oftentimes, the disposition is merely the result of being uninformed or lacking exposure to proper education and training. Thus, McLaren likens their religiosity to an intellectual innocence (*GSM*, 114-18).

21. McLaren, "Everything Old Is New Again," 23-25.

22. Dulles, *A History of Apologetics*, 111-50. Notably, Martin Luther (1483-1546) counteracted this affinity for rationalism by separating faith and logic as qualitatively different. For Luther, reason was incapable of discovering religious precepts and inept at comprehending them, as well. Hence, rationality had to submit to revealed theology, which Christians could only embrace purely on faith (see Lohse, "Reason and Revelation," 337-65).

The emerging sensibilities of the period resulted in a heightened excitement for self-directed reasoning (*EMC* §19, 152; *GO* §8, 132), which prized analytic reductionism in the attainment of knowledge (*FOWA* §6, 53). As he explains, "Modernity loves analysis. Analysis means seeking to understand something by breaking it down into parts, reducing complex wholes into simple components or elements."[23] Part of this analytical period is what McLaren calls "the mechanistic virus," a view of reality as one complex machine (*EMC* §7, 53-54), which has transformed discipleship into an "assembly-line" of conversion manufacturers. Accordingly, Christianity now operates like modern engineering (as opposed to artistry), making religion resemble the Industrial Revolution.[24] As a result, the notion of miracles now required separating the natural realm from the supernatural. Soon, Christians believed their own faith had to look like the same static physical laws as modern science (*NKOC* §2, 23-26).[25] This inclination resulted in "modernism."

4.2.2.1 Enlightenment Modernism

In McLaren's literature, the terms "modern," "modernism," and "modernity" have specific delineations that are not always self-evident. For him, there is a difference between *being* modern and simply *existing* in its cultural milieu. Here, "modern" is the period immediately following the Middle Ages beginning about the sixteenth century (*AMP* §18, 276-77). It is not the same as philosophical "modernism" or the cultural ethos of "modernity" that advances Enlightenment principles. The modern era developed gradually from a number of advances, including the printing press and a new Copernican cosmology.[26] What made this period unique was its "broad,

---

23. McLaren, "A Postmodern View of Scripture," 8. McLaren explains further, "I define analysis as taking a whole and breaking it down into its parts, or taking an effect and breaking it down into its causes—tracing it back to its causes" (*PTP*, 119). Thus, for McLaren, reductionism epitomized the modern era because it believed everything was reducible to its naturalistic processes (McLaren, "Everything Old Is New Again," 24).

24. In this way, explorers became conquerors, evangelists became crusaders, the gospel became a set of spiritual laws, and God became a great clock maker or chief engineer who set physical laws in motion. See McLaren's discussions in *AIFA*, 199-200; *COOS1* §12c, 192-93; *GO* §12, 187; *MRTYR* §1, 25; §5, 53; *SMJ* §7, 52; *SWFOI* §9, 70-71; §30, 223.

25. McLaren writes, "The Christian gospel really has become an argument, and evangelism has located itself rhetorically somewhere between courtroom prosecution and door-to-door sales or cable TV infomercials" (*MRTYR* §1, 25). Interestingly, however, McLaren does refer to God as "an amazing artist, *engineer*, scientist, inventor, [and] manager" in one of his earlier books (*FFR* §1, 28-29; emphasis added), though he also stresses that God cannot be likened to a detached clock maker because a good king does not truly disengage from his kingdom (*SMJ* §7, 53).

26. See Bell, *The Winding Passage*, 275-301 and Featherstone, "In Pursuit of the Postmodern," 203-4. McLaren explains elsewhere, "In some ways, Protestantism is a form of Christianity that could only exist after the printing press because you couldn't have literacy because you couldn't have books in large numbers" (*PTP*, 116).

coherent culture in Western civilization" (*MRTYR* §5, 53) that resulted in industrial-capitalist nation-states.[27]

"Enlightenment rationalism," or "modernism," on the other hand, was a *philosophical* movement that aimed to establish self-sufficient and self-governing people (cf. *AIFA*, 239; *COOS1* §12c, 191); although, it did not fully materialize until the mid-seventeenth century (*AMP* §18, 276-77; cf. *NKOC* §4, 43-46). McLaren describes the Enlightenment as an approach to knowledge where naturalism, rationalism, empiricism, and secularism are the dominant epistemological methodologies (*COOS1* §12c, 190).[28] The resultant skepticism and deism, derived from the Enlightenment, prompted Christian apologists to follow suit and appropriate Enlightenment criteria.[29] As a consequence, the Enlightenment conveyed the mistaken notion that reality is reducible to measurable, "objective" reason, becoming the defining characteristic of both modernity and Christian theology.[30] If there were a slogan for modernism, it would be René Descartes's "I think, therefore I am," which signifies the belief that autonomous reasoning can create an undoubtable foundation upon which absolute certainty can be established. Such a system privileges mathematics, physics, and empirical methods, yet excludes ethereal avenues of knowing (*AIFA*, 62; *COOS1* §12a, 160; §12c, 192-94). The result was a desire for finalized answers in all areas of study (*AIFA*, 217) in hopes of providing rational certitude in all religious truth-claims. Known as the "Enlightenment project" or (strong) "foundationalism," the goal was to eliminate uncertainty and alleviate all epistemic doubt.[31] The problem for McLaren is that these subsequent truth-claims relied on finite human reasoning (*MRTYR* §17,

---

27. Best and Kellner, *Postmodern Theory*, 5; Baudrillard, "Modernity," 67-68; Featherstone, "In Pursuit of the Postmodern," 197-99.

28. Most significantly was the era's intellectual defiance against religious authorities. Hence, McLaren describes the modern era as, essentially, "a cold war between scientific and religious belief systems" (*FOWA* §1, 4). For more on how postmodernists conceive of the Enlightenment, see the essays in Baker and Reill, *What's Left of Enlightenment?* and Gordon, *Postmodernism and the Enlightenment*.

29. Gschwandtner, *Postmodern Apologetics?*, 5-10; van den Toren, *Christian Apologetics*, 39, 69-75; Dulles, *A History of Apologetics*, 145-208; Boa and Bowman, *Faith Has Its Reasons*, 21-25.

30. McLaren, foreword to *What Would Jesus Deconstruct?*, 9. See also, Best and Kellner, *Postmodern Theory*, 2-3. For postmoderns like Myron Penner, the shift from premodern faith to modern skepticism ultimately began with the rationalism of René Descartes (1596-1650), as well as the introduction of "modern science" (Penner and Barnes, *A New Kind of Conversation*, 147).

31. From his writings, it is clear that McLaren and other postmodernists are actually describing "classical" or "strong" foundationalism, not its more moderate expressions, which indicates a gross oversight in philosophical nuance on the part of postmodernists (see Moreland, "Truth," 82-84). In the philosophy of religion, classical (strong) foundationalism asserts that beliefs are only true if they are either "properly basic beliefs" (views that are reasonable to hold without evidence) or have evidential support from other properly derived beliefs. "Properly basic beliefs" are only those assumptions that are self-evident, derived from incorrigible sense experiences, or follow standard procedures of logical inference (see Peterson et al., *Reason and Religious Belief*, 116).

128–29), spawning a "know-it-all judgmentalism" (*FOWA* §6, 53) that became the West's new cultural ethos.[32]

4.2.2.2 Modernity as Cultural Ethos

Significantly, McLaren *is* aware that the modern era was not homogenous (*FFR* §1, 27), recognizing romanticism's dissent from rationalism and the enduring dispute between rationality and religious faith (*AMP* §18, 279).[33] However, as a general ethos, "modernity" represented the effects of the Enlightenment project on philosophy and religion.[34] While he believes modernity led to substantial human advances, such as health care and communication, it also caused significant degradation, as well, including the erosion of community, the alienation of individuals, ecological contamination, and a lack of spirituality.[35] McLaren argues there were several features that did the most societal damage, especially secular scientism, individualism, consumeristic materialism, colonialism, and objective rationalism.[36]

With secular scientism, spirituality is replaced with experimentation and technology.[37] With individualism, people no longer feel accountable to the greater global community (*AIFA*, 81).[38] With materialism, McLaren criticizes both capitalism and communism as the chief tyrannical economic systems of the modern era (*GI*, 253–64), which deceptively caused people to believe that wealth is either the cause of or the solution to society's ills (cf. *COOS1* §2, 34–35; cf. *TWLR*). McLaren also condemns

---

32. Cf. Grenz and Franke, *Beyond Foundationalism*, 28–54 and Rockmore, *On Foundationalism*, 45–62.

33. Contra D. A. Carson, who criticizes McLaren and other "Emergents" for oversimplifying what they deem to be "modernity," suggesting that they are apparently oblivious to the nuances and variations of "modern" thought during the Enlightenment era (Carson, *Becoming Conversant*, 59–64).

34. Baudrillard, "Modernity," 63–64.

35. McLaren even attributes events such as the Holocaust, ethnic cleansings, the slave trade, and the massacre of entire people groups to modernity (*AIFA*, 149–50, 201). In fact, McLaren believes it was the Holocaust that officially collapsed modernity's reveries for a better world. He writes, "Auschwitz showed the ease with which reason could become treason . . . [afterwards], people plumped for scientific rationalism less and less" (*AIFA*, 149). Cf. Baudrillard, "Modernity," 69–70 and Carson, *Becoming Conversant*, 30–32, 71.

36. For details on the following discussion, see *AIFA*, 81, 149, 200–1, 239; *MRTYR* §5, 53; *NKOC* §2, 23–26; and *SMJ* §7, 54. Importantly, McLaren remarks that individualism and consumerism are likely the hardest themes to overcome in the postmodern era (*NKOC* §13, 173).

37. McLaren describes his growing discomfort with the scientific worldview, "In fact, I was caught in a double bind. My religious world gave me one version of fundamentalism that refused to be open to the insights of science, while my secular world gave me this scientific fundamentalism unwilling to see anything brought to the table by faith" (*FFR* §7, 154; cf. *FFS* §3, 87). As McLaren describes elsewhere, the true enemy of critical thinking during the modern age "was rather the 'orthodox choice' scientists made for the objective, mechanistic, value-free, third-person, mind-independent, God-less world of a now discredited 'scientific method'" (*AIFA*, 212).

38. Unfortunately, McLaren argues, individualism has become an intellectual and moral disease spreading throughout the church body (*COOS1* §12c, 195–96). Cf. Rah, *The Next Evangelicalism*, 3–32.

modernity's pervasive rationalism, arguing that the Enlightenment sanctified logic to the neglect of mysticism.[39] He labels this disposition a "modern colonial culture," which perpetrated violence on anyone who differed from Western beliefs (*LWWAT* §2, 15). Describing this phase as "motivation by exclusion," the number of Christian denominations increased rapidly as sects began vying for social control (*MRTYR* §11, 84; *NKOCY* §1, 8).[40] Consequently, modernity engendered a belief that "you absolutely, objectively know the absolute, objective truth . . . with absolute certainty" (*NKOC* §2, 25). This attitude only caused incessant and distracting theological disputes (*PTP*, 116).[41] The reductionistic mentality eventually caused Western society to initiate the postmodern turn in order to regain what was lost in modernity.[42]

4.2.3 Postmodern Turn

Citing Søren Kierkegaard's notion of "the deepest level of despair" (*FOWA* §8, 67), McLaren believes that Christians have unknowingly entangled their faith with the ideals of modernity (*NKOC* §4, 50).[43] According to social theorists, newer generations have a global awareness, spawned from widespread access to data, about the epistemic and ethical problems with modern paradigms (cf. *NKOC* §4, 43-46). Reflecting on the printing press, McLaren asks,

> What happens when we become a screen-based world rather than a paper-based world? What happens when the primary modes of communication are electronic rather than through books? Huge change. Change in the way people think. Change in the way they process information. Change in the way we've got to preach to them. (*PTP*, 116)[44]

Nonetheless, McLaren argues that Western civilization is still in a transitionary period similar to an ecological "ecotone," which is the convergence of two distinct ecosystems (i.e., modernity and postmodernity) as one transitions into the other (cf. *PTP*, 116).[45]

---

39. To McLaren, modernity's goal was to eliminate all mysteries and subjectivity by reducing everything to formularies and procedures (*NKOC* §2, 25-26; §13, 171). Cf. Hiebert, *Transforming Worldviews*, 141-210.

40. Cf. Howard, "The Religion Singularity," 77-93.

41. Cf. Driscoll, "A Pastoral Perspective," 87-93.

42. Cf. McLaren, foreword to *Picturing the Gospel*, 7-8.

43. Frost, "A Snapshot of the Emergent Church," 17. McLaren writes, "And you can imagine what happens to the church . . . when it has so thoroughly accommodated to modernity—so much so that it has no idea of any way Christianity could exist other than a modern way" (*NKOC* §2, 27).

44. See also, Lyotard, *The Postmodern Condition* and the essays in Baudrillard, *Selected Writings*.

45. Cf. Hill, "Troubling Adult Learning," 83-92. The term "postmodern" is a conceptual phrase for the period immediately following the modern era and is not identical with the ensuing philosophy known as "postmodernism" (see Featherstone, "In Pursuit of the Postmodern," 197-99 and Best and Kellner, *Postmodern Theory*, 5). The implication is that philosophical postmodernism is not a period in history but a deliberate challenge to modernistic certitude by embracing the complexities of

For him, this transitional phase is a rejuvenation process that learns from the failures of previous eras in anticipation of future possibilities (*AIFA*, 18-19).[46] He also describes this period as a "liminal time," meaning it is still in its infancy while a mature postmodern philosophy does not, in fact, exist yet (*AIFA*, 27, 239).[47] Accordingly, McLaren defines "postmodernism" as the embryonic philosophy underlying this epochal shift (*NKOC* §2, 28). In terms of metaphysics and epistemology, postmodernism is an extension of poststructuralist theory (cf. *AIFA*, 241) that expressly critiques modernism's philosophical pursuit for universal and totalizing knowledge.[48] It is an outgrowth of, estrangement from, and ultimate repudiation of the modernization effects on society (§4.3).[49]

Stanley Grenz and John Franke explain that Christianity is undergoing a dramatic paradigm shift predominantly because of the failure of modernity's presumed ability to obtain undeniable knowledge about reality.[50] Likening the shift to Martin Luther's Reformation, McLaren suggests that simply questioning the status quo has an ability to change history for the better, particularly as pervasive doubts about the merits of (strong) foundationalism surfaced in the wake of numerous European wars (*AIFA*, 149-50; *MRTYR* §17, 128-29).[51] The result was twofold. First, intellectuals recognized modernity's unwarranted cultural superiority; and second, they recognized modernity's overconfidence, which occasioned colonial exploitation and oppression.[52] In essence, "[Modernity] is a dream gone awry" (*COOS1* §12a, 161). The West now realized that modernity attempted to replace the mysteries of life with scientific reductionism (*AMP* §5, 86), unduly believing that reason was the only reliable source for "truth" (*AIFA*, 267). "For modern man, truth—both mathematical

---

perspectivalism (Woods, *Beginning Postmodernism*, 22-23).

46. Thus, according to McLaren, the postmodern era is about recognizing the unstable and unsustainable beliefs of modernity (*NKOC* §16, 220). See also, Hiebert, *Transforming Worldviews*, 345-46.

47. Steven Best and Douglas Kellner reveal that there is no cohesive or widely agreed upon consensus for defining the parameters of postmodern theory among its advocates (Best and Kellner, *Postmodern Theory*, 1-33). McLaren explains, "'Postmoderns' is a terribly abstract term, as is 'presuppositionalism' (do we mean Cartesian foundationalism? Van-Tillian apologetics? Barthian fideism?). In high-altitudes of abstraction, we can easily think we are talking about the same things when actually we are not, or vice versa" (Streett, "An Interview with Brian McLaren," 10).

48. For a history of the origins, development, and divisions of postmodernism, particularly as an outgrowth of poststructuralist and existential critiques of modernism, see Best and Kellner, *The Postmodern Turn*, 38-123; *Postmodern Theory*, 5-25; Phillips, "Exegesis as Critical Praxis," 7-49; and Baudrillard, "Modernity," 64-66.

49. Featherstone, "In Pursuit of the Postmodern," 197, 202-4; Bell, "Beyond Modernism," 275-301. The result is that postmodernism remains in its deconstructive phase by reacting against modernity, though McLaren anticipates it will still not be homogenous once it fully ages (*AIFA*, 239-40; *CIEC*, 108; *NKOC* §2, 28).

50. Grenz and Franke, *Beyond Foundationalism*, 3-54.

51. McLaren, "A New Quest for Christianity." Significantly, Phyllis Tickle describes McLaren as "the Martin Luther of our current reformation" (Tickle, *Emergence Christianity*, 220).

52. McLaren, "Church Emerging," 144-45.

and spiritual—is arrived at through prose thought, prose logic, prose rationality...not intuition, not imagination, not wonder, not awe, not worship, not reverence, not trust, not faith" (*GO* §9, 147). It is this emphasis on mystery that became the basis for postfoundationalism (§8.2.1.3). "The more we learn, the more we know that we don't know, and the more aware of mystery we become" (*AIFA*, 129).[53]

For McLaren, the Enlightenment was also "the Endarkenment" because of its depreciation of spiritual Truth (§8.3.1.2). He believes that as humanity accepts its rational limitations, mystery will once again abound in everyday life (*AIFA*, 149, 266-67).[54] Postmodernity is now "a [renewed] search for *spirituality*" (*FOWA* §1, 4; italics in original; cf. *AIFA*, 264-65), making the Western emphasis on rational criteria an historical phenomenon that has no universal authority.[55] Subsequently, modernity produced an epistemological arrogance that believed humanity was capable of formulating apodictic truth-claims based on an inadequate understanding of logic.[56] With the realization that rational deductions are not objective endeavors, Western culture will move away from Enlightenment ideals, though McLaren believes this shift will take another century or more. Until then, the effects of the Enlightenment will likely dominate religious expressions for several more centuries (*AMP* §18, 280-81).[57] In the meantime, McLaren employs his own version of postmodernity during this transition.

4.2.3.1 McLaren's Postmodernity

Much like the previous epoch, McLaren employs "postmodernism" and "postmodernity" in distinct ways, suggesting there is a difference between *being* postmodern and existing in its cultural environment. The prefix *post-* is essential to comprehending how McLaren understands this epochal shift. He writes, "*The prefix* post *means 'flowing on from or coming after,' not 'unilaterally rejecting or naively dismissing.' The term suggests*

---

53. McLaren writes, "Although it is never spoken of, hardly ever noticed, to a great degree modern Christianity has bought into foundationalism as much as or perhaps more than the secular culture at large" (*MRTYR* §17, 131). He writes elsewhere, "Nature, it turns out, has a stream of chaos running through it" (*COOS1* §12a, 161), arguing "Absolute certainty is not available on many, if any, things in this life for us" (*FFR* §9, 177).

54. McLaren writes, "Yet as we move into a postmodern world, we reenter a world of mystery and we reenter a world where people are skeptical of those overblown claims to certainty" (*PTP*, 117). Interestingly, McLaren also argues it is an oversimplification to reduce modernity and postmodernity to philosophical epistemology; for him, the issues are simply much more complex than that (McLaren, "Church Emerging," 142-43).

55. van den Toren, *Christian Apologetics*, 157. McLaren argues that whereas modernity excluded faith, postmodernity "is hounded by a spiritually charged universe" (*AIFA*, 239).

56. Best and Kellner, *Postmodern Theory*, 4-5. See also, Ashley, "Postmodernism and Antifoundationalism," 53-75 and Gschwandtner, *Postmodern Apologetics?*, xviii, 10.

57. Cf. Lee and Sinitiere, *Holy Mavericks*, 77-79; Kuhn, *The Structure of Scientific Revolutions*, esp. 66-133; and the essays in Griffin, *The Reenchantment of Science*.

continuity as well as discontinuity" (*CIEC*, 66; italics in original; cf. *GO* §6, 120).[58] Believing that humans do not rely on "abstract logic alone" (*COOS1* §6, 80), McLaren condemns depictions of postmodernity as rejecting logic, commenting, "That's antimodernity, not postmodernity" (*AMP* §18, 278). For example, Phil Johnson argues that postmodernity is actually hostile to biblical Christianity, which generates a wicked mindset that denies objective truth, replaces godly spirituality with mysticism, and rejects all forms of authority.[59] McLaren responds to these alarmist reactions,

> Many Christians who approach postmodernism as a philosophy misunderstand, oversimplify, and hastily critique it from their vantage point within modernity, not realizing how enmeshed with modernity they are and how much they have made modern culture a cult, and not realizing that their own modernity may well have modified their Christianity more than their Christianity has modified their modernity.
>
> As a result, they tend to make *postmodern* a synonym for relativism, moral anarchy (a gross mischaracterization), and in general, utter rottenness. This easy dismissal of all things postmodern will serve to firmly entrench many Christians in modernity. (*AIFA*, 240; italics in original)[60]

For McLaren, science is not enough to explain all of reality particularly since scientism is incapable of answering life's greatest questions (*COOS1* §12c, 191-95; *FFR* §7, 152).[61]

As a socio-historical movement, the postmodern turn in society relies heavily on "discourse theory," which views all of society, especially the communal accumulation of knowledge and belief systems, in terms of semiotics. Here, while information remains static, the significance of that information becomes institutionally molded and, therefore, susceptible to changing cultures.[62] The general assumption is that no discipline can elude the subjective socio-political influences that affect human thought processes.[63] The term "postmodernity," therefore, is not synonymous with philosophical postmodernism but, instead, embodies a particular disposition that results from having survived and outlived the modern era. McLaren uses the word

---

58. For example, a "postgraduate" student does not suddenly become anti-higher education (*CIEC*, 66).

59. Johnson, "You Can't Handle the Truth," 219-45.

60. Sadly, J. P. Moreland echoes these distortions when he writes, "Not only are postmodern views of truth and knowledge confused, but postmodernism is an immoral and cowardly viewpoint that people who love truth and knowledge, especially disciples of the Lord Jesus, should do everything they can to heal" (Moreland, "Truth," 77). See also, McLaren, "Faithfully Dangerous," 33 and "An Open Letter to Chuck Colson."

61. Cf. Featherstone, "In Pursuit of the Postmodern," 202-8. In this sense, McLaren follows the same trend of early twentieth century Roman Catholics and other anti-liberal theologies that rejected Christianity's embrace of modernity. See for example, Pelikan, *Credo*, 268-69 and Grenz and Olson, *Twentieth-Century Theology*, 63-112.

62. Pêcheux, *Language, Semantics and Ideology*, esp. 55-131; Foucault, *Archaeology of Knowledge*, 23-85, 89-95; Best and Kellner, *Postmodern Theory*, 25-27.

63. Lee and Sinitiere, *Holy Mavericks*, 78.

"postpubescent" as an analogy. "To be postpubescent means to have passed through puberty, to have been changed by it, and by virtue of having experienced it, to be now different." The postmodern way of life follows suit. "To be postmodern doesn't imply being anti-modern or nonmodern, and it is certainly different from being premodern (though it is similar in some ways). To be postmodern means to have experienced the modern world and to have been changed by the experience" (*NKOC* §2, 22-23). McLaren subsequently characterizes it as "a broad, diverse, and often paradoxical emerging culture defined as having passed through modernity and being ready to move to something better beyond it" (*AIFA*, 239; cf. *NKOC* §2, 28). This definition exemplifies postmodernism's delineation as a "*resistance movement*" against modernity (*CIEC*, 70; italics in original; cf. *AIFA*, 18-19, 240).

Nonetheless, McLaren seeks to advance beyond negative definitions by supplying readers with a positive description as well, characterizing postmodernity as a mindset, "An umbrella term for an attitude and approach to life, not a single identifiable philosophy or style" (*AIFA*, 239). Here, postmodernity is a developmental temperament that currently evades precise definition except to comment that, for McLaren, postmodernity is a "cultural experience" that wants to correct and improve upon the effects of modernity (*CIEC*, 108). Not surprisingly, then, McLaren describes the Enlightenment as the age of the engineer, the lawyer, and the warrior while postmodernity is the age of the artist (*AIFA*, 40; *AMP* §10, 158-59). Here, the "art of living in the way of Jesus" intricately involves an intersubjective and existential practice of discipleship (*FOWA* §13, 125). Hence, in the postmodern world, theologians will need the help of "poets, musicians, filmmakers, actors . . . dancers, sculptors, painters, novelists, photographers . . . not only to *communicate* an authentically Christian theology, but also to discern it, discover it" (*AMP* §15, 227; italics in original). For postmodernists, this disparity between precritical faith and Enlightenment criteria requires yet another paradigm shift in the standards of justification, especially since modernistic apologetics will likely not work with postmodernists (*COOS1* §3, 47; §8, 101).[64] He writes, "My books in many ways chronicle the story of my own grappling with the challenges of making disciples in the changing context."[65] In essence, McLaren's religio-philosophy has been, in part, the identification and correction of modernization.

4.3 MODERNIZATION EFFECTS ON CHRISTIANITY

What is essential to understanding McLaren's philosophy of religion is that he is not anti-Enlightenment *per se* since some aspects of modernity (e.g., mechanization, science, etc.) are beneficial in many circumstances (cf. *AIFA*, 201; *AMP* §18, 278). McLaren is not anti-modernity, but he is anti-*modernization* (*MRTYR* §5, 52-53), which is the process of superimposing modernity's cultural values (excessive

---

64. Penner, *The End of Apologetics*, 3-4.
65. McLaren, "Becoming Convergent."

individualism, materialism, rationalism, etc.) onto premodern Christianity.[66] It is the process of "arrogant intellectualizing" (*GO* §9, 151) religious faith to the neglect of its intersubjective aspects (§8.2.1).[67] "We must see that analytical thinking without appropriate passion is as unbalanced as passion without consideration" (*AMP* §17, 268). The rationale is that detached reasoning is simply not possible for those who passionately and fervently maintain their existential commitments to religious faith.[68]

According to McLaren, modernity twisted divine revelation in order to create a systematized belief system (§7.3.1) with abstract verbiage designed to make God comprehendible (*GO* §9, 152; cf. *NKOC* §6, 67). It presumed it was possible to reduce ultimate Truth to indisputable propositions (*SWFOI* §14, 102). In so doing, modernization made people believe they could unravel the mysteries of the universe and, thus, control it (*NKOC* §2, 24). The process of discovering religious knowledge became overconfident in its objective standards where an alleged "detached" subject could examine an object of study without subjective interference. In spirituality, this practice meant theologians (the subjects) could somehow inspect God like any other object of study in a standard subject-object relationship (cf. *AMP* §17, 257-59; *NKOC* §2, 25).[69] As McLaren argues, however, "For Christians, objectivity is never the last word, because behind all objects there is always a Subject, God, who is not only the ultimate Subject, but is also the Personal Subject. If this is true, then nothing in the universe is purely objective" (*AIFA*, 163).

The result was an era that forced faith-based religions into opposition with rationality (*COOS1* §12c, 191) and required the construction of universal systematic treatises.[70] The modern mindset forced a distinction between the supernatural and the natural, which was concomitant with the typical dichotomist, either/or mentality of the period (*FOWA* §1, 4; cf. *COOS1* §2, 35). The goal of Christianity was once again apologetic, seeking to create "a bombproof certainty, a state of faith where all our beliefs are at rest, where everything is proven logically" (*MRTYR* §17, 131).[71] Nevertheless, postmodernists argue that Christians today overlook the premodern origins of their own religious language, which forces modern believers to justify premodern dogmas with

---

66. Cf. Smith, *Truth and the New Kind of Christian*, esp. 50-66, 108-34.

67. As a sociological term, "modernization" refers to the economic and societal progression toward an industrialized, urbanistic, capitalistic, and technologically advanced nation-state where the end result is an extensive secularization of society that focuses on self-fulfillment and personal development (see Featherstone, "In Pursuit of the Postmodern," 201).

68. Cf. Lewis, *Testing Christianity's Truth Claims*, 25.

69. McLaren writes, "What was the goal of theology in the modern era, other than this: to describe God as a scientist describes an object—objective, detached, sanitized of subjectivity, removed from the variable of personal relationship?" (*AMP* §17, 262).

70. See Penner, "Postmodern Apologetics," 137-38 and *The End of Apologetics*, 7, 21-46. Cf. Dulles, *A History of Apologetics*, 261-69.

71. Cf. Dorrien, *The Remaking of Evangelical Theology*, 188; van den Toren, *Christian Apologetics*, 40; and McLaren, "An Interview with Brian McLaren: Conversation Partners," 49-52.

criteria foreign to their original context.[72] While precritical metaphysical judgments (e.g., the Trinity) remain orthodox, the conceptual justifications that produced those judgments are now completely absent from Christianity, meaning apologists adopted *ad hoc* standards to rationalize their precritical belief system (cf. *SMJ* §7, 52).[73]

With McLaren, the most disastrous ramification was that Christians began *proclaiming* the truth of Christianity while *living* as though it were not real, having "been taken captive by colonialism, consumerism, and modernity."[74] The resulting arrogance has since become an even greater problem when using "metanarratives" to justify unspeakable horrors around the world.[75] McLaren describes these metanarratives as "framing stories" that condition segments of the population to act out of fear, vengeance, and superiority over others (*EMC* §5, 38-39; §9, 66-67).[76] Hence, postmodernity shifts its emphasis from singular depictions of reality to localized perspectives about the world.[77] Ultimately, a distinction exists between metaphysical inquiries into an ontological, observable, and objective world ("realism") and epistemological assertions that claim to comprehend the world with scholastic neutrality.[78] While accepting the former, postmodernists reject the latter. Rather than embrace skepticism, relativism, or nihilism, postmodernists simply highlight the fact that "truth" and "knowledge" are never exact representations of reality because of humanity's culturally and linguistically conditioned perceptions.[79] Becoming more aware of these distinctions has forced McLaren to reject modernity's liberal-conservative dualism as a manufactured, false dichotomy.

---

72. Penner, *The End of Apologetics*, 5-8. Benno van den Toren believes the decisive difference between modernistic Christianity and authentic Christianity is anthropological, not epistemological, meaning it was the Enlightenment's pursuit for autonomy, rather than its rationalism, that conflicted the most with Christian principles (van den Toren, *Christian Apologetics*, 66-92).

73. McLaren describes how this *ad hoc* process is self-defeating for postmodernists today, "Our lack of example in speech, behavior, love, faith, and purity may also explain why we must rely so heavily on arguments, many of them making claims that appear to postmodern people to be coercive and colonial, and therefore immoral" (McLaren and Litfin, "Emergent Evangelism," 42).

74. McLaren, "A Postmodern View of Scripture," 10.

75. See Slade, "*Hagioprepē*[set macron over e]*s*," *forthcoming*.

76. McLaren, "The Stories We Tell Ourselves," 16. McLaren also defines metanarratives as "framing stores that weave together memoires of grievances that need to be avenged, stories of dangers that need to be avoided, or stories of superiority that explain why one group should be advantaged to dominate over others" (*EMC* §5, 39). While Christianity may be a "*mega*narrative" ("a big story"), it is not a *meta*narrative in the sense of being self-legitimizing and totalizing over all cultural perspectives (see Westphal, *Overcoming Onto-Theology*, xii-xiv). For McLaren, this association with an "alien culture and philosophy" (i.e., modernity) ultimately resulted in the church's "stagnation, domination, [and] containment" (McLaren, foreword to *An Emergent Theology*, 4).

77. Gschwandtner, *Postmodern Apologetics?*, 10; Penner, "Postmodern Apologetics," 142.

78. Cf. Smith, "Reflections on McLaren," 227-41.

79. As McLaren explains, "[Postmoderns are] very aware of the fact that calling something a fact doesn't make it a 'true fact.' They're very sensitive to the ways that we interpret and articulate observations, and thus put a spin on them—so there's some degree of distance between what really happened and how we report what happened as a 'fact'" (McLaren, "An Interview on Christian Publishing"). Cf. Benson, "What Is 'Postmodernism'?," 7; Simmons and Benson, *The New Phenomenology*, 21-22; and

4.3.1 Liberal-Conservative Divide

There was yet another consequence of Christian modernization. For McLaren, liberalism is just as guilty of capitulating to modernity as conservatism (*TWLD*).[80] Gary Dorrien explains,

> Liberal theology has been a straightforwardly modernizing project. It has sought to bring Christian claims into line with beliefs derived from the regnant critical consciousness of modernity. Theological liberalism embraces the Enlightenment modernist wedge between reason and experience; for the most part, it accepts, or at least seeks to accommodate, the modernist valorization of objective, nonparticipatory knowledge.[81]

For McLaren, the late modern period resulted in the infamous liberal-conservative divide that plagued Christianity for decades; but today, the timeworn conflict between liberals and conservatives has quickly become a "relic" of the past (*GO* §8, 138-40).[82] He acknowledges that both divisions have done enormous damage to Christianity's image; and from his perspective, neither side has an acceptable approach to Christian faith (cf. *GO* §8, 135-40; *NKOC* §16, 212). Nonetheless, it was conservatism's strong faith identity that developed a hypercritical attitude toward other beliefs (*JMBM* §5, 40-43), causing a lot of alienation in the process among those outside of the church (*GO* §Intro, 21).

To McLaren, conservatives thrive on "rejecting, and excluding, and shaming, and oppressing the 'other' unless he converts," whereas liberals often overcompensate by abandoning Christianity almost entirely. Thus, McLaren encourages a third alternative that allows a strong Christian identity while also requiring Christ-like love for outsiders (cf. *NKOCY* §17, 175; *WMRBW*, 216-20).[83] "The irony for me, of course, is that I see fundamentalism and liberalism as two ways of being Christian in modernity, and my whole interest is exploring territory beyond modernity and its polarities. I suppose you could say that I'm searching for some new territory that is post-liberal and

---

Penner and Barnes, *A New Kind of Conversation*, 33.

80. Jeffrey Straub compares McLaren to "old liberalism" because he deemphasizes doctrine (Straub, "The Emerging Church," 76-77). However, what Straub and others fail to realize is that McLaren has never once embraced liberalism as a theological or political ideology. Cf. Hawtrey and Lunn, "The Emergent Church," 65-74 and Reed, "Emerging Treason?," 74-78.

81. Dorrien, *The Remaking of Evangelical Theology*, 187-88. Cf. Gray, "The Emergence of The Emerging Church," 27-62.

82. Roger Olson argues that neo-Evangelicals view everything in terms of a liberal-conservative divide with no real awareness that the "war" with theological liberalism has ended (Olson, *Reformed and Always Reforming*, 25-26; cf. Dorrien, *The Remaking of Evangelical Theology*, 185-89). For McLaren, conservative Christians are not just perpetually in opposition to liberalism. They have, in fact, become *anti*-liberal and illiberal in their disposition (cf. *GSM*, 230-31n9).

83.. McLaren, "12 Ounce Interview," 02:59-03:39. See also, McLaren, "Spiritual Formation in Unexpected and Dangerous Places."

post-conservative."[84] From here, McLaren was able to discern yet another modernization perpetuated by both liberals and conservatives: environmental resource depletion.

4.3.2 Environmental Degradation

One ramification of modernization is deeply personal to McLaren: the enabling of callous environmental destruction. For him, creation is vital to spirituality because God's glory manifests in the created order (*FFR* §1, 27-29; cf. *GO* §9, 145-57).[85] However, the adoption of modernity has given rise to hyper-exploitation of the earth (*GSM*, 74-75). Labelling it a "doctrine of dominion," McLaren perceives Christians as rationalizing their ravaging of the earth through a misguided belief that God will destroy the planet anyway (*AMP* §3, 50-51). In McLaren's view, environmental degradation is the consequence of a mechanistic worldview (*SA*, 23).[86] Left unopposed, this approach will generate harmful environmental catastrophes and devastating resource depletion (*COOS1* §2, 37; *JMBM* §8, 65n2; *TWLD*, 35).[87]

McLaren further argues that the Bible depicts creation as "God's self-expression, God's speech act," which eliminates any distinction between the natural and supernatural realms (*SA*, 8). Thus, a truly biblical ontology means everything is interconnected (*COOS1* §2, 34) and unified "in one fabric of creation" (*JMBM* §12, 104). As Lindsay Moseley explains, Christian environmentalists view everything in nature as "essential components in a larger, interdependent web of God's creation."[88] For McLaren, humanity and the environment are inseparable:

> You are made from common soil . . . soil that becomes watermelons and grain . . . and then they become food, and then that food becomes you. As highly organized dust, you are closely related to frogs and tortoises, lions and field mice, bison and elephants and gorillas. Together with all living things, you

---

84. McLaren, "A Postmodern View of Scripture," 7. See also, McLaren, "Red State, Purple Church," 26-29 and Lee and Sinitiere, *Holy Mavericks*, 77-105. From his discussion on theo-politics, it is apparent that McLaren is "more comfortable on the center-left side of the political spectrum" (Reed, "Emerging Treason?," 75).

85. McLaren explains, "This is how I 'live and move and have my being' in God—to walk as a creature among creatures in God's wonderful creation, with my heart open to the Creator, practicing God's presence with me" (*GO* §11, 177-78). For an elaboration on McLaren's theological ecology, see McLaren, *The Galápagos Islands*; "This Good Earth," 166-69; and afterword to *A Faith Embracing All Creatures*, 181-83.

86. Cf. Toly, "Evangelicals and the Environment," 23-40 and Gnanakan, "Evangelicals and Environmental Stewardship," 188-93.

87. McLaren explains that while Americans constitute only 5 percent of the globe, "we are generally acknowledged as the world's most self-centered, consumptive, arrogant, and inconsiderate minority" (*JP* §Intro, 19).

88. Moseley, "Just Ecology," 169. Likewise, Jürgen Moltmann, whose writings McLaren is familiar with (e.g., *AMP* §15, 229; *GSM*, 106), once wrote, "Through his Spirit God himself is present in his creation. The whole creation is a fabric woven and shot through by the efficacies of the Spirit" (Moltmann, *God in Creation*, 212).

share the breath of life. . . .In that story, you are connected and related to everything everywhere. (*WMRBW*, 7-8; see also, *GI*, 74, 85)

In this sense, McLaren views creation as a cosmic temple (*SA*, 7), characterizing it as "God's domain" (*SMJ* §4, 27). "Caring for Creation is, for the emerging culture, caring for the cathedral God built" (*AIFA*, 79-80). He renounces anything that turns "the temple of creation . . . God's true sanctuary" into a den of thieves (*EMC* §27, 227) where the environment becomes nothing more than a temporary warehouse or an expendable sanctuary (*GO* §16, 237-38).[89] With these modernization effects in mind, McLaren is able to develop a postmodern approach to faith.

4.4 POSTMODERN ETHOS FOR CHRISTIAN FAITH

The debate over the nature and prevalence of postmodernity has prompted the rethinking of socio-political systems, as well as the social sciences overall.[90] For some social theorists, the postmodern period has resulted in a blurring between ontological reality and human conceptualizations, suggesting that the relative meanings of local languages, cultures, and imaginations have replaced modernity's universalist metanarratives.[91] Consequentially, Jean-François Lyotard explains that postmodernity is best understood as "a mood, or better, a state of mind."[92] It is, as Myron Penner suggests, "a *condition*, or a set of attitudes, dispositions, and practices that is aware of itself as modern and aware that modernity's claims to rational superiority are deeply problematic" (cf. *COOS1* §12c, 190-91).[93] What is significant to understanding McLaren's philosophy of religion is his depiction of the epochal shift as an "ethos" (*GO* §13, 206) rather than a philosophical belief system (*CIEC*, 108). This ethos signifies a recognition that God is not an objectifiable object but, instead, a Subject with whom to interact in an empathetic way. Following Walker Percy, McLaren believes in changing the conventional theologian-object (I-it) study of God to a subject-subject (I-thou) relationship of intersubjectivity (*AIFA*, 200; *AMP* §17, 257-60).[94] Thus, McLaren's postmodern mentality revels in the "open-endedness" of intimate friendship where

---

89. Cf. Kearns, "Green Evangelicals," 157-77. This doctrine of creation is not without evangelical precedent. Using literary comparisons with the ancient Near East, John Walton argues that Genesis depicts God as establishing the universe as a cosmic temple, whose presence permeates throughout all of creation. See Walton, *Genesis 1 as Ancient Cosmology* and *The Lost World of Genesis One*.

90. For details, see Kellner, "Postmodernism as Social Theory," 239-69; Susen, *The 'Postmodern Turn' in the Social Sciences*; and the essays in Dickens and Fontana, *Postmodernism and Social Inquiry*.

91. Cf. Lyotard, *The Postmodern Condition*, esp. 3-17 and Baudrillard, *Selected Writings*, 169-87.

92. Lyotard, "Rules and Paradoxes and Svelte Appendix," 209. Likewise, Jean Baudrillard describes postmodernity as "a characteristic mode of civilization" (Baudrillard, "Modernity," 63).

93. Penner, *The End of Apologetics*, 13; italics in original. See also, Penner and Barnes, *A New Kind of Conversation*, 5, 30, 32-33, 44-46, 150-52 and Horton, *Christless Christianity*, 64-66.

94. McLaren believes this intersubjectivity is precisely how Jesus approached religiosity (*SMJ* §7, 56-58).

there exist endless possibilities, perspectives, and opportunities to understand God on deeper levels (*AIFA*, 217-18).

The postmodern ethos also rejects the either/or dichotomist thinking of modernity and is unconcerned about possessing absolute certainty. Neither institutional religion nor reductionistic naturalism are capable of providing an existentially livable and sustainable faith (*FOWA* §1, 4-5). Instead, for McLaren, reality consists of *holons*, which are self-organizing systems of both/and qualities ("holarchy") that defy reductionistic analysis (*AIFA*, 144-45).[95] The result is a dialectical synthesis of precritical faith and modern reason, which advocates for "thaumatology" (the study of wonder) by focusing on God as the subject of awe and amazement, not propositional data (*AIFA*, 242, 307).[96] In fact, it was the loss of wonder that explains why McLaren argues "theological quibbling over theological esoterica" is a waste of time (*MRTYR* §12, 95). As he clarifies elsewhere, "Postmodernity more likely seeks to integrate rationality with things *beyond* rationality—things like imagination, intuition and faith . . . we could expect the postmodern era to be a synthesis of faith *and* reason" (*AMP* §18, 278; italics in original).

From the postmodern ethos also comes a realization that no version of Christianity is wholly free of errors (*COOSI* §12b, 172-73; cf. *AMP* §2, 33-34). In essence, all approaches to faith are the product of their socio-historical context (*NKOC* §4, 52), which releases McLaren from the need to establish definitive doctrinal beliefs. "So now I feel free to question church dogma *and* scientific dogma, because I believe that God wants me to seek the truth. And also because anybody—even preachers and scientists alike—can be wrong. I assume that I'm wrong about hundreds of my beliefs, and I hope that God will keep leading me to doubt those beliefs so I can embrace better ones" (*AMP* §16, 245; italics in original).[97] McLaren explains further,

> We are acknowledging that the Christianities we have created—or constructed—deserve to be reexamined and deconstructed, not so that we may slide into agnosticism, atheism, or secular patriotic consumerism, but so that our religious traditions can be seen for what they are. They are not simply a pure, abstracted, and ideal "essence of Christianity," but rather they are evolving, embodied, situated versions of the faith. (*NKOCY* §3, 27)

95. See also, Koestler, *Janus*, 37.

96. For McLaren, the secular, scientific world has made theologians lose the mystery of God's creation (*FFR* §7, 153-54; *NKOCY* §20, 233). He quotes Gregory of Nyssa (ca. 330-395) as saying, "Concepts create idols. Only wonder understands" (*MRTYR* §19, 146).

97. McLaren writes, "I believe Christianity is true, but I do not believe that my version (or yours, for that matter) of the Faith is completely true. (In other words, I believe that all versions are incomplete in some ways, weighed down with extra baggage, and marred by impurities, biases, misconceptions, and gaps). . . . I believe there is no completely true version of Christianity anywhere except, of course in the mind of God. (In other words, incompleteness and error are part of the reality of being human)" (*COOSI* §12b, 172-73). With this tentativeness, McLaren also recognizes the need for a critical approach to postmodern thought, as well (McLaren, "A New Kind of Old Christian," 112).

Today, the difference is not that postmodernity lacks critical thinking: the difference is that the postcritical era also emphasizes thinking critically about modernity (*NKOC* §4, 51).[98] Thus, the postmodern mind perceives reality in post-Newtonian terms, embracing indeterminacy where concepts of God are much more dynamic and indefinite (*SWFOI* §30, 223-24). The implication is a greater emphasis on a suprarational, non-propositional approach to faith.

4.4.1 Rejection of Propositional Systematics

McLaren describes propositional Christianity as adhering to "notional" or "conceptual beliefs" in the sense that its *truth*-claims possess ontological existence and correspondence with perceived reality (e.g., "I believe *that* God exists"). However, "relational beliefs," on the other hand, are not dependent on a claim's ontological existence. Rather, relational beliefs denote the type of existential conviction and fidelity to a particular *faith*-claim ("I believe *in* Christ"). In McLaren's religio-philosophy, relational beliefs take priority because they signify a lifestyle of following Christ whereas conceptual beliefs can be asserted without existential appropriation (cf. James 2:19). For him, Christianity was originally a relational belief system, but it has since been consumed with notional propositions and systematics (*GSM*, 215-16).[99]

Part of the postmodern ethos for McLaren entails a rejection of systematics and theological absolutes, pejoratively labeling them as "conceptual cathedrals" that elevate propositions and arguments above spiritual practices. With him, "systematic theology" is a contradiction in terms and will eventually dissolve as a concept altogether (*GO* §9, 151-52) because it represents modernity's "naïve optimism about theology" (*AIFA*, 282). The origin of McLaren's rejection of systematics stems from his experience in the eighth grade when he took his first biology course and learned about its scientifically detached methodology. He was discouraged by the way it reduced everything to systems, chemistry, and physics (*FFR* §7, 149-50). McLaren rejects the arrogance of systematics because they pretend to "capture all knowable truth in propositions, organized in a master outline, holding for all times and places and people the universal abstractions extracted from the narratives of Scripture" (*AIFA*, 282).

McLaren clarifies that he does not reject the importance of doctrine but, instead, redefines doctrine as the ongoing Christian practice of seeking and teaching truth, a practice the Christian community engages in while pursuing its primary aim of maturing in Christ-like love. For him, this diminution is an appropriation of

---

98. Cf. Hiebert, *Transforming Worldviews*, 211-40. McLaren connects this self-critical process to the spiritual practice of *katharsis* (or *via purgative*), which intends to purge a person's belief system of its own destructive elements through a method of intense and focused self-examination (*FOWA* §15, 147, 151-57). See also, McLaren, foreword to *Manifold Witness*, xi-xiii.

99. McLaren writes, "We're probably at our worst when we present our faith as a system rather than as a story" (McLaren, "Brian McLaren: The Equation of Change").

the mystical-spiritualist tradition of church history where the emphasis is placed on practice (e.g., attending to the poor) rather than abstractions (*WMRBW*, 28-29).[100] Here, McLaren concurs with Grenz and Franke's assertion that theology is not meant to codify propositional truth-claims; it is meant to aid believers in attending to the Spirit's guidance in new ages (*AIFA*, 275).[101] Consequently, the pursuit of deeper existential meaning is more important than theological argumentation (*WMRBW*, 102), especially since systematics have not generated the necessary spiritual transformation in believers (*GO* §14, 220; *NS* §3, 24). Similarly, the Enlightenment did not provide the values, imagination, and passion necessary to convert theological knowledge into wisdom (*COOS1* §12c, 190-91, 194-95). "As I see it, religion is at its best when it leads us forward, when it guides us in our spiritual growth as individuals and in our cultural evolution as a species" (*GSM*, xi). McLaren concludes further, "Instead of rejecting [Christian] doctrines, we need to rediscover, reenvision, and reformulate them in a postimperial, postcolonial, post-Christendom way" (*JMBM* §12, 101). In other words, McLaren believes there needs to be a proper postmodern enculturation of Christian identity.

4.4.2 Postmodern Enculturation

Ultimately, McLaren thinks a new paradigm is needed to correct the modernization effects that have made Christianity irrelevant and untenable for younger generations, though he recognizes that this correction merely looks like a capitulation to postmodernism (*SWFOI* §13, 98). His realizes that his new paradigm is falsely grouped alongside "absolute nihilism, mindless relativism, moral anarchy, and other rotten things."[102] For him, postmodernity merely identifies those parts of conventional religion that need changing (*AIFA*, 170; *COOS1* §2, 34-35). He does recognize, however, that postmodernism can become idolatrous (*SMJ* §8, 70).[103] What McLaren's critics often overlook is that he employs postmodern *rhetoric* as a way of "despoiling the Egyptians," whereby he appropriates pagan wisdom for edification purposes.[104] He remarks,

---

100. This framework aligns with McLaren's "purpose approach" to faith, which intends to answer for what purpose and to what end theology exists (*FFR* §7, 151-52).

101. See Franke, *The Character of Theology*, 135 and Grenz and Franke, *Beyond Foundationalism*, 16.

102. McLaren, "Church Emerging," 142. Cf. Jue, "What's Emerging in the Church?," 20-39 and Hammett, "An Ecclesiological Assessment," 29-49.

103. In fact, McLaren comfortably confesses that there are "seeds of evil in postmodernity just as there are in modernity," and all it will take is a few centuries to reveal its "fatal flaws" (*NKOC* §3, 32-33). Hence, McLaren says he fluctuates "between enthusiasm about the usefulness of the term *postmodern* and feeling sick to death of it." He acknowledges that postmodernity can "launch a kind of fad with attendant slogans, jargon, insider-outsider or us-them sociology, and other unpleasant side effects" (*SWFOI* §Preface, xiv-xv; italics in original). He also agrees that postmodernists often "indulge in facile dualisms" with a smug air of superiority and "New Agey" hype. He sees this tendency among postmodernists as both annoying and stupid (*AMP* §18, 275-76, 279-280).

104. McLaren explains that to be effective evangelizers today, believers need to be less "modern

> I did what scientists do: I allowed new data to correct a long-standing belief. I wasn't simply 'conforming to the world' or 'accommodating to popular opinion,' as my critics frequently asserted. No, I was conforming to reality, to the best current evidence, to a growing bank of experience. I was practicing corrigibility. I was seeking to conform to the way of Christ by being willing to rethink. (*GSM*, 40)[105]

In this sense, McLaren is not so much a postmodernist as he is a "man of the Enlightenment," having become enlightened about the defects of conventional paradigms (*COOS1* §12c, 190).

4.5 CONCLUSION

Harvey Cox describes the current epochal shift as a transition from the "Age of Belief" to the "Age of the Spirit," retaining previous good qualities while preparing for upcoming challenges in the twenty-first century (*NKOCY* §1, 11-13).[106] With McLaren, the issue is not whether Christians ought to resist the postmodern turn: the issue is how to prepare believers for practicing their faith during and after the epochal shift (*COOS1* §Preface, 8-9).[107] Much like his other disillusionments, McLaren's discovery of Christianity's capitulation to a foreign ontology (i.e., "modernity") also resulted in an intellectual disenchantment with conventional paradigms (*NKOC* §2, 19). He eventually learned that neither God nor Christianity is limited to modernistic concepts (*MRTYR* §5, 54). The implication is that McLaren no longer supports prioritizing the objectification of faith in a supposedly objective manner. Though he recognizes the impulse and agony of wanting to retain a modernistic form of Christianity (*LWWAT* §2, 15), he also recognizes that the modern era is quickly fading. Hence, McLaren challenges his readers to have the fortitude to remain faithful to Christ instead of remaining faithful to a misguided Enlightenment paradigm (*AIFA*, 89; *NKOC* §4, 55-56). Having intellectually realized that ideologies and metanarratives are often questionable remnants of a bygone era, McLaren eventually reexamined the very reasoning processes by which he was approaching faith.

---

and more postmodern—not completely of it, of course, but more completely in it" (*COOS1* §12a, 168). See also, McLaren, "Brian McLaren on Outreach," 122; "Church Leaders Wonder?"; *AMP* §18, 275; *CIEC*, 114; *COOS1* §3, 48; §12b, 171; *EMC* §5, 34-35; *GO* §18, 286-87; *JMBM* §12, 101; §16, 138; *SMJ* §App. 1, 221-22; and *WMRBW*, 131-35.

105. He reiterates elsewhere, "Just as new data requires rethinking of old formulations, so our theological constructions must remain flexible, open to correction and expansion and reconception" (*AMP* §2, 43). Cf. Carmody and Carmody, *Catholic Spirituality*, 140; Olson, *The Story of Christian Theology*, 103, 180, 263; Grenz, *A Primer on Postmodernism*, 161-74; and Daston, "Enlightenment Fears," 115-28.

106. Cox, *The Future of Faith*, 1-20.

107. According to McLaren, the type of Christianity that will survive this transition will be those "preparing for ministry in 2040, not 1940" (*NKOC* §16, 208).

5

McLaren and Abduction

5.0 INTRODUCTION

Brian McLaren's disenchantment with conventional paradigms resulted in him distrusting the beliefs of what he considered a discredited "party line" (*FFS* §1, 44). Initially, he saw only two choices: leave ministry or endorse a tradition he no longer accepted. Soon, however, he discovered a third alternative: acquire a new way to be Christian (*FOWA* §6, 58; *NKOC* §Intro, xiii–xiv). He asks, "Could we allow our beliefs to be open to testing and improvement. . . .forever upholding the same passion to learn, even if new learning requires regularly admitting we were previously wrong?" (*GSM*, 37). The thesis of this chapter is that McLaren engages in a logical inference-building known as abductive reasoning. Nevertheless, he purposely conceals his inferences through abductive provocations and rhetorical maneuverings. Four main elements will support this thesis: 1) McLaren's Peircean abduction as his *modus operandi*; 2) his emphasis on practical and aesthetic inferences; 3) McLaren's affection for provocative statements; and 4) his goal to unsettle his readers by stimulating their creativity. Before understanding McLaren's abduction, however, it is first necessary to understand the underlying philosophy for why he pursued an alternative reasoning process in the first place.

5.1 OBLIGATORY SELF-CORRECTION

Derived from the postmodern ethos (§4.4), McLaren's religio-philosophy is premised on the need for humility and self-correction. A major concern for him is that Christians routinely disparage other people's beliefs yet are unwilling to question their own assumptions about reality. Believing Christianity's very nature "challenges all institutions (including its own)" (*GSM*, 3), McLaren argues that a proper faith requires deep introspection. Thus, he routinely includes himself in his criticisms of other Christians, confessing his own hypocrisy in preaching against others in order to camouflage his personal failings (*NS* §10, 88). McLaren even admits to being a poor example of Christian discipleship (*SMJ* §1, 5) since he has ignored the poor and scapegoated society's downtrodden in the past (*EMC* §2, 15-16).[1]

Acknowledging his prior role in promoting erroneous paradigms (*GO* §Intro, 21), McLaren eventually felt his congregation deserved a better pastor (*NKOCY* §Preface, xii). He even empathizes with some of the negative reactions to how his journey has evolved. "While I've tried to model and teach about that better way, many Evangelicals think I've gone too far for them to accept or learn from. I understand that, and don't hold that against them. The 17 year-old me probably couldn't have accepted the 62 year old me either!"[2] However, McLaren insists that Christians should practice the "splinter-and-beam principle," meaning they do not correct others without first correcting themselves. He even co-authored an online article that reads in part,

> We wish to say thanks to our critics for their honest feedback on our books, articles, speeches, blogs, events, and churches. We readily acknowledge that like all human endeavors, our work, even at its best, is still flawed and partial, and at its worst, deserves critique. We are grateful to those who help us see things we may not have seen without the benefit of their perspective. We welcome their input.[3]

McLaren's rationale for self-reflection is simple: confessing one's failures, both as a community and as individuals, stimulates education, humility, and redemption (*FOWA* §4, 33). "If, to put a twist on an old saying, we only learn and tell one sanitized, privileged version of our history, we will repeat the worst parts of it" (*JMBM* §9, 80).

---

1. McLaren, "Church Emerging," 148. McLaren writes elsewhere, "As a teenager I was indignant about the hypocrisy I saw in others, though sadly, not yet in myself. Perhaps I just hadn't lived long enough to develop my own personal style of hypocrisy. I have lived long enough now" (*GO* §Intro, 20; cf. *AMP* §16, 243). McLaren then offers the following prayer: "Creator of the universe, we who have claimed to be your people in our words have betrayed you in our actions" (McLaren, "'Instead of Ruling'—Prayers," 225).

2. McLaren, "Dear White Evangelical Christians . . ." In fact, McLaren apologizes for being overly critical in his own writings (*COOS1* §12b, 176; §13, 204). As Jason Byassee remarks about McLaren, "He offers not another treatise about why everyone else is wrong but his group is right; he insists regularly that he must be as blind to his own vices and oversight as those he criticizes" (Byassee, "An Emergent Voice," 30).

3. Jones et al., "Response to Recent Criticisms."

This humility manifests especially in McLaren's apologetics, which he suggests should begin with an actual apology (*GO* §17, 258-59; italics in original).⁴ "We have got to be honest about our failures, present and past. That way apologetics has a lot more to do with apology" (*PTP*, 123).⁵ He writes elsewhere,

> Instead of defending old answers, the new kind of leader will often apologize for how inadequate they are. In modernity, you gained credibility by always being right; in the emerging culture, you gain authority by admitting when you're wrong and apologizing humbly. . . .Sincere apology is essential to the new apologetic; we Christians will need to repent before we can ask anyone else to do so. (*AMP* §10, 163)

Ultimately, his goal is to defuse negative perceptions of Christianity preemptively, particularly by emphasizing the kind of humility that is inherent to a pilgrim's spiritual journey (cf. *GI*, x).⁶

5.1.1 Continued Pilgrimage

Crucial to McLaren's system is being a *viator in via* (sojourner seeking God's kingdom). Describing life as a "pilgrimage" (*JP* §Intro, 18) and humans as "wayfarers and pilgrims" (*GSM*, x), McLaren stresses the expeditionary nature of theology by questioning his own religion (*AIFA*, 247-49). Indeed, McLaren claims he does not possess faith because he is still pursuing it (*FFR* §Intro, 15). For him, faith is "more a journey than jelled beliefs, more pilgrimage and practices than propositions and principles" (*AIFA*, 303). Hence, he describes believers as "*hopeful pilgrims moving forward in the journey of faith*" (*GSM*, xii; italics in original).⁷

McLaren chronicles his spiritual pilgrimage into five distinct phases (see *JP* §Intro, 18). First, he became disillusioned with mainstream Christianity, entering the second phase by questioning the pragmatic value of religion itself (cf. "Stage 2 faith"

---

4. Though McLaren advocates apologizing for past injustices, he also insists that apologetic humility requires reverence for Christian tradition and those spiritual ancestors who preserved that tradition (*GO* §17, 259).

5. McLaren points to genocidal atrocities in America's history, despite its supposed Christian heritage, to demonstrate why apologists ought to apologize first (*PTP*, 123). This diffident style of apologetics reflects the same contentions of apologist Douglas John Hall, who likewise decried the triumphalism of other apologists. See Hall, *Why Christian?*, ix, 1-2.

6. McLaren explains, "Postmodern apologetics means we say, 'We're really sorry; we blew it. We are just human beings, we are struggling with this. But we are still trying to learn, and we feel that the gospel is calling us to do better in these areas.' That becomes a very winsome apologetic when we talk that way" (*PTP*, 123). Hence, "Your own humility becomes an apologetic. Sometimes the best apologetic is simply to apologize" (*AMP* §6, 98).

7. It is important to note that McLaren was a board member of *Sojourners Magazine* and a founding member of Red Letter Christians (*FOWA* §Author, 216), two organizations that stress the pilgrimage of faith toward social action. See Kim, "'Sojourners' Magazine, 1971-2005" and Claiborne and Campolo, *Red Letter Revolution*.

in *FFS* §3, 89). This questioning then required a reevaluation of theological doctrines, as well.[8] One theological question in particular propelled the third phase: identifying the precise content of Jesus' gospel message and comparing it to the versions of Christianity today (cf. *NKOCY* §14, 137-38). Because so many Christians have tarnished Jesus' name, he felt it was obligatory to reevaluate precisely what Jesus taught (*SMJ* §17, 154). This focus logically necessitated the fourth phase of examining the canonical Gospels in order to read Jesus' original message. The final phase was the realization that Jesus' gospel was more revolutionary than conventional paradigms suggest, with far-reaching implications for social, political, economic, racial, and environmental justice.[9] With these phases in mind, it is now possible to uncover the reasoning processes underlying McLaren's approach to Christian faith.

5.2 ABDUCTIVE LOGIC

Mental reasoning manifests in one of two ways: affective intuition and analytic rationality. With intuition, people reach assumptions based on involuntary instincts; with rationality, people utilize formal logic.[10] Abductive logic (or abduction) is a reasoning process that transcends the typical deductive-inductive dichotomy by also incorporating intuition into the process (cf. *AIFA*, 286-87). Coined by the pragmatic scientist, Charles Sanders Peirce, abduction often manifests in scientific and forensic investigations where experts formulate theories through an imaginative method of educated conjecture and guesswork. The benefit of abduction is that it acknowledges affective discernment but also attempts to restrain impulsive hunches.[11]

In deductive logic, it is *impossible* for the premises to be true and yet the conclusion be false. With inductive logic, however, it is *improbable* (in a Bayesian sense), but not impossible, for the premises to be true and yet the conclusion be false.[12] Abductive logic, on the other hand, indicates it is *implausible* for the premises to be true and the conclusion still be false. It suggests that a particular hypothesis is not immediately

---

8.. McLaren writes, "I have a built-in urge to ask questions, and to me, experts earn their credibility by their willingness to be tested or doubted" (*FFS* §3, 88).

9. Significantly, McLaren's spiritual and philosophical progression is discernable when reading his books in order of publication date. For instance, two of his earliest writings, *Church on the Other Side* (1998) and *More Ready than You Realize* (2002), exemplify McLaren's second phase of addressing practical issues. The third phase involving theological reconsiderations is the predominant theme of *A New Kind of Christian* trilogy (2001, 2003, 2005) and *A Generous Orthodoxy* (2004). The fourth phase is represented in his book, *The Secret Message of Jesus* (2006), while the fifth phase culminates in *Everything Must Change* (2007).

10. Kuhn, "Reasoning," 744-64.

11. Cf. Fann, *Peirce's Theory of Abduction*; Walton, *Abductive Reasoning*, 1-36; and Milkman et al., "How Can Decision Making Be Improved?," 379-83. Various labels for abductive reasoning appear in the relevant literature, including adduction, presumptive argument, defeasible inference, retroduction, and plausibilistic reasoning.

12. Hurley and Watson, *A Concise Introduction to Logic*, 33-40.

outlandish or otherwise fanciful, making abduction immensely important to science.[13] As Peirce once explained, "Deduction proves that something *must* be; Induction shows that something *actually is* operative; Abduction merely suggests that something *may be*."[14] J. P. Moreland and William Lane Craig describe science as a "craft" that employs imagination and intuition derived from years of experience.[15] Notably, McLaren shows familiarity with abduction when he quotes Albert Einstein as saying, "The mechanics of discovery are neither logical nor intellectual. It's a sudden illumination, almost a rapture. . . .initially there is a great leap of the imagination."[16] As McLaren explains further, "Science is a creative process involving many faculties in addition to cold, hard reason" (*FFS* §2, 67).[17] Today, abduction often occurs in the posterior stages of scientific discovery and is associated with an "inference to the best explanation." For Peirce, however, abduction occurred in the anterior stage of theory formation.[18] As G. Schurz explains, Peircean abduction is specifically "a *search strategy* which leads us, for a given kind of *scenario*, in a reasonable time to a most promising explanatory conjecture which is then subject to further test."[19] From these characteristics, it becomes evident that McLaren employs abduction to his own Christian faith.

5.2.1 McLaren and Peircean Abduction

McLaren emphasizes that science is not a set of facts; science is a methodology (*GSM*, 35-37). Embracing the approach of Walker Percy (cf. *WP*, 46-49), McLaren slightly modifies the scientific method to construct a philosophy of religion (*WMRBW*, 29-30) by observing certain phenomena (e.g., spiritual experiences) and then hypothesizing about their implications (cf. *JP* §Intro, 18).[20] Once he develops a theory, he tests whether the model is spiritually viable or not. From here, McLaren concludes

---

13. Walton, *Abductive Reasoning*, 3-4, 17-29, 277n6. In this sense, investigators are able to surmise certain credible beliefs, such as the existence of subatomic particles or the culpability of a murder suspect, based purely on the observation of other phenomena (see Harman, "The Inference to the Best Explanation," 88-95). On the distinction between probability and plausibility, see Rescher, *Plausible Reasoning* and Walton, "Rules for Plausible Reasoning," 33-51.

14. Peirce, *Collected Papers*, 5:106 [5.171]; italics in original.

15. Moreland and Craig, *Philosophical Foundations*, 341-42.

16. McLaren acquired this quotation from Newbigin, *The Gospel in a Pluralist Society*, 31.

17. Peircean abduction, therefore, reveals the inner processes of how some scientists formulate their hypotheses (Fann, *Peirce's Theory of Abduction*, 4-5). See also, Aliseda, *Abductive Reasoning*.

18. Lipton, *Inference to the Best Explanation*, 148-51; Campos, "On the Distinction," 419-42; McAuliffe, "How Did Abduction Get Confused," 300-19; Hintikka, "What: Is Abduction?," 503-33.

19. Schurz, "Patterns of Abduction," 205; italics in original.

20. As a pastor, McLaren developed a passion for studying church history, the Celtics, Eastern Orthodoxy, and Anabaptists. He also had direct encounters with the faith expressions of Christians in the Global South (*NKOCY* §Preface, xii). It was these experiences, along with his passion for philosophy and history, that supplied much of the "scientific" data that eventually caused McLaren to question conventional paradigms (cf. *GSM*, x; *NKOC* §1, 9).

that many conventional beliefs simply do not correspond to existential, historical, or biblical data nor are they practical enough for solving real-world problems (cf. *NKOC* §Intro, xvii–xviii; *NS* §Preface, vii). Case in point, this process led McLaren to believe Christianity had wrongly adopted Neoplatonism, which compartmentalized matter/spirit, body/soul, world/church, and individual/communal categories (§7.1). The result for McLaren was a rejection of these false dichotomies.[21] Hence, he likens his religio-philosophy to a spider's web (§6.1.1) where each doctrine remains in tension with others as new experiential data arises (*MRTYR* §17, 129–30). If further observations disconfirm an old theory, then he will abandon it in search of a better alternative. His loyalty is to the *methodology* and not to long-held paradigms or conventional beliefs.[22] For McLaren, a willingness to change paradigms gives his approach to the philosophy of religion more credibility in its pursuit of truth (*GSM*, 35–37).

While McLaren appeals to science when "doing theology" (e.g., *COOS1* §5, 66), for him, scientific inquiry is Peircean in nature because of its model-making processes:

> Theology is a human attempt to create models of the universe based on beliefs about God. . . .We are not just talking about different beliefs about God; we are talking about different models of the universe.
>
> So in a sense, then, what we do with people is we say, "Let's look at your model of the universe and hold it up against reality. Does it really take reality into account?" . . . "Well, let me show you how mine works. Let's see if mine takes reality into account." . . .[this] becomes a more of a collaborative process. (*PTP*, 125)[23]

It is not surprising, then, that McLaren describes his method in terms concurrent with Peircean abduction, claiming his model-making often "involves a hunch, an intuition, an unproven possibility" with an openness to experimentation and change (*FFS* §5, 122). What is essential is his creativity when constructing religious models.[24] He writes, "Creative thinkers won't have all the *i*'s dotted or *t*'s crossed; they bring us their tentative and unfinished rough drafts. . . .if we ignore their brilliance and focus

---

21. McLaren, "Everything Old Is New Again," 23–24. See also, McLaren, "A Postmodern View of Scripture," 8. McLaren describes the current "postmodern era" as a time of progressing "beyond our deadlock, our polarization, our binary, either/or thinking regarding faith and reason, religion and science, matter and spirit" (*FOWA* §1, 4).

22. Here, McLaren's description of the scientific process is idealistic in nature, particularly when many scientists actually pledge their allegiance to strongly-held paradigms instead of adopting newer models merely because they happen to encounter disconfirming evidence (cf. *GSM*, 236n7). See Kuhn, *The Structure of Scientific Revolutions*.

23. Notably, this comparison of religious belief to a person's experiential knowledge is the primary element of James Fowler's "individual-reflective faith," which attempts to mature away from the more simplistic and unquestioning stages of religiosity (cf. *AMP* §16, 249). See Fowler, *Stages of Faith*, 174–83.

24. See for example, *FFS* §7, 160–62 and McLaren, "Practicing and Loving Diversity," 30. Unlike novices, both expert artists and expert scientists exhibit more creativity and curiosity in their model-making than neophytes. See Csikszentmihalyi, *Creativity*, esp. 21–126.

on their gaffs, we will . . . squander our chance to learn from them" (*COOS1* §12c, 199; cf. *SMJ* §Intro, xvii). These features reveal that McLaren does, in fact, use logic to devise his theories; he simply transcends *formal* logic to include artistic ingenuity.

5.3 MCLAREN'S POSTFORMAL ABDUCTION

John Montgomery describes abductive theology as a dynamic interchange between theory and data, being an interplay between the subjective and objective aspects of religiosity. The process is one of moving back and forth until a theory aligns with the greatest number of data and sustains a multiplicity of needs. The method is concurrently scientific, artistic, and spiritual.[25] For McLaren, the goal is to create an environment for "living in the tension of disagreement and creating communities where civility and acceptance without agreement can be practiced."[26] In this sense, McLaren exhibits an abductive method by insisting that Christians "allow theology, like science and art, to continue in an unending exploration and eternal search for the truth" (*COOS1* §5, 66). The result is a continual process of formulating alternative theories that reflect his own contemplations (*SA*, ix-x).[27] Schurz refers to this process as "creative abductions" (or "second-order existential abductions") where the person introduces new theoretical models based on personal observations.[28] Since the very beginning of his writing career, McLaren's goal has been to present new theological possibilities (*RYC* §Preface, 8).

This process suggests that McLaren is not dependent on restrictive methods to create his beliefs, relying instead on experience to guide his anticipation of future theological problems (*AIFA*, 58; *AMP* §11, 180-81). In essence, abduction displays the flexibility and creativity that is characteristic of other professions (cf. *FOWA* §12, 117; *FFS* §4, 106-7).[29] This reasoning typifies postformal rationality, which is simultaneously malleable, practical, and dialectical by incorporating subjectivity with the ideals of logic (*FFR* §1, 27; *FFS* §1, 46-48).[30] He explains,

> Rather than presenting one answer only . . . I will try to guide you through each of the more plausible answers and encourage you to make your own

---

25. See Montgomery, "The Theologian's Craft," 67-98.
26. McLaren, "Red State, Purple Church," 29.
27. Cf. Walton, *Abductive Reasoning*, 29-31 and Frankfurt, "Peirce's Notion of Abduction," 593-96.
28. "Existential abductions" are different from "selective abductions" where a person merely chooses the best explanation from among already-formulated theories. See Schurz, "Patterns of Abduction," 201-5, 216-19.
29. See Berger, *The Developing Person*, 622-23, 625 and Markofski, *New Monasticism*, 142.
30. For examples of McLaren using suprarational insights to formulate his hypotheses, which combines personal experiences, training, and intuition, see *AIFA*, 40n5; *AMP* §18, 278; *FFS* §2, 66-68; *GO* §3, 87; *LWWAT* §6, 42; and *SWFOI* §31, 229. Significantly, one psychological study suggests that religionists are predisposed to depending more heavily on personal intuition than logical reasoning (Daws and Hampshire, "The Negative Relationship").

choices. Again, I won't pretend to have no beliefs myself, which would be dishonest. Instead, I will try to be open about my own conclusions without imposing them on you. You may agree with me; you may not. I will feel I have been of some service to you either way simply by stimulating your thinking. (FFR §Intro, 17-18; see also, FFS §Intro, 25-26)

Thus, McLaren recognizes the value of multiple avenues of reasoning (§8.4.1), especially as it relates to religion. In fact, those who engage in postformal thinking often have multifaceted concepts of the divine (*MRTYR* §2, 34). Rather than wait for a problem to present itself, postformal abduction anticipates difficulties and preemptively addresses them through creativity and imagination (*AIFA*, 58; *AMP* §11, 180-81).[31] Hence, McLaren describes spirituality as requiring "skill and practice and experience" (*FOWA* §10, 94) just like any other *métier*.

In truth, McLaren's work is replete with this type of postformal abduction. For instance, McLaren's view on original sin stems from his experiences with creation (§4.3.2). For him, traditional dogma is prone to diminishing the goodness and beauty of God's created order (*GO* §16, 234-35). Here, McLaren offers a dialectical alternative by suggesting the possibility that Christians have misunderstood original sin entirely (§7.1.3.1). The greatest difficulty is that his process generates hostility from theological gatekeepers who interpret data only through reigning paradigms.[32] However, McLaren remains undeterred, "When you package old answers to old questions, you have renewal. When you give new answers to old questions, you have reformation. When you're asking new questions, to me that's what revolution is about."[33]

Consequently, McLaren's method generates defeasible possibilities, as opposed to formulating impeccable truth-claims.[34] In schematic form, McLaren's abductive theories develop in a basic (if not oversimplified) pattern as elaborated in Alan Musgrave's work:

> The surprising fact, C, is observed.
> But if A were true, C would be a matter of course.
> Hence, "there is reason to believe (tentatively)" that A is true.[35]

For example, McLaren hypothesizes that all of creation, having derived from the same dust, is related and, therefore, is included in the same salvific gospel message (*JMBM*

---

31. See Sinnott, *The Development of Logic*, esp. 23-49; Griffin et al., "Four Brief Studies," 173-82; Kallio, "Integrative Thinking Is the Key," 785-801; and Benovenli et al., "Three Applications," 141-54.

32. Cf. Moreland and Craig, *Philosophical Foundations*, 342. McLaren's process, therefore, is not "a matter of inference to some unique 'best explanation,' [but] is instead better understood as a pattern of inference to any of several possible explanations." See Callaway, "Abduction," 265.

33. McLaren, "TPC Interviews," 13.

34. McLaren, "Church Emerging," 146-49.

35. Musgrave, "Strict Empiricism," 80-81. Cf. the original schema in Peirce, *Collected Papers*, 5:117 [5.189]. For a detailed analysis of Peirce's original schematic structure, see Buchler, *Charles Peirce's Empiricism*, 36-38, 133n1.

§12, 103-4; *WMRBW*, 8). As a result, McLaren hints at divine *complacentia* ("general good-pleasure") where God's consuming love for every*thing* and every*one* irrevocably unites him to creation.[36] The result is a belief that traditional notions of hell are too narrowly defined (see §7.5.3):

> A defining characteristic of God is *complacentia* (*AMP* §16, 246-47; *LWWAT* §17, 100).
>
> If divine judgment were to end in a divine "embrace" (*LWWAT* §13, 80), then God's *complacentia* would remain intact without inconsistency.
>
> Hence, there is reason to suspect that hell is not the "last word" (*LWWAT* §17, 101).

In following this schema, McLaren does not argue that his theories flawlessly illuminate divine love, nor does he believe his theories are true simply because they involve certain observations.[37] What is essential is the final premise that suggests there is reason to suppose a given explanation might be correct. This part of the abductive structure remains true even if the proposed hypothesis is later defeated with future data.[38] Of course, it is doubtful whether future observations could ever actually falsify McLaren's theological and metaphysical conjectures. To postulate theories about unseen entities is to postulate only the adequacy of a theory's explanation for any given effect. There will never be corroborative evidence that a spiritual theory is true, only that it is tolerable.[39] Because of this fact, McLaren is open to the possibility of discovering information by dialoguing with divergent perspectives and beliefs (cf. §8.4).

5.3.1 Emphasis on Dialogical Discovery

In terms of deconversion, McLaren displayed a nonoptimal person-religion fit, which resulted in him no longer insisting on the supremacy of his own beliefs. This deconversion made him more open to interreligious dialogue and more willing to accept the possibility of truths in other religions (§8.4.1.1).[40] Consequently, McLaren makes inferences through what Douglas Walton describes as an "explanation subsystem of an expert system architecture."[41] Here, human users approach a program (the "expert system") through a user interface to ask questions and receive explanations (an "explanation-seeking dialogue"). In this case, the "expert system" for McLaren is Jesus (§6.1.1.4) supplemented with Scripture and the wider faith community with whom he

---

36. The overarching theme is that God's loving character will never forsake any part of the created order (*FOWA* §8, 72). For the defining characteristics of *complacentia*, see Waldstein, "Covenant and the Union," 140.

37. Contra the demurrals of Frankfurt, "Peirce's Notion of Abduction," 593-96.

38. Walton, *Abductive Reasoning*, 26-27, 36-43; Fann, *Peirce's Theory of Abduction*, 4.

39. See van Fraassen, *The Scientific Image*, esp. 6-40. Cf. Lipton, *Inference to the Best Explanation*, 143.

40. See Barbour, *Versions of Deconversion*, 2, 50-52 and Heinz et al., "The Religious Schema Scale," 151-72.

41. See Walton, *Abductive Reasoning*, 54-56, 66-82.

can interact in dialogue. From this system, McLaren derives preliminary theological and ethical solutions to real-world problems.[42] In fact, McLaren likens the original Jesus movement to the relational process of mentor-student dialectical exchanges (*WMRBW*, xviii-xix; cf. *NKOCY* §9, 94). "We know that insight from multiple perspectives adds wisdom" (*SA*, 12).

Simultaneously, McLaren emphasizes interreligious dialogue among believers by seeking input from multiple sources (*GO* §1, 66-67), particularly marginalized viewpoints (*LWWAT* §6, 42), in order to reveal possible distortions in a belief system (*GO* §9, 152-53, 210; 261).[43] According to McLaren, postmoderns tend to reflect in a group process that first acquires multiple vantage points and then determines truth through interchange and discourse.[44] Not surprisingly, then, intellectuals tend to conceive of God in abstractions; bureaucrats view God in terms of governance; the working class understands God as an advocate for the proletariat; and the social worker recognizes God's love for the poor and oppressed (*MRTYR* §2, 34). Therefore, theology is done with "a spirit of humility and discovery and collaboration, not of partisanship or inquisition" (*AIFA*, 277). As Tony Jones remarks, "The constant desire for more dialogue is not a cop-out, either, because the Christian faith is a journey— a Way— not a destination."[45] Naturally, how McLaren decides which hypothesis is most appropriate revolves around what he personally feels is most significant, namely livability (pragmatics) and beauty (orthonomy).

5.3.2 Inference to a Livable and Beautiful Explanation

With livability, McLaren's standard for "plausibility" is more pragmatic and existential in nature. He argues that Christians need "a new apologetic" that presents faith as socially livable because no one wants to associate with a religion whose outspoken representatives are openly repulsive.[46] Christian explanations are only "plausible" (i.e.,

---

42. McLaren explains, "Each of them sees things the others don't see. Once you listen to them and pay each group the respect of believing they have something to offer, you start to see at least some of what they see. . . .So I feel that I have been enriched from many perspectives, and in the end, the Bible looks bigger, richer, deeper, more dynamic" (McLaren, "A Postmodern View of Scripture," 8).

43. McLaren once stated, "I'm a firm believer—even though I'm a preacher—that people learn more when they're talking than when they're listening. In other words, conversation forms people more than lecture" (McLaren, "A Postmodern View of Scripture," 12).

44. See *AIFA*, 99; *AMP* §5, 78-79; *COOS1* §6, 77; *GO* §10, 164; and *NKOC* §7, 81-82. McLaren explains how this dialogical process helped him fashion an alternative approach to Christian faith, "So by my mid-20s, I had met the conservative Protestant Jesus, the Pentecostal Jesus, and the Roman Catholic Jesus. And by the grace of God, I didn't think of them as different saviors, requiring a lateral conversion to a new denomination each time. Rather I believed that each was a new facet, a new dimension, of the Jesus I had met as a child and rediscovered as a teenager, and that each could enrich my ongoing conversion in my spiritual journey" (*GO* §1, 55).

45. Jones, *The New Christians*, 168.

46. McLaren provides examples, such as when neoconservatives publicly burn copies of the Qur'an, tell their followers that a Haitian earthquake (resulting in hundreds of thousands of deaths

livable) if they address the communal and affective elements of faith, such as whether it will make converts healthier, more joyful, and more kindhearted. Thus, "plausibility" equates to people's perception of the church by considering their feelings of shame when joining a potentially scandalous group like Christianity (*COOS1* §6, 79-80; cf. *NKOCY* §7, 67-70).[47] McLaren asks, "Does the quality of their community life authenticate or undermine their message?" (*FFS* §8, 176). Ultimately, an explanation is only plausible if it creates compassionate people of faith (cf. *GSM*, 177).

With beauty, McLaren's standard for credibility is artistic in nature. Phyllis Tickle explains that the emphasis is now on "orthonomy," which engages aesthetic purity as a method for discerning truth and authority. Elements such as tradition, intuition, community, and reason harmoniously create religious experiences, which then become the basis of authority (§8.5.1).[48] It is no surprise, therefore, that McLaren's writings continually employ "beauty" as a catchall term for orthonomy (cf. §2.3.1) since, for him, beauty is an inherent characteristic of God, truth, and goodness (*AIFA*, 317; *GSM*, 121-22, 127-46). It is synonymous with divine glory and holiness (*AIFA*, 41-42; *FFS* §8, 172-73). In fact, the divine nature is likened to music: God is orderly and yet unconventional, being the very essence of splendor itself (*MRTYR* §13, 98). McLaren labels all revelation from God as "beauty truth" (*AIFA*, 39) and even argues that theology must practice beauty from beginning to end. For "where beauty is, God is" (*GO* §13, 212).

Similarly, McLaren declares that the gospel of Jesus Christ is a "wonderful" and "beautiful message," a "song" so beautiful that believers cannot help but share it; and like the gospel itself, a belief is only beautiful so long as it results in social action (*GSM*, 6, 31; *MRTYR* §Intro, 16). Likewise, beauty is inherent to both creation and mystery (*WMRBW*, 46), being itself mysterious and yet energizing in its ability to establish Christian unity (*FFR* §1, 36-37; *GO* §13, 211-12). Finally, a believer's spiritual pilgrimage finds validation through beauty (cf. *NKOC* §15, 204). From these descriptions, it is evident that McLaren cherishes beauty not just for its external qualities (*AIFA*, 40), such as the outer aesthetics of nature (*FFS* §6, 141-42), but for its mystical, moral, and intellectual attractiveness (*fotosis*) that arouses the spirit's creativity, imagination, and, above all else, fidelity to God (cf. *FOWA* §17, 165; *NS* §22, 194-95). Consequently, McLaren defines beauty in mystical terms: "A vibration or resonance between novelty and order that transports us to heights and depths outside ourselves not otherwise reached. In the presence of beauty we become transformed into artists

---

and millions of lives ruined) was the act of a vengeful God, protest military funerals declaring "God hates fags," continue to give false predictions of the end of the world, or when the Catholic church protects sexually abusive priests (*JMBM* §2, 17-18; *NS* §16, 143). While none of these examples is representative of Christianity as a whole, there is still an ominous silence from the majority of Christians to stop these embarrassments. McLaren asks, "If everyone on earth held this belief, would the results be good. . . .or would it lead to self-destruction and despair?" (*FFS* §8, 176).

47. Cf. Burson, *Brian McLaren in Focus*, 189.
48. Tickle, *The Great Emergence*, 149-50.

of creation engaged in being" (*AIFA*, 39). Hence, to experience beauty is to experience the divine (*FFR* §1, 36-37).[49]

What is significant, however, is McLaren's use of beauty as a criterion for a theory's credibility. He writes, "Plausibility has to do with [an explanation's] beauty and satisfactions . . . as it is lived out in real life" (*COOS1* §6, 79). He writes elsewhere, "If one understands that beauty surrounds us, one understands something unspeakably grand. One can solve a math problem. One can contain a chemical reaction in an equation. But one never 'gets' beauty" (*GO* §20, 291). It is this search for transcendence that propels McLaren to add beauty to his pursuit of faith. According to him, spiritual seekers are concerned with whether Christians display goodness and beauty more than whether Christianity is ontologically true or not. He writes,

> I would say that the dominant thing that we have to prove to a spiritually seeking non-Christian in a postmodern world is not that Christianity is true. We have to prove that it is good and beautiful. And if they are convinced that it's good and beautiful, they will be open to it being true. (*PTP*, 124)

Thus, McLaren recognizes that people do not follow Christ simply because it is rational. Instead, demonstrating Christ's beauty, particularly through sacrificial giving (*FFS* §8, 172-73), is more effective today than sterile logic (*AIFA*, 40; *MRTYR* §7, 65-66).

In this sense, McLaren's rationale is fairly straightforward: the lack of true, good, and beautiful beliefs can result in the intellectual, moral, and physical degradation of God's glory (cf. *AIFA*, 41, 152).[50] "Faith that believes true things but does so in an ugly or inappropriate way is not justified just because it is conceptually correct" (*FFS* §1, 37).[51] Quoting the Romantic poet John Keats, McLaren stresses, "Beauty is truth, truth beauty" (*AIFA*, 39). Today, spirituality tries to find the beauty in other people and other belief systems rather than find fault with them (*NS* §22, 195). If a theory enlarges the world's egotism, then it cannot truly reflect the beauty of the divine (*FFS* §1, 43). Thus, McLaren's rationale requires making beauty a litmus test because it illuminates

---

49. Significantly, McLaren admits that artists (like himself) tend to conceive of deity differently from all other types of people. To them, "God has a wildness and beauty that inspires and attracts" (*MRTYR* §2, 34). Elsewhere, he describes God as "the Shaper of Beauty" (*NS* §5, 46), and expresses his desire for the church to be a community of artists (*AIFA*, 39), "an instrument vibrant with beauty and grandeur and glory" (*FFR* §1, 37).

50. McLaren clarifies, "Don't assume that this sensitivity to beauty means postmodernity is about a 'politically correct' niceness and saccharine sweetness. We are talking about *beauty*, not 'niceness' or 'prettiness.' Full-bodied beauty can contain discord, clash, burn, sting, ugliness" (*AIFA*, 41; italics in original). Likewise, McLaren does recognize that a belief can be partly true, partly beautiful, and partly good.

51. While all three elements (truth, goodness, and beauty) are necessary, beauty is especially noteworthy for McLaren because of its transcendent implications (cf. *FOWA* §14, 131). Thus, he cherishes those who, like himself, have a "profound sensitivity to beauty, dynamism, and complexity" (McLaren, foreword to *Brief Christian Histories*, xiii).

the nature of God and inspires Christ-like living (*FFS* §6, 141-42).⁵² Nevertheless, part of this beauty is in thinking critically and engaging in the *pursuit* of faith. In order to ensure that he does not deprive his readers of thinking for themselves, McLaren purposely conceals his abductive processes through abductive provocations.

5.4 MCLAREN'S ABDUCTIVE PROVOCATIONS

Norman Geisler and Thomas Howe express a common complaint about McLaren, "One of the more difficult aspects of McLaren's writings is his seeming unwillingness to say anything definitive about what he believes."⁵³ John MacArthur concurs, "McLaren suggests that clarity itself is of dubious value. He clearly prefers ambiguity and equivocation, and his books are therefore full of deliberate doublespeak."⁵⁴ What is often overlooked, however, is that ambiguity is a provocative tactic to stimulate abductive thinking. As "prophetic rhetoric," Scot McKnight explains, "The emerging movement is consciously and deliberately provocative. . . . [and] none in the emerging crowd is more rhetorically effective than Brian McLaren."⁵⁵ Because he believes that precision can encumber thoughtful dialogue, McLaren writes with Søren Kierkegaard's "indirect communication" (i.e., a stimulating obscurity) in mind (*GO* §Intro, 22-23; *PTP*, 125).⁵⁶ He labels this approach an "abductive method," which thrives on disorientation, astonishment, and surprise to encourage imaginative discourse (*AIFA*, 31-33). His goal is to motivate contemplation rather than dictate a particular belief system (cf. *COOS1* §Intro, 15), such as when he suggests that he "worshiped the Mola mola this morning, and the black sea turtle, the sea lions, and birds" on a pilgrimage trip to the Galápagos Islands (*GI*, 35; cf. §8.2.2.1).

McLaren explains that people tend to read only those writings that validate their personal judgments (cf. *FFS* §7, 161-62). However, genuine learning best occurs when people think for themselves. "So a playful, provocative, unclear, but stimulating book could actually be more worth your money than a serious, clear book that tells you what to think but doesn't make you think" (*GO* §Intro, 23; see also, *LWWAT* §6, 39). Hence, McLaren employs provocative rhetoric that engages in parodies of the

---

52. McLaren explains, "The appreciation of beauty (along with goodness) is as essential to the pursuit of truth as was the scale or slide rule to the modern scientist" (*AIFA*, 40-41).

53. Geisler and Howe, "A Postmodern View of Scripture," 100. See also, Straub, "The Emerging Church," 76-77 and King, "Emerging Issues," 32-35.

54. MacArthur, *The Truth War*, 18.

55. McKnight further admits, "We sometimes exaggerate. Our language frequently borrows the kind of rhetoric found in Old Testament prophets. . . . [engaging in] deliberate overstatement" (McKnight, "Five Streams of the Emerging Church," 36).

56. The tactic of "indirect communication" is one of the most significant themes of McLaren's master's thesis on Walker Percy and, therefore, one of the most heavily examined topics in McLaren's scholastic career. At one point, McLaren labels this tactic as the "most central to Percy's work as an author as well as Kierkegaard's" (*WP*, 25). The same could potentially be said of McLaren's work, as well.

surrounding culture (*AIFA*, 164-67; cf. *COOS1* §7, 89). What is noteworthy in the book, *A is for Abductive*, is McLaren's use of the term "method," which describes his *communication* technique as a way of disseminating abductive theories in an impactful way. An abductive *method* of communication is associated more with speaking in parables than with formal logic, creating an "abductive experience" that challenges conventional wisdom. This abductive method is designed to transcend linear rationality through art, narrative, and dramatic imagery without succumbing to irrationality (*AIFA*, 31-33; *COOS1* §12b, 181-82). "I am trying to push our thinking about our thinking beyond its normal limits because I believe that doing so can lead us to important insights about faith" (*FFS* §2, 63).

Here, McLaren purposely tries to arouse controversy and stimulate the kind of reflection needed for abductive logic. He seizes people with imagination in order to help them gain a new perspective, thereby removing readers from their world of assumptions (*AIFA*, 31-33). He explains, "As in most of my other books, there are places here where I have gone out of my way to be provocative, mischievous, and unclear, reflecting my belief that clarity is sometimes overrated, and that shock, obscurity, playfulness, and intrigue (carefully articulated) often stimulate more thought than clarity" (*GO* §Intro, 22-23). For McLaren, there is something far better than clarity: profundity (*AIFA*, 131-33). He explains that his method deliberately exploits people's expectations and apprehensions, which can then distort their perceptions of reality. Thus, McLaren's principal objective is to initiate debate, suggest new questions, offer new insights, rouse people's instinctive passions, and stimulate self-reflection (*NS* §21, 179-80; *SMJ* §Intro, 251n2).[57] "I am more interested in stretching your thinking here than tweaking your techniques" (*COOS1* §Preface, 8; cf. p. 26). In fact, McLaren wittingly provokes controversy for the purpose of inciting discussion.[58] As a provocateur, McLaren wants to captivate his audience so as to stimulate their passions. "It's funny how seriousness can impede thought. Playfulness, irony, even whimsy can create space for creativity and imagination."[59] Of course, it is natural to wonder how McLaren learned these tactics in the first place.

5.4.1 Origins of McLaren's Provocations

When McKnight asked McLaren about his "provocative ambiguity" and his "deliberate refusal to clarify" his beliefs, McLaren responded that this was an intentional

---

57. McLaren believes that this tactic was also the approach of biblical prophets who "infect our imagination with pictures of how the world can be, pictures of how we can be" (McLaren, "Conversations," 342).

58. McLaren explains elsewhere, "I don't write books to tell people what to think, nor do I write books so that people don't need to think on their own. . . .To help people learn, I try to stimulate their thinking" (McLaren, "Q and R: Sorry, I'm not going to answer").

59. McLaren, "Practicing and Loving Diversity," 30.

The Logic of Intersubjectivity

tactic he had learned from Kierkegaard.[60] McLaren explains that he has always been inclined to think "a few degrees askew from most people, especially about religion," having been disappointed with predictable questions and unconvinced by conventional answers (*EMC* §1, 3; §32, 275). For him, they create just as many problems as they resolve (cf. *NS* §21, 181-82). The modernization effects on Christianity (§4.3) resulted in establishing a faith of "easy answers and cardboard explanations instead of a window into unfathomable mystery and a pathway into an awesome adventure" (*MRTYR* §3, 42). It was Walker Percy, however, who had recognized this problem and influenced McLaren's philosophical career. Percy observed that a culture-religion was no longer captivating to the West. Thus, he was puzzled with how to reinvigorate an encultured populace about Jesus' message. Imitating Kierkegaard, Percy employed the abductive method. As McLaren writes, "By using cunning and all the tricks of indirect communication, Percy shows himself to be, like Kierkegaard, 'a spy in a higher service'" (*WP*, 100).[61]

Imitating Percy, McLaren learned that writers must present perplexing, comedic, and even scandalous statements, which often captivate younger generations (cf. *COOS1* §7, 87-91).[62] In this case, McLaren employs deliberate caricatures that parody institutional religion and capitalize on the rhetoric of exaggeration and oversimplification. McLaren even argues that the very nature of religious discourse requires these precarious expressions, anyway. All other prose is laughably inadequate (*COOS1* §7, 91-93; *JMBM* §20, 179-80). "Spiritual realities *require* risky language, unless you think they can be reduced to little formulas and formulations. But I guess modern folk do think just that" (*NKOC* §11, 136; italics in original).[63]

McLaren's description of Jesus' parables is a useful illustration: "In some ways, they are intended to hide the truth; they don't reduce truth to simple statements or formulae. Instead, they force the reader to take things to a deeper level, to engage the imagination, to think and think again" (*VL*, 58). For McLaren, propositional elements such as formulas, outlines, and lists are the effects of modernization. Therefore, they

---

60. McLaren and McKnight, "Conversations on Being a Heretic," 00:01:28-00:01:59, 00:04:26-00:05:14. Scot McKnight conducted this interview at the Q Conference, "Conversations on Being a Heretic," in Chicago, Illinois, held between April 28-30, 2010.

61. In reference to "the need for indirect theological 'butt-kicking,'" McLaren further explains Kierkegaard's abductive tactic, "People who are held firmly in the grip of an illusion, he said, need an indirect but real jolt to be awakened" (McLaren, foreword to *A Heretic's Guide to Eternity*, ix). See also, McLaren, foreword to *How (Not) to Speak of God*, ix-xii.

62. In one book, McLaren writes, "What if standard politics, standard communication tactics, standard promotion and marketing and molding of public opinion won't work for a secret message like his? What if Jesus' unprecedented message requires a method so unusual as to be scandalous?" (*SMJ* §8, 62).

63. McLaren explains elsewhere, "A linear prose argument may be the best way to teach engineering or refrigerator repair, but to teach matters of the spirit literary forms work better—with all their . . . imagination and provocation, their spin and sneakiness" (*NKOCY* §14, 144-45). Hence, "You learn . . . to romance your readers with a tiny scrap of punctuation—just as you might do with a gesture or sigh when you preach" (McLaren, foreword to *Secrets in the Dark*, ix).

hinder the sense of wonder necessary for captivating today's spiritual seekers (*MRTYR* §19, 146). From this realization, McLaren learned how to communicate in such a way so as to expose the truth of something without directly confronting it. In other words, the more direct and assertive a religious teacher is with their pronouncements, the less people will be receptive to their messages (*WP*, 22-26). It is this cultural awareness that helps readers fully understand McLaren's provocative heuristic model.

5.4.2 Understanding McLaren's Provocations

McKnight once observed, "McLaren would rather ask a question and create a conversation than propound a solution. This style is an attribute of a good teacher."[64] In his master's thesis, McLaren discussed the tactic of aesthetic writing where much of the literature of Kierkegaard and Percy appear to have the intention of entertaining their audience but, as a form of indirect communication, are actually intended to convey religious messages (see esp. *WP*, 26-33). The same appears to be true for McLaren's writings, as well, particularly his fictional dialogues. Here, McLaren utilizes humor, hyperbole, satire, and sarcasm as a way to conceal the brazenness of his religious message, thereby allowing him to relate more intimately to the struggles and sensibilities of his seeker audience.[65]

In one book, McLaren offers the following discussion questions: "Do you agree with the author's perspective or resist it? Why? If you think [McLaren] is oversimplifying, why might he be doing so intentionally?" (*FOWA* §8, 75). It is the last question that readers ought continually to ask themselves when examining McLaren's work. As John Franke writes, "It is worth remembering that Brian makes clear at the outset his intention to be 'provocative, mischievous, and unclear' for the purpose of encouraging readers to think and enter into the conversation themselves."[66] McLaren again references Kierkegaard as an illustration. When discussing proselytizing methods, Kierkegaard described the ideal evangelist as a person who hides behind a bush and waits for his friend to pass by; the evangelist then runs up and kicks his friend in the rear, jolting his attention. McLaren concludes, "When a person helps another person begin to think about spiritual matters, he dives behind a bush" (*MRTYR* §1, 28).

In many ways, McLaren's style of presenting theology is concomitant with Jesus' parable of the Good Samaritan (Luke 10:25-37), which intended to make a theological and practical argument by exploiting the conventions, expectations, and perceptions of the religious establishment. Jesus' conclusion, that a heretical Samaritan is morally superior to the most dogmatic Jew, would have been offensive and controversial; yet

---

64. McKnight, "McLaren Emerging," 62.

65. One perfect example of McLaren's use of sarcasm can be found in McLaren, foreword to *Love is an Orientation*, 10-12.

66. Franke, foreword to *A Generous Orthodoxy*, 14. As McLaren writes, "Surprise and unpredictability are the key elements to the abductive method" (*AIFA*, 32).

the corrective nature of its message continues to resonate long after the sermon is over (*SMJ* §6, 43-46). While Jesus was not, in fact, encouraging people to adopt Samaritan heterodoxy, the parable helped to solidify Jesus' primary criticism of those claiming orthodoxy, which was that they lacked an existential embodiment of the theology they professed.[67] "I think of Jesus in his parables. He seems more interested in stirring curiosity than in completely satisfying it" (*SMJ* §Afterword, 206-7).

According to McLaren, the most influential religious figures are those who are also the most "stimulating, challenging, provocative, mysterious, and intriguing" because they can relate to spiritual seekers (*AIFA*, 164-67, 247-48). He encourages Christians to communicate as artists of words, utilizing "allegory, rhetoric and poetry, understatement and wild exaggeration for [rhetorical] effect" (*COOS1* §7, 90). For example, he describes today's culture-religion in detestable terms, "The popular and domesticated Jesus . . . has become little more than a chrome-plated hood ornament on the guzzling Hummer of Western civilization" (*EMC* §1, 6). In this way, McLaren is able to incorporate the aesthetics of word art, especially hyperbole and generalizations (cf. *COOS1* §12b, 181-82; *GO* §0, 34).[68] He also routinely exploits the different meanings of similar words in order to make his characterizations memorable.[69] The result is that McLaren's pithy provocations have made him a master of quotable sound-bites.

His writings also capitalize on irony, such as pointing out that in their pursuit of holiness, Christians can become the most inhospitable people. Likewise, merely suggesting Christians should love their enemies can actually engender hostility from them (*JMBM* §1, 6-8; §2, 23). While he attempts to be cautious (*COOS1* §7, 90), McLaren admits his caricatures are sometimes unfair, though he explains that they are meant to tease some of his readers (*GO* §3, 79-80).[70] In fact, McLaren admits that if something he says is an oversimplification, then the statement is likely false with just enough truth to validate making the statement anyway. Regardless, his goal is the same: engender self-reflection rather than sell people supposedly definitive answers (cf. *NKOCY* §22, 257). Overall, McLaren's provocations are merely

---

67. In *A Generous Orthodoxy*, McLaren writes, "You are about to begin an absurd and ridiculous book... . The book is absurd because it advocates an orthodoxy that next to no one actually holds, at least not so far" (*GO* §0, 27).

68. McLaren defines "hyperbole" as "an intentional exaggeration used to convey truth" (*SMJ* §6, 43). Interestingly, however, McLaren writes that there are times he purposely understates certain topics so as not to offend spiritual seekers or the less theologically informed. However, he admits he is not concerned about offending religious gatekeepers or the religious establishment (*EMC* §1, 7).

69. For example, McLaren explains that cooperation with other religions is not only an example of Christian "witness," but it must also involve a "with-ness" in strategy (*JMBM* §26, 242). Elsewhere, he states that the world needs more "violet" Christians (his term for peaceful solidarity that harkens back to being politically purple; §3.4) rather than more "violent" ones (*NKOCY* §20, 235-36).

70. As part of his allegiance to Jesus, McLaren also admonishes his readers, "Avoid 'word inflation' when making vows. Instead, practice clear, straight speech, so simple words like yes and no retain their full value" (*WMRBW*, 145). In one footnote, McLaren writes, "There are plenty of exceptions to my gross (and playful) generalizations here, and my tongue keeps drifting into my cheek" (*GO* §17, 245n122).

an exercise of his inventive and artistic writing style designed to stimulate creative thinking (*COOS1* §Intro, 15).[71]

Suggestively, McLaren declares that Hebrew prophets were also artists with their words (§9.1.1) predominantly because their spiritual message was far too profound for simple prose (*GO* §9, 147). In fact, the "marriage of theologians with artists" is itself an expression of the current epochal shift and its effects on spirituality. Modernization had appealed to the analytic part of the mind; but today, spiritual seekers want something that transcends rationality.[72] "I preach sermons that turn the lights on for spiritual seekers but earn me critical letters and phone calls from the 'veterans' of the church" (*NKOC* §Intro, xix). Overall, his intention is to be sensitive to the complexities of different issues while acknowledging that intrigue is oftentimes more valuable to contemplative listeners.[73] Thus, he rails against the intransigence of Christianity today, "We teach [believers] what to think, not how to think; or we obsessively teach them how to answer yesterday's questions while failing to face today's and or to anticipate tomorrow's" (*AMP* §11, 180–81). Not surprisingly, then, McLaren justifies his provocative nature by appealing to what he thinks is best for discipleship.

5.4.3 Justification of McLaren's Provocations

McLaren summarizes his reading of Jesus' parables, arguing that "Jesus uses dangerous, provocative language" and even "grotesque imagery" (*SMJ* §14, 122, 124) in order to challenge assumptions and offer a higher perspective of reality (*VL*, 43–44). He then concludes, "Jesus' creative use of parables sets an example for us to follow" (*SMJ* §16, 148). According to McLaren, the entire point of Jesus' sermons was to encourage people to think for themselves rather than to coerce them into thinking from only one prescribed perspective (*EMC* §15, 125). Because of these elements, McLaren classifies Jesus as an artist who created short fictional stories for the purpose of stimulating people's curiosity and eliciting further inquiry (*VL*, 58; cf. *FFR* §9, 179; *SMJ* §5, 38; §6, 43–46), something McLaren tries to imitate in his own writings.[74] "The theologian will

---

71. McLaren, "A Postmodern View of Scripture," 9. McLaren's refusal to offer black-and-white answers is often overlooked and, therefore, criticized by those expecting to discover actual solutions in his work (see for example, Reed, "Emerging Treason?," 76-77). Taking the posture of a doctor diagnosing his patient through a series of exams, McLaren qualifies his instance on abductive provocation with an apology: "I'm sorry. The preceding paragraphs probably seem harsh and exaggerated. Remember, they were supposed to be like hammer taps to test your reflex reactions. I wasn't trying to hurt you or be rude" (McLaren, "Ruining Your Ministry for Good," 55).

72. McLaren writes, "The coming theology is one that works in mind *and* heart, understanding *and* imagination, proposition *and* image, clarity *and* mystery, explanation *and* narrative, exposition *and* artistic expression" (*AMP* §15, 227; italics in original).

73. See Taylor, *The Myth of Certainty*.

74. McLaren also uses "semifictional" stories and allegories to communicate his own message about Jesus (*AIFA*, 122; *SMJ* §13, 105-8, 112-13, 164), indicating that his fictional writings are not limited to his novels.

use words, but like Jesus, he will be a weaver of parables, a designer of proverbs, more a sage than a technician" (*COOS1* §7, 90).[75] Ultimately, he hopes his provocations will actually help the disenchanted maintain faith in Christ (*NKOCY* §Preface, xii).

Subsequently, McLaren uses the canonical Gospels as justification for his indirect communication style, arguing that Jesus also used provocations in order to prevent his message from becoming mundane, reductionistic, and ineffectual.[76] Jesus rarely gave propositional answers to questions, choosing, instead, to challenge the conventional wisdom of the religious establishment (*MRTYR* §Intro, 15). McLaren writes, "In conversation after conversation, then, Jesus resists being clear or direct. There's hardly ever a question that he simply answers; instead, his answer comes in the form of a question or it turns into a story or it is full of metaphors that invite more questions" (*SMJ* §5, 39; cf. *JMBM* §27, 252). Expectedly, Jesus' communication style elicited strong reactions from religious gatekeepers, just as they do against McLaren today (*SMJ* §6, 43-46). "Jesus was scandalously risky with his language. He compared God to an unjust judge and an unfair boss. He held up a crooked steward as an example of the kingdom. He said that prostitutes would enter the kingdom before Bible scholars" (*NKOC* §11, 136).[77]

According to McLaren, the same is true for the Apostle Paul, who (like Jesus) was Middle Eastern, not a Western rationalist. Paul's own communication was not linear but poetic and place-dependent (*GI* x–xix). In fact, Paul's language reveals an artistic tendency that capitalized on people's imaginations. To read Paul's metaphor-strewn writings as though they were systematic theologies would be to supplant a Western mindset onto a Middle Eastern man (*NKOCY* §14, 144-45). What is significant is that Paul used his knowledge of different cultures in order to inspire his audience (*VA*, 80). The point was to elevate discussions toward a higher, more spiritual perspective (*MRTYR* §1, 26). Besides, McLaren relates, there is simply no correlation between knowledge of theological esoterica and spiritual vitality. In fact, just the opposite appears to be true. The more people claim to know about God, the less Christ-like they seem to become (*NS* §3, 24).

5.5 CONCLUSION

An essential feature to understanding McLaren's philosophy of religion is the recognition that he is, in fact, a knowledgeable dialectician, whose philosophical propensities are the result of a vivid imagination and thorough cognitive reflection. That is to say,

---

75. Cf. McLaren, Introduction to *Not Religion But Love*, iii-vi.

76. See for example, McLaren, foreword to *Picturing the Gospel*, 7-8; *MRTYR* §App. 1, 160-83; and *SMJ* §1, 4; §4, 34; §6, 43-46.

77. McLaren writes, "[Jesus] doesn't answer their questions; instead, He asks them questions. He seems to decide that the best way to help them is simply by trying to challenge them to think, to question their assumptions, to open them up to new possibilities, to see things from a higher or deeper perspective" (*VL*, 43).

McLaren has not haphazardly formulated new beliefs at the expense of inferential reasoning. He simply chooses not to expound on his reasoning processes in a systematic or structured manner. Instead, McLaren creatively engages his professional training and ministerial experiences in hopes of discovering new paradigms that correlate best with biblical, historical, and experiential data. The result of appreciating this abductive reasoning, as well as recognizing the point of McLaren's abductive provocations, is in learning how to read his work properly.

What is undervalued by most readers is that McLaren intends to maintain a suprarational approach to religiosity, emphasizing aesthetic beauty and pragmatic usefulness over analytic reductionism in theological model-making. He intentionally tries to provoke controversy in order to stimulate reflective dialogue and inferential thinking. He deliberately employs exaggerations and satire because of their rhetorical effect in challenging the superficiality of institutional culture-religions. Consequently, for Christians experiencing a similar identity crisis to his own, McLaren's writings give them permission to question standard paradigms. Failing to understand and value this aspect of McLaren's religio-philosophy will, ultimately, result in distorting his message, his beliefs, and his purpose in writing. From these abductive characteristics and implications, readers are now able to discern precisely how McLaren approaches Christianity by examining his Christological *prolegomenon*.

6

McLaren and Christology

6.0 INTRODUCTION

In Brian McLaren's spiritual evolution (*JP* §Intro, 18), his experiential (chapter 2), moral (chapter 3), and intellectual (chapter 4) identity crises propelled him to adopt abductive inference building (chapter 5) in order to reexamine Christian beliefs. The thesis of this chapter is that much like a sexual orientation (cf. *AMP* §13, 198-210), McLaren possesses a *Christian* orientation, meaning he is naturally attracted to and finds his identity in Christ. McLaren concludes that Christianity is a *faith*-based religion (not a rationalistic one) predicated on paradox and relationship, which further manifests in God's interconnected love for creation. Five aspects will uphold this thesis: 1) McLaren's innate passion for Jesus as Divine Revealer; 2) the necessity of faith and the impossibility of Christian rationalism; 3) the *imago Dei* as denoting humanity's co-creatorship with the divine; 4) *complacentia* as the defining characteristic of God; and 5) McLaren's eschatology of hope. Accordingly, McLaren's Christotelic emphasis on Jesus becomes the *prolegomenon* to his entire philosophy of religion.

6.1 MCLAREN'S CHRISTOTELIC *PROLEGOMENON*

With McLaren, the catalyst for an alternative approach to faith was his simple devotion to the person and message of Jesus Christ; yet, in a deliberately provocative satire of Western Christianity, McLaren suggests the very opposite is true for mainstream churches today:

> I often think that one of the greatest gifts we Christians could give to Jesus at the two-thousandth anniversary of his adult ministry would be to just shut up about him for a few years, during which time we would try to come to terms with what a mess we have made of the simple path that he introduced to planet earth (and which we quickly complicated, confused, and corrupted), during which time we would simply try to practice what he preached, especially the parts about loving God and loving our neighbors, during which time we would stop producing Jesus-junk (pencils, T-shirts, screen savers, bumper stickers, plastic mugs, refrigerator magnets, and the like, with his name embossed upon them, which successfully merchandise and therefore cheapen his name) and try to rediscover some sense of reverence, dignity, and good taste. (*FFR* §8, 164)[1]

It is evident, of course, that McLaren does not actually want to stop talking about Jesus, though he does recognize that doing so often repulses spiritual seekers (cf. *FFR* §8, 160-63).[2] What is essential is his belief that institutional Christianity has tarnished Jesus' gospel message, creating a bifurcation between "Jesus and the Christian religion" in the process (*NKOCY* §20, 293n10).[3]

What may appear surprising is that McLaren still identifies as a "Christian" (and even as an "evangelical"), refusing to abandon his faith in Christ (*GO* §1, 43; *JMBM* §1, 3; §2, 13-24). For him, deserting the church would not resolve anything since no other belief system has the same real-world potential as Christianity (*GO* §Intro, 16n3).[4] He writes, "[Christianity] has the truest news, the deepest views, the highest theme, the most inspiring dream, the plot most full of meaning and magic, vigor and rigor" (*SWFOI* §5, 37). In fact, McLaren likens his spiritual pilgrimage to a "personal obsession" where his life's central goal has been "to understand Jesus—and, in particular, his message" (*SMJ* §Intro, xiii). McLaren explains that he is genuinely in love with Christ (*GO* §2, 70-71; *JMBM* §1, 3).[5] For him, Jesus is the "true source and purpose

---

1. Søren Kierkegaard once wrote, "One can 'know' nothing at all about 'Christ'; He is the paradox, the object of faith, existing only for faith" (Kierkegaard, *Training in Christianity*, 28).

2. See also, McLaren, "Informed, but Not Transformed."

3. McLaren writes, "I believe Jesus is true, but I don't believe Christianity in any of our versions is true. (In other words, we know in part and prophesy in part; we have not yet reached that unity and maturity of faith and knowledge that will come when we know as we are known)" (*COOS1* §12b, 172-73). His concern today is that people have the Christian *religion* in their lives but do not have or know the real Jesus (*LWWAT* §4, 31). See also, McLaren, "A Generous, Not Suspicious, Orthodoxy."

4. Thus, for McLaren, "We often keep faith in spite of religion, not because of it" (*EMC* §2, 13). Nevertheless, McLaren considers it a privilege to be labelled "Christian" (*AIFA*, 83). "I, with all my faults, am very honored to be affiliated with a wonderful religion that condescends to include sinners such as myself, expressing the grace of God in Jesus Christ" (*FOWA* §4, 33). To those saying McLaren is not a "Christian," he responds: "If you want to say I'm not a Christian by your definition, I'll be glad to renounce that definition" (McLaren and Schaeffer, "Brian McLaren Talks with Frank Schaeffer," 00:50:31–00:51:53. Cf. Mattingly, "Time to Pin New Label."

5. McLaren's attraction to Jesus occurred early when he was captivated by stories of Jesus in the Bible (*FFR* §9, 172; *GO* §1, 43). "No one has had a greater influence on my life than Jesus. . . .I keep

of creation," the metaphysical "logic and meaning of the universe" (*JMBM* §16, 137, 143), in whom he has total confidence "as Lord, Savior, Son of God, Son of Man, God incarnate, Word made flesh, and more" (*JMBM* §1, 3). The result is an allegiance solely to the teachings of Jesus (§7.4) by placing him above all religions and creeds (cf. *NKOC* §6, 76; §8, 95; *SMJ* §1, 5; §11, 90; *JMBM* §2, 16). "I am a Christian who does not believe in Christianity as I used to, but who believes in Christ with all my heart, more than ever" (*NKOCY* §20, 294n10).[6]

The term "Christotelic" best describes McLaren's Christian orientation. Peter Enns explains that a "christo*centric*" or "christo*logical*" approach often generates a strained religiosity because it artificially makes everything about the person of Christ. A Christo*telic* approach, on the other hand, views Christ as the *telos* of creation, meaning Christ's ethico-religious teachings imbue everything as its own *causa finalis* ("ultimate purpose;" cf. Rom 10:4).[7] As McLaren writes, "We can only discern God's character in a mature way from the vantage point of the end of the story, seen in the light of the story of Jesus" (*NKOCY* §11, 114; cf. *GO* §13, 199-209). He explains furthers, "The true logic of the universe—the true meaning or syntax or plotline of history—has been enfleshed in Jesus and dwelt among us" (*JMBM* §16, 143). From this Christotelic worldview, McLaren then describes the nature of Christian "authenticity."

6.1.1 Authentic Christianity

Although he recognizes a number of incongruous manifestations of Christian faith, McLaren defines Christianity as "the family of diverse religious traditions based or centered on the life and teachings of Jesus" (*GSM*, 229-30n2).[8] He writes elsewhere, "The message of and about Jesus is in fact a given—it is Christianity's pearl, our treasure, our gift, and it must never be lost" (*GSM*, 11). Being the defining characteristic of Christianity, to minimize the uniqueness of Jesus' message is to abandon Christianity

---

growing in love for the person" (*FFR* §8, 160). He continues, "I have had one lasting obsession: the fascinating, mysterious, uncontainable, uncontrollable, enigmatic, vigorous, surprising, stunning, dazzling, subtle, honest, genuine, and explosive personality of Jesus" (*SMJ* §1, 5). "There's something here that I love and can't stop loving, and that something is actually Someone" (*GO* §Intro, 21). He asserts about the Gospels, "I find someone really there, someone substantial, too real, too vigorous, too alive, too robust to be reduced to a quick formula or set of principles. . . .[Jesus] won't be domesticated, mastered, outlined, packaged, shrink-wrapped, or dialed down" (*FFR* §8, 167).

6. As John Franke remarks, McLaren "maintains a focus on Jesus Christ as the center of the Christian faith. . . .he identifies the centrality of Christ as the single unifying force in a multifaceted tradition" (Franke, foreword to *A Generous Orthodoxy*, 12). Cf. Clark, "Whosoever Will Be Saved," 112-28.

7. Enns, "Apostolic Hermeneutics," 266-70; "Fuller Meaning," 213-15. Interestingly, however, McLaren does describe his reading of Scripture as "Christo*centrically*" focused (*NKOCY* §8, 271n10).

8. Elsewhere, McLaren describes Christianity as having "a sustained and sustaining confidence in Jesus Christ" (*GO* §1, 43), elaborating further "Why am I a Christian? Because I believe Jesus is Savior of the world, Lord, and Son of God" (p. §2, 71; see also, §2, 69).

altogether.⁹ The immediate implication is that if the church merely echoes the ideals of modernity (*NKOCY* §1, 8) or the destructiveness of other religions (*GSM*, 71-74; *SMJ* §9, 78-79), then it cannot be authentic Christianity.¹⁰ He uses the analogy of a spider's web to detail what he believes is an authentically high Christology from which to approach Christian faith. Like a spiderweb, he adopts multiple "anchor points" to stabilize a cohesive system while remaining flexible to new data (*NKOC* §7, 77-78). These anchor points create a *prolegomenon* for McLaren's philosophy of religion by revolving around the incarnation (*AIFA*, 308). "All the stories of Jesus—the ones about him, the ones he told. They become the portal through which I see all the other stories."¹¹ The first anchor point is McLaren's acceptance of the Trinity as the central tenet of Christian faith.

6.1.1.1 Anchor One: Trinitarian Christology

Aligning with his "provocative ambiguity" (§5.4), McLaren does appear to articulate heterodox beliefs in some places.¹² Nonetheless, he clarifies, "I never in any way minimize the classical (and I believe profoundly true) ways of speaking of Jesus in the ancient creeds. I affirm, wholeheartedly and humbly, the mystery of the Trinity and the incarnation, Jesus' role as Savior and Lord and head of the church, the affirmations of the ancient creeds" (*FOWA* §4, 33).¹³ In fact, he argues neo-Evangelicals

---

9. McLaren writes, "So to be a Christian, I believe, is to frame our lives by the unique and particular life and teaching of Jesus. While that doesn't preclude you from learning invaluable lessons from the Buddha or Mohammed—or from Darwin or Hawking for that matter—it means that Jesus is, for you, at the center, and he serves as the gracious host who invites truth, beauty, and wisdom to be welcome, whatever their source." See McLaren, "Q and R: What about the cross?"

10. McLaren explains, "What if God is still more than these modern concepts can contain, the way a poet's language is in a sense more than that of an engineer or scientist, or the way an opera or painting is more than a formula or diagram? And what if our modern depictions of God seem to postmodern people to limit and constrict their imagination about God, rather than inspire it to new heights?" (*MRTYR* §5, 53).

11. McLaren, "A Postmodern View of Scripture," 11. Cf. Bouma, *The Gospel of Brian McLaren*, 47-53.

12. For instance, McLaren sometimes describes God as uniquely infilling Jesus of Nazareth, but the two still appear distinct from each other (*GO* §2, 69). He describes Jesus elsewhere as a "charismatic and enigmatic character . . . whose presence was radiant with the goodness and glory of God." McLaren further appears to distinguish God from Jesus when he remarks, "We have to find ways for people to simply encounter Christ—and God too!" (*MRTYR* §2, 33). If taken in isolation, the implication of these types of comments suggests McLaren believes Jesus was a highly captivating and magnetic person, divinely chosen to be the next Jewish prophet, but still human, nonetheless.

13. McLaren writes, "Let me go on record as saying that I believe sound doctrine is very, very, *very* important (Titus 2:1-3:11), and that bad doctrine, while not the root of all evil, is a despicable accomplice to a good bit of the evil in the world" (*GO* §0, 32; italics in original). McLaren's philosophy of religion "consistently, unequivocally, and unapologetically upholds and affirms the Apostles' and Nicene Creeds" (*GO* §0, 28). Elsewhere, he states, "I am completely orthodox in all of my beliefs about Christ. I affirm all the ancient creeds" (McLaren, "Interview with Brian McLaren," interview by Stephen Knight).

actually lack a sufficiently high Christology because they often present Christ as a mere formula where Jesus is simply "equal to God," believing that whatever "is true of God is true of Christ" (*JMBM* §16, 139). For McLaren, however, a proper Christology should not presume that any conception of deity is correct, even those of the ancient Israelites. As a committed trinitarian (*AMP* §17, 261), Christology should mean "God is like Jesus," not the other way around (*NKOCY* §11, 114; §12, 119). Thus, he warns, "There are a number of other Jesuses in play in today's world, various distortions and domesticated images of Jesus trimmed to fit comfortably and conveniently within the existing societal machinery" (*EMC* §18, 143).

McLaren explains that later trinitarian beliefs resulted from the primitive church's encounter with Jesus, which fundamentally altered their understanding of deity, conceiving of the Trinity in order to balance lopsided misconceptions about God and Christ (*MRTYR* §2, 33).[14] Using *perichōrēsis*, the early church envisioned an "eternal dance" between Father, Son, and Holy Spirit. According to McLaren, even creation is part of this same ballet (*GO* §1, 56).[15] What is significant is that Jesus, being the authentic incarnation of the divine *Logos* (*JMBM* §16, 143), altered how people perceived God rather than *vice versa*, making Jesus the very meaning and substance of divine logic (*WMRBW*, 12–13).[16] The theological implication is that Christ reveals "the essence" and "genetic code" of deity (*GO* §2, 72); his very presence becomes "the highest, deepest, and most mature view of the character of the living God" (*NKOCY* §11, 115). Hence, McLaren's trinitarian beliefs, integrated with his belief in God as Creator (§4.3.2), make Christ's incarnation into the created order the principal source for understanding the divine (§6.1.1.4). This trinitarian emphasis naturally leads to a focus on the incarnation and Jesus' dual natures.

6.1.1.2 Anchor Two: Chalcedonian Christology

The second anchor point is a Chalcedonian Christology. McLaren's acceptance of the ecumenical creeds (*GO* §0, 28), particularly Chalcedon (*FOWA* §4, 33; *JMBM* §15, 127), indicates a belief in the hypostatic union. He even accuses some Christians of being "closet adoptionists or Arians, unconscious Nestorians or Apollinarians, or implicit

---

14. McLaren writes, "I make it clear that the trinity is an attempt to protect us from making false statements about God the Father, Jesus, and the Holy Spirit; the doctrine is far from a mathematical equation" (*AMP* §6, 99). Cf. Yoo, "A Critical Analysis," 100.

15. Cf. Simmons, "Quantum Perichoresis," 137–50.

16. Here, McLaren defines the "incarnation" as a "theological term for God's embodiment in Jesus" (*GO* §1, 57) where Christ is one with the Father and preexisted as deity prior to his human enfleshment (*NKOCY* §11, 115). Being more than a prophet, McLaren states, "[Jesus] is the true image of God, the true firstborn destined to inherit the throne, the true source and purpose of creation, the true head of the body politic, the true embodiment of the fullness of God, the true source of peace and reconciliation" (*JMBM* §16, 136–37; cf. *SMJ* §12, 97–98).

monophysitists or monothelitists" (*JMBM* §15, 127).¹⁷ Professing that "those who had seen [Jesus] had in some real way seen God" (*SMJ* §4, 31; cf. *GO* §1, 54), McLaren presupposes Jesus was the perfect expression of human nature (*GO* §2, 72; *VL*, 163–64) and "the true embodiment of the fullness" of deity (*JMBM* §16, 137, 139). Though McLaren does not speculate, his lack of a distinction between human and divine actions suggests a monergistic Christology, which perceives Christ as a single and unified God-man. The implication is that Christianity is predicated on a metaphysical paradox where two incongruous natures coexisted within the same person (§6.2.2). Jesus, therefore, is the personification of divine mystery (*EMC* §15, 120; *SMJ* §2, 15-16).

Significantly, Søren Kierkegaard also viewed the incarnation as the "absolute paradox" because of the irrational concept of God becoming a man (the *Gud-Mennesket*), making him refuse to defend Christian faith using rational concepts.¹⁸ Kierkegaard recognized faith as the very tool that transforms absurdities into existential realities. In following Kierkegaard, McLaren can state that certain metaphysical truth-claims are valid simply because he has faith in the Absolute Paradox (*AMP* §17, 269; *NKOC* §8, 94). In fact, the acknowledgment of divine mystery allows believers to exercise a heightened sense of faith in God, which further results in making the impossible a reality in the mind of the believer.¹⁹ Hence, for both Kierkegaard and McLaren, the problem of Christology is not the dual natures of Christ but rather how finite humans can intersubjectively and existentially relate to the purpose of the incarnation (cf. *WMRBW*, 122).²⁰ To answer this dilemma, McLaren adopts a form of christological kenoticism.

6.1.1.3 Anchor Three: Kenotic Christology

McLaren uses *kenōsis* to describe Christ in a paradoxical fashion, defining it as a deliberate "self-emptying" through which Jesus can then empower others (*GSM*, 91–92).²¹ What McLaren's kenoticism highlights is that "the true nature

---

17. Thus, McLaren describes Jesus in both divine and human terms (*NKOC* §10, 128; *NKOCY* §14, 149). He writes, "I cherish the church's attempts to articulate the mystery of Christ, including the language of Chalcedon. Our great creeds from the 4th and 5th centuries were doing important work for their time: seeking to articulate an evolving understanding of God in contemporary thought forms and cultural settings" (McLaren, "Q and R: Hints of Kierkegaard."). However, unlike many Chalcedon-affirming Christians today, McLaren would say that to follow the example of Chalcedon is to articulate their understanding of Christ in "thought forms" as relevant to today's contemporary "cultural settings," just as the ancients did in theirs (§4.4.2).

18. Kierkegaard, *Practice in Christianity*, 14, 82; Hong and Hong, *Søren Kierkegaard's Journals and Papers*, 3:3083. See also, Walsh, *Kierkegaard*, 117.

19. See Pojman, "Kierkegaard," 167–69.

20. Cf. Dawe, *The Form of a Servant*, 157; Law, *Kierkegaard's Kenotic Christology*, 269–70; and Walsh, *Kierkegaard*, 114-15, 117, 131.

21. A paradoxical notion of *kenōsis* is further implied when McLaren describes his *prolegomenon*, "This new kind of strong Christology begins by redefining strength itself

of God" reveals itself in self-sacrifice, not conflict or subjugation (*JMBM* §16, 137). Thus, in the incarnation, Christ reveals a God who is neither attached to nor defined by "his transcendence, his safety, [and] his glory" (*COOS1* §11, 149). Notably, in Kierkegaard's system, belief in the incarnation is valid precisely because it is absurd, referring to Christ's humiliation as "the most profound *incognito*."[22] Whereas other kenotic theologians intended to explain away how an impassible God could suffer during Christ's passion, Kierkegaard highlighted Jesus' anguish as confirmation of his divinity. Christ's "sensuous media" was an act of both hiding his divine nature while simultaneously revealing it by employing omnipotence to retain his human existence.[23] Similarly, McLaren's Christology reflects Kierkegaardian kenoticism by focusing on the incarnation's existential implications rather than rationally defending its historicity. He highlights Christ's "open handed humility," "self-giving," and "preference for others" by remarking, "Christ as a true image bearer of God does not climb to a place of prominence and glory through the normal means of rivalry and conquest. Rather, he descends—down into common humanity, down into servanthood, down into suffering, down into death" (*JMBM* §16, 137).

Moreover, according to McLaren, Jesus allowed corrupt authorities to murder him in order to reverse imperial notions of strength and power (§7.5.2), revealing a nonviolent deity who ridicules the futility of violence (*GDT*; *GSM*, 91-93). McLaren explains, "We see God as one who identifies, serves, and suffers with creation as Christ did, who would rather be tortured and killed than torture or kill" (*WMRBW*, 228). Here, he uses the Philippians hymn to stress Christ's humility and even adopts Kierkegaard's "incognito" terminology:

> Philippians 2 might be more a hymn about the humanity of Christ than the deity of Christ, presenting him not as "existing in the form (or nature) of God," . . . but rather as "existing in the image of God"—as the true human, content in being human, not seeking to grasp for more. . . . When Christians present Jesus as one who demands that others acknowledge his deity (crudely put, "Bow down and say I am God or I will send you to hell!"), they contradict the whole spirit of Philippians 2. To add to the irony: if Jesus truly is the image of God (or "in nature God" or "in the form of God"), then he reveals that God's true nature is not to grasp at deity! That suggests that God is willing to go "incognito." . . . if God is humbly manifest in the most unexpected form of a servant hanging on a cross,

---

in light of Christ's strength-through-weakness, gaining-through-losing, rising-through-descending" (*JMBM* §16, 138).

22. Kierkegaard, *Practice in Christianity*, 131; emphasis added. See also, Dawe, *The Form of a Servant*, 160; Walsh, *Kierkegaard*, 112-16, 129; and Law, *Kierkegaard's Kenotic Christology*, 267, 271-72.

23. Hinkson, "Luther and Kierkegaard," 27-45; Law, *Kierkegaard's Kenotic Christology*, 19-33, 267-88; Walsh, *Kierkegaard*, 12-30. Significantly, McLaren endorses divine anthropopathy, writing, "The God of Abraham and his descendants is a God who feels, a God who suffers" (*FOWA* §18, 177).

> then perhaps we should expect God to be humbly manifest in unexpected ways in the contexts of other religions, too. (*JMBM* §16, 142n11)[24]

The Philippians 2 hymn is central because it presents the opposite of what McLaren calls "omnitheology" (e.g., omniscience, omnipresence, and omnipotency), which conveys the idea that God's sovereignty manifests as a "controlling, dominating, dictatorial power." Philippians 2, on the other hand, portrays God as one who rules by serving others. While Christ is the Supreme Being, he is "supreme" in the sense of being the epitome of love and aliveness (*GSM*, 92-93); and in this way, Jesus redefines what it means to be supreme.

Likewise, Kierkegaard's notion of "contemporaneity" (*Samtidigheden*) with Christ, which conveys the sense of imitating Jesus' humility and focusing on subjectively actualizing Christ's solidarity with humanity, dominates McLaren's belief system (cf. *AIFA*, 277; *AMP* §2, 41; *COOS1* §5, 65-66).[25] He summarizes, "Jesus' incarnation (an event in the past that is always *contemporary* and always has a claim on us as Christians) sets an example of showing up on time, of being in touch with one's world in the present—not of it, but truly in it" (*COOS1* §11, 148; emphasis added). For McLaren, Christianity is about the story of Jesus and the existential appropriation of Jesus' humility during the incarnation (*CIEC*, 200-5). The difference is that McLaren's philosophy also emphasizes an unassuming faith (§6.2.1) by identifying Jesus (and only Jesus) as the noetic basis for Christian truth-claims.

6.1.1.4 Anchor Four: Noetic Christology

In seemingly deliberate tension with kenoticism, McLaren's Christology also accentuates Christ's divinity to a loftier degree than conventional paradigms. For McLaren, Christ's divinity means that any other conception of deity apart from Jesus must be wrong. He explains,

> The doctrines of the incarnation and deity of Christ are meant to tell us that we cannot start with a predetermined, set-in-stone idea of God derived from the rest of the Bible and then extend that to Jesus. Jesus is not intended merely to fit into these predetermined categories; he is intended instead to explode them, transform them, alter them forever, and bring us to a new evolutionary level in our understanding of God. An old definition of God does not define

---

24. The Philippians hymn has special significance to McLaren, writing, "Philippians 2:5-11 is indeed important to me" (McLaren, "Q and R: Hints of Kierkegaard"). See also, McLaren, *Is Jesus the Only Way?*

25. This theme also appears in the Eucharist as "a continual rendezvous with the risen Christ" (*GO* §1, 54). For details on Kierkegaard's concept of "contemporaneity," see Homer, *On Kierkegaard and the Truth*, 283-91 and Law, *Kierkegaard's Kenotic Christology*, 276.

> Jesus—the experience of God in Jesus requires a brand-new definition or understanding of God. (*NKOCY* §11, 114)[26]

In other words, Jesus is the ultimate discloser of transcendent Truth (§8.3.1.2), to which all other religious claims must align with, including the claims of Scripture, church tradition, spiritual experience, and logic. Because the incarnation challenged conventional wisdom about God, McLaren argues that a "robust" Christology is one that views the Godhead only through the life and teachings of Jesus. What is true of Jesus is true of God, not *vice versa* (see *JMBM* §16, 139-40).[27] This noetic Christology contends that the incarnation ought to be the church's sole cognitive foundation for all claims about God. As such, Scripture alone cannot provide a complete theological system because of its derivative, heteroglossic, and polyphonic nature (§8.4.1).[28] Only Jesus provides the necessary information from which to derive all primary knowledge of the divine. Thus, the person of Christ is more important than the Christian religion, christological speculations, or church tradition (cf. *NKOC* §6, 76; §8, 95; *JMBM* §2, 16).

The rationale for McLaren's emphasis on Jesus as Divine Revealer is simple: "Jesus presents us with a radically new vision of God, a non-violent God, a suffering and serving God, descending and disrupting preexisting categories, opening up previously unrealized possibilities" (*JMBM* §16, 143). Hence, McLaren presents Jesus as the divine corrective to how ancient Israelites and Second Temple Jews imagined God.[29] He explains further,

> If I see a tension in scripture, rather than appealing to Augustine, Aquinas, Luther, Calvin, Scofield, or the pope to resolve it, I should first turn to Jesus. If Jesus truly was the highest and fullest revelation of God, if Jesus was truly the *logos*, the radiance of God's glory, the exact representation of God's nature, the fullness of the godhead in bodily form, and in very nature God, then his life and teaching mattered in tensions like this. And if the Bible was intended, as Jesus said, to bear witness to Christ . . . then "when in doubt, consult Jesus" seemed like good advice.[30]

---

26. Endorsing a "theology of resistance," McLaren declares that the believer's sole authority ought to be "the Word of God made flesh in Jesus Christ" (McLaren, foreword to *Solus Jesus*, xv). Cf. F Shults, *Christology and Science*, 4-11.

27. Significantly, McLaren suggests that the God of the Hebrew Bible often acts very "un-Christlike" (*NKOCY* §10, 98). Likewise, McLaren does not accord Pauline soteriology or Petrine ethics the same status as Jesus's teachings from the Gospels (§7.4). Hence, McLaren rhetorically asks, "Who would be so pristinely arrogant or demonically naive to claim to be right on par with Jesus?" (*NKOCY* §3, 26).

28. Hatch, "Hearing God Amid Many Voices," 23-47.

29. McLaren writes, "The character of God, seen in Jesus, is not violent and tribal. The living God is not the kind of deity who decrees ethnic cleansing, genocide, racism, slavery, sexism, homophobia, war, religious supremacy, or eternal conscious torment" (*NKOCY* §11, 118).

30. McLaren, "Is God Violent?," 19; italics in original. As McLaren explains further, a proper Christology is about "*letting* Jesus serve as the Word-made-flesh revelation of God's character" (*NKOCY* §13, 128; emphasis added).

The incarnate Christ reversed many of Judaism's theological assumptions about deity, such as God being violent (*GO* §2, 72-76; *VL*, 43). Because Christ revealed "the true nature of God" (*JMBM* §16, 137) and offered "a new vision" of divinity (*GSM*, 3), McLaren contends that Jesus is the paradigm through which believers must still seek to understand God's character (*WMRBW*, 159). Being both "wild and alive," however, God is recognizable predominantly through the canonical Jesus (*MRTYR* §7, 64; cf. *NS* §2, 17). Hence, other ancient books, such as Leviticus, and other humans, such as the Apostle Paul, are *not* co-equals to Christ. Jesus is Lord above all and is "the zenith of God's self-revelation" (*NKOCY* §17, 179). McLaren explains,

> In Hebrews, we do not read, "Long ago God spoke to our ancestors in many and various ways by the Jewish prophets, but in these last days he has spoken to us through the Christian apostles. . . .Their writings are the reflection of God's glory and the exact imprint of God's very being." [. . . .]
>
> Nor do we read in the Gospel of John, "In the beginning was the Word, and the Word was with God, and the Word was God. . . .And the Word became Scriptures and was published among us. . . .The Bible is the light of the world . . . and the way, and the truth, and the life. Whoever has understood the Bible has seen the Father. . . .The Bible and the Father are one." (*NKOCY* §11, 115; unbracketed ellipses in original).

Rather than diminish the Bible, McLaren believes he is honoring Scripture by recognizing its proper status as a derivative *witness* to the living Word of God, Jesus Christ, and therefore should not receive the same veneration as Jesus himself (*NKOCY* §11, 116).[31] Since Jesus identified himself as the new Moses and new lawgiver (cf. Mark 10:3-12; John 1:17), the implication is that Jesus is fully capable of overriding any biblical material that does not correlate to his own self-revelation (cf. *SMJ* §4, 30).[32] Thus, McLaren confidently argues that Jesus' command to love one another "supersedes all Torah" (*GO* §10, 170).[33] The significance for McLaren's philosophy of religion is the belief that humans cannot fully contemplate the divine (§6.2.2.2); yet, in the incarnate Christ, humans can encounter an embodiment of Truth so unique that neither the Bible (as a collection of verses) nor the creeds (as a collection of propositions) can replace him (§8.3.1.2). From this high Christology, McLaren infers that the incarnation is principally about God's union and solidarity with creation itself.

---

31. Cf. Barth, *Church Dogmatics*, §1/I 4.2-4.

32. See also, Allison, *The New Moses*). In fact, McLaren interprets the Gospels as a hermeneutical corrective to other portions of Scripture: "We can't tell the story about Elijah (1 Kings 18) calling down fire on the prophets of Baal without hearing Jesus' rebuke of his disciples for recommending the same violent response to the 'religiously other' (Luke 9). We can't tell the story of Moses sending people to kill their brothers (Exodus 32) without also telling the story of the Transfiguration, where the nonviolent words and ways of Jesus are honored over those of Moses" (*JMBM* §20, 194).

33. McLaren concludes, "If Jesus truly reveals and images God, this vision of God is vastly different from the tough, macho judge and angry male potentate that many people think of when they think of God" (*GO* §2, 75).

The Logic of Intersubjectivity

6.1.1.5 Anchor Five: Solidarity Christology

The final anchor point is McLaren's emphasis on an all-embracing "solidarity," which derives from the primitive church's intersubjective experience with Jesus and the succeeding belief that their lives had been absorbed into the divine (*SA*, 332).[34] In this sense, God has embraced all of creation history, "The Incarnation is about God's solidarity with our world. It is about God leaving his distance, his transcendence, his safety, his glory, and getting caught up with the muck and blood and tears and spit and history of our world" (*COOS1* §11, 149). In fact, McLaren declares that solidarity was the entire purpose of Christ's incarnation. Here, God not only united himself to human nature, but God also united himself to the entire universe (cf. *JMBM* §16, 141), creating a "profound solidarity between creator and creation" (*FFS* §6, 142). "I think that God is *in* nature as well as outside of it (God fills all things, Scripture says), that God is totally *with* nature as well as totally other from it (the Incarnation of Jesus demonstrates God's solidarity not only with humanity, but with all of creation)" (*AMP* §12, 194; italics in original).[35] Thus, Christ not only saves humanity; he saves *all* things, including the entire cosmos and human history (*GO* §1, 58-59; cf. *LWWAT* §3, 21). McLaren's fictional character, Dan, clarifies,

> Jesus really was, and *is*, about saving more than just human souls after they die. He really *is* about saving the world—human history, creation, the whole thing. . . . So I guess what you're helping me see is that the whole idea of the incarnation of Christ is far more radical than we realize. It's not just God entering creation, and especially human history. It's God taking creation, including human history, into his heart, and declaring eternal solidarity with it. He's really with us in . . . the process, the story, the unfolding. (*SWFOI* §31, 230-31; italics in original; cf. *LWWAT* §3, 21)

Accordingly, McLaren implicitly follows the ancient maxim that whatever is not absorbed in Christ is not saved.[36] In other words, because humans are interconnected to all of creation (see §6.2.3), Christ's appropriation of human nature means that he is now connected to all aspects of the universe, which allows the eschaton (§6.3) to involve the redemption of everything in the cosmos (cf. *JMBM* §12, 103-4; *WMRBW*, 8). Following Eastern Orthodoxy, McLaren theorizes,

---

34. McLaren defines "solidarity" in existential terms where people choose to experience the energies and resources of a particular group identity that they did not originally possess at birth (*JMBM* §8, 69-70n5).

35. McLaren emphasizes, however, that he rejects theological pantheism and panentheism because of its immoral implications on the nature of God's goodness and God's relationship to evil (*BMF*, 296; *FFS* §6, 134-36).

36. Contra Christopher Peppler's impulsive claim that McLaren holds the "typical liberal view" for presenting Jesus "as a social, not a spiritual, savior" (see Peppler, "A New Kind of Liberalism," 196).

> First, God takes the human life of Jesus into God's own eternal life, and in so doing, Jesus' people (the Jews), species (the human race), and history (the history of our planet and our whole universe) enters into—are taken up into—God's own life. . . . In this way Jesus will ultimately bring blessing to the whole world, to all of creation.
>
> Second, as humanity (and all creation) enters into God through Jesus, God also enters Jesus' people, species, and history. . . . [and] is forever bound to [all creation] in solidary, faithfulness, loyalty, and commitment. (*GO* §1, 56-57)

Describing the cosmos as "a universe in interactive relationship with God" (*SMJ* §7, 53), McLaren envisions how doing something for the least in society is, in fact, doing something for Christ himself (*AIFA*, 215-16). Essentially, McLaren's Christology culminates in a "mystic doctrine of redemption," which suggests that liberation rests in Christ's total being, not merely in his actions, because Christ actually represents the totality of the redeemed cosmos (cf. §4.3.2).[37] Hence, McLaren can offer the following prayer to God: "When we launched inquisitions and persecuted heretics, we hunted and persecuted you. When we marginalized religious minorities, we marginalized you. When we divided from others we deemed less orthodox than ourselves, when we taught our children to distrust or avoid those different from us, when we tried to convert and assimilate what we didn't respect or understand, you suffered at our hands."[38] The implication for McLaren's philosophy of religion is that humanity becomes co-creators of social justice (§6.2.3.1), which seeks to redeem everyone and everything in the world (cf. §7.4.2).

6.2 CHRISTOTELIC IMPLICATIONS

McLaren describes his religious evolution as a "three-step process" where he first "acknowledged that honest doubt can't be a sin;" he then centered his faith on the person of Jesus while he "simultaneously de-centered passages from the Bible that make dubious claims;" lastly, he placed "primary focus on Jesus's teachings of love" (*GI*, 157). From these evolutionary stages, four direct consequences to McLaren's Christotelic *prolegomenon* present themselves: 1) the necessity of faith and the inevitability of doubt; 2) paradoxy as the essence of Christianity and, therefore, the impossibility of Christian rationalism; 3) a corrective sense of cosmic anthropology; and 4) a heightened sense of divine love and goodness.

---

37. See Grillmeier, *Christ in Christian Tradition*, 1:531.
38. McLaren, "'Instead of Ruling'—Prayers," 225.

6.2.1 The Necessity of Faith

The most immediate implication of McLaren's Christology is the assertion that Christianity is a *faith*-based religion predicated on seemingly illogical paradoxes.[39] Unlike modernism, postmodernity realizes that nothing is absolutely certain, everything is taken on faith, and humans are incapable of grasping the inexplicable mysteries of reality, both human and divine (*COOS1* §12b, 175; *WMRBW*, 227).[40] Here, the postmodern ethos recaptures what was once an assumed premise: *faith* and *mystery* are the essence of Christianity. McLaren writes, "The bigger our understanding about God, the bigger the mystery that we must acknowledge" (*WMRBW*, 29). Quoting historian Harvey Cox, McLaren concurs that the "first era" of Christianity was the "Age of Faith," describing it as a time of "diversity, energy . . . persecution, courage, and rapid growth" (*NKOCY* §1, 11). In fact, for McLaren, a mature faith realizes that only God knows everything and, therefore, mystery is an inherent part of life (*AMP* §16, 249).

In patristic theology, Augustinian *sapientia* ("wisdom") was the predominant principal where "faith seeking understanding" preceded human reason; yet, medieval scholastics later adopted Aristotelian *scientia* ("scientific knowledge") that relied on rationality.[41] In postmodernity, however, faith once again takes precedence because every religious truth-claim has a measure of circular reasoning.[42] Here, "faith" does not signify epistemic fideism in league with foundationalism (cf. *AMP* §16, 247; *FFS* §1, 41). Instead, it recognizes that all religious truth-claims are *presumed* correct. As Mark Hanna explains, "Metaphysical presuppositions are implicit in every epistemology, and epistemological presuppositions are implicit in every metaphysic."[43] Hence, McLaren defines faith as "a state of relative certainty about matters of ultimate concern

---

39. See *AIFA*, 231, 233; *GO* §15, 229; §17, 262; §20, 297; *JMBM* §15, 127; *SWFOI* §14, 102.

40. McLaren states, "There is no certainty apart from faith, and the only kind of understanding possible for us humans grows in the environment of faith" (*COOS1* §12b, 175). "We all live by faith, not certainty" (*FFS* §2, 64). Or as Kierkegaard once wrote, "All Christianity is rooted in the paradox" (Hong and Hong, *Søren Kierkegaard's Journals and Papers*, 3:3083).

41. See Lewis, "Faith and History in St. Augustine," 39-50; *Testing Christianity's Truth Claims*, 45-66, 76-94, 293-94; Boa and Bowman, *Faith Has Its Reasons*, 15-17; and Penner and Barnes, *A New Kind of Conversation*, 62-63. For an examination of *sapientia* and *scientia* in theological methodology, see Clark, *To Know and Love God*, 208-19.

42. Frame, *The Doctrine of the Knowledge of God*, 131; "Presuppositional Apologetics," 217-18; Peterson et al., *Reason and Religious Belief*, 59-74, 113-29; Boa and Bowman, *Faith Has Its Reasons*, 131, 159.

43. Hanna, *Crucial Questions in Apologetics*, 100. Kenneth Boa and Robert Bowman likewise conclude, "There appear to be *no universally accepted criteria of truth that can be applied without already assuming the truth of a particular worldview*. . . .one's perspective on what is reasonable, factual, and practical is largely determined by the worldview one has already espoused" (Boa and Bowman, *Faith Has Its Reasons*, 131-32; italics in original). Thus, even if empirical evidence for Christianity were possible, it would still require an act of faith to accept orthodox Christianity's interpretation of the evidence. For instance, Gordon Lewis remarks, "Historical data may be variously interpreted by people from different perspectives. The same events may seem to show very different things to Christians and non-Christians" (Lewis, *Testing Christianity's Truth Claims*, 97).

sufficient to promote action" (see his entire discussion, *FFS* §1, 38-50).⁴⁴ The notion of "true faith" is even more nuanced with McLaren since it involves an intersubjective trust in God and in the church's ability to better the world without exclusionary in-group/out-group polarities (*GDT*; *WMRBW*, 25-25). This faith is not the same thing as being religiously dogmatic, which is incorrigible and pretentious (*COOS1* §12a, 168-69). Instead, faith means "to trust God and God's dreams enough to realign our dreams with God's."⁴⁵ Accordingly, hubris becomes the greatest obstacle to faith (cf. *FFS* §1, 46-47; §2, 64), which forces McLaren to decry the overconfidence of conventional paradigms (*MRTYR* §19, 150; *NKOCY* §1, 8).⁴⁶ Not surprisingly, then, religious doubt becomes an essential element to possessing authentic faith.

6.2.1.1 Accepting Doubt

In dogmatism, religionists are adamant that their beliefs are true, generating pride and bigotry in the process (*COOS1* §12a, 168-69). In McLaren's "perplexity" stage of faith, however, the complexity of religious knowledge forces many to doubt their beliefs (*AMP* §16, 249), which can then engender greater trust in God (cf. *SMJ* §13, 108). For McLaren, doubt is an entryway to spiritual maturation that is often very painful but essential to embracing divine mysteries (*AMP* §16, 243-51).⁴⁷ Therefore, Christianity is best seen as a self-contained approach to embracing the divine that risks being mistaken and misguided. Attempting to "prove" Christianity diminishes the distinctiveness of faith by asserting an unwarranted hyperconfidence in the validity of its truth-claims (*COOS1* §12a, 168-69; *EMC* §6, 303n3).⁴⁸ In this sense, McLaren does not promote fideism but, instead, "paradoxtrine" as the crux of the church.

44. McLaren explains further, "Faith is about admitting that many of life's greatest truths are going to remain mysteries to us, due to the limitations of our tiny brains that weigh less than a cantaloupe. Faith is about reaching out to God to guide us, and asking for God's help so we can be honest, good-hearted seekers. That's what child-like faith is" (*AMP* §16, 247).

45. McLaren, "Found in Translation," 16-17.

46. For McLaren, the universe is full of "mystery, order, complexity, life, and wonder" (*AMP* §6, 97). He writes, "In the twenty-first century the new church will feed the seeking mind with the savory mysteries of Creation, Incarnation, Trinity, Atonement, transformation, and unity," and emphasizes divine mystery as "the place to work with your questions, live your questions, explore possible answers, and find direction to live by. . . .life is at heart a mystery to be explored, using faith" (*COOS1* §6, 78-79). Cf. Caputo, *Philosophy and Theology*, 50 and Simmons and Benson, *The New Phenomenology*, 182.

47. Cf. Benson, "Theology and (Non)(Post)Foundationalism," 66-67 and Suk, *Not Sure*. As one postmodern blogger remarks, "There is a freedom in the insecurity of postmodernism. I don't know anything more than you do and what we can know is limited anyway" (quoted in Penner and Barnes, *A New Kind of Conversation*, 30).

48. McLaren does recognize that too much doubt can be detrimental. "If one is left without commitment, without moral obligation, without any sense of justice or hope or meaning . . . then one's doubt has become like an auto-immune disease. The best remedy to that kind of doubt, I think, is to doubt it!" (McLaren, "An Interview with Brian McLaren on Faith"). Kierkegaard famously wrote, "If I can grasp God objectivity, then I do not have faith, but just because I cannot do this, I must have faith. If I wish to stay in my faith, I must take constant care to keep hold of the objective uncertainty, to be

6.2.2 Orthodoxy as "Paradoxtrine"

McLaren describes the essence of Christianity as "Stage One orthodoxy ... what some have called paradoxy—the realization that every true statement about God (including this one) cannot fully contain the true majesty and wonder of God" (*NS* §Part IV, 189). McLaren explains that paradoxes are a vibrant display of uncontainable transcendental Truth (§8.3.1.2) where "paradoxtrine" represents the core of faith in God (*AIFA*, 233; cf. *GO* §15, 229; *SWFOI* §14, 102). Because Christianity is predicated on paradoxes, and Christ is the essence of reality (*AMP* §17, 261; *NKOC* §8, 94), McLaren believes that "mystery and poetry" must, therefore, permeate *literally* everything (*GO* §9, 157). For him, paradoxy is its own category of ontological reality (*FFS* §2, 67-68), especially since God's very nature is inexplicable (*NS* §2, 17; §5, 40). Thus, he concludes, "Orthodoxy is paradoxy. One/Three; Transcendent/Immanent; Human/Divine; Saint/Sinner; Revealed/Hidden; Ascension/Presence" (*AIFA*, 102).[49]

The nature of a theological "paradox" is such that when coalesced together, multiple well-founded statements about God result in an apparent contradiction in human logic or intuition.[50] Synonymous with the technical term "antinomy," or the lay word "mystery," theological paradoxes produce mystical profundity once believers attempt describing God through human language. Paradoxes caution theologians from overemphasizing one facet of religious faith to the dilution or neglect of another (equally important) facet. Rhetorically, paradoxes also capitalize on contradiction in order to seize the imagination and compel critical reflection about perceived theological absolutes. The result is that God and Christ are neither subject to critical inspection nor reducible to propositional statements.[51] Significantly, paradoxtrine makes Christianity appealing once again to postmodern seekers (*COOS1* §6, 84), particularly since mystery enhances people's awe at the prospect of experientially knowing God. "Our words will seek to be servants of mystery, not removers of it as they were in the old world. They will convey a message that is clear yet mysterious, simple yet mysterious, substantial yet mysterious" (*COOS1* §7, 89).[52] Hence, McLaren accentuates Jesus'

'on the 70,000 fathoms deep' but still have faith" (Kierkegaard, *Concluding Unscientific Postscript*, 172). Cf. Dulles, *A History of Apologetics*, 305-10.

49. Metaphysically, despite the prevalence of numerous theories about reality, mysteries continue to persist, making any system of belief incapable of explaining all known data (Hebblethwaite, "The Nature and Limits," 210-36).

50. Kandiah, *Paradoxology*, 1-6.

51. Schwartz, "Antinomy," 1:81; Elwell, *Baker Encyclopedia of the Bible*, s.v. "Paradox." Cf. Dulles, *Models of Revelation*, 84-97.

52. As Louis Pojman remarks, "Only in the absurd does the possibility of seeing God arise" (Pojman, *The Logic of Subjectivity*, 8). Likewise, Tony Jones explains, "Emergent churches are full of persons who faithfully follow Jesus but do not fear paradox" (Jones, *The New Christians*, 168). According to McLaren, the propensity for modernistic churches to develop creeds and precise doctrinal statements beyond the Apostles' and Nicene Creeds appears like an elaborate attempt to demystify the paradoxes of Christian orthodoxy (*AIFA*, 231; *GO* §9, 145-46).

otherworldliness: he is a magnificent song and a mystery to enjoy, not a thesis to argue (*MRTYR* §19, 149-50). As Philip Bentley explains, religionists who embrace paradoxy do not substitute objectivity for relativism; they highlight the pursuit of truth while recognizing its unreachability.[53] The result is recognizing that Christian truth ineludibly transcends rationality, being a suprarational wonder, instead.

6.2.2.1 Paradoxtrine as Suprarational Wonderment

For McLaren, "God is real yet immaterial, peaceful yet dynamic, powerful yet gentle, and comprehensible yet incomprehensible. . . .[who] relativizes time and space and thus renders us part of something big and beautiful and fast and timeless and mysterious and wonderful" (*FOWA* §17, 163). The rationale for stressing paradoxy is because of Christianity's reliance on the Trinity (in association with the incarnation) and the kingdom of God, which together produce an acute sense of wonderment. With the Trinity, orthodox Christianity insists (paradoxically) that there is only one God but three persons.[54] Whereas abstract monotheism confines God to human expectations, the notion of God in trinitarian form is, in fact, rationally perplexing. Cornelius Plantinga summarizes the conundrum of trying to grasp the Trinity:

> Given the modern concept of a person (a self-conscious subject, a center of action, knowledge, love, and purpose), how many persons does God comprise? Barthians admit to only one. Social trinitarians argue for three. But there is also a traditional position. . . .These trinitarians seem to want to answer the central question both ways. God comprises three persons in some full sense of 'person.' But since each of these is in fact identical with the one divine essence, or each is in fact a center of exactly the same divine consciousness, the de facto number of persons in God is finally hard to estimate.[55]

This doctrine of the Trinity formed because Jesus forced his followers to conclude that God's nature was more dynamic than originally thought. "Over time, [theologians and mystics] tried to describe this mysterious paradox. After much dialogue and debate, a radically new understanding and teaching about God emerged. They had to create a whole new term to convey it: *Trinity*" (*WMRBW*, 226; italics in original). To McLaren, the doctrine of the Trinity defies modern notions of rationality, which is an asset, not a

---

53. Bentley, "Uncertainty and Unity," 191-201. For McLaren, even Christianity's destabilization (and perhaps eventual ruin) means, paradoxically, recapturing an authentic faith in Christ (McLaren, "Bless This House?," 96).

54. For a review of the socio-historical, philosophical, and theological developments that eventually established the Trinity as orthodoxy, see Hill, *The Three-Personed God*, 29-52 and Letham, *The Holy Trinity*, 89-268.

55. Plantinga, "The Threeness/Oneness Problem," 40. For a detailed discussion on the numerous theoretical conceptions of the Trinity in contemporary theology, see Hill, *The Three-Personed God*, 81-237.

liability.[56] As Tony Jones remarks: "The Trinity is too beautiful *not* to be true."[57] Subsequently, to presume that this triune deity incarnated one of its persons as a first century peasant becomes especially offensive to human reasoning. Here, paradox disrupts people's understanding of God while forcing them either to be offended at or to embrace (in faith) the ludicrousness of these mysteries (cf. *GO* §3, 83-84; *SMJ* §2, 15-16).[58]

A final paradoxical element that McLaren emphasizes is the economy of God's kingdom. The biblical story begins with a Creator who precedes creation yet who is, paradoxically, the same loving Christ who suffers and dies with mortal creatures (cf. *WMRBW*, 19-23). This Christotelic view of history develops further in Jesus' ministry, most notably through his teachings that exemplify the foolishness and mystery of the gospel.[59] Using the prophet Hosea as an illustration, McLaren associates Christ's death with the "prophetic paradox" of God delivering good news through the life of a victimized laborer (*CPA*, 114-16; *WMRBW*, 119). For McLaren, the significance of Christ's servanthood is itself a paradoxical message where Christians must imitate God's "victory through defeat, glory through shame, strength through weakness, leadership through servanthood, and life through death" (*WMRBW*, 119).[60] In sum, the very economy of God requires a believer's total embrace of paradoxical ideas that defy the status quo of logical thought and the analytic rationalizing of conventional paradigms.

What these paradoxes entail is a sense of humility (*GO* §20, 291), which eliminates the reductionistic urge to analyze the Almighty. "It is clear that this new epistemology challenges our modern approach to theology, which suggests that 'God' can be studied 'objectively,' like any other object of inquiry" (*AIFA*, 233). Accordingly, an authentic Christian faith is one that embraces the ineffable beauty of divine mystery (*MRTYR* §19, 149-50). The problem is that humans attempt to resolve these paradoxes in a logical manner, thereby eliminating the faith necessary to be an orthodox

---

56. See McLaren, "Rethinking the Doctrines," 13-14, 56-59.

57. Jones, *The New Christians*, 166; italics in original. The rationale is similar to the church father, Tertullian (ca. 150–212), who believed that the more explainable a deity becomes, the more likely it is that the religion is a figment of human imagination. Thus, for Tertullian, the incarnation was an assured historical and theological fact precisely *because* it was an absurd paradox (see Tertullian, *Carn. Chr.* 5).

58. Cf. Elrod, *Kierkegaard and Christendom*, 203; Roberts, *Emerging Prophet*, 36, 42-43, 131; and Evans, *Kierkegaard's*," 148, 212.

59. McLaren refers to this paradoxical kingdom as the "alternative economy" of God where "the last are first and the first are last. Leaders serve, and the humble—not the arrogant—inherit the Earth" (*WMRBW*, 22).

60. This paradoxical economy is replete with examples directly from Jesus himself. Most profound is the notion that Christ's death could somehow bring new life. Other examples unite both the mundane and the metaphysical: adult believers need to be reborn and have the mindset of a child; people need to lose their lives in order to find it; people who love their lives will lose it and people who hate their lives will obtain eternal life; the first are last and the last are first; and the highest ranking should become lowly servants (see Elwell, *Baker Encyclopedia of the Bible*, s.v. "Paradox"). See also, McLaren, "Dorothy on Leadership."

Christian in the first place.[61] In fact, the dialectical nature of the church's ancient ecumenical creeds intended to maintain a tension between opposing viewpoints about God and Christ, which allowed for ecclesial diversity without endorsing one extreme over another.[62] Thus, as McLaren infers, theologians must apply poetry and imagination to counter the inadequacy of human reasoning (*SWFOI* §6, 41). To do otherwise would be to commit "conceptual idolatry" by presuming humans can elucidate the divine nature.[63]

Theologically, Enlightenment ideals have described God as a rational being and, therefore, predisposed to endowing humanity with his own cognitive abilities. In response, Myron Penner comments, "One looks in vain for direct biblical warrant for the claim that logic is part of God's essential nature."[64] Here, rational theology merely consigns God to analytic formulas and analysis; but, as Bruce Benson notes, God is hardly an unbiased rationalist. "The modern category of 'objectivity' is falsely attached to God, who is far from being a neutral, detached observer."[65] For McLaren, "The moment that we have all the bolts screwed in tight and all the nails hammered in, it's at precisely that moment that we *cease* being faithful."[66] As a result, the embrace of theological paradoxes is not intended to replace rationality but to transcend and surpass it, ultimately making Christian rationalism both misguided and wrongheaded.[67]

6.2.2.2 Discounting Christian Rationalism

What is noteworthy is that the term "paradox" does not imply a formal, logical contradiction or even an apparent negation through self-referential incoherence. Rather, dialectical existentialists, such as McLaren, merely highlight the deficiency of rationality in corroborating theological truth-claims. "Paradox" is simply another way of describing wonder and mystery, but it is not equivalent to affirming magical nonsense.[68] This emphasis on paradoxy is also why McLaren discards reductionistic or logical attempts to articulate Christian belief in propositional and systematic

---

61. Jones, *The New Christians*, 164. Bruce Benson remarks that Christianity's theological foundations, such as the incarnation, the hypostatic union, the trinity, and many of Christ's teachings on the kingdom of God are predicated on paradoxes and not rationality (see Penner and Barnes, *A New Kind of Conversation*, 78, 80).

62. Pelikan, *Credo*, 186-215.

63. Benson, "Theology and (Non)(Post)Foundationalism," 68. Cf. Simmons and Benson, *The New Phenomenology*, 140-41, 165.

64. Penner and Barnes, *A New Kind of Conversation*, 26. For a defense of divine logic, see Geisler and Brooks, *Come, Let Us Reason*, 6-8 *Baker Encyclopedia of Christian Apologetics*, s.v. "Apologetics, Need For."

65. Benson, "Theology and (Non)(Post)Foundationalism," 67. Cf. Penner, *The End of Apologetics*, 8.

66. Quoted in Jones, *The New Christians*, 168; italics in original.

67. Cf. Smith, "Systematic Theology and Ministerial Efficiency," 591.

68. Hence, McLaren still evaluates a religious belief system according to its intellectual and coherent credibility (*FFS* §8, 176). See also, Evans, *Kierkegaard's*, 213-25.

form. It is simply unviable to explain life's absurdities in a logical way, particularly with religion (§4.4.1). Thus, paradoxes deepen a person's faith by illuminating diverse, often opposing beliefs within a single statement of faith.[69] This results in McLaren upholding a faith-based tension among conflicting truth-claims (cf. *AIFA*, 28; *COOS1* §12c, 195), which transforms Christianity from a system of dogmas into a "paradoxical message" that embraces the mystery of Christ's incarnational solidarity with the world (*WMRBW*, 119).

Consequently, paradoxtrine dismisses comprehending the incarnation cognitively because the incarnation's purpose was not to provide an intellectual dilemma but, instead, to provide an example of servanthood (cf. *GO* §1, 57). Since orthodoxy ought to be ridiculous to human reason, a different approach to faith is needed, one that accepts the absurdity of the incarnation and embraces Christ as Lord.[70] "This sense of mystery may offend our rationalistic minds. . . .But the mystery itself is part of the message" (*COOS1* §11, 153). For McLaren, Christianity must be about "spirituality," not dogma, which is McLaren's way of describing the relational aspects of faith that integrate rationality with intersubjectivity (*FOWA* §1, 4; *NS* §2, 14-15). However, faith first demands admitting ignorance about God (*FFS* §1, 46-47).[71] Hence, the most direct way to "know" the divine relationally is to encounter God through spiritual disciplines.

6.2.2.3 Rediscovery of Christian Mysticism

Since rationalism is no longer viable for relating to Christ, McLaren argues that believers need to reappropriate Christian mysticism (*COOS1* §12c, 195; *GO* §9, 151). According to him, God divinely directed the evolution of *Homo sapiens* beyond abstract analytics to include developing a higher sense of meaning associated with spiritualism (*NS* §8, 68-70). In a process McLaren labels "theotropism," where humans naturally turn towards the light of God (*FOWA* §17, 160-61), mysticism is not only essential to Christian orthodoxy but to human mental stability, as well (*GO* §9, 149).[72] However, McLaren advocates for a balance that does not endorse over spiritualizing or over rationalizing Christianity (*SWFOI* §7, 53; §8, 60-62). Rather, by describing the "mystical consciousness" of the postmodern shift, McLaren views spiritualism as

---

69. Bosserman, *The Trinity*, 175-96.

70. Law, *Kierkegaard's Kenotic Christology*, 29, 277, 286-87.

71. Cf. Henry, *I am the Truth*, 12-52. Ken Howard argues that because of the Trinity and the incarnation, Christians ought to admit their reliance on paradoxical mystery and allow it to deepen their relationship to the divine (Howard, *Paradoxy*, 138-62). See also, Kierkegaard, *Philosophical Fragments*, 13-18; Pojman, *The Logic of Subjectivity*, 8, 56-57, 121-22; and Evans, *Kierkegaard's*, 148, 212.

72. According to McLaren, this experiential mysticism will eventually be the preeminent authority for religious and socio-political issues (*AIFA*, 267; McLaren, foreword to *Solus Jesus*, xvii), especially as Christian faith returns to ancient and medieval mystical practices (*AIFA*, 201-204; *NKOC* §13, 167). See also, McLaren, "Spiritual Formation in a Postmodern Context," 183-89.

an acceptance of everyday mystery, as well as miracles, without becoming a religious eccentric.[73] Both rationality and spiritualism are necessary parts of reality (*AIFA*, 201-204); but to connect with the divine personally, believers need a mystic's mindset. "The scandalous truth, known by mystics throughout history and affirmed in the pages of our sacred texts, is that when we connect with God, it is as if we are plugging our souls into a pure current of high-voltage joy. The joy that surprised me under the stars in my teens was exactly what the ancient psalmist knew (16:11), that God is a joyful being" (*NS* §8, 66). "More and more of us are imagining a wild theology that arises under the stars and planets" (*GI*, xv). McLaren even argues that spiritualists have an awareness of God's glory in every aspect of creation (*FFR* §1, 29), meaning mystics, visionaries, prophets, and poets are better able to enter the "non-prose world" of religious faith than others (*GO* §9, 146). Naturally, from mysticism comes a sense of cosmic interconnectedness.

6.2.3 Cosmic Anthropology

With Kierkegaard, the problem for McLaren was not the dual natures of Christ but, rather, how humans could relate to such a paradoxical Being.[74] He infers that God simply did not design humans to intellectualize the divine. "Who do we think we are—we small creatures with three-pound brains, a few limited senses, and life spans barely long enough to get to know our neighborhood, much less the planet, and much less the galaxy, and much less the universe, and much less still its creator!" (*FFS* §7, 146). This tension intensifies, however, since McLaren also asserts that humanity is supposed to represent God (*SA*, 7) and his good character (*WMRBW*, 19), having been created to live in harmony with the rest of creation (*GI*, 59-79; *NS* §7, 57; *JMBM* §12, 103).

McLaren initially derives his anthropology from Genesis where he concludes that "the true essence of humanity is to be in the true image of God" (*GO* §2, 72n33). Nonetheless, the creation accounts also indicate that humanity is interconnected to the universe (*AIFA*, 50), being "made from common soil" (*WMRBW*, 7).[75] This cosmic anthropology, which McLaren labels "nonlocalism" (*AIFA*, 215-16), indicates that humans are not any more special than any other species. "Personally, I find myself emphasizing humanity as *part of* creation, not *above* it" (cf. *AMP* §12, 194-95; italics

---

73. See also, McLaren, "An Interview with Brian McLaren," interview by Joshua Graves. Cf. Pless, "Contemporary Spirituality," 347-63; and Rhodes, "The Maze of Mysticism," 6-8.

74. Dawe, *The Form of a Servant*, 157; Law, *Kierkegaard's Kenotic Christology*, 269-70; Walsh, *Kierkegaard*, 114-15, 117, 131.

75. McLaren writes, "The Bible could not link the story of life to the story of the earth any more intimately than is implied in God's creation of Adam out of *adamh*—the dust of the earth" (*AIFA*, 78). The phrase "cosmic anthropology" here originates from the Apostle Paul's own conception of human nature as having been created good and having been elevated through the incarnation (see Isaak, *New Testament Theology*, 88), as well as Sanford Schwartz's analysis of *Out of the Silent Planet* by C. S. Lewis, who emphasizes humanity's ability to misapply and transcend rationality simultaneously when connecting to transcendental Truth (Schwartz, "Cosmic Anthropology," 523-56).

in original).⁷⁶ McLaren confidently concludes that God loves all humans without any national or religious preferences (*JMBM* §12, 103; cf. *SA*, 13-14). "Whatever our religion or race or marital status, whatever our nationality or culture. . .we *all* bear God's image, no exceptions" (*WMRBW*, 8; ellipses and italics in original).⁷⁷ Subsequently, he identifies two "essential truths" about human nature: its goodness and its cosmic unity.

First, McLaren highlights the Bible's depiction of humans as "very good." He writes, "Along with all our fellow creatures, we were created with a primal, essential goodness that our Creator appreciates and celebrates" (*WMRBW*, 8).⁷⁸ Therefore, human nature is not reducible simply to being evil and damnable (*JMBM* §28, 260; *SA*, 13). Second, since God enjoys his creation, he intimately interacts with every*one* and every*thing* in creation (*SMJ* §4, 26-27).⁷⁹ Even the *imago Dei* suggests that humans are "a small imitation or echo" of God as caretakers of the earth, being interconnected to the universe in one cosmic relationship (*WMRBW*, 8). In fact, humanity exists to exercise solidarity with all life wherever it is found (*JMBM* §12, 110-11). What is most important is that the "image of God" represents a need for humans to have a loving relationship with the divine, with each other, and with creation. At the very least, being God's representative indicates that humans should "reflect the goodness, creativity, and freedom of God . . . [it] evokes the idea of God's kingship, with humans having the responsibility to be agents of God's kingship in their care for the earth" (*SMJ* §4, 27).⁸⁰

As divine ambassadors, McLaren insists that humans need to imitate their Creator's incarnational servanthood. In the case of Christians, Jesus' nonviolent call for the revolutionary defeat of social and institutional evils (§7.4) must also be the call of believers who are united to everything in creation (*WMRBW*, 17-18, 80, 88, 137). McLaren remarks,

76. This statement appears to contradict McLaren elsewhere when he writes, "Yes, people matter even more [than plants and animals], but it's not a matter of either/or; it's a matter of degree in a realm where everything that is good matters—where everything God made matters" (*GO* §16, 238). It is likely that McLaren views humans and (for example) wild animals as *ontologically* equal, both being good creations of a good God, but not *spiritually* equal, since only humans can represent the divine. Thus, McLaren argues that the greatest implication of his anthropology is on how people view life, "including, but not limited to, unborn human life, aged human life, human life under oppression and damaged by poverty" (*AIFA*, 265). He merely seeks to equalize all of God's creation in order to eliminate the tendency to exploit and misuse creation on the basis of human superiority (cf. *EMC* §17, 137), what he labels a "doctrine of dominion" that will result in "geocide," the mass destruction of the earth (*GSM*, 88).

77. Regarding sexism in particular, the story of Adam and Eve's creation indicates to McLaren that males and females are equal in value and authority. Thus, granting one sex dominance inside the church or outside in the world counters the biblical trajectory toward solidarity and harmony (*JMBM* §12, 104). See also, Nicole, "Biblical Egalitarianism," 4.

78. Interestingly, McLaren understands the adverbial modifier "very" to confirm his epistemology regarding value judgements. "Even the idea of 'very' applied to 'good' suggests a world marked not by absolute perfection, but by relative goodness" (*NKOCY* §5, 47).

79. Cf. Bouma-Prediger, "Yearning for Home," 188.

80. For a defense of humans as divine vice regents, see Walton, *Genesis 1 as Ancient Cosmology*, 74-86, 175-78 and Batto, *In the Beginning*, 96-138.

> We have learned that we are all interconnected ecologically. . . .We are learning how we are interconnected economically. . . .We are learning how we are interconnected politically. . . .To live in our world today means to think globally, and thinking globally requires addressing bigger problems that involve bigger time frames. This, then, is the way we as Christians must learn to think, simply because of the Incarnation. . . .It says that caring means entering and feeling solidarity with the problems of our world, so that "their" problems are our problems, too. . .out of faithfulness to Christ, whose solidarity with this sinful world brought its salvation. (*COOS1* §11, 148-49)

McLaren's interpretation of Genesis enhances this conviction, suggesting that God created everything so that "man would live in a network of relationships" (*SWFOI* §7, 51). With this understanding, a believer's new identity in Christ means being "more fully in solidarity with our neighbors everywhere" (*JMBM* §23, 219; cf. 138n8), which should promote alleviating the suffering of others through social, political, ecological, and economic transformation.[81] As David Law summarizes, "We are true followers of Christ not when we construct clever theories that eliminate the tension of the Christian faith, but when we take up our cross and follow him."[82] Thus, McLaren expands his anthropology to include a worldwide perspective concomitant with the globalization of the twenty-first century, which ultimately results in a bold assertion by McLaren that "*God is not enough*" (*SWFOI* §7, 52; italics in original), meaning God wants humanity to establish an empowering relationship as co-creators of the created order.[83]

6.2.3.1 Co-Creators with the Divine

For McLaren, the purpose of the incarnation was to bring justice, peace, and joy to the world (*GO* §1, 57) by creating a new humanity (a "new Genesis") who will liberate the poor and oppressed (a "new Exodus") from the evils created by the old humanity (*NKOCY* §13, 130-32; cf. *SMJ* §4, 31; §12, 100-1). He concludes, Jesus "truly is the logos that reveals the heart of God and the ultimate inner logic by which the universe arcs toward justice and peace" (*JMBM* §18, 160). Nevertheless, as divine image bearers, humanity now has the burden of establishing these same ideals in their own lives

---

81. McLaren writes, "From the emerging viewpoint, God's concern is more holistic or integral, seeing individual and society, soul and body, life and afterlife, humanity and the rest of creation as being inseparably related" (*EMC* §10, 81). Cf. Kelly "Solidarity," 44-64 and Pattyn, "The Emotional Boundaries," 101-8.

82. Law, *Kierkegaard's Kenotic Christology*, 287.

83. According to McLaren, globalization suggests humans identifying as a united *species* rather than religio-ethnic or nationalistic identities. For him, the notion of physical borders will soon dissipate just as the internet has eliminated conceptual borders in religion. Thus, globalization makes people more aware of the interrelatedness of all humans and how each individual impacts the lives of others across the globe (*AIFA*, 138-41).

(*FFR* §5, 108-19).[84] Just as God creatively transforms people today (*GO* §20, 292-93), McLaren believes God designed humanity to be "apprentice artists, co-creators" of the world (cf. *SWFOI* §8, 57-58; §Reader's Guide, 298n10). "We're masterpieces in progress, so creation is continuing in us. Right now!. . ..it's all about creation, from beginning to ending" (*SWFOI* §8, 63). With Genesis as the beginning of humanity's "true story," all of human history depicts creation as a present reality in people's lives. Here, God acts as a master artist while humans are his co-creators of future possibilities.[85] Thus, humanity's ultimate *telos* is to co-establish the kingdom of God on earth (§7.4.2), joining the divine in bringing light to the rest of the world (*FOWA* §18, 172). He wants to see humanity move from spreading violence to "co-conspiring only beauty" (*TSS*, 35). The result is an emphasis on divine love and goodness as the quintessential characteristics of God.

6.2.4 Divine Love and Goodness

Stemming directly from McLaren's solidarity Christology, the final implication is a dogged belief that God's goodness (*complacentia*) is so overwhelming that it exceeds comprehension (*LWWAT* §Intro, xi). For McLaren, this goodness is important because it affects how people will practice their faith. "Vastly different ways of living can be promoted under the name 'Christianity.' Jesus can be a victim of identity theft, and people can say and do things with and in his name that he would never ever do" (*NKOCY* §12, 119).[86] Too many Christians today conceptualize Jesus as "more wolf of God than lamb of God," whose mission is to defend only those whose doctrine is "correct" while expressing hostility to everyone else (*JMBM* §16, 135).[87] However, Christ's

---

84. McLaren argues that the most profound way humans can represent God is not intellectually but creatively where humanity creates cultures that are "a spring of pure water gushing into the world" concurrent with God's ideals for the world (*CIEC*, 240). "The purpose of existence isn't money or power . . . [it is] to participate in the goodness and beauty and aliveness of creation. And so we join the Creator in good and fruitful work" (*SA*, 10).

85. This description is similar to Darrel Falk's admonition that Christians should avoid an engineering model for describing God, proposing that they stop using the term "Designer." Instead, Falk asserts that deity's role in creation resembles an artist who subtly guides brush strokes to produce a painting (Falk, *Coming to Peace with Science*, 13-15). Significantly, McLaren's remarks also indicate his growing appreciation for open theism (*BMF*, 299-300).

86. McLaren explains further, "If our *concept of God* is nonviolent, we will be transformed into that nonviolent image, whether or not that concept is true. We might say that whatever our God is like, whether or not our God exists, our God is still powerful because our image of God transforms us. Like an image in a mirror, our God concept reflects back to us the image of what we aspire to become" (*GSM*, 94; italics in original).

87. For McLaren, many Christian churches adhere to a theology that would change the Bible (if they could) to read: "For God hated the world so much that he sent his only Son, so that whoever believes in him could be removed from the world, so he can save the believers and go ahead and damn the world, which he really hates. . .For God sent his Son into the world to condemn the world and to save the church" (McLaren, "Ruining Your Ministry for Good," 53-54; ellipses in original).

central definition of deity was that "God is Love" (*AIFA*, 171), and Jesus himself was "the embodiment of love."[88] In fact, more than any other attribute, God is "triune love" (*GO* §12, 195), who will judge humanity "with love in his eyes" (*CIEC*, 236).[89] "To me, God means holy, loving presence, connection and flow, deep encounter and creativity, and the very human aliveness dancing in Christ" (*GI*, 186).

According to McLaren, Jesus' "unflinching emphasis" was on practicing an ethic of love, which should take priority over everything else (*GSM*, 42-44). Hence, what is important today is a faith that focuses on what Jesus declared most imperative (*CIEC*, 256): the premise that God is "completely good, all the time" (*SWFOI* §12, 89), who commands his followers to love others (*JMBM* §16, 143).[90] Significantly, McLaren describes "spirituality" and "religion" as synonyms for "love," defining all three terms as "seeking vital connection" with God and others. The implication is that despite the diversity of religious traditions, faith in God should lovingly reconnect people in solidarity (*NS* §2, 14-15). Philosophically, from McLaren's view, both Christ's divinity and love constitute an indivisible set of "symmetrical identicals," meaning that whatever is true of love must be true of deity, as well. Thus, McLaren claims he has not only encountered God through an overwhelming sense of love, but humans are also able to encounter the divine through acts of love toward each other (*FFR* §1, 39-40; §5, 115). McLaren stresses an *actus fidei* (the "actualization of faith") where proper solidarity translates to an existential appropriation and outward actualization of divine love. "This logos of love reveals to us the true heart of God and therefore the true hidden logic and meaning of the universe" (*JMBM* §16, 143).

These conceptions, however, are not meant to discard the notion of Jesus being a subversive revolutionary (§7.2.2.1).[91] In fact, McLaren contrasts his current view, what he labels "God 5.0," with an earlier conception ("God 2.0") that defined deity as overly sentimental (*GSM*, 98). Arguing that God is not "the divine doting Auntie in Heaven, full of sweetness and smiles," McLaren cautions his readers from turning God into a mascot who tolerates humanity's violence and racism without judgment (*LWWAT* §Intro, xiii). Hence, he does not worship a "teddy-bear" Jesus, but McLaren does believe God wants universal harmony (*GSM*, 101-4). Naturally, because of his adherence to *complacentia*, McLaren reenvisions the notion of divine election.

---

88. McLaren, "'Instead of Ruling,'" 227. Cf. Woodcock, *Hell*, 489-518.

89. Not surprisingly, McLaren's passion for God's love results in poetic imagery: "[God is] an essential goodness, an inexpressible beauty, a light beyond all seeing, an infinite song" (*SWFOI* §6, 39-40), and "a master artist and lover" (*MRTYR* §7, 63). Elsewhere, he describes God as "the fine wine of justice, joy, and peace; the uncontained wind of creativity, comfort, and liberation; the living water of holiness, beauty, and love" (*NS* §2, 18).

90. Akin to his discussion on the "big" questions in apologetics, McLaren describes Christianity's central value as loving God and loving people. Other discussions can become unnecessary distractions that hinder a relationship with the divine (*GO* §12, 184-85). Cf. Penner and Barnes, *A New Kind of Conversation*, 151.

91. See also, McLaren, "Beyond Fire and Brimstone," 16.

6.2.4.1 Divine Election

A recurring theme throughout McLaren's literature is his rejection of predestination and theistic determinism (*GO* §12, 186-88; *SMJ* §19, 173), viewing divine election in missional terms, instead (*JMBM* §17, 151). He explains, "We should understand that God doesn't bless some to the exclusion of others, but rather God blesses some for the benefit of others. So, being blessed isn't simply a privilege: it's a responsibility."[92] Instead of obtaining privilege and status, God elects his chosen specifically to better the world.[93] Embracing the "priesthood of all believers," McLaren then argues that Christians must direct their attention to bearing the burdens of others through compassion and love (*MRTYR* §20, 154; *NS* §15, 132-34). Moreover, Christians are not just priests; they are, in fact, Christ on earth because of God's "unification and interpenetration" with humanity (*FOWA* §10, 92).[94] God's radical inclusiveness means that he consecrates "insiders" in order to bless "outsiders" (*MRTYR* §7, 63).[95]

For McLaren, blessing others is the entire point of Christian faith, and its greatest heresy is the "individualistic, narcissistic, and nationalistic understanding of the gospel" that claims exclusive incentives for only a chosen few.[96] However, to appropriate Christ's incarnation is also to unite with all people (*JMBM* §8, 69-70n5). Thus, McLaren imagines that an all-loving father would not only want a relationship with his children, but he would also want his children to have a relationship with each other (*FFR* §4, 90). With this rationale in mind, McLaren constructs a more inclusive approach to faith in hopes of building a better eschatological future for humanity, something he calls "evotheology" (*GI*, 183-201).

6.3 MCLAREN AND *STAR TREK* ESCHATOLOGY

Interestingly, the television and film series, *Star Trek*, plays a significant role in understanding McLaren's eschatology.[97] In short, McLaren is an avid *Star Trek* fan, as evi-

---

92. McLaren, "TPC Interviews," 13. See also, McLaren, "Emerging Values," 34-39.

93. McLaren, "Ruining Your Ministry for Good," 57; ellipses in original.

94. McLaren elaborates, "The Holy Spirit is God-in-us or God-upon-us or God-among-us everywhere and anywhere" (*JMBM* §17, 150).

95. Or, as McLaren articulates it, "Some of us for all of us" (*TSS*, 124). In essence, the church's purpose is to be God's instrument for blessing others by establishing God's kingdom on earth (McLaren, "Underneath the Cosmetics").

96. McLaren, "Practicing and Loving Diversity," 30. See also, McLaren, "Chosen for What?," 59-60; "A Memo on the Arc of the Universe," 57.

97. As a pop-culture phenomenon established in 1966, *Star Trek* has spawned (to date) eight television series (spanning over three decades of on-air production with a few more forthcoming series rumored), countless novels, several academic books, and thirteen movies. In addition to being the inspiration for numerous technological inventions, *Star Trek* was a groundbreaker for civil rights (by featuring a prominent African-American female lead), as well as for cultural collaboration (by having a Japanese helmsman and a Russian navigator as main characters during the Cold War), and sexual orientation acceptance (by displaying transgendered and non-gendered species, as well as

denced by his numerous references to the show (e.g., *CIEC*, 181; *COOS1* §11, 156-57). Philosophically, what separates *Star Trek* from other science-fiction operas, such as *Star Wars*, *Doctor Who*, *Battlestar Galactica*, or *The Twilight Zone*, is that it specifically appeals to the fundamental virtuousness of humanity. Like other shows, *Star Trek* imagines complex scenarios that delve into deep philosophical and ethical questions, but with one caveat. *Star Trek* imagines how a fully enlightened humanity, having united to eradicate war, poverty, disease, racism, and religious tension, could use science, technology, and solidarity to promote social justice and equality.[98] In this vision of the future, humans have become the quintessential peace-makers, explorers, and cultural unifiers of the galaxy.[99] Here, McLaren likens the original *Star Trek* to modernized man, embodied in the character Spock and his devotion to pure logic. *Star Trek: The Next Generation*, on the other hand, reflects the shift into postmodernity where the character, Data, reincorporates a sense of humanity to supplement unbalanced rationalism (*AMP* §17, 260-61).[100] As McLaren expounds, "When we read or watch . . . *Star Trek* . . ., we don't think the writers and filmmakers are trying to predict the future. No, we understand they are really talking about the present, and they are doing so in hopes of changing the future" (*NKOCY* §12, 123).

Furthermore, *Star Trek* cinematically depicts McLaren's optimistic eschatology. "I enjoy pondering the vision of the future unfolded in the series. . . . Don't you think it is time to embrace an eschatology that will . . . launch us through the clouds and maybe even to the stars?" (*COOS1* §11, 156). For him, the eschaton is about living Jesus' kingdom ideals today, not escaping a doomed planet (*AMP* §3, 47; *EMC* §1, 4). Echoing Jürgen Moltmann, McLaren's "eschatology of hope" believes that God is drawing humanity toward himself, located in a much better future (*COOS1* §11, 152).[101] Like Moltmann, McLaren promotes the kind of human solidary that would

---

asexual and homosexual relationships).

98. Cf. Neece, *The Gospel According to Star Trek*, 60-67. As Captain Jean-Luc Picard (*Patrick Stewart*) explained in one film, "The economics of the future are somewhat different. You see, money doesn't exist in the twenty-fourth century. . . . The acquisition of wealth is no longer the driving force in our lives. We work to better ourselves and the rest of humanity" (*Star Trek: First Contact*, 50:05-50:30). Interestingly, McLaren echoes these same thoughts when he describes the kingdom of God as a "commonwealth" or an "alternative economy" of God, which involves fixing the world at the individual and institutional levels (*WMRBW*, 22). He writes elsewhere, "Becoming fully human involves defecting from mimetic rivalry" (*TSS*, 170).

99. For details, see Hanley, *The Metaphysics of Star Trek*; Barad and Robertson, *The Ethics of Star Trek*; Eberl and Decker, *Star Trek and Philosophy*; and Decker and Eberl, *The Ultimate Star Trek and Philosophy*.

100. McLaren, "Honey, I Woke Up in a Different Universe!," 35-46. The influence of *Star Trek* on similar theologians and philosophers is visible in Grenz, "Star Trek and the Next Generation," 24-32; "*Star Trek* and the Postmodern Generation," 1-10; and Kimball, *The Emerging Church*, 229-30.

101. Cf. Neece, *The Gospel According to Star Trek*, 33-39. McLaren cites Moltmann for his "new kind of eschatology," characterizing it as one of "hope, anticipation, and participation" (*NKOCY* §18, 206). In line with his prophetic action, McLaren argues, "Prophets in the Bible have a fascinating role as custodians of the best hopes, desires, and dreams of their society. They challenge people to act in

actualize God's dreams of justice, liberation, and peace (*AMP* §15, 229-30).[102] With John Dominic Crossan and N. T. Wright, McLaren's eschatology imagines people living as though the kingdom were real while collaborating to ensure it becomes real for others (*COOS1* §11, 156).[103] His goal is to transcend the compulsive uniformity of conventional paradigms by inspiring a global network of subversives who will plot to spread love and hope throughout the world.[104]

6.4 CONCLUSION

What is most evident is that McLaren begins his philosophy of religion with a deeply-held commitment to orthodox Christology, embracing trinitarian, Chalcedonian, and kenotic beliefs about the incarnation. The result is a heightened sense of Christ's divinity and subsequent solidarity with the created order. McLaren theorizes that if the central dogmas of Christianity are paradoxes, then mystery and perplexity must necessarily permeate reality. Therefore, every assertion in McLaren's religio-philosophy is a consequence of the incarnational paradox where 1) Christianity is necessarily a *faith*-based religion; 2) the incarnation unifies all of creation; and 3) God's *complacentia* requires imitation through humility and benevolence. The consequence of this interconnectedness is a fundamental rejection of Western spirituality's distinction between the sacred and the profane.[105] For McLaren, there is no such distinction (*JMBM* §17, 151); and so long as the church remains impervious to change, it will never progress for the better. Having been ineffective at making Christ-like disciples, however, McLaren contends that institutional Christianity needs deconstructing in order to identify both its problem and its possible solution.

---

ways consistent with those hopes" (*WMRBW*, 64). Thus, "People need a vision of a good future. Our imagination needs images that celebrate peace, justice, and wholeness towards which our dismal, conflicted, polluted, and fragmented world is moving" (*AMP* §15, 229).

102. See Moltmann, *Theology of Hope*, esp. 325-29. Pursuing what he labels as an "ethic of anticipation," McLaren's central message seeks "to have our present way of life shaped by our vision of God's desired future" (*NKOCY* §18, 200; italics in original). Stated differently, he asks, "What kind of world does God wish our world to be, and how can we see that world become more and more real?" (McLaren, "Religious Right or Wrong?," 10).

103. See Crossan, "Jesus and the Challenge," 105-52 and Wright, *Surprised by Hope*, 189-232, 255-89. McLaren states that Wright's work is a major influence on his eschatology (cf. *LWWAT* §Intro, xv, 192; *NKOCY* §18, 284n9; *SMJ* §2, 252nn2-3), and he uses the same terminology as Crossan when labeling his vision a "participatory eschatology" (*NKOCY* §18, 200).

104. McLaren, foreword to *A Generous Community*, vii-ix; "Unterror Cells," 114.

105. Cf. Durkheim, *The Elementary Forms of Religious Life*, 35-41.

7

McLaren's Deconstructive Rationale

7.0 INTRODUCTION

From Brian McLaren's pursuit of an authentic Christianity (chapter 6) came the search for Jesus' original gospel message (*JP* §Intro, 18). As he relates, "The meaning-rich stories of what Jesus said and did form the unique heart of Christian faith that must always pulse within us" (*GSM*, 11). However, McLaren feels he must first deconstruct institutional Christianity in order to identify the gospel. The thesis of this chapter is that McLaren's deconstruction emphasizes the imperial context of Jesus' ministry. By applying an aesthetic hermeneutic to his focus on the canonical Gospels, McLaren infers that institutional Christianity has supplanted Jesus' message with Neoplatonic philosophy. Four areas will support this thesis: 1) McLaren's view of the Greco-Roman (meta)narrative; 2) Jewish beliefs about the kingdom of God; 3) McLaren's artistic reading of Scripture; and 4) the subversive nature of Jesus' gospel. McLaren begins his deconstructive process by first examining the institutional church.

7.1 DECONSTRUCTING INSTITUTIONAL CHRISTIANITY

As an introduction to postmodern thought (*AIFA*, 240), deconstructionism questions traditional assumptions by disassembling their cultural underpinnings. It is a process of stripping away socio-political influences to reigning paradigms so that a better one can emerge in its place. McLaren clarifies that deconstruction is not *destruction*; rather, it is a "careful and loving attention to the [evolutionary] construction of ideas, beliefs, systems, values, and cultures" (*NKOCY* §6, 55). For him, deconstructing Christianity revealed its Neoplatonic influences.[1]

7.1.1 Neoplatonism and Ontotheology

McLaren launches his investigation by questioning whether "Greco-Roman philosophical categories" should be normative today (*JMBM* §16, 138), inferring it was the "love affair with Greek philosophy" that originally obscured Jesus' gospel message (*SMJ* §App. 1, 221–22). Although early apologists had to engage with Greek philosophy, McLaren believes they mistakenly transplanted Jesus' Jewish message into foreign soil, which twisted its original intention (*LWWAT* §28, 168–69; *NKOCY* §18, 193–94; *SWFOI* §10, 72–74).[2] "[Christianity] unwittingly traded its true heritage through Jesus from Judaism for an alien heritage drawn from Greek philosophy and Roman politics" (*NKOCY* §4, 41).[3] What eventually defined Christianity was its Neoplatonic focus on abstract Ideals, changing the earthly emphasis of Judaism into a Gentile concern for the afterlife (*LWWAT* §28, 168–69). McLaren writes, "This [Neoplatonic] mind-set would predispose readers of the Gospels to interpret Jesus's message in light of timeless abstractions and miss the historically particular references to contemporary political realities and social movements."[4] The result became "ontotheology," which conceives of deity in Greek classifications of "being," transforming the biblical God into a philosophical *causa sui*.[5] Ontotheology focuses primarily on what is supposedly intrinsic to personhood (*EMC* §13, 104).[6]

---

1. See *AIFA*, 87–90; *FOWA* §11, 108; *GO* §3, 83; *GSM*, 114–18; *LWWAT* §7, 43; §17, 105–6; and McLaren, "Everything Old Is New Again," 23–24. McLaren explains further, "Deconstruction is disassembling anything that has acquired a pat and patent set of meanings for the purpose of reassembling in new ways. It means allowing the interpretation of a familiar text, image, or experience to unravel and become unstable so that new insights and old revelations can be found and reclaimed" (*AIFA*, 95). For details, see Derrida, *Deconstruction in a Nutshell*, esp. 31–48.

2. For McLaren, the ancient church over utilized Greek philosophy to make Christianity more respectable, which became weaponized for imperialistic agendas (*SA*, 332; *WMRBW*, 227). He does recognize, however, that the Trinity is also the result of Greek philosophy (*GO* §2, 76). For details, see Dillon, "Logos and Trinity," 1–13; Gaston, "The Influence of Platonism," 573–80; and Olson, *The Story of Christian Theology*, 36, 54–67, 80, 85–98, 103–6, 174–93.

3. See also, *GO* §19, 280–81; *NKOC* §14, 184–85; *NKOCY* §18, 193–94. In a personal interview, McLaren once remarked, "I think so many of the problems we have now flow from that Platonic world where essences are higher and existence is lower" (McLaren, interviewed by Darren M. Slade, Denver, CO, May 14, 2015). Cf. Wright, *Surprised by Hope*, 25; Moltmann, *The Coming of God*, 58–65; Schwarz, *Eschatology*, 272–80; and Pattison, *God and Being*, 17–55.

4. McLaren, "The Secret Message of Jesus," 20. For McLaren, Neoplatonism has since conditioned Christianity to adopt a perpetual dualism that continues today: sacred versus profane; spiritual versus carnal; conservative versus liberal; etc. (*NKOCY* §4, 37–39; *SWFOI* §10, 73).

5. For the relationship between deconstruction and ontotheology, see Ruf, *Religion* and Ingraffia, *Postmodern Theory*, 101–22, 226.

6. See also, Gschwandtner, *Postmodern Apologetics?*, 21, 29, 237–41 and Simmons and Benson, *The New Phenomenology*, 89–98. The term "ontotheology" dates to Martin Heidegger's 1936

Charles Davis illuminates this Hellenizing of Christian faith, "Ontotheology is the attempt to translate the content of the Christian myth into the theoretical concepts and statements of metaphysical philosophy. . . .It makes knowledge not love foundational."[7] Here, ontotheology signifies a "presupposition that there is an analogy of being between our philosophical ideas about (the structures of) the world as such and God as its absolute ground."[8] As Merold Westphal defines it, "Each [form of ontotheology] puts its God, whether it be the Unmoved Mover, or Nature, or Spirit, or the Market to work as the keystone of a metaphysical theory designed to render the whole of reality intelligible to philosophical reflection."[9] Consequently, theology is now fixated on universal meaning and a "metaphysics of presence" that presumes God has imbued religion with monosemous, static qualities.[10] George Pattison clarifies,

> Metaphysical thinking is thinking that offers an account of all that is and does so by tracing this 'all' back to its most basic ground, to what makes it be what and as it is, its first cause, or ultimate reason or ratio. This means that it can be described as onto- . . . because it views the world with regard to its being, theo- . . . because it deals with the ultimate cause of the world, and 'logical' because it offers an account or discourse . . . of its subject matter.[11]

Accordingly, God becomes the "transcendental signified," who "*functions* as the purported locus of truth that is supposed to stabilize all meaningful words" about the divine.[12] For postmodernists, however, ontotheology is what created the arrogance of modernity, which in turn perpetuated a desire to maintain Neoplatonic forms of absolutist, imperial Christendom.[13]

---

lectures on Friedrich Schelling. See Heidegger, *Identity and Difference*, 42–74; Hemming, "Nihilism," 95; and Gardner, "Sartre," 247–71.

7. Davis, *What Is Living*, 60–61. Heidegger once explained, "When metaphysics thinks of beings with respect to the ground that is common to beings as such, then it is logic as onto-logic. When metaphysics thinks of beings as such as a whole, that is, with respect to the highest being which accounts for everything, then it is logic as theo-logic" (Heidegger, *Identity and Difference*, 70–71).

8. Jonkers, "God in France," 6. According to Heidegger, Western philosophy absorbed Platonism's preoccupation with articulating the essence of "being," which became the defining presumption of later theology and apologetics (see Pattison, *God and Being*, 17–55 and Heidegger, *Identity and Difference*, 42–74).

9. Westphal, *Transcendence and Self-Transcendence*, 18.

10. See Heidegger, "Kant's Thesis about Being," 340; Derrida, *Of Grammatology*, 47–70; and Gschwandtner, *Postmodern Apologetics?*, 21. Cf. Thiselton, *New Horizons in Hermeneutics*, 83; Grenz, *A Primer on Postmodernism*, 138–50; and Erickson, *Postmodernizing the Faith*, 86.

11. Pattison, *God and Being*, 5.

12. Taylor, *Erring*, 105; italics in original. Cf. Alessi, "L'essere e la croce," 53–111 and Simmons and Benson, *The New Phenomenology*, 142.

13. Cf. Baron, "The Theology of Gerald O'Collins," 18; Prickett, *Words and The Word*, 4–36; Auerbach, *Mimesis*, 143–73; Westphal, *Transcendence and Self-Transcendence*, 15–90; and Erickson, *Postmodernizing the Faith*, 107, 127–44. As Christina Gschwandtner explains, "Onto-theology is characterized by calculative and representational thinking that eliminates God's transcendence, [and] puts the divine at the disposal of human knowledge" (Gschwandtner, *Postmodern Apologetics?*, 239).

7.1.2 *Imperium Christianum*

According to McLaren, the influence of Neoplatonism allowed the Roman Empire to exploit Christianity, starting with the emperor Constantine (ca. AD 285–337), who transformed the church into a body politic that spread through violence and coercion (*SMJ* §17, 153–54).[14] Eventually, Romanized Christian clergy obtained imperial support by enforcing loyalty to their emerging theocratic empire in the form of dogmatic creeds. This collusion now meant the near-total domestication and imperialization of Jesus' gospel, resulting in tens of thousands of murders (cf. *JMBM* §10, 82–84; §11, 90–94).[15] McLaren summarizes his general viewpoint:

> From Constantine to Columbus to the other Conquistadors to the Colonizers to the present, we have mixed authentically Christian elements of love, joy, peace, and reconciliation with strictly imperial elements of superiority, conquest, domination, and hostility. We have created a new religion with an identity far different from the one proclaimed and embodied by Jesus in Galilee, or by James and Peter in Jerusalem, or by Paul around the Mediterranean, or by the Christian scholars of the second and third centuries. In other words, what we call Christianity today has a history, and this history reveals it as a Roman, imperial version of Christianity. (*JMBM* §10, 84)

In time, Christianity became "Christendom," a codified belief system of social control (*NKOCY* §1, 11–12) where "saving souls" became, wittingly or unwittingly, camouflage for colonizing other people groups (*GSM*, 9).[16] The most long-lasting consequence was Christendom's transformation of believers into "inquisition-aholics."[17]

Merold Westphal concurs, "Perhaps onto-theology consists in the pride that refuses to accept the limits of human knowledge" (Westphal, *Overcoming Onto-Theology*, 7).

14. Cox, *The Future of Faith*, 1–20. Here, McLaren defines "violence" as "force with the intent of inflicting injury, damage, or death" (McLaren, "Is God Violent?," 16). He calls this embrace of violence a "dysfunctional marriage" between the kingdom of God and imperial Rome (*GSM*, 76). In discussing Constantine's supposed conversion to Christianity, McLaren writes, "It would be better said that Constantine converted Christianity to the values and mission of the Roman Empire than to say the reverse" (*GSM*, 243n9; cf. *SMJ* §App. 1, 222). "It's nightmarish to consider this: that the very language of 'kingdom of God' would eventually be co-opted by leaders of the failing Roman regime and their successors to legitimize their use of violence in the name of Jesus Christ" (*SMJ* §17, 154). For McLaren, at this stage in church history, it was no longer viable for theologians to challenge imperial practices; hence, they redirected their focus to abstract esoterica, instead (*SMJ* §App. 1, 222).

15. McLaren defines "imperialism" as the imposition of cultural, geographical, and economical structures to maintain inequality and subordination over other people (*AIFA*, 58–59; *JMBM* §10, 84–85n5). He argues that while the ecumenical creeds were necessary, the church has subsequently created more unnecessary doctrines and creeds, hampering Christian faith by overloading it with excessive dogmas. This doctrinal inflation makes Christianity less able to progress or adjust to changing cultures and information (*MRTYR* §2, 33).

16. Cf. Nietzsche, *Thus Spoke Zarathustra*, esp. 207–87; *The Gay Science*, esp. 178–97; *The Will to Power*; and Verduin, *The Reformers and Their Stepchildren*, esp. 21–62.

17. McLaren, foreword to *A Heretic's Guide to Eternity*, x. For McLaren, "Christendom" is "Roman-Imperial Christianity" (*JMBM* §10, 81–86; §11, 87–95; §12, 99n2). Also labelling it as

McLaren explains, "Religious gatekeepers gain one of humanity's greatest powers: to excommunicate or expel. In this way, belief-based systems centralize power and provide an easy way to test compliance with authorities: *will you recite the required beliefs?*" (*GSM*, 30; italics in original).

Sadly, church history reflects the worldly pattern of oppressed people ascending to a position of power only to reverse course and subjugate others (cf. *JMBM* §9, 74).[18] McLaren refers to this heresy-hunting as a story of "purification" and "scapegoating," which presumes that wickedness exists because of theological dissenters. Therefore, it is now necessary to purge or suppress heretics for the good of the world. "It's easy for inquisition-launchers to go on fault-finding missions; they have lots of practice and they're really good at it."[19] Naturally, McLaren wonders how the church so easily degenerated, and he concludes Greek philosophy is to blame.

7.1.3 The Greco-Roman (Meta)Narrative

McLaren implicitly questions why Christianity became a bastion of racism, slavery, and murder (*JMBM* §19, 168–70). For him, it was the "Greco-Roman narrative," a catchall term for the centuries-long tampering, redacting, and supplementing of Jesus' gospel message (§7.4) with colonialist agendas (cf. *GSM*, 11–12). This worldview victimized Jews, Muslims, indigenous peoples, and other Christians; and it continues today through American exceptionalism (§3.2.1.1).[20] To McLaren, it was Christendom's alien philosophy that established several inauthentic doctrines, such as original sin, which helped solidify the gospel's mutation.

"post-Christian," McLaren explains that the most prodigious failing of church history was its "official or unwritten alliance of church and state" (*GO* §4, 92n42).

18. McLaren, "Finding the Seventh Story," 124–25. Here, McLaren describes religious imperialism as "a system of Christian thought and practice that functions within (and often as a fractal of) the Roman Empire's prime model of domination, subordination, expansion, and assimilation" (*JMBM* §10, 85). Religious "colonialism" is similarly defined as possessing a mindset of conquest and subjugation where one group believes God has chosen them to rule over other groups (*JMBM* §11, 94), typically resulting in exporting and imposing a cultural version of the Euro-American "gospel" (*GO* §5, 106).

19. McLaren, foreword to *A Heretic's Guide to Eternity*, ix. Cf. McLaren, "Finding the Seventh Story," 125; "Conditions for the Great Religion Singularity," 40–49; Dixon, "Whatever Happened to Heresy?," 219–20; and "'Five by McLaren," 217–71.

20. McLaren, "'Instead of Ruling'—Prayers," 225; "Finding the Seventh Story," 128. In light of McLaren's discussion on "framing stories" (§4.3), it is appropriate to change his "Greco-Roman narrative" to a "Greco-Roman *meta*narrative." In fact, he actually labels it a "Greco-Roman *framing story*" in one instance (*NKOCY* §12, 126; emphasis added). Cf. McKnight, "Rebuilding the Faith from Scratch," 59–66.

7.1.3.1 *The Fall and Original Sin*

In McLaren's retelling, the Greco-Roman (meta)narrative begins with a fall into original sin (*FFS* §3, 87). Now, humanity is fated for eternal damnation unless it receives salvation. For McLaren, this narrative is obviously Platonic in origin since it clearly parallels Greek philosophy (*NKOCY* §13, 128; *SWFOI* §10, 72–74). Here, the storyline declares that people once existed in a state of perfection (i.e., Platonic Ideals), fell into a "cave of illusion," and now need rescuing from Hades.[21] This Creation-Fall-Redemption plotline, however, is *Greek*, not *Hebraic* and, therefore, was not the same belief held by Jesus himself (*NKOCY* §4, 33–45).[22]

Accordingly, concepts like human nature, original sin, and an ontological fall are Greek rather than Jewish, and therefore are not native to the Genesis story (*JMBM* §12, 110–11; *WMRBW*, 16, 19). As an artistic metaphor (§7.3.2), McLaren interprets the Garden of Eden as depicting humanity's penchant for trying to judge "good" and "evil." The Genesis message is that humanity often creates *more* iniquity by claiming to detect it in others.[23] By feasting on "the Tree of Aliveness," people can appropriate their *imago divina*, value creation, and further spread God's life-giving creative activity (cf. 5.2.3.1). By feeding from "the second tree," on the other hand, people reject partnering with God to heal the world (*WMRBW*, 8–10).[24]

D. A. Carson notes that Genesis's description of creation as "good" appears prior to the Fall, something he feels McLaren unjustifiably glosses over.[25] From McLaren's perspective, however, creation's goodness still remains intact (*SWFOI* §9, 76), particularly since Genesis does not indicate that humanity is forever engulfed in a sin nature (cf. *SMJ* §7, 54). While Christians should take sin seriously, they should not

---

21. Cf. Bernstein, *The Formation of Hell*, 21–49.

22. McLaren does admit that his reconstruction is reductionistic and, ironically, engages in the same dualism as Platonism. He also recognizes that both Greek and Hebrew thought were not monolithic; but he insists that the conventional plotline of Creation-Fall-Redemption is not original to Jesus (*NKOCY* §4, 263–64n1). Cf. Hengel, *Judaism and Hellenism*; *The "Hellenization" of Judaea*; and Olson, *The Story of Christian Theology*, 36, 54–67, 80, 85–98, 103–6, 174–93.

23. McLaren explains, "God sees everything as good, but we will accuse more and more things of being evil," and writes further, "If we humans start playing God and judging good and evil, how long will it take before we say this person or tribe is good and deserves to live, but that person or tribe is evil and deserves to die?" (*WMRBW*, 9). Statements like these do not indicate McLaren denies the existence of "evil." Rather, it is intended to eliminate what he perceives to be a "hostile identity" within humans that creates an artificial in-group/out-group combativeness among people. Instead of being lovers of peace, notions of "evil" oftentimes lead to opposing the well-being of others because of a shared belief in their inherent wickedness (see *JMBM* §7, 61–63).

24. Historically, the early desert mothers and fathers asserted that humanity's primary vice was judgmentalism while its ultimate virtue was compassion. These same hermits opposed moral absolutism and rejected the formation of theological systems and ideologies for the sake of living according to God's paradoxical kingdom ideals (see Schwarz, "What the Thunder Said," 139–57).

25. Carson, *Becoming Conversant*, 183–84. For the emphasis on creation as "good" in postmodern thought, see Bouma-Prediger, "Yearning for Home," 189–93. For McLaren's rejection of deterministic theodicies, see McLaren, "Faith Beyond All Answers."

over exaggerate its metaphysical effects on creation, which he believes is still good in God's eyes (*GO* §16, 234–35; *NKOCY* §5, 49–50). Adam's sin merely hindered the emergence of human potentiality (*FFR* §5, 109; *GO* §19, 282; *SA*, 25), thereby making all humans "disabled," not depraved (*AIFA*, 96–97). Besides, McLaren argues, Genesis reveals a patient and merciful God, who refuses to enact punishment simply for one couple's foolish and destructive choice. Though humans must live with the effects of sin, God does not disown or torture his creation because of it (*NKOCY* §5, 49–51).

Of course, to reject belief in original sin seems to imply Pelagianism.[26] Nevertheless, McLaren objects to this implication as a category error. He argues that Pelagianism is a position that makes sense only in the context of Neoplatonism and, since he is not working within that context, the term no longer applies (*BMF*, 14–15). Moreover, God's solidarity with creation pre-empts the problem of original sin because God has redeemed all of human history through the incarnation (cf. *WMRBW*, 249), divinizing everything in creation in the process (§6.1.1.5). Intertwined with the notion of original sin is also Neoplatonism's belief in a wrathful deity.

7.1.3.2 *The Myth of Redemptive Appeasement*

Walter Wink argues that the most archetypal plotline in imperial cultures, as early as the ancient Near East, is the "myth of redemptive violence," which suggests that people often conceive of deity with violent characteristics who will righteously vanquish "evil" from the world, which empires then exploit for colonialist agendas (cf. *GDT*).[27] According to McLaren, the problem is not so much a myth of redemptive violence; the problem is a myth of redemptive *appeasement*, which suggests that God's own wrath is what needs vanquishing. "Oppression theology and supremacist spirituality developed in the belief ecosystem of an angry God who needed appeasement in order to dispense grace . . . who welcomed the favored into religious institutions that accumulated and hoarded privilege and protected the status quo" (*GSM*, 196). As this myth proliferated, Christ's message mutated into salvation specifically from a wrathful deity (*NKOCY* §4, 43). McLaren quotes one associate, "In all the church services I attended, I only heard one sermon. . . . 'You are a sinner and you are going to hell. . . .Jesus might come back today, and if he does . . . you will burn forever in hell'" (*EMC*

---

26. Burson, *Brian McLaren in Focus*, 247; Hixson, *Getting the Gospel Wrong*, 223-251. McLaren states, "I am in no way denying sin (original, social, whatever) . . . rather I'm suggesting we try to avoid the damage that a distortion of the doctrine has done to our understanding of the goodness of original creation" (*GO* §16, 235). See esp., *JMBM* §13, 105–14.

27. As Walter Wink writes, "This myth of redemptive violence is the real myth of the modern world. It, and not Judaism or Christianity or Islam, is the dominant religion in our society today" (Wink, *The Powers That Be*, 42). McLaren further explains that the Roman Empire capitalized on this myth because its own prime directive was to "decisively crush any and all opposition to the emperor. Then, unified under the emperor's supreme will, the empire will defeat its enemies and punish its criminals so that all will experience prosperity, equity, and peace" (*EMC* §9, 84).

§3, 18–19). For McLaren, this myth of redemptive appeasement in no way reflects what is learned from the historical Jesus (cf. §7.4.2).

7.2 DECONSTRUCTING THE HISTORICAL JESUS

McLaren reasons that if conventional paradigms are, in fact, aligned with Christ, then surely they would create more Christ-like disciples.[28] What he discovered while disentangling Jesus from Anglo-American depictions (*JP* §Intro, 18; *NKOCY* §1, 6–7) was that the church obscured Jesus' teachings by forever merging him with Neoplatonism (*EMC* §28, 243; *SMJ* §11, 90). By the end of the second century, Jesus' original Jewish sect morphed into an anti-Semitic Gentile religion, abandoning Jesus' gospel in the process (*NKOCY* §16, 163–64; *SMJ* §App. 1, 221). "If I were a conspiracy theorist, I would write a book about how Christianity has successfully dethroned Jesus as Lord to such a degree that the 'Jesus' who is preached, pasted on bumper stickers, serenaded in gooey love songs on religious radio and TV, and prayed to is an imposter" (*GO* §3, 85–86).[29] He infers this change by first examining Jesus' Jewish heritage.

7.2.1 The Jewish Matrix

McLaren declares that the church has neglected Jesus' upbringing within Second Temple Judaism.[30] "Without understanding his Jewishness, one doesn't understand Jesus" (*SMJ* §1, 7; cf. *NKOCY* §4, 33–45).[31] Unfortunately, instead of accounting for the historical *Jewish* Jesus, situated in the Jewish stories of Adam, Abraham, Moses, and the prophets, Christians have inverted the practice by approaching Jesus in the context of Neoplatonic controversies from centuries later. In other words, through most of its history, Christians have largely defined Jesus through his descendants rather than his ancestors and contemporaries (*NKOCY* §4, 41; *SMJ* §App. 1, 222–24). The result is an adoption of the Greek god, *theos*, who reigns by excluding others, while neglecting

---

28. As Richard Kearney remarks, "Despotic theology . . . leads directly to despotic theocracy. Tyrannical Gods breed tyrannical humans. And vice versa" (Kearney, *Anatheism*, 147).

29. Here, McLaren approaches the historical Jesus synchronically, meaning he focuses on the Gospels in their final form rather than diachronically, which would require a form-critical and traditio-historical analysis. As he explains, "We're not claiming some new revelation or new authority figure. We're following the best Christian tradition of going back to Jesus and the Scriptures, so our quest for a new kind of Christianity is, in fact, a most conservative quest. . . .We're simply going back to the original Evangelists, apostles, and especially Jesus and making sure we're as in sync with them as possible from this point forward" (*NKOCY* §14, 141).

30. *AMP* §5, 85; *EMC* §10, 308–9n4; *FOWA* §4, 34–35; §8, 69; *LWWAT* §7, 46; §13, 77; §Comm., 192; *NKOC* §14, 184–85; and *SMJ* §3, 19–25; §20, 184. McLaren derives much of his beliefs about the Jewish matrix from N. T. Wright; for example, Wright, *The Challenge of Jesus*. Highlighting Jesus' Jewishness is now a hallmark of historical Jesus research; see Eddy and Beilby, "The Quest for the Historical Jesus," 48–49.

31. Cf. Penner, *The End of Apologetics*, 5–6 and Zimmermann, *Incarnational Humanism*, 66–67.

the Jewish God, *Yahweh* (*GSM*, 153).³² Eventually, Christendom used the Heraclitean notion of *theos* and *logos* to justify social inequality and legitimize slavery, plutocrats, and militarized oligarchies. McLaren argues that the Gospel of John actually rejects this Greek deity by depicting Christ as the new *Logos* of love and peace (*JMBM* §16, 141–44). From here, Christianity became a religion focused almost exclusively on a Greek afterlife.

7.2.1.1 The Afterlife and Cartesian Souls

Emphasizing the Jewishness of Jesus results in McLaren rejecting the kind of dualism that is associated with Neoplatonism (*NKOC* §14, 184–85). Here, McLaren explains that ancient Israelites principally emphasized earthly affairs more than they speculated about the afterlife (*AMP* §5, 85; *LWWAT* §7, 46).³³ As a product of Israelite religion, Jesus adhered to proto-liberationist visions of the kingdom of God as expressed in many Second Temple writings. While McLaren believes the afterlife is still meaningful (*NKOC* §10, 126–27), he discards the church's preoccupation with the hereafter because Jesus himself did not stress this issue (*EMC* §12, 96; cf. *LWWAT* §7, 46). According to McLaren, humanity's focus should be on a kingdom revolution that seeks to relieve the plight of others in the here and now (*EMC* §13, 105–8).³⁴

By viewing Jesus in his Jewish matrix, McLaren attempts to diminish notions of Cartesian souls, as well. Although he believes in a distinction between the mind, body, and spirit, he specifically rebuffs the "[N]eoplatonic and Cartesian ghost-in-a-machine" (*GO* §19, 280–81) that has dominated church history (*FOWA* §8, 69). For him, science has confirmed what Jews already believed: characteristics traditionally

---

32. McLaren explains that this Greco-Roman *theos* is fully Platonic in nature, meaning this concept of deity elevates spirit and belittles physical matter. *Theos* is absolutely perfect in the sense that there is no change, no story, and no existential becoming. The result is a deity who is fixated on perfection and, therefore, seeks to destroy or torture anything that is not perfect, including his own creation. According to McLaren, this deity cannot possibly be the same God as Jesus' *Abba* (*GO* §2, 76; *NKOCY* §4, 42–43; §10, 98–99). As McLaren writes elsewhere, "Our concept of God risked having more in common with the Greek *theos* of Plato and Plotinus than the *Yahweh* of Abraham, Isaac, and Jacob" (*LWWAT* §28, 168; italics in original).

33. McLaren, "Finding the Seventh Story," 128. He explains that even the concept of resurrection did not originally involve an afterlife, being an earthly renewal of life, instead (*LWWAT* §10, 60). Cf. Maier, *Zwischen den Testamenten*, 281; Green, "Heaven and Hell," 371–73; Bernstein, *The Formation of Hell*, 133–77; Wright, *Surprised by Hope*, 25; Moltmann, *The Coming of God*, 58–65; and Schwarz, *Eschatology*, 31–41, 272–80.

34. McLaren does specifically mention that Jesus definitely believed in an afterlife (*WMRBW*, 112). Interestingly, from McLaren's viewpoint, a focus on that afterlife in the ancient world would not have been surprising considering life for the ancients was short and unbearable; thus, a message about a better existence really would seem like "good news" to an ancient worldview (cf. Stark, *The Rise of Christianity*, 147–62). The problem is that this focus on the afterlife eventually exempted the Christian church from its responsibility toward helping fix the socio-political problems that now marginalize and oppress entire people groups. In this way, the church has managed to retain the people's loyalty but without any need to bear actual fruit here on earth (*LWWAT* §28, 169).

associated with a soul (e.g., reasoning, volition, personality, etc.) are a product of the whole person, not an immaterial specter inhabiting the body (*NKOCY* §17, 175–76). Hence, "the soul is the 'bigger' reality, the higher emergent reality, differentiated from the body and mind but never disassociated from them" (*GO* §18, 281).[35] McLaren stresses that while it is appropriate to be "heavenly minded," focusing singularly on the afterlife causes Christianity to lose relevance for people here on earth (*COOS1* §11, 145–47). Additionally, the idea of heaven as a place to experience God's Spirit appears to discount his presence throughout creation (*SMJ* §20, 183–84). It has been McLaren's experience that the church's focus on rescuing souls results in an anthropocentric selfishness and an unregenerate church body. The consequence is that Christians no longer concern themselves with living according to kingdom principles (§7.4.2.1); instead, they concern themselves with saying a few magic words to avoid hellfire (*LWWAT* §14, 85; *NKOC* §10, 119). This eschatological model merely creates a focus on private rewards instead of earthly justice (*EMC* §26, 219; *GO* §4, 100; §5, 107). According to McLaren, while Jesus did speak of an afterlife, his discussions almost always shifted back to God's kingdom as a counter to imperialist agendas.[36]

7.2.2 The Imperial Matrix

For McLaren, the entire Christian faith centers on the incarnation of God into a specific culture and socio-historical context (*MRTYR* §1, 23). In order to understand this incarnation, however, believers must situate Jesus within the oppressive and imperialistic matrix of his time (cf. *SMJ* §2, 11). To do otherwise would be to superimpose a foreign worldview onto Jesus and his message. As McLaren explains, since at least the sixth century bce, Jews had been under foreign occupation, first from the Assyrians, then Babylonians, Medo-Persians, Greeks, and eventually Romans, which created a perpetual sense of subjugation under an idolatrous empire. From this context of poverty and marginalization, Jesus emerged as a revolutionary to announce God's new kingdom (*FFR* §5, 113; *SMJ* §2, 12; *SWFOI* §23, 173). Of course, this matrix also meant the swift and violent punishment of all revolutionaries under the *pax Romana*.

7.2.2.1 Pax Romana

In this context, Jesus' ministry revealed a blatant difference to the methods of the Roman Empire. Having no soldiers, no weaponry, no wealth, and no home, Jesus inaugurated a kingdom of peace in order to subvert Rome's violence (*SMJ* §4, 26–34).

---

35. See also, *AIFA*, 47; *AMP* §4, 71; §6, 105; §15, 237; *FOWA* §10, 92; *SMJ* §20, 259n4. Cf. Moltmann, *The Coming of God*, 100–1. This monism was also the contention of the second century apologist, Tatian (ca. AD 120–190), who rejected the notion of an immaterial soul (*Or. Graec.* 12–13, 15).

36. McLaren, "Beyond Fire and Brimstone," 16–20. See also, McLaren, "The Report Back to Mars," 112.

It was a *"radical rejection of dominating supremacy in all its forms"* (*GSM*, 90; italics in original). Here, Jesus intentionally set up a rivalry between two sets of kingdom ideals (*NKOCY* §12, 124–26): the *pax Romana* ("Roman peace") and the *pax Christi* ("peace of Christ").[37] According to John Dominic Crossan, whom McLaren studies (*EMC* §15, 122; *GSM*, 119; *JMBM* §Ack. 275), the Mediterranean Basin believed that Rome would be the final world power, eventually securing peace through conquest. Jesus' kingdom, however, envisioned a transfiguration of the world as a challenge to the empire's politically violent authority (cf. John 18:36). Instead of the *pax Romana*'s "Peace Through Violent Victory," Jesus introduced a Jewish version of "Peace Through Nonviolent Justice," or what McLaren labels the *pax Christi* (*SMJ* §12, 99).[38] As Crossan explains, people already referred to Caesar as the "Son of God," "Lord," "Redeemer," and "Savior of the World." For the early church to apply these same titles to Christ indicates that the church viewed Jesus as a political rival to Caesar. Even the phrase "good news" suggests a political opposition to Rome (*EMC* §15, 122). Significantly, though, Rome never had Jesus' disciples executed as revolutionaries, indicating that his ministry was purposely nonviolent.[39]

More importantly, Jesus was *crucified*, "the dark side of the *pax Romana*" (*EMC* §10, 86; italics in original), which is proof positive that Rome considered Jesus to be a political insurrectionist (*EMC* §10–§11; *GO* §3, 83; *WMRBW*, 103). "Anyone who dared to defy the power and authority of Caesar would be executed in this public and humiliating way. The cross, then, became a symbol of the invincible and dominating power of Caesar and his empire; and Jesus is crucified as a revolutionary" (*VL*, 158).[40] While the *pax Romana* was meant to establish peace by crucifying dissenters, Jesus transformed the cross into an instrument of love and nonviolence, which explains why his followers would rather suffer from hostility than inflict it on others (*SMJ*

37. McLaren writes, "The Pax Christi, in which Christ rules by a reconciling word, is more powerful than the Pax Romana, in which Caesar rules by the dominating sword" (*NKOCY* §18, 284n8). As one proof, McLaren points to Jesus' first public speech as an example of his political rejection of first century Palestine's power structures of the day (*SMJ* §4, 29). He also highlights the Gospels portrayal of the empire as weak and inferior when in contact with Jesus. He uses the story of the Roman centurion as an example (*SMJ* §8, 66–67).

38. These political allusions expand further when comparing early Christology to that of the imperial *Pax Augusta* cult. See Cotter, "Greco-Roman Apotheosis," 127–53.

39. Crossan, "Jesus and the Challenge of Collaborative Eschatology," 107–11, 131–32, 185–87. Cf. Moltmann, *The Coming of God*, 318. According to Paula Fredriksen, the most fundamental historic anomaly of the passion narratives is Pilate never arresting or punishing Jesus' followers (Fredriksen, *Jesus of Nazareth*, 9–11, 240–57).

40. Interestingly, McLaren's retelling of Acts (*VA*, 23) recognizes that the early church blamed the Jews, not the Romans, for Jesus' death (see for example, Acts 5:28, 30; 7:52). Elsewhere, McLaren admits that it was the Jewish religious establishment who felt threatened by the incarnation and coerced Rome to execute Jesus (*FFR* §5, 114). Even McLaren's acknowledgement that the Gospels actually portray Jews, particularly the Pharisees, as the enemy of God makes him admit that the Gospels are partly responsible for the church's anti-Semitism. "The tragic reality of anti-Semitism through history is connected to the negative portrait of the Pharisees in the [G]ospels" (McLaren, "Hurtful Stereotypes," 4).

§17, 152–53). Consequently, McLaren views Jesus as an imperial rebel specifically because he promoted a nonviolent revolution and challenged the *pax Romana* with his message of peace and compassion (*NKOCY* §12, 125). Jesus' death was, essentially, a *political* execution (*WMRBW*, xvii), not a sacrificial bloodletting designed to appease an angry God, as Roman sympathizers would later want Christians to believe (§7.5). From this deconstruction, McLaren turned his attention to rereading Jesus' *socio-political* gospel message.

7.3 SCRIPTURE AS LITERARY ART

Despite the numerous publications on McLaren's hermeneutic, one characteristic remains almost completely ignored: his artistic inclinations.[41] As McLaren reiterates, the only way to know and understand God is to focus on the central message of Jesus Christ (*MRTYR* §7, 64; cf. *NS* §2, 17). However, to know Jesus, believers must focus almost exclusively on the canonical Gospels because the writings of other humans, such as the Apostle Paul, do not take precedence over the actual teachings of Christ himself.[42] Considering McLaren's passion for literature and art (§2.3.1), it is no surprise that he approaches Scripture as narrative and poetry (*NKOCY* §8, 79), which is to say, *not* "literal."[43] For McLaren, the Bible is a divinely inspired library (*GO* §10, 161–62; *NKOCY* §8, 83), containing the perceptions, reflections, and experiences of precritical people.[44] It is a collection of ancient documents (*AMP* §5, 75) that displays diversity in theological and ethical thought (*JMBM* §22, 204; *NKOCY* §8, 83). As an ancient library, the Bible is not concerned with Western abstract theories or systematized propositions. It tells stories, instead (*NKOC* §3, 35).[45]

41. For example, see the extended (and sometimes laughable) portrayals of McLaren's hermeneutic in Shogren, "'The Wicked Will Not Inherit the Kingdom of God,'" 95–113; Kim, "An Evangelical Critique," 49–204; and Hatch, "Hearing God Amid Many Voices," 23–47.

42. See *NKOCY* §3, 26; §11, 115; §17, 179; *SMJ* §4, 30. When McLaren began to re-read the Gospels with a new set of questions, he "started noticing dynamic things in the Bible and especially in the teachings of Jesus that had been there all along but I—like most Christians—had been trained not to see them and to focus on other things" (McLaren, "Making Waves," 29). McLaren writes, "The one I believe to be the real Jesus—the Jesus of Matthew, Mark, Luke, and John, the Jesus of Acts, the letters, and Revelation too (wisely interpreted)—cannot be understood and must not be trimmed to fit within the Greco-Roman framing story" (*NKOCY* §12, 126). Cf. Burk, "Editorial," 2–4.

43. McLaren defines a "literal" approach to Scripture as an insipid reading that disregards the different genres, socio-political contexts, and cultural influences that comprised the biblical world. This hermeneutic results in treating the Bible as a textbook designed to provide modern-day readers with absolute certainty regarding modern-day problems (*FFR* §5, 116). As he explains, a "literal" reading of Scripture is not the only (or favored) way to possess a "high view" of Scripture (cf. *GSM*, 112). Cf. Longman, "What I Mean," 137–55.

44. *NKOCY* §8, 79; *SA*, 12; *WMRBW*, 58–59, 172. McLaren writes, "[The Bible] is at once God's creation *and* the creation of the dozens of people and communities and cultures who produced it" (*GO* §10, 162, italics in original), concluding that Scripture is both "God's book" and a "human book" (*SWFOI* §16, 113).

45. McLaren writes, "After all, that's what the Bible is—a collection of stories" (McLaren,

For McLaren, these stories are a gift from God (*GO* §10, 159) with real-world import (*FFR* §5, 102, 117; *MRTYR* §9, 75), but Scripture is also morally reprehensible in many passages.[46] If the Bible is a collaboration between divine and human authors, as McLaren believes (*GO* §10, 162; *SWFOI* §16, 113), then these passages appear inconsistent with Christ's own teachings. The two main solutions, either unquestioningly accept everything the Bible says (*FOWA* §6, 57) or dismiss it as Bronze Age myths (*GO* §10, 163; *JMBM* §22, 197–98), are not sufficient (*FFS* §2, 63–65). Rather, McLaren believes the problem derives from modernity (*AMP* §5, 77; *GO* §10, 166) and its erroneous dogmatism, which requires an uncritical loyalty to biblical literalism (*GO* §8, 133–34), or what McLaren terms a constitutional hermeneutic.[47]

7.3.1 Constitutional Biblicism

McLaren argues that both liberal and conservative approaches to Scripture are the result of the Enlightenment's influence on religious thought and, therefore, are woefully defective (cf. *GO* §10, 164; *JMBM* §22, 197). Liberals often dismiss the Bible for not adhering to modern notions of credibility. Conversely, conservatives react by forcing the Bible to fit modern criteria (*LWWAT* §7, 43), reducing a "tradition of spiritual storytelling to the modern constraints of journalism or historiography" (*GSM*, 233n11; cf. *AMP* §5, 76–77).[48] The result is a dogmatic devotion to an ideology known as "biblicism."[49] Here, McLaren's concern is that conservatives have trans-

---

"Conversations," 343). See also, Streett, "An Interview with Brian McLaren," 8 and McLaren, "Changing Faith," 16–17. As a former English literature professor, McLaren's academic training and boyhood passion was in discovering plot lines, protagonists, character development, and conflict resolution. Therefore, as a literary scholar, McLaren does not expect to find doctrinal systems, objective ontological truths, or systematic theologies in an ancient library filled with multiple voices and perspectives of the world (*NKOCY* §6, 55; cf. *SMJ* §6, 43).

46. For examples and details, see *EMC* §19, 153; *FFR* §1, 33; §5, 117–118; *GO* §10, 166; *GSM*, 112; *MRTYR* §8, 69–71; *NKOCY* §10, 98; *WMRBW*, 47; and McLaren, "Is God Violent?," 16–20.

47. McLaren, "The Problem Isn't the Bible." As Roger Olson remarks, investing interpretations with absolute authority "is functionally to place a set of human statements on the same plane with Scripture; they become a written magisterium placed on a pedestal above question or reconsideration even on the basis of fresh and faithful biblical scholarship" (Olson, *Reformed and Always Reforming*, 19).

48. McLaren disapproves of liberalism's dismissal of biblical miracles and the divine origins of Scripture, but he also objects to conservativism's atomistic reduction of the text into propositional content. Liberals restrict the value of Scripture by substituting its authority for modernistic ideals while conservatives attempt to argue for a consistency and historical accuracy that simply does not exist. Their constitutional approach results in an authoritarian view that demands everyone adhere to their particular interpretations and religio-ethical sensibilities (*JMBM* §22, 204n13; *LWWAT* §7, 43; *NKOC* §7, 80; *NKOCY* §8, 81; §9, 96). For the impropriety of approaching biblical narratives as historical treatises, see Sternberg, *The Poetics of Biblical Narrative*.

49. Christian Smith defines "biblicism" as an ideologically uncritical devotion to the notion that the Bible possesses exclusive and foolproof authority on all matters, and that its self-evident meaning is plainly understandable, universally applicable, and perfectly consistent in all its pronouncements (Smith, *The Bible Made Impossible*, viii, 4–5). Peter Enns likewise defines "biblicism" as "*the tendency*

formed the Bible into a type of legal brief (like the American Constitution) with the false expectancy of deriving objective knowledge, moral certainty, and metaphysical absolutes from its texts.⁵⁰ This constitution model is injurious because it mistakes Scripture for an encyclopedia of "facts" about the universe (*COOS1* §6, 77); and when put in the wrong hands, "the Bible [becomes] as suspicious as an abandoned suitcase at an airport . . . because [it has] been used and will be used again to inspire hate, fear, killing, even mass murder."⁵¹ Charles Hodge exemplified this constitutional approach when he wrote, "The Bible is to the theologian what nature is to the man of science. It is his store-house of facts; and his method . . . is the same as that which the natural philosopher adopts."⁵²

As McLaren quips, if God intended to create a textbook, he would have included an index for topical reference (*FFR* §5, 106); but the truth is, the Bible is a pitiful textbook because it lacks technical precision, pragmatic schemas, academic rigor, theoretical abstractions, and internal consistency (*COOS1* §6, 77; *SWFOI* §Pref. Pbk. ed., viii). "If we want the Bible to be a constitution, it isn't enough. It isn't at all. Nor is it enough as a road map for successful living, as a set of blueprints for building a life, institution, or nation, or as an 'owner's manual' with handy-dandy information guaranteed to make your life run smoothly" (*NKOCY* §9, 96). It is, thus, unrealistic to treat the Bible as a "codebook" to life because its original tradents, as well as later scribes, were products of their own socio-historical and cultural contexts.⁵³

---

to appeal to individual biblical verses, or collections of (apparently) uniform verses from various parts of the Bible, to give the appearance of clear, authoritative, and final resolutions to what are in fact complex interpretive and theological issues generated by the fact that we have a complex and diverse Bible. Put another way, biblicism is a tendency to prooftext—where the 'plain sense' of verses are put forth as final and incontrovertible 'proof' of a given theological position" (Enns, "Biblicism"; italics in original).

50. Cf. *AIFA*, 282; *GO* §10, 160; *JMBM* §22, 204; *NKOC* §7, 79–80; *NKOCY* §7, 68. Of course, as McLaren explains, the Bible is not capable of providing humans with objective certainty because finite humans are still interpreting and transmitting the information, which is an impossibly subjective process (*FFS* §2, 63–65). Readers should note that McLaren does not object to the Bible teaching believers what is true, ethically right, or correcting behavior (cf. *GO* §10, 164). Rather, he objects to the notion of treating Scripture as a how-to manual and blueprint for contemporary life because this distorts its multivocal and polysemic nature (cf. *NKOCY* §9, 87–97).

51. McLaren, foreword to *Compassion or Apocalypse?*, 2. See also, McLaren, foreword to *The Jesus Driven Life*, xiii–xiv.

52. Hodge, *Systematic Theology*, 1:§5A, 10. See also, Dulles, *A History of Apologetics*, 321–22 and Smith, *The Bible Made Impossible*, 55–60.

53. Cf. *FFR* §5, 104–5, 119; *LWWAT* §7, 43; *NKOCY* §8, 80; §14, 146. Even as an ethics manual, Scripture is tragically inadequate. McLaren writes, "The Bible, when taken as an ethical rule book, offers us no clear categories for many of our most significant and vexing socioethical quandaries. We find no explicit mention, for example, of abortion, capitalism, communism, socialism, schizophrenia, bipolar disorder . . . systemic racism, affirmative action, human rights, nationalism, sexual orientation, pornography, global climate change . . ." (*NKOCY* §7, 68). As Terry Eagleton elaborates, "The value-judgements by which [literature] is constituted are historically variable, but that these value-judgements themselves have a close relation to social ideologies. They refer in the end not simply to private taste, but to the assumptions by which certain social groups exercise and maintain power over others" (Eagleton, *Literary Theory*, 14).

What is most alarming for McLaren is that biblicism can promote social injustice. "We hear claims that 'God' or 'the Lord' actively commands or blesses actions that we would call crimes against humanity. Many religious scholars have assumed that because the Bible makes these claims, we must defend them as true and good. That approach, however, is morally unacceptable for growing numbers of us" (*WMRBW*, 47–48; cf. *NKOCY* §7, 69, 75–76).[54] He contends that contemporary hermeneutics are neither culturally detached nor politically nonpartisan, causing dogmatic conservatives to spread self-aggrandizing narratives that serve only their particular sociopolitical interests.[55] McLaren likens this approach to having a "know-it-all" mentality where biblical passages become mathematical formulas to condemn whichever segment of society they dislike most (*COOS1* §9, 110–11; *NKOC* §6, 71–72). Of course, not all conservatives endorse the bigotry, genocide, polygamy, or infanticide as typified in Scripture, but this is in spite of their biblicism, not because of it. Christians (for the most part) have a "grid of decency" that prevents them from applying the morally reprehensible portions of Scripture to contemporary life (*NKOC* §6, 70–71).[56] However, as Masood Raja explains, Christians today use the Bible as a "prop" to bolster their own prejudices, inconsistently "cherry-picking" only those verses that suit them (cf. *NKOCY* §8, 80).[57] McLaren warns that the careless mixing of Scripture's abhorrent passages with biblicism will result in more Christians justifying "anti-Semitism, slavery, segregation, the inferiority of women, or the earth-centered universe" (*GSM*,

---

54. McLaren continues by parodying conservatives, "'Don't argue with me—argue with God. I'm just preaching the Word,' they would say, as if their preaching involved no interpretation at all" (*CIEC*, 180–81). As the disreputable maxim states, "If the Bible says God said it, then God said it and that settles it" (*NKOCY* §9, 94), and thus, McLaren used to believe his job was to accept every image of God in the Bible without question (*GSM*, 111). McLaren objects to this blind obedience (*VL*, 4-5) particularly because a "bad faith" is one that adopts a hardline doctrinaire system simply because authority figures say to do so. This inflexible devotion to an ideology inhibits critical thinking and is characteristic of brainwashing, thought control, and menticide (*FFS* §1, 41–42). Thus, for McLaren, a constitutional-literalist approach to Scripture is no different than what radical Muslims do with the Qur'an, which ultimately treats the Bible like *Robert's Rules of Order* or some tax code that, if faithfully observed, would require Christians (like their Muslim counterparts) to live according to a Bronze Age or first century worldview complete with racial and religious bigotry and violence (McLaren, "A Postmodern View of Scripture," 11).

55. Consequently, neo-Evangelicals tend to read the Bible as though it were written *by* American Republicans *for* American Republicans (Raja, *The Religious Right*, 49). For details on the effects of biased interpretive communities, see Fish, "Interpreting the *Variorum*," 164–84.

56. Although biblicism suggests that the entirety of Scripture is divinely inspired, in practice neo-Evangelicals are willing to insist that only a few biblical norms become the law of the land (e.g., heteronormative, monogamous marriages) while deliberately ignoring other biblical mandates. "Fortunately, evangelicals don't say that people who disobey their parents should be stoned, as the Bible teaches in Leviticus, or that people whose genitals are mutilated should be excluded from worship, as the Bible also teaches in Leviticus, or that it's a sin for women to wear jewelry or have a short haircut, as the Bible teaches in some of Paul's writings" (*NKOC* §6, 70–71). Nor do conservatives push for laws that accord with Jesus' commands to lend money to those who cannot repay, give a shirt to someone who demands their coat, turn the other cheek, or forbid divorce (*AMP* §13, 205).

57. Raja, *The Religious Right*, 54.

12). Similar to pro-slavery advocates who once used Scripture to justify oppressing minorities, so too will oppressive interpretations continue to prevail, such as excluding monogamous lesbian and gay relationships from church life.[58] This bigotry will ultimately discredit Christianity for all future generations (*MRTYR* §2, 29–31; *NKOCY* §7, 69, 75–76; §17, 177).[59] Thus, McLaren adopts an alternative hermeneutic that has strong affinities with Paul Ricoeur.

7.3.2 Ricoeurian Poetics

It is important to understand that McLaren's hermeneutic views Scripture as *literature*, comprised mostly of poetry and narrative; and as literature, the Bible is properly viewed as artwork, which requires an *artistic* interpretation (*COOS1* §6, 77).[60] According to McLaren, the Bible tells stories to communicate deeper meanings and truths (*GSM*, 113–21). "It's easy to miss the point of ancient stories. Those stories didn't merely aim, like a modern textbook, to pass on factual *information*. They sought people's *formation* by engaging their interpretative *imagination*" (*WMRBW*, 52; italics in original).[61] Hence, McLaren opts for a "mystical/poetic approach," which views the Bible as literary art with very little prose (*GO* §9, 155). In fact, to stress this point, McLaren quotes Sara Maitland's definition of theology "as (1) the art of telling stories about the divine and (2) the art of listening to those stories" (*AIFA*, 205).

Storytelling shapes communities by providing the linguistic and interpretive grid through which they can then experience God (cf. *TSS*, 83–134). In a modernistic

---

58. Reed, "Emerging Treason?," 74. For a treatment of homosexuality in the Bible that aligns with McLaren's interpretation, see Via, "The Bible," 1–39; Snyman, "Homoseksualiteit en tydgerigtheid," 715–44; and Brownson, *Bible, Gender, Sexuality*, 2013).

59. See esp., Slade, "*Hagioprepē*[set macron over e]*s*," forthcoming.

60. McLaren writes, "Instead of a dictated rulebook, we have this wildly inspired collection of stories, songs, fiction, nonfiction, history, fable, and poetry. Sometimes it's hard to tell where one genre begins and the other ends. But put together, it gives us the rhythm and shape of a story that gives meaning and context and purpose for our lives" (McLaren, "A Postmodern View of Scripture," 11). For him, even prophetic and epistolary literature are artistic "narrative" in the sense that they fit into the Bible's overarching storyline (*AIFA*, 206–7).

61. Regarding whether McLaren believes biblical stories are "true" in the sense of having factual historicity, he explains that he is not concerned with the Bible's accuracy. He is concerned with its depth of wisdom and insight. If he learns, either from God or critical research, that certain stories are merely imaginative metaphors for deeper realities, then he is content to activate the same suspension of disbelief that is required of all fiction. If he learns that the stories are, in fact, historically accurate, then better still. The meaningful intent of the text has not changed (*NS* §5, 255n2). For McLaren, it is an Enlightenment failing to divide the Bible into "historical" and "mythological" categories (*FOWA* §3, 206n1). Significantly, however, McLaren does believe in the historicity of the virgin birth and Christ's resurrection, remarking, "Not only do I believe in the resurrection of Jesus Christ, I base my life on it" (Metzger, "Brian McLaren Responds"). McLaren continues, "These [biblical] stories are so improbable, so unexpected, so challenging to the status quo . . . that they simply seem to have the ring of truth to them" (*FFR* §9, 177). "What if their purpose is to challenge us to blur the line between what we think is possible and what we think is impossible?" (*WMRBW*, 68).

framework, however, Scripture loses its experiential impact once academics dissect the stories for analysis.[62] Reading the Bible as a constitutional document forces Christians to become makeshift lawyers, arguing for interpretive precedents according to authorial intent while failing to grasp the deeper, existential intentions of storytelling (cf. *NKOCY* §8, 78–79; §12, 120–21). What McLaren rejects is the "mythic-literal" simplicity of a constitutional hermeneutic because it ignores Scripture's use of metaphor and symbolism.[63] Here, Walker Percy's understanding of art is instructive:

> The purpose of art is to transmit universal truths of a sort, that in art, whether it's poetry, fiction or painting, you are telling the reader or the listener or the viewer something he already knows, so that in the action of communication he experiences a recognition, a feeling that he has been there before, a shock of recognition. And so, what the artist does, or tries to do, is simply to validate the human experience and to tell people the deep human truths which they already unconsciously know. (Quoted in *WP*, 49)

Referring to this approach as "rhetorical hermeneutics," McLaren argues that Christians need to focus more on what artists are trying to accomplish ("what they're *doing*") more so than the words they are saying (*LWWAT* §13, 81; italics in original; cf. *AIFA*, 294). For him, the Bible is "valuable not for what it proves, but for what it reveals" (*AMP* §6, 101).[64]

He begins his hermeneutical process with socio-historical research into the biblical texts (cf. *LWWAT* §7, 44), but this only provides preliminary background information. The most important hermeneutical element is reading Scripture *literally*, paying particular attention to its artistic use of language and metaphor (*WMRBW*, 51–52). He looks for *meaning* within the stories of the Bible, not necessarily facts (*GI*, 215). McLaren explicitly compares biblical hermeneutics to the interpretation of a painting where changes in visual distances and angles can alter a person's sensitivity to different meanings. Thus, just as beauty is in the "eye of the beholder," so too are people's contextualized interpretations of Scripture.[65] "We train people in languages—grammar, vocabulary—but not in literacy, which involves learning genre, imagery, rhetoric, and imagination. . . .I'd make [my seminary students] read poetry until they got it. . . .I'd

---

62. McLaren, "There's A Bigger Story." See also, Lindbeck, *The Nature of Doctrine*, 113–24 and Frei, *The Eclipse of Biblical Narrative*.

63. Fowler, *Stages of Faith*, 135–50.

64. See also, McLaren, "A New Kind of Bible Reading." Historically, neither biblical writers nor ancient readers practiced so-called ("literal") hermeneutics. For the agenda-driven expediency of biblical interpretation throughout history, see Rogers and McKim, *The Authority and Interpretation of the Bible*; Froehlich, *Biblical Interpretation in the Early Church*; Snodgrass, "The Use of the Old Testament in the New," 29–51; Kugel, *Traditions of the Bible*; and Fairbairn, "Patristic Exegesis and Theology," 1–19.

65. Cf. *LWWAT* §Intro, xvii; *MRTYR* §10, 77; *NKOCY* §8, 84–85. Thus, for McLaren, *sola Scriptura* is not nuanced or sufficient enough to decide socio-ethical questions for today (McLaren, foreword to *Solus Jesus*, xv–xvi).

also take them to lots of movies, art galleries, and plays because most of the Bible is art, and without sensitivity to art, students will read the Bible like tax accountants."[66]

The problem for Enlightenment-based exegetes is that art generates divergent and often incompatible interpretations. Therefore, appealing to authorial intentionalism, where hermeneuts seek a supposed "correct" interpretation from the work's creator, initially seems to be the best interpretive method.[67] However, there exist numerous problems with this approach. For one, authors often change their minds over time or are unclear about their own "original intent" (or purposely have no intention at all). Sometimes, authors update or alter their work to convey new meanings or convey multiple meanings simultaneously. Literary artists even have ambivalence about their meaning or possess (consciously and subconsciously) multiple layers of ambiguous subtext. Sometimes, the true "meaning" of an artwork is unknowable and never will be known, making authorial intent impractical as the sole hermeneutical grid from an epistemological stance. In fact, part of the beauty of art is its ability to generate differing personal experiences through creativity, suggesting that meaning is not static if divergent people can have divergent interpretations based on their experiential encounter with the artwork. Finally, since all creations are situated in a particular socio-historical milieu, merely identifying a text's cultural context implies that it derives its meaning (at least partially) from something outside of the creator.[68]

With this in mind, McLaren's hermeneutic aligns with Paul Ricoeur's belief that Scripture's emphasis is not theological dogma but, instead, the polyphonic nature of experiencing the divine (cf. *AIFA*, 98–99; *GO* §10, 166–67; *WMRBW*, 7). More importantly is Ricoeur's notion of "philosophical poetics," which suggests Scripture is metaphorical art that transcends definite speech acts in order to draw its audience into participation with the text. As art, the nature of religious discourse is more poetic than prose (cf. *FFR* §5, 119; *GO* §9, 155).[69] As McLaren writes, "If we enter the text together and feel the flow of its arguments, get stuck in its points of tension, and struggle with its unfolding plot in all its twists and turns, God's revelation *can happen to us*" (*NKOCY* §9, 91; emphasis added). The point is to allow Scripture's "*metaphorical truth*" to shape the human imagination through intuitive readings. However, these truths are not absolute or fixed; they are akin to the "*timely insight*" that occurs within fluctuating socio-political and cultural contexts (*GSM*, 113–14; italics in original).

Notably, Ricoeur likens textual interpretation to an orchestra, much the same way that McLaren likens the Bible to a symphony (*NKOCY* §9, 95). Just as composers

---

66. McLaren, "A Postmodern View of Scripture," 12.

67. See Irwin, *Intentionalist Interpretation* and Livingston, *Art and Intention*. For a defense of intentionalism as it relates to biblical hermeneutics, see Vanhoozer, *Is There a Meaning in This Text?*

68. Tallman, "Was It All a Dream?," 22–26.

69. Ricoeur, *Essays on Biblical Interpretation*, esp. 75–102. Cf. *NKOCY* §9, 93–94; *SWFOI* § Pref. Pbk. ed., viii; §33, 252–53. Significantly, for McLaren, art is best *enjoyed*, not analyzed (McLaren, foreword to *Secrets in the Dark*, ix–xi).

relinquish control over their musical scores, so too must literary artists allow conductors and ensembles to interpret and apply the text in their own creative ways. How the musical score reads and plays is more important than what the original composer intended. While the musical notes confine some aspects of the composition, they do not dictate how it is experienced. Thus, while an author's intent acts as a framework from which to approach literature (most markedly by restricting interpretations to the type and amount of lexical data), the dynamic and contextual nature of artwork suggests that intentions are not fixed and, therefore, are not imposable by the author. Hence, for McLaren, the goal of interpretation is to identify the *sense* of mental communication taking place by experiencing literature as a whole (cf. *GSM*, 25).[70] Because biblical writers were concerned with declaring true *meaning*, not always factual accuracy, their intention would ultimately have been to generate an intersubjective and existential faith in Christ (§8.2).[71]

Accordingly, rather than approach Scripture as a forensic scientist, believers ought to approach it as a teenage boy flirting with a girl. In other words, they should approach Scripture with personal investment, adventure, and a romance that allows for the reciprocity of dialogue between God and reader. The focus is on allowing the Bible to transform Christians holistically in order to actualize God's kingdom ethics, but this transformation can only occur when readers encounter God through the biblical texts (*NKOC* §7, 77–85; *NKOCY* §9, 95–96). Therefore, as art, Scripture is a divinely inspired library that intends to encourage a deep pursuit for Christ's kingdom (*LWWAT* §12, 71–73; §13, 81). As a consequence, McLaren's artistic hermeneutic indirectly appropriates the art philosophy of Arthur Danto.

7.3.2.1 Dantoian Aesthetics

According to Danto, artwork is rarely forthright in its meaning or intention. In fact, art often defies its audience's expectations; but for Danto in particular, artwork automatically invites people to complete its creative process. The rationale is that since literary art is public, it avails itself to the experiences of the public, thereby creating multiple and divergent subjective perceptions. By relinquishing control over people's experiences, an artwork's meaning transcends the artist as it continues to inspire new meanings (cf. *GSM*, 25). Because the Bible is open to interpretation (in the sense that its tradents did not place restrictions on how people could experience their stories), its meaning is not confinable solely to each author's intentions. This "multiplism" or "perspectivalism" suggests that several interpretations of literary art, even conflicting ones, are valid so long as they are consistent with the text's syntactical data.[72]

---

70. Ricoeur, *Interpretation Theory*, 71–88; *Hermeneutics and the Human Sciences*, 184–208.

71. *COOS1* §7, 90; *NKOC* §7, 80; *NS* §20, 173; *SA*, 34; *WMRBW*, 172.

72. See his full discussion in Danto, *The Transfiguration of the Commonplace*, esp. 54–89, 115–35 and *What Art Is*, 53–75. Cf. Clinchy, "Beyond Subjectivism," 15–30 and Tallman, "Was It All a

McLaren contends that an artistic approach does not completely abandon authorial intent since the author's perspective is still important to the interpretive process (*MRTYR* §10, 78; *VL*, 1). It does mean, however, that believers should fully recognize the divine dimension of Scripture by practicing *lectio divina* ("spiritual reading"), which allows them to experience "the light of God" as it permeates readers (*FOWA* §17, 161, 165) and inspires them to action (*WMRBW*, 69).[73] Rather than privilege only *one* authoritative interpretation that claims to have found only *one* meaning in the text, McLaren's hermeneutic prizes the multiplicity of contextualized interpretations because they add depth and perspective to the artwork. This then invites people to share in each other's experiences (*AIFA*, 87–88; *GI*, x–xix).[74] Of course, McLaren does not believe *all* readings are equally valid, such as with proslavery Christians, for example, in their interpretations of Scripture (*NKOCY* §8, 271n10). For McLaren, the interpretation that most accounts for God's beauty (*COOS1* §4, 63) is the one that most elevates people's relationship to the divine and stimulates them to loving others (*NKOC* §6, 74; *NKOCY* §4, 35).[75] With these practices in mind, readers can now understand how McLaren interprets the canonical Gospels.

7.4 THE REVOLUTIONARY JESUS

In recognizing Jesus as divine, McLaren focuses on the canonical Gospels in order to know God and his priorities.[76] What this means for McLaren's philosophy of religion is that following Jesus does not necessarily equate to following his successors. For

---

Dream?," 26–29. Cf. Hatch, "Hearing God Amid Many Voices," 23-47.

73. Because of the Jewish-imperial context, McLaren interprets the Gospel narratives as a sociopolitical commentary on Rome's use of violence against dissenters. For example, McLaren suggests that Jesus physically healing the blind is indicative of God wanting to heal humanity's distorted view of life. Likewise, Jesus healing the lame indicates the power of God's kingdom to inspire the downtrodden toward social action. Jesus quieting the storms exhibits God's pursuit of world peace while his exorcisms signify a desire to liberate people from economic, political, social, militaristic, and spiritual oppression (*WMRBW*, 101). It should be noted, however, that McLaren does not deny these miracles actually, physically occurred (*GO* §1, 61). They just have deeper meanings according to their sociopolitical context that a superficial "literal" reading too easily misses (*GSM*, 113–21). He would classify arguments over whether the events in question occurred as secondary to and even a distraction from the reason for their being told, whether they were intended as fiction or non-fiction.

74. As McLaren writes, the Bible is like an art gallery, not a single photo (*GSM*, 120). "We have become aware of how easily communities of interpretation can create a bubble where they are certain they are in touch with reality, but to those on the outside, it doesn't look that way at all" (*AIFA*, 89).

75. See also, McLaren, foreword to *Disarming Scripture*, xvii–xxi and "Brian McLaren Reflects on 25 Years of Emergence."

76. Cf. *COOS1* §6, 82; *EMC* §2, 13; §9, 72–73; *GO* §3, 80–85; *GSM*, 229–30n2. For McLaren, it is essential to discover precisely what Jesus taught about the gospel, especially since he places primary importance on aligning his philosophy of religion with Jesus' own worldview (cf. *GO* §0, 37). As John Dominic Crossan suggests, the most important method for understanding the historical Jesus is to understand his eschatological message about the kingdom (Crossan, "Jesus and the Challenge of Collaborative Eschatology," 131).

him, the person of Christ is far more important than whatever religion is constructed around him (*JMBM* §2, 16). This perspective puts McLaren out of sync with the Roman Catholic concept of *magisterium*, along with other approaches that suggest later commentators can end conversation about the meaning of Jesus' words and deeds. Throughout his literature, McLaren focuses his interpretation on four main aspects of Jesus' ministry: the Sermon on the Mount; the stories of Jesus interacting with individuals; Jesus' miracles; and the Olivet Discourse (cf. *JMBM* §19, 172–73). From these passages, McLaren believes that Christianity is predominantly about an existential way of life, not a doctrinaire system that relies on assenting to prescribed dogmas or creeds (*AIFA*, 303–5).[77] He writes, "Before Christianity was a rich and powerful religion, before it was associated with buildings, budgets, crusades, colonialism, or televangelism, it began as a revolutionary nonviolent movement promoting a new kind of aliveness on the margins of society" (*WMRBW*, xviii). Not surprisingly, then, McLaren often substitutes the word "doctrine" for the phrase "healing teachings" precisely because notional Christianity is rooted in the compulsion to dominate others. Reenvisioning doctrine's purpose as "healing" makes arguments over theological interpretations and other esoterica even more irrelevant (*JMBM* §18, 163).

Sadly, according to McLaren, Christianity has since domesticated Jesus so he no longer looks like a socio-political radical. Instead, he has become the mascot for American political and national self-interests.[78] "We sometimes try to enlist God to condemn those we want to condemn, deprive those we want to deprive, even kill those we want to kill. But God isn't willing to be domesticated into our little tribal deity on a leash" (*WMRBW*, 24).[79] In McLaren's reading of the Gospels, Jesus was a revolutionary who led a nonviolent coup against the imperial status quo (*SMJ* §4, 31), becoming an agitator for rebuking worldly kingdoms of conquest (*WMRBW*, 122). In this sense, Jesus is not only an insurrectionist: he is the archetypal anti-Caesar.

7.4.1 Jesus and Caesar

McLaren concludes that traditional paradigms, where Christ's primary concern was the salvation of individual souls, do not account for the totality of Jesus' teachings

---

77. McLaren calls the Sermon on the Mount Jesus' "kingdom manifesto" (see *SMJ* §14, 117–28) and describes following Jesus as "a better, more responsible, wiser, and more sustainable way to be human" (*GSM*, 10). He explains further, "If we think Jesus was right, we have to stop obsessing over beliefs. Our opinions, our conceptual formulations, our doctrinal statements may be interesting. They may even be important. But they aren't the point, and they can easily distract us from the point. Our problem isn't simply a matter of having the wrong beliefs. It's a matter of believing that right beliefs are what matters most" (*GSM*, 22).

78. See *EMC* §22, 183–84; *SMJ* §2, 16; *VL*, 158–59.

79. Cf. Benson and Heltzel, *Evangelicals and Empire*; Horsley, *Jesus and Empire*, 15–34, 129–49; and Gushee, *The Future of Faith in American Politics*, 121–39.

(*SMJ* §App. 1, 220–21).⁸⁰ Rather than fixate on purity laws or cultic observances, Jesus obsessed over exhorting people to actualize his kingdom ideals, which in turn would liberate people from institutional evils (cf. *GO* §5, 111; *GSM*, 20–22). For McLaren, the decisive conflict portrayed in Scripture is the proclamation of Jesus as the new eschatological king, which directly challenged the reign and prestige of Caesar (*EMC* §14, 111; *WMRBW*, 116–117).

In the ancient world, kings were considered divine-human hybrids who manifested their power through violence and conquest; yet, Jesus reversed this belief by revealing a nonviolent and just deity (*WMRBW*, 69). Jesus' entry into Jerusalem is a prime example of this conflict. While Caesar would have entered on a white steed with luminaries and soldiers brandishing weapons, Jesus entered on a lowly donkey, attended by commoners brandishing tree leaves. Caesar maintained peace through conquest, whereas Jesus promoted peace through sacrificial humility (*VL*, 132). In fact, when Jesus began his ministry, he came as a lamb under the sign of a dove, both symbolizing peace and nonviolence (*WMRBW*, 89).⁸¹ Jesus did not inaugurate his kingdom through domination; he conquered powers and principalities through vulnerability and sacrifice (*EMC* §14, 312n3). Caesar maintained his authority by crucifying others; Jesus established his authority by allowing himself to be crucified (*GO* §3, 83). Of course, Rome's attempt to stop Jesus' revolution backfired when they learned that Jesus' message was unkillable, revealing that God's love triumphs over imperial conquest (*SWFOI* §23, 173; *VL*, 158–59).

When interpreted through this Jewish-imperial matrix, the primitive church's employment of christological titles begins to reflect an even stronger political dimension (see *JMBM* §19, 170). The title "Christ" and "Messiah" signify Jesus as the people's liberator.⁸² To highlight this role, McLaren renders Luke 1:31 as, "You will have a Son, and you must name Him 'Liberation,' or Jesus," and he later retranslates Luke 2:11, "Today, in the city of David, a Liberator has been born for you! He is the promised Liberating King, the Supreme Authority!" (*VL*, 7, 15; italics in original). As an imperial "liberator," Jesus was thoroughly dedicated to ending the social and institutional

---

80. Labelling it a theology of "integrality," McLaren sees both the afterlife and this life as two aspects of the same kingdom message. See *FOWA* §8, 74; cf. *AMP* §15, 228–32; *COOS1* §2, 35–36.

81. Thus, according to McLaren, it is no surprise that the first people to learn of Jesus' birth were not dignitaries or wealthy landowners. They were "minimum-wage" shepherds, which signifies God's preference (contra Caesar) for the poor and marginalized of society (*VL*, 16). "The kingdom throws down a direct challenge to the supremacy of the empire of Caesar centered in Rome, for in the kingdom of God, the ultimate authority is not Caesar but rather the Creator" (*SMJ* §2, 17).

82. McLaren describes "Christ" as a "revolutionary term. . . . meaning 'the liberating king promised by God'" (*EMC* §12, 97). Thus, paraphrasing Acts 2:36, McLaren writes, "God has made Jesus both Lord and *Liberating King*" (*VA*, 10; italics added). As he explains elsewhere, "The liberation mind-set gives special attention to the activism of this brand of disciples in relation to systems of oppression. Through them, with them, Jesus works for liberation of all oppressed people" (*GO* §1, 63). Originally, the Greek word *Christos* "denotes someone who has been ceremonially anointed for an office," including kings, but the connotation of a political savior-king developed later in Jewish messianism (see Rengstorf, "Jesus Christ," 2:334–43).

evils of his day.[83] Moreover, the title "Son of Man" conjures the book of Daniel's image of liberation while "Lord," according to McLaren, implies Jesus' political authority over Caesar (*EMC* §12, 98).[84] As the "Lamb of God," Jesus chastised Caesar's persecution of dissenters; and as the "Word of God," Jesus revealed the compassionate nature of deity (*JMBM* §19, 170). Even Mary's *Magnificat* (Luke 1:46–55) fosters a "social, economic, and political revolution" (*VL*, 9) that culminated in Jesus reversing Caesar's practice of shedding an enemy's blood by shedding his own (*EMC* §19, 158–59; *SWFOI* §20, 148).

With Caesar's imperial dominance, McLaren's historical reconstruction unveils four main Jewish responses to the Roman Empire, resulting in one major social corollary.[85] According to McLaren, the Sadducees and Herodians allied with the Romans and, in turn, enabled the colonialist oppression of other Jews. They did nothing but legitimize society's inequalities and injustices. Zealots, on the other hand, pursued violent revolt against any and all collaborators. They intended to provoke a war with the ruling power structures. The Pharisees responded to Rome by scapegoating other Jews, blaming sinners for their subjugation. They often compartmentalized the socio-economic and political status quo by separating their public life from their religious life.[86] Finally, Essenes responded by isolating themselves from society in hopes that God would eventually destroy everyone they deemed an infidel.

The result of these responses was an increase in economic disparity where wealthy land owners, politicians, and the religious aristocracy horded as much power and wealth as possible to the marginalization of impoverished Judeans, Samaritans, and Galileans. What is significant for McLaren is that Jesus, a member of the victimized proletariat, offered an alternative to these responses. Here, Jesus preached the kingdom of God, which demanded generosity, solidarity, inclusivity, and the empowerment of the other (§8.4.2). His goal was to make God's kingdom the new societal norm.[87] McLaren further explains,

---

83. Cf. *EMC* §13, 105–8; *NKOCY* §12, 124–26; *WMRBW*, 118, 147. As the subtitle to Part II of *The Great Spiritual Migration* suggests, Jesus came to transform people's approach to religion, "*From a Violent God of Domination to a Nonviolent God of Liberation*" (*GSM*, 69; italics in original).

84. McLaren, therefore, paraphrases Acts 17:24 by replacing the term "Lord" with a Roman designation, "This is the God who made the universe and all it contains, the God who is *the Caesar*, the King, of all heaven and all earth" (*VA*, 78–79; italics in original).

85. For explanations and examples of these responses, see *CIEC*, 15; *EMC* §11, 89–90; §33, 285; *SMJ* §2, 17–18; §19, 179; *SWFOI* §23, 165–68; McLaren, "Finding the Seventh Story," 124–31; and Riess, "Emerging Star," 52.

86. In McLaren's literary reading of Scripture, the "Pharisees" represent the self-righteous, hypocritical, apathetic, and judgmental elements of debauched religiosity, which transcends all peoples, traditions, and denominations (cf. McLaren, "Hurtful Stereotypes," 4–5).

87. For McLaren, one of the most destructive elements to promulgating justice is Christianity aligning with secular political parties (*AMP* §7, 120–21). "I think there are many [Christians] who are rendering to Caesar everything that is Caesar's, and they are also rendering to Caesar much of what they think they are rendering to God" (*NKOC* §13, 164). In fact, McLaren attacks Democrats and Republicans for their enablement of American religious imperialism (cf. *EMC* §20, 162–63; *TWLD*;

> Jesus' alternative framing story, as we've seen, involves God's bringing down those in power (Luke 1:52-53) so that the poor can be legitimized (Luke 4:18), and so that the religious collaboration with the empire can be exposed as hypocrisy. The empire uses crosses to punish rebels and instill fear and submission in the oppressed: Jesus will use a cross to expose the cruelty and injustice of those in power and instill hope and confidence in the oppressed. (*EMC* §15, 124)

Expectedly, McLaren sees contemporary parallels to these responses. There are Essene Christians who insulate themselves with their own broadcastings, writings, and universities. Zealot Christians promote warfare terminology in order to "take America back for Jesus." Pharisaical Christians blame scapegoats for the decline of Christianity by condemning their favorite sinners, such as homosexuals and liberals. Herodian and Sadduceeic Christians defend the economic and political status quo regardless of who is in power (*EMC* §11, 89–90).[88] From McLaren's perspective, however, Jesus' gospel message was about countering these narratives.

7.4.2 Jesus' Alternative Kingdom

McLaren sees six main storylines that have governed human behavior: 1) domination over others; 2) violence against others; 3) seclusion from others; 4) discrimination toward others; 5) victimization by others; and 6) privation of others. Nevertheless, Jesus offered a seventh story that focuses on reconciliation among all people groups (*CSS*; *TSS*). McLaren highlights the fact that Jesus never intended to establish a new religion. He merely announced the inauguration of God's kingdom, which undercut Rome's authority by stressing love and self-sacrifice.[89] Subsequently, McLaren's reconstruction suggests that Jesus' original gospel message was *explicitly* about the kingdom of God (*NKOCY* §14, 142) in defense of society's marginalized and oppressed (*WM-RBW*, 12–13). "The message of Jesus is not what most Christians assume it to be: information on how to go to heaven after you die. Instead, it is a radical message about

---

TWLR). "So for the conservatives, God is conservative (surprise!); for the liberals, God is liberal" (*MRTYR* §2, 34). He further remarks, "Democrats and Republicans, left and right, even 'terrorists' and 'free world' are generally playing by the same rules and part of the same system—in much the same way as in Jesus' day, complacent Herodians and Sadducees and activist Pharisees and Zealots were, for all their squabbles, playing within the same system: defining their lives in relation to Caesar" (*EMC* §33, 285).

88. See also, McLaren, "Found in Translation," 14. Interestingly, McLaren equates the Sadducees with contemporary conservatives and the Pharisees with contemporary liberals. The former because they were traditionalists while the latter syncretized and borrowed from other religious philosophies, such as Zoroastrianism. Thus, McLaren interprets Jesus as claiming both were perilously wrong just as conservatives and liberals are wrong today for making Jesus conform to their socio-political "boxes" (McLaren, "A Postmodern View of Scripture," 9).

89. *EMC* §15, 123; *FOWA* §4, 34–35; *GSM*, 93; *SMJ* §2, 10. In fact, McLaren believes Jesus' "revolutionary love" is the church's "*raison d'être*" (McLaren, "Conditions for the Great Religion Singularity," 46).

the possibility of a new social and spiritual order available and possible here and now, evoked in the pregnant yet elusive phrase *kingdom of God*."[90] Here, God's presence is found in serving others, unlike the practices of colonialism (*GSM*, 3), making Jesus' goal the creation of a missional community in pursuit of God's kingdom ideals (*AIFA*, 197–98).

Perhaps the greatest paradox for McLaren (§6.2.2) is that Christ's kingdom manifestation is completely backwards to worldly expectations (*FFR* §5, 113–114) and is indiscernible to the uninitiated (*SMJ* §7, 60).[91] For McLaren, the phrase "kingdom of God" does not reference the afterlife (*SMJ* §2, 14), nor does the phrase "eternal life" mean living in heaven after death. Rather, both relate chiefly to an earthly kingdom of God, being synonymous with other phrases such as "new life," "life in the Spirit," and "life in Christ."[92] The key to understanding Jesus' gospel is the Lord's Prayer, which implores God's heavenly kingdom to manifest itself here on earth (cf. *AMP* §3, 47; §4, 65; §15, 229–30). As Heinz Schürmann explains, the Lord's Prayer is the firmest method for understanding how Jesus viewed the kingdom of God.[93] Correspondingly, the appositive clause, "your kingdom come," equates to actualizing God's "wish" or "dream" for creation. Thus, McLaren translates Matthew 6:10 as, "May all your dreams for your creation come true" in a total display of *shalom* peace (*SMJ* §16, 140–41; §17, 161). From McLaren's perspective, God's dream is similar to "a mother who has great dreams for her child, or an artist who has great dreams for a novel or symphony he is creating."[94] As he clarifies,

90. McLaren, "The Secret Message of Jesus," 19; italics in original. McLaren remarks elsewhere, "Like many people, I formerly understood kingdom of God to refer to heaven after this life, with a kind of backlight cast on this life. Now, I see the kingdom as primarily being about God's will being done on earth, in history, with a forward light cast beyond this life" (Streett, "An Interview with Brian McLaren," 7). Thus, while he is "all for people going to heaven," McLaren is far more interested in the "gospel of the kingdom of God (not just the gospel of how to go to heaven after you die)" (McLaren, "Conversations," 342).

91. McLaren's reading of the Gospels suggests that the kingdom of God requires more than just logic to understand its implications, it requires the work of human imagination, as well (McLaren, "*PW* Talks with Brian McLaren," 62).

92. *EMC* §12, 311n2; *LWWAT* §13, 77–78; §24/25, 150–152; *SMJ* §5, 36–37; *WMRBW*, xvi n1. McLaren writes, "Could Christian faith lose the bitter taste of colonialism, exclusion, judgment, hypocrisy, and oppression, and regain the sweet and nourishing flavor of justice, joy, and peace?" (*GSM*, 2).

93. Schürmann, *Gottes Reich*, 135, 144. This verse is so integral to McLaren's philosophy of religion that it appears repeatedly throughout his writings. See for example, *AIFA*, 93, 113–14; *AMP* §3, 47; §7, 121; §15, 230; *EMC* §1, 4; §3, 20–21; §26, 219; *FOWA* §8, 69; *JMBM* §8, 69; *MRTYR* §18, 142; *SMJ* §16, 140; §19, 171; §20, 184; *SWFOI* §32, 240; *WMRBW*, 103. In fact, McLaren argues that loving God translates to supporting and establishing Jesus' desire to see the kingdom of God established on earth (*WMRBW*, 213). "It's the Kingdom of God, the dream of God coming true when people harmonize their wills with God's will" (*LWWAT* §23, 143). For McLaren, the kingdom of God is specifically about the Spirit's active work in the universe (*NKOC* §10, 120–21).

94. McLaren, "Found in Translation," 16. According to McLaren, however, "kingdom" language is anachronistic and may even sound despotic to today's hearers without proper explanation. Thus, McLaren infers that Jesus would not utilize this same political metaphor in the twenty-first century. Rather, McLaren thinks Jesus would use phrases such as "dream of God," "revolution of God," "mission

> *The kingdom of this world is (or has) become the kingdom of our Lord and of his Messiah*. We look around us, and what do we see?. . ..we see regimes of violence, threat, abuse, conflict, danger, pollution, corruption, domination, and oppression. The kingdom has not yet fully come. There is much to do—beginning with our realizing that there is such a thing, such a possibility, as the kingdom of God, and adjusting and arranging our lives to be part of it." (*SMJ* §21, 203; italics in original)

Here, God's kingdom signifies more than just charity work; it is about ensuring the poor and needy are protected from further destitution (*JMBM* §25, 237–38).[95] McLaren makes a strong distinction between "mercy" and "justice," explaining, "Unjust systems throw people into misery and mercy brings us to relieve some of their misery, but until we confront the unjust systems by doing justice we're never going to make a change."[96] Hence, "The kingdom of God . . . calls rich people to stop working to increase their personal wealth portfolio; instead, it challenges them to join God by using their wealth and power on behalf of the poor" (*VL*, 115).

Ultimately, the kingdom of God is characterized as benevolence toward all creation (*COOSI* §2, 31; *JMBM* §19, 171–72n6) where believers act out of compassion on behalf of the poor and the oppressed (*NS* §15, 139). The results are a radically different understanding of God and his priorities as preached in conventional paradigms:

> We come to know a God who consistently refuses to support a pyramid economy with a few at the top and the masses at the bottom. We come to trust a God who consistently opposes the oppressors and consistently takes the side of the humble, the vulnerable, and the poor. We eventually come to understand God as one who consistently prefers nonviolence over violence, equality over dominance, and justice over injustice. Taken together, these stories make one of the most audacious claims in all of history: the living God doesn't uphold the status quo . . . but repeatedly disrupts it and breaks it open so that something better can emerge and evolve. (*WMRBW*, 21; ellipses in original)

Rather than coming to save people from eternal damnation, McLaren interprets Jesus' original gospel message as the actualization of God's kingdom ethics, which would save people from injustice, inequality, violence, and other structural evils (cf. *GO* §3, 86; *JP* §Intro, 14).[97] As such, social issues were not mere annoyances to Jesus; they

---

of God," "party of God," "network of God," and "dance of God." These updated metaphors are meant to convey Jesus' opposition to social injustice, the need for an existential relationship with the divine, and the celebratory nature of God's hope for creation (pp. 14–19).

95. Accordingly, this kingdom is exceptional because it seeks to place others first through service and humility rather than the type of arrogant exceptionalism displayed in America today (§3.2.1.1). To be anything other than sacrificially generous in all areas of life is to be an embarrassment to Jesus' gospel message (*NKOC* §13, 161). See also, McLaren, "America the Exceptional," 19.

96. McLaren, "Author Brian McLaren." Cf. Belcher, *Deep Church*, 113–16.

97. McLaren, "*PW* Talks with Brian McLaren," 62. According to McLaren, the New Testament Greek word *dikaios*, often translated as "righteousness," is best understood as social, communal, and

were his entire focus (*NKOCY* §13, 127–28), and he is still deeply concerned about them today (cf. *EMC* §3, 19). In the end, Jesus did not intend a new culture-religion: he intended to redeem earthly cultures through a nonviolent socio-political insurgency known as the *pax Christi* (*NKOC* §9, 107; cf. *VA*, 78–79).[98]

7.4.2.1 Pax Christi

While the *pax Romana* pursued peace through violence and domination, Jesus' alternative kingdom reversed imperial methods through an incarnational solidarity with others (*EMC* §17, 138–39). The *pax Christi* is specifically a strategy for pursuing peace through empathy, humility, and self-sacrifice. Engaging in a "ministry of presence," where Jesus simply dwelt among the suffering of humanity, was the essence of Christ's incarnation and his subsequent ministry in the Spirit (*CT*, 19–22). "The suffering of others invariably puts each of us in a predicament of our own, a moment of choice. Will we, in our chosen response to the suffering of others, become more calloused, uncaring, embittered, or overwhelmed? Or will we strengthen the sacred connection with God and others, feeling compassion and desiring relief for our fellow creatures in pain?" (*NS* §14, 126; cf. *AIFA*, 72–73).

McLaren labels this *pax Christi* a "cruciform" lifestyle, which embraces suffering for the sake of others with the impression that denying the self and taking up the cross is at the heart of Christian tradition (see *GSM*, 185–88). More generally, the *pax Christi* is a method for establishing God's kingdom on earth in an existential act of faith that reverses worldly ideals of power and control. "What if our only hope lies in this impossible paradox: the only way the kingdom of God can be strong in a truly liberating way is through a scandalous, noncoercive kind of weakness; the only way it can be powerful is through astonishing vulnerability; the only way it can live is by dying; the only way it can succeed is by failing?" (*SMJ* §8, 70). The point of realizing God's kingdom is, ultimately, to pursue equality and peace (*EMC* §22, 177) by serving others (*AIFA*, 91) and eliminating systemic injustices (*GSM*, 152). However, the *pax Christi* does not mean Jesus was a mere "political action committee leader" (*AIFA*, 82n51); rather, he was a "wild" and untamable insurrectionist (*MRTYR* §7, 64). The difference is that he promoted nonviolent transformations, not violent ones (*WM-RBW*, 122; cf. *CIEC*, 94–95).[99]

---

global justice, not a privatized sense of piety (*EMC* §22, 319n4). For McLaren's definition of "justice," see *JP* §Justice, 21–22. Cf. Bouma, *Reimagining the Kingdom*, 143-68.

98. McLaren comments, "Jesus indeed was a revolutionary. He didn't come to proclaim a new religion, but a new kingdom—a new way of life. He was indeed a threat to Caesar's way of doing things, a way that had coopted the religious leaders" (*VL*, 158). He states elsewhere. "What if [Christ] didn't come to start a new religion—but rather came to start a political, social, religious, artistic, economic, intellectual, and spiritual revolution that would give birth to a new world?" (*SMJ* §1, 4).

99. Hence, "[Jesus] advocates an identity characterized by solidarity, sensitivity, and nonviolence. He celebrates those who long for justice, embody compassion, and manifest integrity and nonduplicity"

For McLaren, the problem is that Christianity soon forgot Jesus' original kingdom message by colluding with the Roman Empire (*JMBM* §11, 89; *WMRBW*, xviii–xix). Now, churches have become so compromised that they tell stories about Jesus but contradictorily support or enable the suicide machine (*EMC* §16, 128–132; cf. *SMJ* §19, 181; *VA*, 90).[100] Stated simply, the religious establishment's endorsement of any imperial or national power is the pinnacle of biblical hypocrisy because Jesus himself was put to death by those religious powers who conspired with wealthy imperialists (*EMC* §15, 124). Hence, the kind of spirituality that McLaren promotes is one that concedes to God's will for the betterment of humanity and the promotion of the common good. He objects to a faith that does the will of individual humans, religions, countries, and other alliances (*NS* §5, 44; §14, 126; *VA*, 11). "At the end of the day, being a Christian isn't about being ancient, medieval, modern, or postmodern. It's about following Jesus, becoming more like him, participating in the kingdom he announced and invited us into" (*COOS1* §12c, 201; cf. *CIEC*, 113). Of course, the question arises that if Jesus' original gospel message was about establishing God's kingdom, then how did the Apostle Paul and the early church misconstrue this message so drastically.

7.4.2.2 Pauline Christianity

McLaren responds by arguing that the apostles did not, in fact, misinterpret Jesus' message.[101] In reality, it was later Christians who mistook Paul as offering the "real" gospel while mistakenly presuming the four *Gospels* were mere stories about Jesus (cf. *GO* §3, 86n39; *EMC* §9, 308n4). "Paul wasn't trying to define or explain the gospel at all. . . .Paul never intended his letter[s] to be an exposition on the gospel" (*NKOCY* §14, 142–43). For McLaren, the problem is that Christians have retained Jesus as Savior but have promoted his successors to Lord and Teacher (*GO* §3, 86). This issue compounds as Christians today adhere to (for example) Jerry Falwell's *interpretation* of John Wesley's *interpretation* of Thomas Aquinas's *interpretation* of Augustine's *interpretation* of Paul. The practice, however, ought to be "frontwards" where Jesus' message is understood through Adam, Abraham, Moses, David, the prophets, and finally John the Baptist.[102] Besides, argues McLaren, even if Paul was elucidating Jesus'

(*WMRBW*, 128). In describing *Sojourners*, Robert Johnston writes, "Jesus' life is politically axiomatic. They believe, therefore, that Jesus neither calls his people to a personal, individualistic salvation, nor to a life of secular commitment to social action and class struggle, but rather to a participation with him in the kingdom of God" (Johnson, *Evangelicals at an Impasse*, 91).

100. Csinos and McLaren, "Breaking the Bubble Wrap," 18.

101. See *FOWA* §5, 41–49; *NKOCY* §16, 166–70; *SMJ* §11, 92–93; and McLaren, "A Postmodern View of Scripture," 14. McLaren does acknowledge, however, that soon after Jesus' death and resurrection, "pseudo-apostles" had already begun distorting Christ's message (*CIEC*, 180).

102. *NKOCY* §4, 36–37; §6, 59; §14, 140; cf. *NKOC* §9, 113–14; *SWFOI* §28, 209. McLaren quotes a friend in asking, "Don't you think we should let Jesus tell us what the gospel is?" (*SMJ* §11, 91). See also, McLaren, foreword to *Healing the Gospel*, ix–xi; Peppler, "A New Kind of Liberalism," 187–201; and Shogren, "'The Wicked Will Not Inherit the Kingdom of God,'" 95–113.

"real" gospel message, it makes no sense to interpret Jesus through *Paul*. In fidelity to Christ, Christians ought to interpret Paul through *Jesus* (*FOWA* §5, 41; *GO* §13, 206–7). As McLaren remarks, "To grant Jesus no more authority than Paul renders me speechless" (*NKOCY* §11, 274n6), especially since Paul was a second-generation latecomer to *Jesus*' revolution (*SMJ* §8, 66). In using Paul to interpret Jesus, believers have since converted to "Paulianity," not Christianity (*SMJ* §11, 90–94). Therefore, when traditionalists insist on making Jesus' death the main point of the incarnation, McLaren objects to their narrow understanding of Jesus' ministry and the cross.

7.5 DECONSTRUCTING THE CROSS

Concluding that Jesus' gospel focused on the kingdom of God, McLaren laments that Christians have overemphasized abstractions, like atonement theory and the second coming, to the neglect of more important issues (cf. *EMC* §10, 79–80; *WMRBW*, 52).[103] Adopting what he labels an "Eco-Christianity," which recognizes the biblical pattern of God coming down in solidarity with creation instead of humanity going up to be with God, McLaren reorients himself by emphasizing the poetic nature of Jesus' ministry and how it should affect the way Christians live (*COOS2* §11, 164; *CPA*, 117–18).[104] As he summarizes, Western Christianity has been so preoccupied with God's wrathful punishment of sinners that it has effectively turned God into the enemy of humanity. The cross simply becomes a means of rescuing people from God's vicious anger. For McLaren, however, the true enemy is humanity itself, especially its propensity towards violence. With this in mind, McLaren concludes that God wants to save people not from himself but from perpetuating injustice and inequality (cf. *EMC* §22, 179–80).[105] In this way, Jesus' death is illustrative of God's sacrificial and loving character, not his violent wrath.

7.5.1 Rejecting a Violent God

McLaren objects to penal substitutionary atonement theory because it depicts God as a wrathful Father seeking revenge, which then requires Jesus to rescue the world from his own Father. In this schema, God unjustly punishes an innocent man to avoid penalizing the people he actually loves (*EMC* §10, 79–81). Even worse, God violently

---

103. As he questions, "Should Jesus' life, teaching, signs and wonders, resurrection, and ascension be marginalized, as if the only thing about him that really matters is his substitutionary death?" (*JMBM* §23, 211n8). Cf Haykin, "Recovering Ancient Church Practices," 62–66.

104. McLaren, "Brian McLaren Reflects on 'Seizing An Alternative' Conference," 05:32–06:34. McLaren says he is interested in applying Celtic, Franciscan, Anabaptist, Quaker, Eastern Orthodox, and liberationist interpretations of Jesus' atonement (*EMC* §10, 309n5; *JMBM* §18, 157).

105. McLaren, "Darkwood Brew Interview," 03:18–05:07. McLaren writes elsewhere, "[God's] anger is never against *us* (or *them*); it is against *what is against* us (and them). [God's anger] is not out to destroy us; it is out to destroy what is out to destroy us" (*JMBM* §28, 260; italics in original).

murders his own Son, being somehow incapable of forgiving others without first torturing someone else (cf. *JMBM* §23, 210; *SWFOI* §20, 143). As one fictional character remarks, "That just sounds like one more injustice in the cosmic equation. It sounds like divine child abuse" (*SWFOI* §20, 143).[106] For McLaren, this mentality cannot be the same God who demanded loving and forgiving one's enemies (cf. *EMC* §12, 99). "If violence and hostility characterize God's identity, is it realistic to aspire to be better than God by being nonviolent and nonhostile?" (*JMBM* §23, 211n8).[107]

Theologically, according to McLaren, substitution theory fails precisely because God does not actually desire nor require blood sacrifices like other pagan deities (*JMBM* §23, 212–13; *WMRBW*, 58–59). In fact, McLaren suggests the Hebrew Bible's demand for animal sacrifices originally represented God's longing for people to relinquish things of value in order to prioritize placing the good of the community above themselves.[108] He explains,

> After ritualized human sacrifice was left behind forever, prophets and poets arose among Abraham's descendants who made the shocking claim that God doesn't need animal sacrifices, either. They realized that God could never need anything *from* us, since God provides everything *for* us. Not only that, but they realized God isn't the one who is angry and hostile and needs appeasement. We humans are the angry ones! Our hostile, bloodthirsty hearts are the ones that need to be changed! (*WMRBW*, 30; italics in original)

For McLaren, substitutionary atonement reduces people's relationship with the divine to a mere transactional agreement, "a get-out-of-hell-free card, a way of managing a nasty legal problem by striking a deal with the judge" (*CPA*, 118). The result is a religion full of "'vampire Christians' who want Jesus for his blood and little else" (*GO* §1, 48n18).[109] Rather than establish a selfish religion, McLaren believes Jesus' death was really a confrontation with imperialism.

---

106. McLaren's statement echoes one book (endorsed by McLaren) that describes the cross as "a form of cosmic child abuse - a vengeful Father, punishing his Son for an offense he has not even committed. . . .If the cross is a personal act of violence perpetrated by God towards humankind but borne by his Son, then it makes a mockery of Jesus' own teaching to love your enemies and to refuse to repay evil with evil" (Chalke and Mann, *The Lost Message of Jesus*, 182–83). From McLaren's accentuation of Jesus' life, it is clear that both God and Jesus are thoroughly good and nonviolent (McLaren, foreword to *Solus Jesus*, xvi–xvii).

107. He explains elsewhere, "If you really believe that calling God by the right name can spell the difference between eternal happiness and eternal suffering, then it becomes quite reasonable to treat heretics and unbelievers rather badly" (*JMBM* §7, 55). "If God tortures for eternity, might it be OK for us to do the same in our next war or political upheaval?" (*WMRBW*, 256). In his estimation, the future of Christianity depends on disarming it of its violent elements (McLaren, foreword to *Disarming Scripture*, xvii–xxi).

108. *The Bible Rules*, 25:59–26:07.

109. Here, McLaren borrows the phrase "vampire Christians" from Willard, *The Divine Conspiracy*, 403n8. These sentiments echo Jürgen Moltmann, who pejoratively referred to the penal substitutionary theory as a divine "emergency measure" (Moltmann, *The Trinity and the Kingdom*, 114). Much

7.5.2 Reversing Imperial Violence

McLaren's atonement beliefs most closely align with *Christus Victor* theory (*GO* §1, 54) where Jesus' death and resurrection is actually a clash with the unjust power structures that oppose God's kingdom (*SWFOI* §20, 146). As Gustaf Aulén explains, "Its central theme is the idea of the atonement as a divine conflict and victory; Christ—*Christus Victor*—fights against and triumphs over the evil powers of the world, the 'tyrants' under which mankind is in bondage and suffering, and in him God reconciles the world to himself."[110] Sharing N. T. Wright's view, McLaren understands Jesus' death as inherently political, not metaphysical, where Jesus reverses Roman political violence by flaunting the ineffectiveness of using might to achieve peace (*EMC* §10, 308–9n4; §19, 158–59).[111] Hence, the crucifixion and resurrection were prophetic actions condemning institutional oppression and injustice. Using the book of Hosea, McLaren views God as prophetically speaking through victims of society. The cross becomes a symbol for humanity's selfishness and the pain it causes God personally (*CPA*, 114–20). He writes,

> By becoming vulnerable on the cross, by accepting suffering *from* everyone, Jews and Romans alike, rather than visiting suffering *on* everyone, Jesus is showing God's loving heart, which wants forgiveness, not revenge, for everyone. Jesus shows us that the wisdom of God's kingdom is [self-]sacrifice, not violence. It's about accepting suffering and transforming it into reconciliation, not avenging suffering through retaliation. (*SWFOI* §20, 148; italics in original)

From this perspective, the phrase "Jesus died for our sins" now becomes, "[Jesus died] to help cure [our sins]" or "because of [our sins]." It no longer means appeasing a bloodthirsty deity (*JMBM* §23, 212n11). As William Payne remarks, "[Liberationists] stress Jesus' unjust suffering and victimization at the hands of corrupt religious and government establishments."[112] The resurrection, therefore, is political because it indicates the triumph of the *pax Christi* over the *pax Romana* (cf. *TSS*, 48–55). With these inferences in mind, it becomes much harder for McLaren to conceive of the afterlife, heaven and hell, through conventional paradigms.

---

like McLaren, Moltmann argued that the incarnation created a solidarity between God and humanity that allowed God to suffer genuinely as a "poor slave" in his kenosis. "This is a path of self-emptying. If we look at that solidarity with the helpless and the poor which it manifests, it is the path of the divine love in its essential nature" (Moltmann, *The Way of Jesus Christ*, 178).

110. Aulén, *Christus Victor*, 20. Cf. Boyd, "Christus Victor View," 23–46 and Weaver, *The Nonviolent Atonement*, 20–69, 282–83.

111. McLaren mentions that his ideas about eschatology are largely due to N. T. Wright and Lesslie Newbigin (*LWWAT* §Intro, xv; "Why Everything Must Change: A Conversation with Brian McLaren"). See the numerous liberationist imagery in Wright, *Jesus and the Victory of God*, 2:383–611 and Waters, "It's 'Wright,' but Is It Right?," 188–210.

112. Payne, "Discerning an Integral," 91–92. Cf. Bouma, *The Gospel of Brian McLaren*, 41–46.

7.5.3 Heaven and Hell

For Greg Gilbert, a McLaren critic, the notion of hell is pretty straightforward: neither Jesus nor the apostles "intended to convey with their teaching about hell anything other than that it is a real experience of eternal conscious torment of *God's enemies*."[113] For many others, however, this belief maintains a macabre notion of God being "superficially exacting" about doctrine yet unconcerned with humans experiencing "rage, condemnation, punishment, torture, and vengeance" in hell (*NKOCY* §10, 102). The result is that a so-called compassionate Father not only views his own children as an "enemy," but he seems incapable of making peace with them (*GO* §13, 207). "Our way of talking about hell sounds absolutely wacky. 'God loves you and has a wonderful plan for your life,' we say, 'and he'll fry your butt in hell forever unless you do or believe the right thing.' 'God is a loving father,' we say, 'but he'll treat you with a cruelty that no human father has ever been guilty of—eternal conscious torture'" (*LWWAT* §13, 75).[114] From McLaren's viewpoint, Jesus' remark on the cross demonstrates that he insists on forgiving those who reject him, not condemning them (cf. *LWWAT* §17, 102; *WMRBW*, 160, 164).

While McLaren explicitly discards conventional universalist, exclusivist, and inclusivist paradigms (*GO §5, 113*–14; *LWWAT* §Intro, xv), he does embrace an alternative framework based on "rhetorical hermeneutics."[115] Here, McLaren argues that Jesus' comments on hell are not meant as ontological details; instead, they are standard apocalyptic images designed as a rhetorical device to expose the duplicity of the religious establishment (see *LWWAT* §12/13, 71–81; §Comm. 188–89). To suggest otherwise would mean Jesus was guilty of embracing Roman tactics of violence and cruelty, the very thing he denounced.[116] As Richard McBrien explains, "When Jesus used this imagery, he did so not to describe a particular place but to dramatize the urgency of his proclamation of the Kingdom and the seriousness of our decisions for or against the Kingdom. . . .Neither Jesus, nor the Church after him, ever stated that persons actually go to hell or are there now."[117] Accordingly, McLaren thinks Jesus

---

113. Gilbert, "Saved from the Wrath of God," 260; emphasis added. See also, Robertson, "A Critical Analysis," 133–39.

114. McLaren continues, "Jesus said God is good, like a caring father. Caring fathers don't torture their children" (*LWWAT* §17, 100). Later, when discussing the death of a Holocaust survivor, one of McLaren's fictional characters pointedly asks, "How am I supposed to believe that after all Shirley's father suffered, he's going to burn in hell forever, eternally tortured, because he didn't believe in Jesus? What kind of God would add his own torture to the obscenity of human torture her father suffered?" (*LWWAT* §14, 85).

115. Cf. Dixon, "'Five by McLaren,'" 217–71 and Craigen, "Emergent Soteriology," 177–90.

116. McLaren, "Finding the Seventh Story," 128; italics in original. Besides, McLaren argues, billions upon billions of human beings perpetually existing in agonizing torment for all eternity is not "good news," nor is it just, loving, or life-affirming (*LWWAT* §1, 8–9). See also, McLaren, "Making Eschatology Personal."

117. McBrien, *Catholicism*, 1176.

reversed conceptions of hell specifically to counter the exclusive arrogance of dogmatists (*LWWAT* §22, 136; *WMRBW*, 111–13). "Ironically, it wasn't the whores and crooks that Jesus threatened with hell. . . .it was the religious who heard the rhetoric of fire and brimstone!" (*FFR* §9, 176).[118]

Because of his belief in divine *complacentia* (§6.2.4), it is hard for McLaren to think that God needs to torture sinners just to satisfy a dichotomistic and unnuanced sense of justice. It would not be difficult for Jesus to show grace toward creation while still remaining hostile toward human greed and violence (cf. *SWFOI* §20, 141–50). Hence, McLaren highlights "the deeper and wider existential, social, systemic, historical, ecological, and economic dimensions of sin" (*JMBM* §23, 211n8). In McLaren's alternative model, the notion of hell should force Christians to focus less on personal salvation and more on social justice (*BMF*, 291; *EMC* §5, 33).[119] He hypothesizes that upon death, each individual will have two different experiences of the same reality. There, a person's character before death will determine whether being in God's presence is heavenly or not. For instance, McLaren asserts that God's presence is alive with unspeakable goodness and love. For those who have lived a life of hate and selfishness, however, this experience is likely to be at least temporarily hellish (*NKOC* §10, 122–31).

7.6 CONCLUSION

McLaren's philosophical rationale demands deconstructing institutional Christian beliefs about the nature and content of Jesus' original gospel message. Believing that Jewish subjugation is the primary matrix through which to interpret the Gospels (*SMJ* §2, 12), McLaren concludes that Jesus' original message was about establishing the kingdom of God in defiance against Rome. Theologically, the most significant consequence is the notion that Jesus would likely *not* be a "Christian" today. As McLaren suggests, "I don't think Christians would like Jesus if he showed up today as he did 2,000 years ago. In fact, I think we'd call him a heretic and plot to kill him, too" (*GO* §3, 80).[120] Thus, McLaren openly admits that he would rather be a follower of Jesus and not associate with Christianity than be affiliated with Christianity and not follow Jesus' liberationist ways (*FOWA* §4, 33); but this proclamation engenders another

---

118. He comments elsewhere, "Who was going to hell? Rich and successful people who lived in fancy houses and stepped over their destitute neighbors who slept in the gutters outside their gates. Proud people who judged, insulted, excluded, avoided, and accused others. Fastidious hypocrites who strained out gnats and swallowed camels. The condemnation that the religious elite so freely pronounced on the marginalized, Jesus turned back on them" (*WMRBW*, 113; see also, *EMC* §25, 208). However, asking who is going to hell explains why McLaren rejects Calvinism and Arminianism; they are both premised on a faulty belief in eternal conscious torment (*BMF*, 297–98).

119. McLaren writes, "If our theologies make us focus only on the eternal and the individual (i.e., getting my soul into heaven) so that we avoid God's concern for the historic and the global (i.e. God's will being done on earth as well as in heaven), then the more people we win over to our theologies, the fewer people will care about God's world here and now" (*AMP* §3, 57).

120. Kristof, "What Religion Would Jesus Belong To?"

dilemma. Some may dismiss McLaren's views as nothing more than the appropriation of liberation theology, or equating his philosophy of religion with a proclamation of the "social gospel."[121]

He does make distinctions between his approach and liberation theology, and he rejects parodies of the social gospel that replace, rather than augment, the spiritual and personal dimensions of Jesus' message with social and political concerns. He believes Jesus' message of the kingdom of God applies to all of life, including public matters like poverty, ecology, corruption, and racism, as well as personal matters like lying, cheating, greed, lust, and pride. Ultimately, he sees personal and public dimensions to Jesus' vision of building an "authentic community, for the good of the world" (see *CIEC*, 211–15). For him, liberation theology correctly identified the economic problems of South America but mistakenly aligned with Marxist and Communist ideologies (*GO* §1, 62–64). As such, "real liberation" means actualizing God's kingdom in all contexts (*AIFA*, 183–84) while seeking to learn how Jesus would respond to both local and global twenty-first century problems (cf. *SMJ* §16, 139). In this sense, Christians, and religionists in general, need to evolve in how they conceive of God and their role in his kingdom (*GI*, 190–94). Hence, McLaren's philosophy of religion has both a personal and global outlook, laying the foundation for his existentially intersubjective approach to faith.

---

121. McLaren writes, "I've been convinced that [Jesus' message] has everything to do with public matters in general and politics in particular—including economics and aid, personal empowerment and choice, foreign policy and war" (*SMJ* §2, 10). See also, McLaren, "Brian McLaren Responds."

8

McLaren's Existential Intersubjectivity

8.0 INTRODUCTION

Utilizing abductive inferences (chapter 5) to expand his understanding of the incarnation (chapter 6), Brian McLaren's deconstruction of institutional Christianity (chapter 7) resulted in an alternative religio-philosophy that distinguishes between *doctrinal beliefs* and a *meaningful faith*. For McLaren, although theology is important, it is not central to a relationship with God (*AMP* §6, 102-3). Hence, he argues that someone can cognitively assent to beliefs *about* God without ever possessing faith *in* God; and just like Abraham, believers should be able to enjoy faith without needless esoterica (*GSM*, 47-46, 215-28).[1] The thesis of this chapter is that McLaren's philosophy of religion is the appropriation of divergent theological perspectives in order to embody an existentially intersubjective relationship with God (cf. *BMF*, 302). Here, McLaren evaluates Christian paradigms according to experience and the ability for disciples to internalize and actualize Christ's kingdom ethics. Four proposals will support this theory: 1) McLaren's post-ontotheology; 2) his nuanced distinction between types of truth and knowledge; 3) the emancipatory ethics of postcolonialism; and 4) his criteria for assessing Christian paradigms. With McLaren, a proper philosophy of religion begins with overcoming ontotheology.

---

1. As McLaren writes, "Having faith is really about seeking something beyond faith itself: we are seeking truth, love, purpose, and a sense of place in the universe" (*FFR* §Intro, 16).

8.1 POST-ONTOTHEOLOGY

An "analytic" approach to the philosophy of religion applies logical axioms to an emotionless and often apathetic interpretation of empirical data.[2] From the postmodern perspective (§4.4), however, academia's approach is simply too indifferent to the real-world implications of religious faith (§6.2.1), particularly since rationality cannot corroborate Christian paradox (§6.2.2) or answer life's deepest questions (cf. *AMP* §6, 103; *COOS1* §6, 78-79).[3] Those utilizing a "continental" philosophy of religion, however, recognize that *propositional* reasoning necessitates *propositional* content.[4] Here, continental philosophers have a general mistrust of abstract theorizing because faith possesses its own existential logic.[5] As Myron Penner explains, "Christianity, however, is a *way of being* . . . a way of living with and before God—and not just a cognitive event involving intellectual assent to a set of propositions."[6] Curbing this ontotheology is the best way to recapture the ineffable Otherness of deity while avoiding "the arrogant humanism that puts God at our disposal."[7] While McLaren believes doctrines are vital (*GO* §0, 32), they cannot substitute the existential command to love others (cf. *GSM*, 20).[8] Thus, he approaches faith through "nonconceptual thinking (intuition, aesthetic inclinations, spiritual enlightenment, emotions, images), through

---

2. This tradition dates to at least the scholasticism of the high Middle Ages and has continued throughout modernity. See Caputo, "Who Comes After the God of Metaphysics?," 2-3 and Dulles, *A History of Apologetics*, 98-132.

3. Cf. Lewis, *Testing Christianity's Truth Claims*, 45-98, 287; Levine, "Contemporary Christian Analytic Philosophy of Religion," 89-119; Boa and Bowman, *Faith Has Its Reasons*, 49-69; Caputo, *Philosophy and Theology*, 50; and Gschwandtner, *Postmodern Apologetics?*, 10. For an example of this analytical approach to Christian faith, see Geisler, *Christian Apologetics*.

4. Simmons and Benson, *The New Phenomenology*, 182-83. As John Caputo remarks, "The God of the traditional philosophy of religion is a philosopher's God explicating a philosopher's faith, to be found, if anywhere, only on the pages of philosophy journals, not in the hearts of believers or the practice of faith. This philosopher's God is a creature of scholastic, modernist, and Enlightenment modes of thinking that deserve nothing so much as a decent burial" (Caputo, "Who Comes After the God of Metaphysics?," 3). McLaren elaborates further, "I think most Christians grossly misunderstand the philosophical baggage associated with terms like *absolute* and *objective* (linked to foundationalism and the myth of neutrality)" (McLaren and Litfin, "Emergent Evangelism," 43; italics in original).

5. Heidegger, *Identity and Difference*, 42-74; Meynell, "Two Traditions and the Philosophy of Religion," 267-74; Trabbic, "Aquinas and Continental Philosophy of Religion," 210-28; Smith, "Continental Philosophy of Religion," 440-48; Westphal, "Inverted Intentionality," 233-52; Gschwandtner, *Postmodern Apologetics?*, 19-30; Caputo, "Who Comes After the God of Metaphysics?," 2-3.

6. Penner, "Postmodern Apologetics," 139; italics in original.

7. Westphal, *Overcoming Onto-Theology*, 24. Merold Westphal reiterates, "We must think God as the mystery that exceeds the wisdom of the Greeks. We must think God as the voice that exceeds vision so as to establish a relation irreducible to comprehension. We must think God as the gift of love who exceeds not merely the images but also the concepts with which we aim at God" (p. 270; italics removed from original). See also, Westphal, *Transcendence and Self-Transcendence*, 93-114, 133, 140; Benson, *Graven Ideologies*, 110-24; Simmons and Benson, *The New Phenomenology*, 145-50; and Gschwandtner, *Postmodern Apologetics?*, 237-41.

8. According to McLaren, the fundamentals of Christian faith are to love God and to love others (*GO* §12, 184), and expressing love for others is the truest form of loving God (*GSM*, 56-57).

mystical enlightenment, through anomalous and peak experiences, and through soul journeys" (*AIFA*, 202).

According to McLaren, Christianity's stagnation stems partly from ontotheology's epistemic arrogance (§7.1.1), which claimed it could provide absolute truth (*FFS* §1, 46-48). Christianity has since become reductionistic in its attempt to eliminate divine mystery while ignoring the socio-historical contexts through which "God-talk" arises. The result is an artificial religion founded on human imagination, not a relationship with the divine.[9] A renouncement of the "philosopher's God" is now necessary to combat the arrogant intellectualizing that has transformed Christianity into just another metaphysical system of thought.[10] Echoing Martin Luther, McLaren labels this protest a "naked spirituality" (*NS* §Intro, 3). For Luther, God is *Deus nudus* ("naked God"), who "is unknowable exactly because....[t]here is no medium through which one can reach *Deus absconditus*."[11] The implication here is that rationally-inspired dogma cannot guide spirituality because it fails to appreciate divine mysteries. The point is not that classical abstractions are baseless; the point is that they are ineffectual for the relational aspects of faith that require emulating Jesus' way of life (*AMP* §6, 95-96; *COOS1* §6, 78).[12]

8.1.1 Emulating Jesus

The ultimate goal of post-ontotheology is to unite believers under something other than dogmatic (and unprovable) pronouncements about the essence of a God who surpasses human knowledge (cf. *GSM*, 220-28). Hence, McLaren's approach begins with focusing on questions of empathy and social justice, not with abstract doctrines.[13] "Some might argue that the esoteric arguments [of the past] were necessary;

---

9. As Christina Gschwandtner comments, "This is not the God to whom Christians (or others) pray, but it is the philosophical concept of the divine" (Gschwandtner, *Postmodern Apologetics?*, 20); or, as Martin Heidegger remarked, "Man can neither pray nor sacrifice to this god. Before the *causa sui*, man can neither fall to his knees in awe nor can he . . . dance before this god" (Heidegger, *Identity and Difference*, 72; italics in original). Cf. Ingraffia, *Postmodern Theory and Biblical Theology*, 241; Hemming, "Nihilism," 96; Siniscalchi, "Knowing that God Exists," 60-61; Simmons and Benson, *The New Phenomenology*, 96-98, 140-50, 182; and Westphal, *Transcendence and Self-Transcendence*, 15-40, 115-16.

10. Cf. Caputo, "Who Comes After the God of Metaphysics?," 2-3; Simmons and Benson, *The New Phenomenology*, 91, 97, 142, 182-83; and Ingraffia, *Postmodern Theory and Biblical Theology*, 101-22, 226.

11. Laats, "Luther's Idea of *Deus Absconditus*," 172. Merold Westphal utilizes similar language, "It is the task of the intellect to apprehend God naked" (Westphal, *Overcoming Onto-Theology*, 239), meaning the self-revelation of God intends to flout human wisdom precisely because it is the revelation of a "hidden" and mysterious God (Muller, *Dictionary of Latin and Greek Theological Terms*, 90).

12. Cf. Alessi, "L'essere e la crose," 53-111; Heidegger, *The Phenomenology of Religious Life*, 79; and Webber, *The Younger Evangelicals*, 94-106.

13. McLaren, "Reflection on Postcolonial Friendship," 14. Cf. Simmons and Benson, *The New Phenomenology*, 90-91 and Hemming, "Nihilism," 96.

otherwise, Christian theology would have lost its doctrinal integrity. . . . .But if it did indeed succeed in saving its doctrinal integrity, one wonders if it lost its ethical integrity in the process, and one wonders what profit there is in saving the former while losing the latter."[14] Stated differently, the incarnation was not about providing esoteric information; it was about establishing relationships so no single religion or group of people could claim supremacy over others (cf. *AMP* §6, 102-3). Thus, McLaren insists he merely follows "the [old] way of Jesus," which is the way of love (*GSM*, 51-56).[15] He wants Christianity to transform from "*a religion organized for self-preservation and privilege to a religion organizing for the common good of all*" (*GSM*, 153; italics in original).[16] For him, emulating Jesus necessarily requires an existentially intersubjective faith.

8.2 EXISTENTIAL INTERSUBJECTIVITY

As "Son of Man," McLaren believes Jesus is the "ultimate embodiment of humanity" and, therefore, has an intersubjective relationship to every person on earth (*GO* §2, 72). At its core, McLaren's religio-philosophy is about an intersubjective relationship with God, whereby an existential internalization and actualization of God's priorities manifest in his followers. Thus, McLaren characterizes being "spiritual" in relational terms: "living in an interactive relationship with God" (*SMJ* §10, 83; cf. *MRTYR* §18, 135). The result is a shared emphasis on living *authentically*, "a better way of being Christian, and a better way of being human" (*GSM*, xiii). Sylvia Walsh explains further, "What Christianity seeks to communicate to individuals is not *knowledge* about Christianity . . . but an *inward capability* for existing authentically through a relation to God."[17] In essence, an existentially intersubjective paradigm entails a set of

---

14. McLaren, "The Secret Message of Jesus," 20.

15. Cf. Burson, *Brian McLaren in Focus*, 189-92; Clark, "Reformed Epistemology Apologetics," 278-83; Penner and Barnes, *A New Kind of Conversation*, 45, 51; Penner, *The End of Apologetics*, 77-108; Gschwandtner, *Postmodern Apologetics?*, 211; Webber, *The Younger Evangelicals*, 104-18; and Simmons and Benson, *The New Phenomenology*, 219.

16. Here, McLaren is insisting on reprioritizing more important things (§3.4.1) than being doctrinally correct (*NKOC* §8, 86-96). As he describes it, he wants to transform Christianity "*From a System of Beliefs to a Way of Life*" (*GSM*, 17; italics in original). Thus, the new era of Christian faith is characterized by action and attitude, not doctrine. "The farther back we go [in church history], the more we see that our forebears saw truth and belief as essential for an even higher goal: a way of life lived in community" (McLaren, "Everything Old Is New Again," 25). As one blogger explains, "I desire to be part of a church that holds more loosely to its defining propositions and more tightly to its defining actions" (Penner and Barnes, *A New Kind of Conversation*, 54). According to McLaren, this intersubjective connection between humans and the divine is precisely what Jesus had with the Father. Their bond was not institutionalized or cultic; it was relational and familial, which explains why Jesus referred to God in Aramaic as *Abba*, or "daddy" (*GO* §2, 73-74). Cf. Barr, "Abbā Isn't 'daddy,'" 28-47.

17. Walsh, *Kierkegaard*, 26; italics in original. McLaren clarifies the role of authenticity in his pursuit of faith, "I began wondering what it means to be an authentic follower of Jesus in my daily life" (*SMJ* §1, 5).

characteristics that are both isolable, in the sense of possessing their own limits for study, and contingent, in the sense of needing insights from each other in order to comprehend the whole. Before examining these features, however, it is first necessary to define "intersubjectivity."

8.2.1 Defining Intersubjectivity

Describing the kingdom of God, McLaren writes, "A kingdom is a network of relationships. It's a relationship with a king, and then it's a relationship with all the other citizens in the kingdom, and then that puts you in relationship with the land the kingdom occupies and with people in other kingdoms."[18] He simplifies elsewhere, "God the ultimate subject has created us for an intersubjective relationship with himself, with one another, and with creation. . .I am created for intersubjective relationships—that is, for love" (*AMP* §17, 261-62).[19] This "interactive family relationship" (*FFR* §4, 90) is the essence of intersubjectivity, which is the sharing of people's conscious experiences (i.e., empathic communication). It results in a belief that "all public, objective events are in actuality shared subjective experiences."[20] In other words, intersubjectivity is the interchange of thoughts and emotions between persons sharing empathy for one another. In both philosophical constructivism and social constructionism, this empathy suggests that relational networks *co-create* perceived reality (cf. §6.2.3.1). Thus, intersubjectivity may properly be defined as the reciprocity of experiential knowledge (§2.1) that ensues from intimate interactions (cf. *TSS*, 32).[21] As McLaren clarifies, to "know" God means to "be in an interactive relationship with" the divine (*LWWAT* §25, 151), being a different kind of "knowing" than what develops from abstract theorizing (*CIEC*, 249). "We find ourselves as beings-in-relationship with that which we interact. We live, move, and have our being in relationships, because God the ultimate reality is at heart a triune relational being" (*AMP* §17, 261).[22]

Describing it as being "post-objective" (*AIFA*, 242), McLaren first learned about intersubjectivity from Walker Percy, who described the perils of theological objectivity, which effectively cheapens God into a non-relational dyad ("object") of study (an "I-it" relationship). Conversely, in subjectivity, theologians align dyads to fit their own self-conceptions (an "I-I" relationship). Intersubjectivity, on the other hand,

---

18. McLaren, "*PW* Talks with Brian McLaren," 62. Thus, McLaren's definition of God is "*the one through whom we are related and connected to everything*" (*WMRBW*, 8; italics in original).

19. Significantly, McLaren also defines spirituality as "*seeking vital connection*" with God and the created order, which McLaren argues is, in essence, just another synonym for "love" (*NS* §2, 15; italics in original). "Loving a distant and theoretical God who must be approached through complex belief systems can indeed be tough—even exhausting, mentally and emotionally. But loving the God who is experienced in love for neighbor, self, and creation comes as naturally as breathing" (*GSM*, 61).

20. VandenBos, *APA Dictionary of Psychology*, s.v. "Intersubjectivity."

21. Cooper-White, "Intersubjectivity."

22. Cf. Moon, "God as a Communicative System *Sui Generis*," 105-26.

transcends these subject-object dealings (i.e., *intra*subjectivity) to allow an exchange of experiential data between persons (an "I-thou" relationship). Here, God becomes a second Subject in the knower-known, friend-friend relationship. This connection allows for a mutual rapport between humans and the divine, which then affects each other's subjective perception of reality (cf. *AMP* §2, 39-40; §17, 257-62).[23] Ultimately, intersubjectivity transcends the false dichotomy of objective-subjective faith (cf. *COOS1* §12a, 169). The implication is that people should not only reform their beliefs about God as their experiential intimacy with him deepens (*GO* §12, 191-93), but it also suggests becoming so personally invested in God that injustices perpetrated in his name are personally unbearable (*AMP* §17, 260-62). In this sense, an intersubjective faith transcends false notions of objectivity.

8.2.1.1 Post-Objectivity

Benjamin Warfield once argued that rationality can authenticate Christianity and that believers should accept Christ precisely because it is logical to do so.[24] For McLaren, however, objectivity is illusory (*AIFA*, 162) and is maladaptive to the existential duties of religious faith. To him, believers should supplement logic with emotion and experience (*COOS1* §6, 80).[25] In fact, the church is failing today partly because it excludes other epistemic sources, such as spiritualism, imagination, service, suffering, and love.[26] Jaroslav Pelikan summarizes the problem, "In an effort to demonstrate the plausibility of the Christian faith, many Orthodox theologians made extravagant claims for reason and philosophy, so that to many an observer it must have seemed that there was very little actually remaining for divine revelation to supply."[27] Ultimately, logic cannot provide the passion necessary to follow Christ.[28] "For a new kind of Christian, there is no objective laboratory (seminary, study, pulpit) where we can remove the subjective

---

23. McLaren summarizes, "God can't ever really be an object to be studied" (*NKOC* §16, 231), because "we as personal subjects interact with other personal subjects" (*AIFA*, 164; cf. *CIEC*, 256). Hence, intersubjectivity entails the "move from aggressive reasoning to receptive understanding. From knowing about to knowing-in-relationship. From facts to meaning. From taking things apart to seeing things whole. From knowledge to love, from prose to poetry, and from invocation and thanksgiving to the awe of worship" (*NS* §8, 69-70).

24. Warfield, *The Works of Benjamin B. Warfield*, 9:8-9, 15. Norman Geisler concurs, "If logic is the basis of all thought, it is the basis of all thought about God. . . . A reasonable Christian merely uses reason to *discover* truth that God has revealed, either by general revelation or by special revelation in the Bible" (Geisler, *Baker Encyclopedia of Christian Apologetics*, s.v. "Logic;" italics in original). See also, Geisler and Feinberg, *Introduction to Philosophy*, 255-70.

25. McLaren writes, "Unfortunately for defenders of objectivity, this reality isn't real. It is a figment of the Enlightenment, and it never really existed" (*AIFA*, 163). Cf. Sinnott, *The Development of Logic in Adulthood*, esp. 23-49 and Berger, *The Developing Person*, 521-22.

26. Cf. Craig, *Reasonable Faith*, 29-60, esp. 51-56; Boa and Bowman, *Faith Has Its Reasons*, 71-77; and Lewis, *Testing Christianity's Truth Claims*, 291-93.

27. Pelikan, *From Luther to Kierkegaard*, 77.

28. Pojman, *The Logic of Subjectivity*, 39-47; Elrod, *Kierkegaard and Christendom*, 202-03.

'variables' of who we are, and where we are; rather, those very variables are essential factors in how we see God, life, ourselves, everything" (*AMP* §17, 262).

In response to conventional paradigms, post-objectivists try to reclaim a pre-critical emphasis on intuition in order to avoid an overly analytical faith (*AIFA*, 164). They do not want to discard logic; rather, they renounce using rationality to transform Christian paradox into flat propositions, particularly since logic is incapable of scrutinizing God.[29] Penner clarifies,

> The 'absolute truths' of God's revelation are not rationally compelling in the universal and objective reason of modernity. . . . It takes something else—what modernity would call an appeal to subjectivity—to recognize and accept God's revelation. . . . modern apologists who attempt to establish the authority of revelation according to the standards of modern criteria for rationality implicitly deny the apostolic source of authority, which was always and only God's revelation to them (cf. 1 Corinthians 1:18–2:16).[30]

Hence, post-objectivists postulate that the first Christians did not embrace Christ because it was rational to do so; instead, they accepted him because they had a personal encounter with him.[31] In fact, for McLaren, everything is inherently subjective because God subjectively values everything in creation (*AIFA*, 163).[32] Christianity should incorporate both reason and emotion (*FOWA* §1, 4; cf. *FFR* §7, 154–57) while espousing a "radical orthodoxy" that denies objectivity as the arbiter of spiritual truth (*AIFA*, 251–53).[33] He clarifies elsewhere, "Faith is an attempt to orient oneself to and

---

29. John Franke eloquently summarizes, "Postmodern theory does not support the rejection of rationality but rather supports rethinking rationality in the wake of modernity. This rethinking has resulted not in irrationality, as is often claimed by less informed critics of postmodern thought, but rather in numerous redescriptions and proposals concerning the understanding of rationality and knowledge" (Franke, foreword to *A Generous Orthodoxy*, 10). See also, Penner and Barnes, *A New Kind of Conversation*, 18–19, 34; Penner, "Postmodern Apologetics," 137; Dulles, *A History of Apologetics*, 210–22, 261–64; Boa and Bowman, *Faith Has Its Reasons*, 71–72, 132, 157–59, 216, 346–51; and Simmons and Benson, *The New Phenomenology*, 89–98.

30. Penner and Barnes, *A New Kind of Conversation*, 152. Cf. Dulles, *A History of Apologetics*, 221; Gschwandtner, *Postmodern Apologetics?*, 219. As Gordon Lewis summarizes, "The rational man who employs his laws of logic to recognize the true revelation will also employ it to stand in judgment upon revelation" (Lewis, *Testing Christianity's Truth Claims*, 133).

31. Penner and Barnes, *A New Kind of Conversation*, 17.

32. McLaren does offer a more nuanced dimension to this discussion, explaining, "If God exists and God is a personal subject, then I'm not sure that objectivity is even possible in God's universe. In other words, if I assume God knows both rationally and affectively, then God can't know a created thing without loving it, or love something without knowing it, since for God, as I understand God, knowing and loving would simply be two words we humans are trying to apply to something beyond words. I'd say that the highest knowledge would not be [objectivity], but rather, would be subjectively [existing] in alignment with God's affective understanding" (McLaren, email to author, January 5, 2019). McLaren writes elsewhere, "The subjectivity that really counts . . . is what the Ultimate Subject feels and knows and says!" (*CIEC*, 256).

33. McLaren expounds, "There's something more to life, something that can't be reduced to the formulas or mechanisms of organized religion or reductionist science" (*SMJ* §Intro, xv). In

concern oneself with what is real and true both 'in here' (subjectively) and 'out there' (objectively)" (*FFS* §1, 39). Consequently, the best approach to Christian faith is to maintain an apophatic ("negative") theology in dynamic tension with a kataphatic ("positive") theology. Here, post-objectivists declare God to be so mysterious that positive statements about him are never sufficient, while simultaneously arguing that people can speak of the divine by having an intimate, loving relationship with God.[34] Similar to David Law's "kenosis of understanding," Christians must empty all preconceptions about how God should be, act, and think.[35] McLaren argues that without this humility, believers will feel theologically superior, which can then lead to hostility (*JMBM* §16, 135). For him, the concern is defining God in such a way that promotes only one socio-political ideology, which neglects new phenomenology's proposal that dissenters can experience God directly, as well (cf. *COOS1* §12a, 164-67).[36]

8.2.1.2 New Phenomenology

Because of apophaticism, post-ontotheologists must appeal to "phenomenology" as a rationale for engaging in "God-talk."[37] Here, the term describes a return to human experience that believes there is an intimate correlation between natural phenomena and their appearance to human consciousness ("phenomenality").[38] Its defining be-

---

postmodernity, the term "radical orthodoxy" signifies a form of Christianity that is separated from rational or evidential justifications (Webber, *The Younger Evangelicals*, 99–100). McLaren explains further, "For Christians in particular, our faith must always draw us beyond objectivity, because there is no sphere of life where we live as pure, abstracted, uninvolved subjects who objectify the world" (*AMP* §17, 261). Thus, he employs both objectivity and subjectivity, as exemplified in his rationalistic book, *Finding Faith—A Search for What Makes Sense*, and in his romanticist book, *Finding Faith—A Search for What Is Real* (*FFR* §1, 27; *FFS* §Intro, 25). It is important to note that McLaren's use of the phrase "radical orthodoxy" does not mean he ascribes to the "Radical Orthodoxy" school of John Milbank, Catherine Pickstock, and Graham Ward (for details, see Shakespeare, "The New Romantics," 163-77 and Insole, "Against Radical Orthodoxy," 213-41).

34. This apophaticism is why McLaren states, "We know next to nothing of Jesus, so we should say next to nothing for a change" (*FFR* §8, 164; cf. *SMJ* §1, 3-4). See Jones, *The New Christians*, 165. As Westphal explains "Negative theology is a reflection on the transcendence of God. . . . It tells us how not to speak of God, namely not to speak of God as if any images derived from our perceptual powers or any concepts derived from our intellectual powers, including the divinely authorized images and concepts of biblical revelation, were adequate to the divine reality. God is never at the disposal of our cognitive equipment" (Westphal, *Transcendence and Self-Transcendence*, 115-16).

35. Law, *Kierkegaard's Kenotic Christology*, 286-87. McLaren writes, "Perhaps we can agree that whoever and whatever God is, our best imagery can only point toward God. . . . In fact, the more we know about God, the more we have to acknowledge we don't know" (*WMRBW*, 29).

36. See also, McLaren, foreword to *How (Not) to Speak of God*, ix-xii.

37. In fact, the ineffability of God is a common theme throughout McLaren's writings, which is succinctly summarized in his description of human naiveté: ". . . the being of God, which is (and obviously must be) *way* beyond the comprehension of our puny three-pound brains" (*AMP* §6, 99-100; italics in original).

38. See Husserl, *The Paris Lectures*, 12-18; Simmons and Benson, *The New Phenomenology*, 13-41; and Gschwandtner, *Postmodern Apologetics?*, 13-14. Literarily, the embryonic origins of classical

lief states, "Phenomena must be accepted simply as they are. . . .but *also only within the limits in which it is presented there.*"[39] Soon, however, continental philosophers recognized classical phenomenology's inability to study ethereal phenomena, such as moods, dreams, art, and spiritual experiences. Therefore, they established "new phenomenology" with the assumption that mysticism can possess experiential significance.[40] According to Dominique Janicaud, new phenomenology constitutes a naïve "theological turn" in the science of phenomenology.[41] Conversely, however, if God is relational, then spiritual experiences would be consciously perceptible. Thus, appealing to new phenomenology helps legitimize subjective experiences as an empirical basis for truth.[42] Like Hans Küng's work, post-ontotheology means all religious authorities are disputable if rivalled against experiential knowledge, which implies the need to transcend strong foundationalism.[43]

8.2.1.3 Postfoundationalism

The Enlightenment notion of "truth" resides in correspondence theory, meaning that a belief is true only if it correlates to tangible facts or a state of affairs.[44] Epistemologically, modernity embraced strong foundationalism with correspondence theory

---

"phenomenology" first appeared in Immanuel Kant's distinction between the abstract, nonempirical world (*noumena*) and the sense experience of the natural order (*phenomena*), especially with his suggestion that experiences appear differently to different people. Nonetheless, the term itself derives from Edmund Husserl (1859-1938) and Martin Heidegger (1889-1976), who sought to understand how human consciousness relates to objects in the world (see Simmons and Benson, *The New Phenomenology*, 2-3, 46-48 and Gschwandtner, *Postmodern Apologetics?*, 13-14).

39. Simmons and Benson, *The New Phenomenology*, 19, italics in original. See also, Thompson, *Mind in Life*, 16. The process by which phenomenologists find meaning in subjective experiences is through description of first-person accounts, as opposed to third-person explanations of the data (Gschwandtner, *Postmodern Apologetics?*, 13-14; Simmons and Benson, *The New Phenomenology*, 15, 18, 22).

40. Simmons and Benson, *The New Phenomenology*, 1-4, 6; Gschwandtner, *Postmodern Apologetics?*, 14. Husserl appears to have excluded God-talk from classical phenomenology precisely because people would be incapable of having an immediate sense-experience of a transcendent, non-relational deity (Husserl, *Ideas Pertaining*, 133-34).

41. For Janicaud, phenomenology ought to focus on the lived experiences of actual phenomena, not the metaphysical conjectures of supernatural invisibility. See the entire discussion in Janicaud, "The Theological Turn," 16-103.

42. New phenomenology seeks to answer one question: "Is there a way to speak of God that both makes God present and allows God to remain other to us?" (Benson, *Graven Ideologies*, 169). See also, Welz, "God - A Phenomenon?," 4-24; Caputo, "Methodological Postmodernism," 284-96; Benson, "Theology and (Non)(Post)Foundationalism," 66; Simmons and Benson, *The New Phenomenology*, 84-89, 114, 192-99; and Gschwandtner, *Postmodern Apologetics?*, 209-10.

43. See for example, Küng, *On Being a Christian*. As Bruce Benson remarks, "Postfoundationalists assume instead that *all* respective starting points of theological or philosophical belief systems can *always* be questioned by others" (Benson, "Theology and (Non)(Post)Foundationalism," 67; italics in original).

44. For a Christian defense of correspondence theory, see Groothuis, "The Postmodernist Challenge," 11-19; Geisler and Feinberg, *Introduction to Philosophy*, 235-51; and Craig, *Reasonable Faith*, 29-60.

in mind, positing that "nonbasic" or "derived" beliefs about religion require evidential support from other independently verified foundational or "properly basic" beliefs.[45] The postmodern ethos, on the other hand, replaces universal foundations with the idiosyncrasies of cultural, linguistic, and historical contexts.[46] Consequently, McLaren criticizes classical foundationalism for being self-referentially incoherent, being unable to uphold its own criteria for most other justifiable beliefs (*FFS* §2, 61–62). Foundationalism is not only unfeasible, but it also limits people's exposure to the potentially edifying nature of differing perspectives.[47] Of course, postfoundationalism is not *anti*-foundationalism; rather, it broadens what is considered incorrigible data to include, as properly basic beliefs, the existential "aliveness" of experience and intuition.[48]

8.2.2 Existential Aliveness

The problem for McLaren is that Christianity has become a collection of doctrines instead of an actualized faith put into action.[49] In his judgment, religion's greatest worth is in its ability to inspire and fulfill a "quest for aliveness," which McLaren describes as the importance of holistic health, personal and communal harmony, a feeling of blessedness, and overall serenity (*WMRBW*, xv). The result is a philosophical difference between mere living (without meaning) and being "alive" (with a sense of worth and purpose).[50] Here, McLaren not only echoes Percy's existentialism (cf. *WP*, 1, 103n4), but he also embraces his view of humanity as "wanderers" toward actualizing an authentic faith (cf. §5.1.1). For both writers, the religious life is inherently linked to divine mystery (§6.2.2).[51] Hence, Christians "need to function less as problem solvers and answer givers, and more as problem identifiers and question askers" (*AIFA*, 235).

---

45. Peterson et al., *Reason and Religious Belief*, 115–24. Cf. Lewis, *Testing Christianity's Truth Claims*, 45–66, 76–94 and Boa and Bowman, *Faith Has Its Reasons*, 71–77, 155–64.

46. For details, see Kenneson, "There's No Such Thing as Objective Truth," 155–70 and Penner and Barnes, *A New Kind of Conversation*, 144–45.

47. McLaren writes, "We must understand the essence of our faith to be something other than a list of opinions, propositions, or statements that our group holds but cannot prove" (*GSM*, 22). Guarino, "Contemporary Theology," 311–22; Benson, "Theology and (Non)(Post)Foundationalism," 67–68; Simmons and Benson, *The New Phenomenology*, 44.

48. McLaren, foreword to *Solus Jesus*, xvi; van den Toren, *Christian Apologetics*, 44; Penner and Barnes, *A New Kind of Conversation*, 74–80; Simmons and Benson, *The New Phenomenology*, 175. Cf. Smith, "Some Suggestions," 67–85.

49. McLaren, "Everything Old Is New Again," 25.

50. McLaren explains, "The rising numbers of church dropouts don't want to be part of a flat spiritual malformation community" (*FOWA* §13, 126); thus, he concludes, "To be alive is to imitate God's generous desires . . . to create, to bless, to help, to serve, to care for, to save, to enjoy" (*WMRBW*, 17; ellipses in original). McLaren develops the notion of "aliveness" more fully in his book, *Seeking Aliveness: Daily Reflections on a New Way to Experience and Practice the Christian Faith* (2017).

51. See Boisvert, "Walker Percy's Postmodern Existentialism," 639–55. In fact, three of Percy's novels, *The Last Gentleman* (1966), *Love in the Ruins* (1971), and *The Moviegoer* (1977) are fictionalized renderings of Kierkegaard's existentialism and the pursuit of an "authentic self" in the midst of

Implicitly, McLaren addresses the question: What is the point of living if there is no objective meaning to life? His answer is grounded in Christian faith: the meaning to life is accentuating the resolute and personally meaningful embodiment of Christ's incarnation while deliberating on its practical relevance for daily existence and real-world dilemmas. "Orthodoxy . . . is seen as a kind of internalized belief, tacit and personal, that becomes part of you to such a degree that once assimilated, you hardly need to think of it. We enter it, indwell it, live and love through it" (*GO* §0, 33). Here, McLaren does not abandon orthodoxy, though he does reject certain doctrines, such as substitutionary atonement (cf. *CPA*, 110-21). Rather, he argues that truth encompasses "more than factual accuracy. It means being in sync with God" (*NKOC* §8, 88). To exist *Christianly* means to embody Christ's example of humility, lowliness, and sacrifice (§6.1.1.3) for the sake of establishing God's kingdom (*GSM*, 20-22). Referring to believers as "living examples," McLaren declares, "Loving relationships would be the ultimate evidence that [Jesus] is real" (*AMP* §6, 102-3). In this way, "The gospel is no longer a disembodied message; it is a message embodied in a community" (*PTP*, 123). Thus, McLaren labels faith *in* God as "be-living" in order to highlight the existential effects of following Jesus' teachings (being a "be-liver"). Thus, any Christian paradigm that does not accentuate the internalized consequences of faith cannot sensibly worship God as modeled during Christ's ministry (cf. *AIFA*, 42-44).

8.2.2.1 Worship and Doctrinal Reticence

The rationale for an existentially intersubjective paradigm is that it is the natural outgrowth of worship and ritual (*AIFA*, 232-35). McLaren outlines worship as the determination that someone or something is "worthy of our time, our attention, our pursuit, our availability. We worship them by forgetting ourselves in their presence, humbling ourselves to be benign elements of their environment. We let the reverence and awe they deserved rise within us and wash over us like a wave from mysterious, unseeable depths" (*GI*, 35-36). Implied here is the patristic notion of *lex orandi, lex credendi* where "the rule of prayer is the rule of belief," or (more pragmatically) "*how* a person prays dictates *what* a person believes." This dictum suggests that common prayers, liturgies, and other spiritual disciplines actually prescribe orthodoxy.[52] From here, McLaren then derives further implications, "If the ancient formula *lex orandi lex credenda* [sic] . . . is true, then it is equally true that *lex orandi lex vivendi* (the way we worship is the way we live). If we want to live in greater strength and kindness, then strength and kindness must be more central to our liturgical lives" (*JMBM* §19, 178).[53]

---

existential despair (Taylor, "Walker Percy's Knights of the Hidden Inwardness," 125-51).

52. Pelikan, *Credo*, 158-85, 336-64; Allen, *Theological Method*, 28, 46, 57-58, 67-68; Volz, "Lex Orandi Lex Credendi," 17-22.

53. McLaren writes elsewhere, "[Christians] will behave themselves into a better way of believing before they will understand themselves into a better way of believing" (*PTP*, 119).

The effect is that McLaren's intuitive approach to worship (*GO* §9, 147) guides both his doctrinal beliefs and outward lifestyle.

Consequently, McLaren implicitly adheres to the philosophical distinction between simple *belief* and factual *knowledge*. The former is more psychological than the latter, where beliefs are not a claim to objectivity but, rather, a preparation for action. He is more interested in the emotion-sensitive venture of believing than justifying those beliefs with rational proofs. Accordingly, his philosophy of religion attends mostly to the affective and intuitive characteristics of religiosity while still offering a reasonable (though not objective or analytical) basis for belief (see §8.5).[54] When making these distinctions, however, it is important to understand precisely how McLaren nuances his epistemology.

8.3 DISTINGUISHING EPISTEMOLOGIES

McLaren once commented, "I often hear people saying we deny the existence of truth (which is, frankly, ridiculous). . . .Some reduce everything we're talking about to a rather esoteric and un-nuanced debate about epistemology."[55] Agreeing that it is still God's will "to seek the truth" (*AMP* §16, 245), McLaren argues that humans are irreparably finite and, therefore, need epistemic humility (*AMP* §2, 41; *COOS1* §5, 65-66). "Our attempts to understand and articulate [God's] message and truth are always approximations. . . .At some level of profundity and accuracy, we are bound to be inadequate or incomplete all the time, in almost anything we say or think" (*COOS1* §5, 65). His philosophical approach to faith results in the construction of a *religio-epistemology* that McLaren believes is more appropriate to the participatory nature of Christian living.[56] Of course, in his estimation, epistemology is a wholly *Western* dispute with little practical import. Thus, he seeks to refocus attention toward more important matters.[57] Nevertheless, it is still necessary to understand the different *types* of truths that he embraces.

54. Cf. Frijda et al., "The Influence of Emotions on Beliefs," 4 and Fiedler and Bless, "The Formation of Beliefs," 144-70.

55. Streett, "An Interview with Brian McLaren," 8. Cf. MacArthur, "Perspicuity of Scripture," 141-58 and *The Truth War*, 18-19, 34-40. The suggestion that McLaren "hates" truth is even more ridiculous when considering he retweeted a *Washington Post* article detailing President Trump's 8,158 lies in his first two years in office, commenting, "Let's look for a person who loves truth as our next president—as a baseline!" (McLaren, "This is not normal").

56. Cf. Grenz, *A Primer on Postmodernism*, 49-56. McLaren writes, "The ascertainment of truth is indeed the highest aim of mental life" (*FFS* §5, 120) because "God is all about truth" (*FFR* §6, 128). He insists elsewhere, "That doesn't mean we give up language, and it certainly doesn't mean we stop trying to describe reality or pursue truth" (*LWWAT* §12, 72). However, the pursuit of truth is only credible so long as people are willing to reform their beliefs (cf. *GSM*, 35-37).

57. McLaren, "Church Emerging," 151. He writes elsewhere, "Arguments that pit absolutism versus relativism, and objectivism versus subjectivism, prove meaningless or absurd to postmodern people: They're wonderful modern arguments that backfire with people from the emerging culture" (McLaren and Litfin, "Emergent Evangelism," 43).

8.3.1 Types of Truth

With ontological truth (lowercase 't'), or what McLaren often labels "absolute" truth, he acknowledges that what people think they "know" is actually a result of socially, culturally, and historically constructed preconceptions about reality. With transcendental Truth (capital 'T'), McLaren insists that people can attain spiritual Truth only when in relationship with the divine.[58] The effect is that McLaren possesses two distinctive but interrelated epistemologies: one for sublunary discussions (e.g., economics, ecology, etc.), and one for the "category of truth called spiritual truth" (*FFS* §5, 120). More specifically, ontological truth is most appropriate for argument-based assertions expressed in propositional form. The "spiritual" category, on the other hand, is applied directly to the person of Jesus Christ and is accepted purely on faith (cf. *FFS* §2, 57-69). These two classifications are interrelated in the sense that natural and supernatural explanations of reality are no longer mutually exclusive.[59] For example, God's appearance in a dream can be both a natural incident (having derived from the inner psyche) and a revelation from the divine. The phenomenological significance of the dream is still transformative for a person's spiritual journey (*MRTYR* §13, 97-98; *NS* §1, 10; *WMRBW*, 169).[60] Nevertheless, McLaren believes Christians often make a category mistake when discussing ontological truth.

8.3.1.1 Ontological Truth

Metaphysically, McLaren acknowledges that absolute-objective truth exists and is present in an ontological reality (cf. *SWFOI* §6, 41-43). He simply doubts whether anyone (himself included) can acquire, comprehend, and then communicate that truth using finite human language (cf. *FFS* §7, 155-56).[61] Thus, McLaren cautions believers from elevating their own religious sensibilities to the level of absolute truth.[62] With him, ontological truth is so important that he refuses to exalt elements of a

---

58. Cf. Benson, "What Is 'Postmodernism'?," 6-7.

59. Although there is a distinction between his epistemic reasoning, McLaren is not, thereby, making a distinction between so-called natural and supernatural realms of reality (*FOWA* §1, 4-5; *SWFOI* §9, 69-70).

60. Cf. the insightful remark by Thomas Hobbes (1588-1679), who commented, "To say [God] hath spoken to him in a Dream, is no more than to say he dreamed that God spake to him" (Hobbes, *Leviathan*, 411).

61. Cf. Benson, *Graven Ideologies*, 110-24; Simmons and Benson, *The New Phenomenology*, 145-47; and Webber, *The Younger Evangelicals*, 99-105.

62. Questioning whether contemporary Christians really value the notion of ontological truth as much as they claim, McLaren asks, "Why can you turn on late-night cable TV and see a dozen different Christian preachers, with a dozen different spins on the truth, all proclaiming with apparent certainty that their version is right and everyone else's is wrong?" (*COOS1* §12a, 167). He remarks elsewhere, "I hear preacher after preacher be so absolutely sure of his bombproof answers and his foolproof *biblical* interpretations (in spite of the fact that Preacher A at 9:30 a.m. usually contradicts Preacher B at 10:00 a.m. and so on throughout the day)" (*NKOC* §Intro, xviii; italics in original).

faith-based belief system (§6.2.1) to the status of absolute certainty because this would confuse subjective perspectives with objective reality (*COOS1* §12a, 166-67). "We are aware perhaps as never before of the gap between what we subjectively 'know' and what is objectively true. . . . We can only aspire to relative certainty, which involves relative uncertainty . . . which actually requires—faith" (*FFS* §2, 68).[63]

In social constructionism, ontological reality is a socialized (*not* relativized) concept in the sense that people's subjective perceptions are further influenced by group experience. Each person's brain constructs models of reality that, in turn, influence other brains in their perception of the world, thereby creating empathy for other perspectives (§7.3.2).[64] A constructivist epistemology accounts for the sociological, anthropological, psychological, and linguistic processes that combine to create a group's particular sense of meaning.[65] Hence, comprehending the world is actually the socio-political socialization of reality, or the "disabling realization that one can be objective about anything, but only from a subjective point of view" (*AIFA*, 162). For instance, when discussing sexuality, constructivists argue that cultural views have changed throughout history and that a particular subculture's viewpoint today will not align with the sensibilities of other cultures (ancient or contemporary).[66] Hence, "You begin to see that what seemed like pure, objective certainty really depends heavily on a subjective preference for your personal viewpoint" (*NKOC* §4, 51). In this sense, people are "behaving organisms," and the same environmental variables that influence behavior will also affect a person's view of reality.[67] Accordingly, ontological truths differ from McLaren's notion of spiritual Truth.

8.3.1.2 Transcendental Truth

This constructionist understanding of socialized truth percolates into McLaren's understanding of how an intersubjective relationship with God affects believers. He

---

63. As Kierkegaard once wrote, "It depends, then, not only on what a man sees, but what a man sees depends on how he sees it; for all observation is not only a receiving, a discovery, but also a creation, and insofar as it is that, the crucial thing is what the observer himself is" (Kierkegaard, *Edifying Discourses*, 1:67).

64. Berger and Luckmann, *The Social Construction of Reality*, esp. 19-28. Cf. McLaren, foreword to *Manifold Witness*, xii. As McLaren writes, "All truth is contextual" (*NKOC* §12, 152)

65. Rogers, "Nature of the Third Kind," 393-412; Roukema-Koning, "Het sociaal constructionisme," 48-64; Cooper-White, "Intersubjectivity." In a paradoxical process known from quantum mechanics as the "observer effect," all persons actually alter ontological reality just by observing it. The exchange between consciousness and physical matter will, therefore, interfere with and determine the kind of contextualized reality that people experience (cf. Walker, *The Physics of Consciousness* and Lyon, "The Necessity to Rethink Magic," 208-27).

66. Szesnat, "Human Sexuality," 335-61. See also, Gergen, "Relativism," 365. For McLaren, the result is that "if we understand truth to be always human and contextual, then the way I quote the Bible [e.g., against homosexuality] changes" (*PTP*, 118).

67. Cf. Poling et al., *Fundamentals of Behavior Analytic Research*, 2.

writes, "You cannot escape subject-object interaction in any arena of life, especially worship" (*AIFA*, 232). For him, there exists a deeper notion of "truth" that is neither an abstract thought nor an internal conviction, and it requires separating Christian *faith* from the conceptual dogmas that pervade religion (*GSM*, 220-28). McLaren defends this feature of his religio-epistemology:

> Of course I believe in propositional truth. Any statement is propositional truth. Even the statement, "I don't believe in propositional truth" is a proposition—so arguments about propositional truth can become absurd very quickly. But the truth of God can never be limited to propositions- it always is expressed in incarnation and action and relationships as well. An awful lot of superficial things are being said in the various arguments about propositional truth, and we need to reach down to deeper levels of understanding.[68]

In essence, he believes in a distinct category of reality that surpasses all other epistemic sources because of the sheer enormity and profundity of the "truth" it possesses. Knowledge of this type evades human comprehension and is, thus, attainable only through faith (*FFS* §2, 67-69). He brands this Truth as "matters of ultimate concern" (*FFS* §1, 39; cf. *NKOC* §8, 94). In short, spiritual Truth equates to the person of Jesus Christ (*AIFA*, 169-71; *GO* §2, 69; *JMBM* §16, 143). As Tony Campolo remarks, "God's truth is not a theology, but a person. Our faith is not about Jesus Christ, not based on Jesus Christ—it *is* Jesus Christ. But that's where the certainties end. Christians explain their personal encounters with Jesus differently."[69] More generally, transcendental Truth is the intuitive realization that Jesus is the main epistemic source from which to judge what is real and ethical.[70]

Because Jesus "embodied a true, full, dynamic, pure, and undomesticated image" of God (*MRTYR* §2, 35), the implication is that a specifically *Christian* notion of truth must be relational in nature (cf. *NKOCY* §11, 114), being neither neutral nor mathematical. It is an existentially intersubjective relationship to *the* Truth, which then renders Jesus' gospel affectively, spiritually, and cognitively real on a personal level.[71] As one postmodern blogger eloquently explains,

68. Frost, "A Snapshot," 21-22.

69. McLaren and Campolo, *Adventures in Missing the Point*, §2, 35; italics in original. McLaren also writes, "The ultimate truth is not an objective concept, not an objective principle, but rather a Person" (*AMP* §17, 269; cf. §2, 34-35). Walsh further explains, "The object of faith is not a *teaching* about Christ that is to be comprehended through philosophy or theology but rather the *teacher* himself, who is the absolute paradox and thus not subject to mediation or a higher understanding in knowledge" (Walsh, *Kierkegaard*, 156; italics in original). Noticeably, however, McLaren is not consistent with capitalizing "truth." For example, he labels the Father as the "God of truth" (McLaren, "'Instead of Ruling'—Prayers," 227), but elsewhere, he writes, "Jesus is Absolute Truth, the Subject/Object, the objective referent that relativizes everything else. Jesus is the infallible, inerrant image of God. . . .[the] single universal truth" (*AIFA*, 169).

70. Cf. Dulles, *A History of Apologetics*, 326-27 and Simmons and Benson, *The New Phenomenology*, 61-63.

71. Penner, *The End of Apologetics*, 109-33. Hence, if confronted with the position that Scripture,

> If, however, truth is a person, we come to know that truth in a different way. Terms such as 'objective' and 'absolute' make a lot less sense. More importantly, 'understanding' takes on different meaning. 'Understanding' a person is very different than 'understanding' a concept or an object.
>
> If truth is a person, then truth that is entangled in culture, language, personality, perspective, and experiences is not only permissible but can be seen to be the primary way in which its content may be apprehended. Furthermore, the question of 'content' is less urgent, as we realize the discernment of the 'content' of a person makes little sense to us. . . . This further implies that we interact with truth relationally, rather than abstractly.[72]

A helpful explanation also appears in Kierkegaard's work where Truth transcends propositional claims about reality, being instead the existential appropriation of Christ's very being:

> Christ is the truth in such a sense that to *be* the truth is the only true explanation of what truth is. . . . That is to say, the truth, in the sense in which Christ was the truth, is not a sum of sentences, not a definition of concepts, &c., but a life. . . . the truth was in Christ, for He was the truth.
>
> And hence, Christianly understood, the truth consists not in knowing the truth but in being the truth. . . . Only then do I truly know the truth when it becomes a life in me.[73]

Consequently, rather than focus on propositional truth-claims, a proper Christian epistemology concerns itself with "*embodied truth*" (*AMP* §6, 98, 102-3; italics in original) by internalizing Christ's kingdom ethics (cf. *FFS* §2, 67-69; *GSM*, 42-44). Aligning with Paul Ricoeur's manifestational truths, McLaren views epistemology poetically where the goal is to manifest the transformative power of the kerygma.[74] The result is that for McLaren, "spiritual" truth-claims are a matter of faith and are not subject to scientific corroboration. Hence, the basis of Christian truth is the humble awe of divine mystery and its ability to better the world (*AMP* §2, 41; *COOS1* §5, 65-66). Nevertheless, these truths do not suggest a total lack of propositional knowledge.

---

as the "word of God," also disseminates transcendent Truth, McLaren responds by pointing out that the Bible never describes itself this way. Only Jesus "reveals the true nature of God" (*JMBM* §16, 137; cf. *NKOC* §6, 76).

72. Penner and Barnes, *A New Kind of Conversation*, 86-87.

73. Kierkegaard, *Training in Christianity*, 200-2; italics in original.

74. See Ricoeur, *Figuring the Sacred*, esp. 48-72 and Gschwandtner, *Postmodern Apologetics?*, 85-104, 210-11. McLaren's reading of Genesis embodies this approach: "It is a story that gives us *information* . . . a story that *forms* us *inwardly* with truth and meaning (*SWFOI* §7, 46; italics and ellipses in original). From here, people can join God in healing and restoring the world (*TSS*, 44).

8.3.2 Types of Knowledge

Significantly, throughout Kierkegaard's literature, he made a careful distinction between objective "knowledge" as truth and subjective "truth," which for him was the appropriation of religio-ethical beliefs.[75] In virtually the same way, by suggesting there exists a distinct type of transcendental Truth, McLaren's philosophy necessitates a distinction between several different classes of knowledge: absolute, objective, *provisional* (implied), and the kind of knowledge accessible only through a personal appropriation of Christ's living presence (*transcendental* knowledge).[76] While the goal of the first three is the discernment of ontological reality through dispassionate analysis, the method for acquiring transcendental knowledge specifically relies on a believer's existentially intersubjective embrace of faith. Again, McLaren argues, Christians are liable to making a category mistake when claiming to possess religious knowledge.

8.3.2.1 Absolute and Objective Knowledge

McLaren suggests that "absolute knowledge" actually equates to "incorrigible knowledge," which is the formulation of inerrant pronouncements about reality; but McLaren realizes that people have an astonishing capacity for self-deception. Hence, only God can possess absolute knowledge. Similarly, "objective knowledge" naïvely suggests that people are capable of knowing something without bias or distortion. Again, only God can possess objective knowledge (*AIFA*, 289).[77] Regardless, McLaren does not abandon the pursuit for knowledge any more than he abandons truth (cf. *LWWAT* §12, 72); he merely concludes that any and all knowledge about reality is provisional at best. Though humans can know *some* things, it is impossible to know anything with absolute or objective certainty (*FFS* §2, 67-69).

In this case, McLaren recognizes the existence of absolute objective truths "out there" in reality (*COOS1* §12a, 166-67), but he avoids making a commitment to correspondence theory simply because he is sensitive to creaturely limitations, being compounded by the complexities of social location and personal bias. For him, "knowledge" is the subjective aspect of human comprehension. Whatever objective truth may be, any person's subjective knowledge of reality is susceptible to further correction.[78] Ultimately, to "know" something is true necessarily involves numerous complexities that can only provide a tentative degree of certainty while still acknowledging that what is "known" today may be invalidated in the future. Therefore, what is subjectively *believable* is not the same as what is objectively true (*FFS* §2, 57-69). This distinction is even more pronounced within Christian mysticism. When it comes to

---

75. Watkin, *The A to Z of Kierkegaard's Philosophy*, 259-60.
76. Cf. McLaren, "Virtual Virtue and Real Presence," 110 and *Why Don't They Get It?*
77. Elsewhere, McLaren remarks, "Only God understands everything" (*AMP* §16, 249).
78. Cf. McLaren, *Why Don't They Get It?*

religion, "facts" are rationally elusive and often impossible to attain since, as McLaren argues, there is no "objective" human observer. All facts require subjective interpretation. Hence, instead of doctrinal precision, McLaren seeks a faith that prioritizes the passions of a sincere spirituality (*AIFA*, 120, 232), derived mainly from transcendental knowledge of the divine.

8.3.2.2 Transcendental Knowledge

According to McLaren, "thinking" in the West has become synonymous with reductionistic analysis, which mistakenly ignores all other forms of thought, especially imagination and intuition. An excessively rational epistemology merely concludes that mysticism is nothing more than superstition (*NKOC* §2, 24-25). However, McLaren believes there exists too many examples of spiritual mysteries in reality to be so easily discounted. Thus, there must be more to reality than humanity's incomplete knowledge of the physical world.[79] "What if all forms of knowledge, which are appropriate for every single other entity in the universe, were in this one case inappropriate for 'knowing' God—since an uncreated God would, by definition, be in a separate category from every created thing?" (*FFS* §5, 121). Being that rationality is "earthbound and limited" (*SWFOI* §7, 49), he adopts a type of knowledge that transcends both organized religion and reductionistic scientism (*SMJ* §Intro, xiii-xvi). In this sense, the kind of knowledge offered in Christ translates into a "metaphorical truth" that derives specifically from a believer's mystical sensitivity to God's Spirit. McLaren explains,

> We have a traditional idea of how people get knowledge. People get knowledge by getting educated, by the authorities. So Jesus says it is not just getting educated by sitting in classrooms or by sitting at the feet of rabbis and listening to them. There is a heart attitude toward this thing, too. There is an experiential attitude. You are going to know my teaching; you are really going to understand it and know its validity when you try it and when you obey God's will. . . .knowledge isn't about just gaining abstract information. There is a moral dimension to the gaining of knowledge. (*PTP*, 118-19)

The result is a type of spiritual insight that transcends the mundaneness of "earthbound" knowledge (cf. *GSM*, 113-14). Nevertheless, because of the intersubjective nature of faith, the only real knowledge a person can have of God must be relational (*FFS* §7, 146-47).[80] Hence, if asked how McLaren "knows" his religious beliefs about Jesus are "true," he merely comments, "The only answer can be, 'I don't know; I just know!'" (*GO* §3, 88). Transcendent knowledge is intuitive in nature, "knowing something without knowing how we know it" (*AIFA*, 40n5), whereby believers recognize

---

79. *AIFA*, 129; *AMP* §6, 97; *COOS1* §6, 78-79; *SMJ* §Intro, xiii-xvi.

80. Using the metaphor of a father and his children, McLaren writes, "True, their limitations as [eight-year-old] children gave them certain disadvantages in understanding their father, but their [intimate] relationship as my children gave them other incomparable advantages" (*FFS* §7, 146-47).

the divine with suprarational insight (*FFS* §2, 66-68). Here, this "inner perception," as Husserl described it, expands knowledge beyond the physical senses.[81]

Accordingly, believers can possess two types of transcendental knowledge: familial and experiential. In the former, direct experiences with the divine are acquired through the same type of special (if not deeper) intimacy that characterizes matrimonial relationships between humans.[82] The believer now has an intuitive knowledge of God's thought processes that is not easily verbalized. In the latter, experiential knowledge results from being more aware of God's daily involvement in the world. McLaren describes this knowledge as the "contemplative tradition," which ranges from subtle to dramatic encounters with God (*FOWA* §10, 89-97).[83] In both cases, the suggestion is that humans are capable of gaining direct knowledge beyond the confines of rationality, which then elevate participants to an intersubjective awareness of an ineffable Other (*AIFA*, 303–5).[84] Here, there is an implicit distinction between knowledge *de dicto* and knowledge *de re*. The former suggests that while believers come to know elements of God's nature and character (with relative certainty), they only learn this information *about* God. The latter, on the other hand, emphasizes a firsthand knowledge *of* God through personal familiarity.[85] As Kyle Roberts explains, "Emergent Christianity, by and large, is empathetic to the mystical and Apophatic traditions of theology, those that emphasize the cognitive elusiveness of God; they are drawn toward the experiential and relational knowledge of the divine."[86] Of course, for McLaren, this type of knowledge does not, therefore, necessitate epistemic relativism.

8.3.3 Relativism

The accusation that McLaren endorses relativism, either in the sense that all beliefs are equally valid or that "truth" has numerous equivocal meanings, are simply unwarranted, particularly since they do not take into consideration his evaluative criteria (see §8.5). Instead, McLaren's position is far more nuanced.[87] He views ontological "truth" and "rationality" as encultured concepts, acknowledging the ethnocentric

---

81. Husserl, *Logical Investigations*, 2:277-78.

82. Cf. Csinos and McLaren, "Breaking the Bubble Wrap," 20.

83. In this sense, something as simple as a bird's song can have the same impact as a miraculously burning bush (*FOWA* §2, 15; see also, *FFR* §1, 29).

84. McLaren, "Found in Translation," 17-18; McLaren and Litfin, "Emergent Evangelism," 42-43.

85. Morris, *Our Idea of God*, 86-87.

86. Roberts, *Emerging Prophet*, 62.

87. For instance, John MacArthur suggests that McLaren's postmodern ideals are incapable of distinguishing truth from error. "Practically speaking, then, his system embraces such doctrinal and hermeneutical subjectivism that, essentially, any view is accepted" (MacArthur, "Perspicuity of Scripture," 149). These accusations are merely the result of a dichotomistic and oversimplified view of epistemology that uses alarmist rhetoric to declare, "Once the foundation for absolute truth is destroyed, relativism and subjectivism follow" (Geisler and Howe, "A Postmodern View of Scripture," 65).

characteristics intrinsic to truth-claims. Because of the plasticity of "truth" and its diverse expressions, the exact referent of a "truthful" belief does not always possess an ontological correspondence to reality.[88] The problem for intersubjectivists is that Western notions of rationality are presumed to be universal; yet, this analytic approach compromises an authentic faith in Christ by making reality conform to the fluctuating dictates of a culture's rationalism. Claiming absolute certainty about religion is no longer sustainable in a world comprised of various socio-cultural preferences.[89] As John Caputo remarks, "Postmodernism is thus not relativism or skepticism, as its uncomprehending critics almost daily charge, but minutely close attention to detail, a sense for the complexity and multiplicity of things, for close readings, for detailed histories, for sensitivity to differences."[90]

Regardless, McLaren has repeatedly renounced relativism throughout his work.[91] Even D. A. Carson acknowledges this fact, "Many forms of postmodern thought do in fact lead to some kind of religious relativism, and McLaren knows that for the Christian that is not an option. He clearly wants to steer a course between absolutism and relativism."[92] McLaren emphatically declares the importance of truth. He writes, "First, relativism offers no standard for stopping the crazies," elaborating further that some beliefs are simply "misguided, untrue, and evil. . . .Second, relativism tends to trivialize the very beliefs it is trying to promote tolerance for," warning his readers that relativism induces apathy (*COOS1* §6, 83). Thus, McLaren's epistemology recognizes the absurdity of claiming either absolute certainty or total relativity when considering multiple vantagepoints (cf. *AMP* §2, 42; *NKOCY* §20, 232). In other words, McLaren rejects "absolute knowledge" and "objective knowledge," but he does not reject absolute truth. "Having a universe full of absolute truth but a world full of people incapable of grasping and conveying it with absolute accuracy is almost—but not exactly—the same as having no absolute truth at all" (*COOS1* §12a, 166). His fictional character, Dan, summarizes, "The only thing I'm confident about is that I don't have all the answers anymore" (*NKOC* §2, 18).[93]

---

88. See the discussion in Rorty, *Objectivity, Relativism, and Truth*, 1:23-24. Here, Richard Rorty provides an accurate description of a post-foundationalist epistemology: "There is nothing to be said about either truth or rationality apart from our descriptions of the familiar procedures of justification which a given society—*ours*—uses" (p. 23; italics in original). For an example of postmodernists adopting Rorty's neo-pragmatic concept of truth, see Kenneson, "There's No Such Thing as Objective Truth," 155-70 and Penner and Barnes, *A New Kind of Conversation*, 22.

89. See Gschwandtner, *Postmodern Apologetics?*, 10; van den Toren, *Christian Apologetics*, 5; and Penner and Barnes, *A New Kind of Conversation*, 6-7, 33, 41, 122.

90. Caputo, *Philosophy and Theology*, 50.

91. See for example, *COOS1* §6, 83-84; *FFR* §4, 88-89; *GO* §19, 285-88. McLaren writes, "First of all I think that there is so much sloppy thinking among relativistic people, and some of it is just downright silly. I think it's appropriate for us in a very gentle, humble way to point out some of that silliness" (*PTP*, 124).

92. Carson, *Becoming Conversant*, 35.

93. Or as Merold Westphal articulates, "We speak most appropriately about God when we fully

Instead of succumbing to the polarization of either modernistic certitude or postmodern relativism, McLaren seeks a "proper confidence" in his religio-epistemology, meaning those with faith can possess a conviction that their beliefs are real so long as they acknowledge both the diversity within Christian tradition and the impossibility of absolute certainty.[94] He concludes, "Relativists are right in their denunciation of absolutism. . . .absolutists are right in their denunciation of relativism. . . .they are both wrong because the answer lies beyond both absolutism and relativism" (*GO* §0, 37-38). Not surprisingly, then, McLaren embraces religious pluralism; yet, unlike its ideological implication that a society cannot (or should not) identify a supreme worldview, McLaren does not actually advocate for the legitimacy of all belief systems. Rather, he embraces religious pluralism descriptively as "learning to live with diversity in daily life" (*COOS1* §6, 82).[95] In fact, McLaren associates ideological pluralism with epistemic relativism, describing both as erroneous and potentially dangerous because of their tendency toward socio-spiritual apathy.[96] Instead, McLaren's overarching goal is to establish an alternative approach to religious faith that prevents people from using their holy texts or traditions to oppress others and, thus, further colonialist agendas (*NKOCY* §7, 67-77).

8.4 POSTCOLONIAL ALTERITY

Since subjectivity involves the idiosyncratic perception of reality by individuals, *inter*subjectivity involves a convergence of these personalized perceptions by multiple people. It is no surprise, then, that the concept of alterity, or "otherness," becomes significant for intersubjectivists because of its avoidance of totalizing theologies and its welcoming of "the other."[97] As McLaren describes it, "The good news of Jesus encompasses and integrates all of life—how we treat a person of a different race, religion, or sexual orientation . . . how we structure our church so that outsiders can become insiders."[98] In colonialist modernity, however, the aim was to make others conform to

---

realize and acknowledge the inadequacy of whatever we say" (Westphal, *Transcendence and Self-Transcendence*, 114).

94. Cf. McLaren, "Church Emerging," 146-49.

95. For a distinction between the ideological and descriptive notions of "pluralism," see Newbigin, *The Gospel in a Pluralist Society*, 14 and Carson, *The Gagging of God*, 13-22. Cf. Rah, *The Next Evangelicalism*, 180-99 and Duncan, "A Critical Analysis," 55-57.

96. McLaren elaborates, "I am not recommending the absurdities of 'absolute relativism' or radical postmodernism—where we say that everything is relative and nobody can know anything with certainty, conveniently ignoring the fact that we seem to believe we know with complete certainty that everything is relative! To argue such a point is itself illogical" (*FFS* §2, 63).

97. Here, McLaren defines "the other" as "anyone who is considered to be an outsider, not 'one of us,' belonging to a differing group, gender, orientation, party, community, religion, race, culture, or creed" (*JMBM* §2, 19n11). See also, Haroutunian, "Postmodern Ministry," 163-66 and Cooper-White, "Intersubjectivity."

98. McLaren, foreword to *Intelligent Church*, 10.

Western ideals, something that is now vehemently rejected in postmodernity.[99] The result is a felt obligation from McLaren and others to correct colonialism by highlighting the viewpoints of society's marginalized. As McLaren explains, the current paradigm shift demands the uplifting of other divine image-bearers (*AMP* §17, 261). "This movement would never forget how 'the neighbor' can be so easily dehumanized into 'the other,' and how, according to Jesus, if one wishes to encounter God, one must do so through the loving encounter with the stranger, the other, the outcast, the outsider, and the enemy."[100] For him, "there is no them" (*TSS*, 55), as exemplified in Scripture's heterophily.

8.4.1 Bibliological Heterophily

McLaren's conversational model of divine revelation (§7.3) is instructive for his approach to postcolonial alterity. He first recognizes that Scripture makes a poor textbook because it fails to anticipate (or even prevent) theological heresies and human rights violations (*FFR* §5, 104).[101] Because he believes in a divinely inspired Bible from a wholly good God (§6.2.4), he argues that the problem is not with Scripture but with modern notions of revelation (*NKOCY* §8, 82; §9, 92; *NS* §20, 171). He writes, "I'm recommending we read the Bible as an inspired library. This inspired library preserves and inspires an ongoing vigorous conversation with and about God, a living and vital civil argument into which we are all invited and through which God is revealed" (*NKOCY* §8, 83). For him, the Bible exhibits an evolutionary development of thought, engaging in heteroglossic discussions over theological and ethical issues. The result is a conception of deity that matures toward peace and justice.[102] He elucidates,

---

99. See the discussion in Penner and Barnes, *A New Kind of Conversation*, 115-35. McLaren defines "colonialism" as the spread of the sovereignty or belief systems of a nation or people group over other territories in order to control their resources, labor force, and economic markets with the intention of legitimizing the belief that the colonizers are superior to the colonized (McLaren, "Church Emerging," 143-44). According to McLaren, nearly all religions have morphed into something unrecognizable from each of their founder's initial conception, becoming "constricted, change-averse, nostalgic, fearful, obsessed with boundary maintenance, turf battles, and money" (*GSM*, 5). For him, this antagonistic temperament is not surprising considering an imperial mindset fosters four dominant characteristics: 1) group anxiety, where a dominant culture-religion is perpetually afraid of losing its prestige and power; 2) paranoia, where all religious competitors are viewed as a threat to the culture-religion's authority; 3) a desire for the eradication of the other, believing that only the religiously "pure" are worthy of life while diversity is seen as impurity; and 4) a mentality that views everything as a battle between good versus evil, right versus wrong, conservative versus liberal, and us versus them (*NKOCY* §19, 212-214; cf. *JMBM* §10, 82-84).

100. McLaren, "Finding the Seventh Story," 130.

101. McLaren uses the example of racist Christians to illustrate how easy it is to use the Bible in justifying horrendous crimes against people (*NKOC* §6, 71-72). He remarks, "Wouldn't it make sense for us to try to understand how so many Bible-reading, Bible-believing, Bible-quoting, and Bible-preaching people could be so horribly wrong for so terribly long?" (*NKOCY* §7, 72).

102. McLaren uses the book of Job as an illustration of this conversational model, which depicts multiple dialogues and multiple voices declaring both true and false beliefs. While God identifies

> I'm *not* saying that the Bible is free of passages that depict God as competitive, superficially exacting, exclusive, deterministic, and violent. But neither am I saying that those passages are the last word on the character of God. I am *not* saying that the Bible reveals a process of evolution within God's actual character, as if God used to be rather adolescent, but has taken a turn for the better. . . . I *am* saying that human beings can't do better than their very best at any given moment to communicate about God as they understand God, and that Scripture faithfully reveals the evolution of our ancestors' best attempts to communicate their successive best understandings of God. As human capacity grows to conceive of a higher and wiser view of God, each new vision is faithfully preserved in Scripture like fossils in layers of sediment. If we read the Bible as a cultural library rather than as a constitution, and if we don't impose a Greco-Roman plotline on the biblical narrative, we are free to learn from that evolutionary process—and, we might even add, to participate in it. (*NKOCY* §10, 103; italics in original)

Here, McLaren's bibliology makes harmonizing Scripture both tortured and artificial (*LWWAT* §7, 43; *WMRBW*, 7). He not only treats Scripture like an artistic symphony, but he also identifies God's Spirit as an orchestral conductor (§7.3.2), assembling the different theo-political agendas of priests, prophets, poets, sages, and storytellers to engage in dialogue with humanity.[103]

McLaren reasons that God purposely designed Scripture to elicit the contemplation of divergent perspectives (*FFR* §5, 105).[104] "In fact, the whole Bible can be seen as a library containing documents that show different views of God interacting and evolving together, serving as an invaluable record of human theological development. In this light, the Bible should not be seen as a ceiling or road block inhibiting further progress, but rather as a launch pad" (*GSM*, 248n2). Hence, the Bible does not totalize religious beliefs; instead, it exposes the restricted, fleeting, and unprivileged nature

---

some of the ideas as wrong, the book still leaves some questions about important social, ethical, and theological subjects unanswered (cf. *COOS1* §6, 81–82; *NKOCY* §9, 87–89). For the rationale of his multivocal and polysemic model, see *FFS* §7, 160–62; *GSM*, vix-xi; *LWWAT* §Comm., 189; *NKOCY* §10, 99–105; §11, 108–10; *WMRBW*, 20–23, 56–60.

103. See *NKOCY* §8, 79; §9, 95; *WMRBW*, 58–59, 172. McLaren notes that the Bible is discrepant not just in small details (cf. *EMC* §19, 316n12) but in major areas, as well (*WMRBW*, 172–73). The only consistency he sees is its persistent struggle with the same religio-ethical questions throughout the ages, addressing these questions from different vantagepoints and contexts (*NKOCY* §8, 81). In fact, the creative storytelling of the Gospel writers specifically, where they relocate or modify stories for their audiences, reveals why a literalistic reading is incongruous with the spiritual intent of the authors (*GSM*, 233n11). As Terrence Tilley remarks, "Narrative theology recognizes the irreducible and provocative multiplicity in Christianity. . . . The stories of God cannot be captured in a [single] system" (Tilley, *Story Theology*, 16). Cf. Bernstein, *The Formation of Hell*, 18, 133–34, 167, 171–72, 175–77, 196–97.

104. McLaren, "A Postmodern View of Scripture," 12; Csinos and McLaren, "Breaking the Bubble Wrap," 20. From this model, McLaren believes it is safe to assume that God wants periodic revolutions in the reigning theological paradigms (*COOS1* §8, 101) since the Bible is "a record of people who had authentic spiritual experiences with God" (*AMP* §6, 98).

of religious convictions (*MRTYR* §9, 76). "I think the Bible is more of a question book than answer book; it raises questions that bring people together for conversation about life's most important issues" (*SWFOI* §16, 116).[105] It is this conversational model that becomes the basis for McLaren's theology of religions.

8.4.1.1 Theology of Religions

In essence, what a multivocal and polysemic bibliology means is that God endorses what Janet Soskice labels "theological perspectivalism," which chronicles and contemplates people's experiences with the divine (*NS* §20, 171).[106] As McLaren writes, "Revelation occurs *not* in the *words and statements of individuals*, but in the *conversation among individuals and God*" (*NKOCY* §9, 89-90; italics in original).[107] As with any other library, believers can identify which voices they assent to and which perspectives they disagree with (*AIFA*, 98-99). However, they should not ignore those disagreeable portions because God inspired them to facilitate dialogue about religio-ethical issues (*AIFA*, 98; *AMP* §5, 81n*; *JMBM* §22, 204-5). Therefore, believers are free to abrogate or dissent with portions of Scripture just like Jesus and the Apostles did (*JMBM* §22, 204).[108] It is here that McLaren's bibliology extends into a theology of religions.

At the outset, McLaren desires to see Christianity transform from a colonialist religion of conquest and control to one that collaborates with other religions for the good of the world (*GDT*; *NKOCY* §7, 67-77).[109] McLaren wants to "call people to

105. Hence, McLaren describes himself as "irenic rather than polemic" whose "aim isn't to argue why one version of Christian faith is better than all others . . . [it] is to help readers get a sense of how all the versions are interrelated and how all share commonalities" (McLaren, foreword to *Brief Christian Histories*, xiv). See also, Hatch, "Hearing God Amid Many Voices," 23-47.

106. Soskice, "The Truth Looks Different from Here," 50. Soskice further explains, "If we are to continue within what is recognizably Christian orthodoxy when we embrace a diversity of perspectives, we must cleave to the idea that it is 'the truth' that we are approximating, however inadequately, and 'the truth' that looks different from here. That is, a concern for 'that which is certain in itself but subjectively uncertain to us' will continue to be at the heart of the Christian message" (p. 51).

107. Hence, McLaren views revelation as an *event* that occurs when readers encounter the divine through conversations in the biblical texts (*NKOCY* §9, 91). Divine "revelation" no longer implies a purely intellectual making-known of God or propositional self-disclosure. Instead, McLaren's system is more akin to a divine epiphany, the unmediated inspiration of the Holy Spirit on the biblical authors, and the internal testimony of the Spirit on subsequent believers. In this sense, Christians can recognize revelation on an intuitive level as they engage and experience God (*NKOCY* §9, 272n6). "The Word, or Self-Revealing of God, in this light, isn't a bunch of lessons, morals, doctrines, or beliefs that God dictates or otherwise encodes. It is an event, a turning point, a breaking open, a discovery, a transforming and humbling and ennobling encounter that occurs to readers when they engage with the text in faith—the text with all its tensions and unresolved issues intact" (*NKOCY* §9, 91).

108. Cf. McCasland, "Matthew Twists the Scriptures," 143-48 and Mead, "A Dissenting Opinion," 279-89. McLaren further remarks, "An integral approach allows us to see that different voices in the biblical library held opposing viewpoints, and the tension between those viewpoints forces us to see both the wisdom and the weaknesses of both sides. . . .they challenge us to think individually and grapple with unanswered questions in community" (*GSM*, 119-20).

109. McLaren, "Church Emerging," 149. He clarifies, "The world has been getting smaller, but

join a mission, to sign up in the fight against evil. . . .The church must call people from being part of the problem to becoming part of the solution" (*COOS1* §6, 83). This collaboration is due to the Holy Spirit's presence throughout humanity, meaning people of other religions may not only experience God directly, but their religions also exhibit some Truth as the Spirit works in and through divergent belief systems (*COOS1* §6, 81-84; *PTP*, 123; *WMRBW*, 203-206). Consequently, McLaren adheres to the notion of *semina Verbi* ("seeds of the Word"), or the post-Vatican II belief that every religion points to Christ in some way.[110] "The Spirit is ubiquitous—everywhere, always, in all creation" and, therefore, necessarily "preexists all religions, cannot be contained by any single religion, and therefore can't be claimed as private property by any one religion."[111] McLaren cites First Thessalonians to argue that new theological ideas deserve at least to be "tested, sifted, [and] considered carefully" (*AMP* §2, 43). His fictional character, Neo, explains,

> Instead of saying, "Hey, they're wrong and we're right, so follow us," I think we say, "Here's what I've found. Here's what I've experienced. Here's what makes sense to me. I'll be glad to share it with you, if you're interested."
>
> Instead of conquest, instead of a coercive rational argument or an emotionally intimidating sales pitch or an imposing crusade or an aggressive debating contest where we hope to "win" them to Christ, I think of it like a dance. You know, in a dance, nobody wins and nobody loses. Both parties listen to the music and try to move with it. In this case, I hear the music of the gospel, and my friend doesn't, so I try to help him hear it and move with it. And like a dance, I have to ask if the other person wants to participate. (*NKOC* §8, 88-89; quotation marks in original)

The rationale is that because of Christ's human solidarity (§6.1.1.5), Christians should perceive the divine's image in all people, especially those of other faiths (cf. *WMRBW*, 34-35).[112]

---

now we are in a place where the world gets ever smaller, ever faster, because the whole world becomes linked through the Internet and television, radio and airplanes. That changes the way we think about people from other cultures. It is not so easy to create caricatures of them; it is not so easy to see them as bad and us as good" (*PTP*, 116). McLaren reasons that because humans are incapable of objective knowledge *about* God, it is pretentious to discount the experiential knowledge that others have *of* God. Thus, McLaren argues that emphasizing theological distinctives to the point of creating in-group/out-group divisions is hazardous to the Christian faith and the world in general (*GDT*; *NKOCY* §16, 164; *JMBM* §15, 125-32; *WMRBW*, 216-20). For McLaren, a "good religion" is characterized by its ability to unite people together for a common cause of justice and peace (*NS* §2, 14-15). See also, McLaren, "Suicidal vs. Life-Giving," 64-67.

110. For details, see Mannucci, "Il teo-finalismo nel quarto vangelo," 15-30.

111. McLaren, "Rethinking the Doctrines," 58.

112. See the discussion in Reed, "Emerging Treason?," 77-78. Matthew's infancy narrative embodies McLaren's theology of religion. Both the Magi and the Egyptians were members of different religions, yet they participated in the life of Jesus. This partnership is how McLaren envisions different religions relating to each other. "They remind us that members of Earth's religions don't need to see

The Logic of Intersubjectivity

Of course, for McLaren, collaboration does not mean "giving tacit approval to everything they believe and do."[113] While he believes that Christ alone is God and King (cf. *LWWAT* §17, 103-4; *NKOC* §14, 189), he also respects other religionists because they can correct, augment, or deepen his own faith in Christ (*PTP*, 122-23; *WMRBW*, 83).[114] As Jason Byassee explains, McLaren considers all religionists to be spiritual pilgrims in pursuit of transcendent Truth. Where they are incorrect in their beliefs, McLaren can empathize because of his own deficiencies. Where they are correct, he can appropriate their insights.[115] McLaren concludes,

> We can understand human religions—all human religions, including our own—as imperfect human responses to our encounters with the Spirit who is present in all creation. That is not to deny the presence of divine revelation in any one religion, nor is it to affirm that all religions are the same. Instead, it is to propose that each religion, based on its unique location and history, would have a unique and evolving perspective from which to encounter the Spirit in a unique way. That would mean that differences between religions would not necessarily mean contradictions. They could simply mean additional data, expressed in different systems of imagery and language, based on differing encounters with the same Spirit of God. (cf. *GDT*)[116]

From his theology of religions develops a dialectical perspectivalism that attempts to eliminate the obstinacy and obscurantism of conventional Christian paradigms.[117]

8.4.1.2 Dialectical Perspectivalism

McLaren labels obstinate paradigms as "Type 1" churches where the only people who can integrate best are those who already agree with everything taught. There is little room for religious dissenters, reflective questioners, or other spiritual seekers (*FFR* §4, 87). Discussing Christianity in general, McLaren writes, "Too often seminaries recruit students who already know what they think and are not interested in having their thinking stretched or challenged. . . . They'd rather learn stronger defenses and justifications and proofs for their current beliefs" (*AMP* §11, 180). He continues, "We like a Jesus who . . . hates the people we hate and likes whatever we like" (*NKOCY* §12,

---

their counterparts as competitors or enemies. Instead, we can approach one another with the spirit of gift-giving and honor, as exemplified by the Magi. We can be there to welcome and protect one another, as exemplified by the Egyptians" (*WMRBW*, 83).

113. McLaren, "Practicing and Loving Diversity," 30.

114. Cf. Zovkic, "Dhelovanje Duha Bozjega," 55-83.

115. Byassee, "An Emergent Voice," 29. Vern Poythress explains further, "Other people have both good and bad ideas. By looking for the 'grain of truth' even in some bad idea, we can sometimes find a starting point for a new perspective or a piece of truth that we ourselves had overlooked" (Poythress, *Symphonic Theology*, 52).

116. McLaren, "Rethinking the Doctrines," 59. See also, McLaren, *Is Jesus the Only Way?*

117. For more details, see Bray, "Evangelicals," 214-36.

121).¹¹⁸ Part of this obstinacy derives from a fear of syncretism with the surrounding culture or with other religions (*AMP* §8, 130).¹¹⁹ Hence, McLaren argues, Christian tribes often practice hospitality only toward those with the same beliefs (*GSM*, 98). However, McLaren relates, "We in no way want to relativize Christian truth by any historical or cultural category. . . .We're just trying to play our role in the part of [God's] story we happened to be born into, and to do so faithfully" (*CIEC*, 114). For him, theological myopia is not a virtue. He seeks, instead, to celebrate theological diversity while focusing on the unified goal of creating Christ-like people who outwardly express Christ-like love to all other persons (*NKOCY* §16, 164).¹²⁰ His post-formal emphasis on cognitive flexibility recognizes the magnitude of diverse religious perspectives today (*NS* §2, 14).¹²¹

Spiritual knowledge for McLaren is, therefore, functional and dynamic simply because it derives from numerous subjective perspectives. He engages in a dialectical thinking that synthesizes opposing viewpoints in order to enrich his own spiritual knowledge (§2.3).¹²² For McLaren, gaining the perspective of other traditions is actually a divine gift that aids in viewing "the other" more properly as "the neighbor" (*WMRBW*, 84). Seeing God through multiple viewpoints broadens people's encultured outlook and can even expose some of the biases that have compromised Western theology.¹²³ "Theology that arises in human-made, human-controlled architecture . . .

---

118. Interestingly, one study showed that more than any other socio-economic factor, inculcated Christian beliefs are the single greatest inhibitor of people seeking higher education (see Darnell and Sherkat, "The Impact of Protestant Fundamentalism," 306-15). What is significant to note is that the most powerful predictor of tolerance for other people's beliefs is the attainment of further education (Nunn et al., *Tolerance for Conformity*, 169; Nie et al., *Education and Democratic Citizenship in America*, 148-49).

119. Cf. Taylor, "An Introduction to Postconservative Evangelicalism," 22-24; Kinnaman and Lyons, *Unchristian*, 26; 121-52; and Raja, *The Religious Right*, 47.

120. In one story, McLaren details his friendship with a young Muslim boy named Armin where he explains, "The standard approach to Muslims from my Evangelical upbringing was to be nice to them when necessary in order to evangelize them; otherwise, see them as spiritual competitors and potential enemies." Eventually, McLaren's relationship with the boy helped him to understand and respect those different from himself (McLaren, "Entering without Knocking," 3-6). See also, McLaren, "Brian McLaren on Outreach," 123.

121. McLaren writes, "What if the Christian faith is *supposed to* exist in a variety of forms rather than just one imperial one? (*NKOCY* §16, 164; italics in original). "I sincerely love and see beauty in all expressions of Christian faith" (McLaren, foreword to *The Way of Jesus*, xi). Cf. Grenz, *A Primer on Postmodernism*, 138-50 and Middleton and Walsh, *Truth is Stranger Than It Used to Be*, 31-33.

122. See Lemieux, "Post-Formal Thought," 399-406 and Berger, *The Developing Person*, 522-26. According to Edmund Husserl, the subjective nature of faith suggests that believers will experience religious phenomena from individualized perspectives. He insists that obtaining multiple viewpoints on God is the best way to understand the divine (Husserl, *Ideas Pertaining*, 40-62; *Logical Investigations*, 2:113). Jason Byassee explains that McLaren is able to celebrate and have an openness to different religious traditions because they each display features of the incarnation observable through different perspectives (Byassee, "An Emergent Voice," 29).

123. Frost, "A Snapshot of the Emergent Church," 20. See also, Cooper-White, "Intersubjectivity" and Middleton and Walsh, *Truth is Stranger Than It Used to Be*, 28-45. As Simmons and Benson

will surely reflect the prejudices and limited imaginations of its makers" (*GI*, xiv–xv). This perspectivalism not only involves differences of theological opinion or interpretation; it involves the entirety with which people perceive the world. The result is a symphony of many beautiful voices, "Through [the other] we are hearing new melodies and harmonies, new rhythms and overtones in the rich world music of the gospel that we had never before heard, and that music makes us want to dance. The Good News is richer, fuller, better, more radical than we had ever realized!"[124]

Indeed, McLaren's embrace of "Social Trinitarianism" (cf. *NS* §21, 183) means God's very nature glorifies the reciprocity of a dynamic and interdependent community. An unfathomable unity *through* diversity, or "undifferentiated homogeneity" (*JMBM* §15, 128-31), is reflected in the Godhead (*MRTYR* §18, 136; *NKOCY* §16, 164-67).[125] Hence, as each tradition emphasizes a different aspect of God, it either balances or supplements the emphases of other traditions.[126] McLaren's religio-philosophy, thus, reveals itself in a "dynamic tension" among seemingly disparate traditions, whereby he is able to counter reductionistic paradigms by assenting to a multidimensional (sometimes conflicting) sense of the divine (*GO* §1, 66-67; §13, 210; §17, 261). In this sense, believers cross-pollinate the "diverse streams of Christian spirituality" with each other's viewpoints (*COOS1* §4, 59-60; cf. *FOWA* §6, 57-58; §14, 138-39). Hence, he can declare, "Since you (as God) are so much greater than each of your individual children, and since they are so limited, no one of them can know more than a sliver of you. But if they each share their unique perspectives, all can gain a broader experience of you. Not only that—but they will have a lot of fun together too" (*FFR* §4, 90).[127] What develops from this cooperation with other theologies is an emancipatory view of marginalized perspectives.

---

remark, "We never encounter the world free of ideas about it, but instead always only as such an encounter can occur: internal to our social, cultural, historical, and biographical contexts" (Simmons and Benson, *The New Phenomenology*, 49).

124. McLaren, "Church Emerging," 148. McLaren explains further that religious uniformity was sold like a product for many centuries but this uniformity causes social ossification (McLaren, foreword to *A Generous Community*, vii–ix). "By never letting my mind reduce God to one image or one name, I keep my mind opened up and awake rather than shut down and half asleep and, in so doing, I maintain reverence" (*NS* §5, 46).

125. McLaren writes, "In the Pentecost story, we discover a third option: not unity without diversity, and not diversity without unity, but unity and diversity in harmony" (*WMRBW*, 205). In fact, according to McLaren, even creation exhibits God's love for diversity (*AIFA*, 66). "In that loving community of creation there is both unity and diversity, both melody and harmony, difference without division" (*NS* §Afterword, 240). "The Spirit of God . . . is a team spirit, and in the holy team Spirit, we experience a unity that is energized by diversity" (*WMRBW*, 217).

126. For example, Roman Catholics and Protestants highlight Christ as savior of the individual. However, the Eastern Orthodox balance this dimension by emphasizing Christ as savior of the entire universe (*GO* §1, 55).

127. Elsewhere, McLaren describes the same divine's-eye perspective, "What do You do about all these versions of You, made in human images? Of course there is an element of truth in nearly everyone's image of You. But on the other hand, each has its distortions, its imbalances, its gap, its excesses, its voids" (*MRTYR* §2, 34).

8.4.2 Emancipatory Ethics

McLaren explains that Jesus' gospel necessarily unites him to all people groups. To reject others because they differ theologically or politically "is a dreadful compromise of Christian identity and calling."[128] He recounts that originally, when writing *A New Kind of Christian* (2001), he used the term "postmodern" because it was convenient. Six years later, he realized that it was really only one aspect of the current epochal shift. While postmodernity rejects overconfidence, post*colonialism* rejects modernity's attempt to control other people's religious beliefs, which eventually just exploited and oppressed non-Westerners.[129] Labelling it a "theologically infused arrogance" that decimated indigenous peoples (*GI*, 50), the colonialist gospel message spread under the guise of "world missions" in order to dominate other cultures by emphasizing hellfire and damnation for dissenters (cf. *BMF*, 294).[130]

Akin to the codependency of personality cults, colonialist leaders often proffer easy, authoritative, black-and-white answers while warning their followers about the wickedness of outsiders (*NS* §Part I, 30). Here especially, the Americanized culture-religion resembles cultic brainwashing when it ignores the effects of its theological imperialism on minority groups (*MRTYR* §1, 23). According to Westphal, however, this type of xenophobia actually stems from Neoplatonism's influence on theology and its elimination of God's otherness ("divine alterity").[131] The value of post-ontotheology is its emancipatory ethos that seeks to reverse the centuries-long marginalization of others (*GSM*, 90). "[Jesus] sent us into the world to teach what he had taught—love, compassion, mutuality, reconciliation, benevolence, and concern for the common good. We twisted that commission and turned it into a mandate to conquer, control, subjugate, dominate, assimilate, exclude, convert, and ruin."[132] The trinitarian God is now seen as "a sacred choreography of self-giving, other-receiving; honoring, being honored; fully seeing the other, fully revealing the self. Imagine an eternal

---

128. McLaren, "Religious Right or Wrong?," 10.

129. McLaren, "Reflection on Postcolonial Friendship," 13-15. Heidegger helped establish this postcolonial alterity by suggesting that rationality was just another way for the West to control the world. To counter this imperialism, theologians ought to adopt an external sense of poetic language that conceives of "truth" and "being" apart from the arrogant claims of the Enlightenment (Heidegger, "Letter on 'Humanism,'" 239-76).

130. See Horkheimer and Adorno, *Dialectic of Enlightenment*, esp. 63-136. According to McLaren, the threat of temporal punishments (e.g., shame, excommunication, death, etc.) and eternal torture (hellfire, damnation) are used in creating superficial allegiances to prescribed belief systems. Internally, people oftentimes refuse to admit the inaccuracy of their belief systems for fear of admitting they are wrong or to avoid the anxiety of cognitive dissonance (*GSM*, 216). As a result, almost one-third of evangelicals believe laws protecting freedom of speech "go too far," which is over 10 percentage points higher than the average American; and upwards of one-quarter to one-half of evangelicals adamantly agree with the need to restrict and censor groups they disagree with, particularly homosexuals, atheists, and communists (Smith, *Christian America?*, 209-10, 213-16).

131. Westphal, *Overcoming Onto-Theology*, 238.

132. McLaren, "'Instead of Ruling,'" 227.

one-anotherness who is by nature non-assimilating, non-isolating, non-dominating, non-eliminating, non-overthrowing, non-competing, and non-victimized or -victimizing."[133] Because of human solidarity and intersubjectivity, there is an awareness that the disadvantaged have, in actuality, keen insights into religious suppression and hostility (§3.2.3). Hence, their subjective perspectives, which expose the oppressive power structures that control theological narratives, need a fair hearing.[134]

In McLaren's estimation, being attentive to God's Spirit equates to defending scapegoats from unwarranted slander (*MRTYR* §16, 121–23; *WMRBW*, 233). Indeed, Christians today need to grasp just how their hermeneutical and evangelistic practices, in defense of totalizing metanarratives, still resemble those who have supported slavery and genocide in the past (*GSM*, 85).[135] Hence, believers should rectify the perception that Christianity is "at war" with all other worldviews (*COOS1* §6, 81–83) and take into consideration the beliefs of "Jews, Muslims, Mormons, liberals, doubters, agnostics, gay folks, whomever" (*JMBM* §3, 31). The point being that fidelity to Christ does not demand ignoring the wisdom of other traditions. If McLaren were to design a biblical studies course, he would "expose [students] to the most offbeat interpreters I could find, too, and get some rip-roaring (but hopefully good-natured) arguments going on, to help people hear 'the voice of the other' both in and about the biblical text."[136]

Therefore, McLaren's philosophy of religion is "post-conquest," meaning it accentuates the preservation of diverse traditions through dialogue and cooperation (cf. *AIFA*, 19, 242; *NKOC* §2, 27).[137] For him, "Denominations are inevitable. They are simply relational networks. They are a family, preserving history and distinctives. But we do have to get beyond sectarianism. We have to get beyond the dominating or intimidating idea that everyone else has to capitulate to our opinion and submit to our

---

133. McLaren, "Rethinking the Doctrines," 14, 56–57. Hence, when discussing evangelism, McLaren relates that he capitalizes on the diversity of thought within Christianity, remarking that Christians have always struggled to conceptualize their faith accurately and precisely throughout church history, which has ultimately created the need for a delicate balance between differing points of view (*AMP* §6, 99–100). "And this diversity didn't compromise God's unity but made it more beautiful and wonderful" (*WMRBW*, 226).

134. Cooper-White, "Intersubjectivity."

135. Cf. Westphal, "Onto-theology," 141–53. The problem for McLaren is that throughout church history, Christians have interpreted Scripture in such a way so as to create political and economic supremacy for only one portion of society, most notably for white, heterosexual males today. McLaren writes, "I am in full agreement that we need to understand the real [Christian] story in terms of a shift away from white, Western, male hegemony and homogeneity" (McLaren, "Overcoming Resistance," 19).

136. McLaren, "A Postmodern View of Scripture," 12. Cf. McLaren, "Out of the Echo Chamber," 110. Myron Penner clarifies that a supposedly "objective" approach to Christian defense "also inclines Christian apologists to overlook the fact that their arguments may be used to support an oppressive and socially unjust form of Christianity, and therefore to that degree fail to justify *actual* Christianity" (Penner, "Postmodern Apologetics," 140; italics in original).

137. As Louis Markos explains, McLaren "relies less on systematic doctrine than on conversation and spirituality" (Markos, *Apologetics for the Twenty-First Century*, 270). McLaren's endorsement of religious cooperation is especially true for world missions (McLaren, foreword to *The Missionary Letters*, ix–xiii). See also, McLaren, foreword to *The Gospel in Christian Traditions*, vii–ix.

way of doing things."[138] What is important is the emancipatory ethics that derive from an existentially intersubjective religiosity. "By advancing the conversation from postmodern to postcolonial, we build from theoretical matters of knowledge, language, truth, and certainty to intensely practical and ethical matters of violence, domination, justice, and power."[139] Thus, a postcolonialist gospel is about solidarity in establishing God's kingdom (*EMC* §3, 22; *GSM*, 75), believing that an authentic faith must be *seen* in the world, not just heard (*COOS1* §2, 28).[140] Being exposed to people who suffer injustice or are on the margins of society, such as Eco-feminists, liberationists, and mimetic theorists, is now a vital part of following Christ.[141] "God isn't the one who favors the rich and righteous. God isn't the one who ordains the rich to be in the castle and the poor to be in the gutter. God is the one who loves everyone, including the people the rest of us think don't count."[142] With this alterity in mind, McLaren is able to establish criteria with which to evaluate Christian paradigms.

8.5 EVALUATIVE CRITERIA

Because McLaren endorses perspectivalism, the final component of his philosophy of religion pertains to assessing Christian belief systems, or paradigms, such as evangelicalism.[143] Here, McLaren seeks a synthesis of both rational and romanticist values

---

138. Quoted in Frost, "A Snapshot of the Emergent Church," 22. McLaren does not believe that denominations are outdated or harmful to the church (McLaren, foreword to *Anabaptist Preaching*, 7–8), but he also argues, "To follow Jesus is to change one's understanding of God. . . .we are rising to a higher and deeper understanding of God as pure light, with no shadow of violence, conquest, exclusion, hostility, or hate at all" (*GSM*, 93). Hence, "The living God is a God who cares for the marginalized, disadvantaged, and forgotten" (McLaren, "Everything Old Is New Again," 27). Cf. Pettegrew, "Evangelicalism," 159-75.

139. McLaren, "Church Emerging," 151.

140. For McLaren, if the colonial message about heaven and hell were really "good news," it should have had a greater impact on civilization, but it simply has not made people better. A genuine gospel message, he feels, ought to oppose systemic injustice, offer hope for a better world, and result in a rich, fulfilling life (*EMC* §5, 34). As one of McLaren's fictional characters states, "I couldn't figure out how anything with 'eternal conscious torment' in it could be called 'Good News'" (*LWWAT* §5, 35). Thus, for McLaren, theology is not a rational discourse about deity as much as it is a retelling and personal participation in the story of God. "This narrative approach. . . .helps turn the Bible back into what it is, not a look-it-up encyclopedia of timeless moral truths, but the unfolding of God at work in a violent, sinful world, calling people, beginning with Abraham, into a new way of life" (*GO* §10, 171).

141. See Csinos and McLaren, "Breaking the Bubble Wrap," 20 and McLaren, "From Organized Religion." An example of McLaren appropriating a feminist perspective to supplement his beliefs is viewable online: McLaren, "'Women on the Edge': Brian McLaren Sermon."

142. McLaren, "Beyond Fire and Brimstone," 18–19.

143. These criteria are different from McLaren's evaluation of specific Christian doctrines. For instance, when evaluating particular claims about God, humanity, or creation he uses the Wesleyan quadrilateral to ensure his theology "squares up with Scripture, and common sense, and church tradition, and that internal discernment from God's Spirit" (*SWFOI* §31, 229). For details on his *theological* method, see *GO* §13, 210-12; *LWWAT* §6, 41; *NKOC* §7, 77–79, and McLaren, "Rewriting Brethren Distinctives," 39–42.

(*FFR* §1, 25-27; §2, 52-53) to distinguish plausibly beautiful worldviews (§5.3.2) from destructive ones (*COOS1* §6, 83). "All of this has to be integrated with our own experience, with how our beliefs work out in our daily lives, with what kind of fruit they bear" (*LWWAT* §6, 42). Accordingly, McLaren's criteria look for the following elements in a Christian belief system: 1) firsthand experience; 2) personal meaningfulness; and 3) real-world import (*AIFA*, 42-44). These three conditions are self-correcting to ensure that no single criterion is allowed to justify a belief system without also meeting the other benchmarks.[144] They also recognize the unfalsifiability of most religions and, therefore, concentrate on the participatory nature of an existentially intersubjective faith (cf. *FFS* §2, 68). In other words, he wants to determine whether a Christian belief system is real enough to make better disciples for the good of the world (*COOS1* §3, 42). With him, Christianity's authenticity is ultimately dependent on whether it *becomes* true for the believing community. "When people trust [that Jesus' message] is true, they act upon it, and it *becomes* true. Our faith unlocks its potential. Our faith *makes* it real" (*WMRBW*, 122; emphasis added).[145] The first of McLaren's criteria is personal experience, especially mystical encounters.

8.5.1 Firsthand Substantiation

McLaren begins his evaluation process by asking certain questions: "Does the belief make sense?....Does it fit reality as I know it?....Is it probable, convincing, believable?" (*FFS* §8, 176).[146] He elaborates further, "My data isn't numbers. My data is my experience—my general experience as a committed Christian and my specific experience as a pastor" (*NKOC* §Intro, xviii). Foundationally, McLaren argues that humanity has pursued encounters with the divine throughout history (*SWFOI* §8, 60). According to Edmund Husserl, first-person accounts constitute a type of empirical "evidence" because the mere act of "experiencing" something would have the same legitimacy as any other empirical sensory data.[147] However, for McLaren, a phenomenological ex-

---

144. For instance, a religious belief can generate intense spiritual experiences that create a sense of purpose and, yet, still be false because it fails to meet the standard of "bearing good fruit" (see *AIFA*, 122; *FFS* §8, 175-76; *GO* §9, 156; and *MRTYR* §13, 97; §14, 104-5). See also, McLaren, foreword to *Paradoxy*, ix-xi.

145. McLaren writes elsewhere, "When people believe it is true, it becomes true" (*SMJ* §4, 32).

146. The issue of homosexuality is illustrative in this case. McLaren explains that neoconservatives claim that homosexuals are immoral, rebellious, diabolical soldiers of a "gay agenda." However, people's actual experiences with their gay family members and friends reveal a genuinely good, healthy, and sincere people, many of whom appear to exemplify Christ's love for others more than their angry Christian counterparts. These experiences are enough to warrant questioning those neoconservative claims (cf. *NKOCY* §17, 177).

147. Husserl, *Cartesian Meditations*, 12. Simmons and Benson explain further, "When we say that something is 'objectively true,' we mean that we all experience it in the same way, which makes it transcendentally true (since it transcends any particular experience)" (Simmons and Benson, *The New Phenomenology*, 25). From a psychological standpoint, the idea that subjective occurrences provide "evidence" is common since heightened emotional arousals tend to concretize

perience does not constitute transcendent Truth in itself. Subjective encounters with God, instead, are capable of revealing transcendent Truth but only through an intersubjective relationship with God (cf. *GSM*, 7).[148] Leith Anderson succinctly explains, "The old paradigm taught that if you have the right teaching, you will experience God. The new paradigm says that if you experience God, you will have the right teaching."[149]

Correspondingly, the act of experiencing ("a mental seeing") translates into first-person testimony that is thought to corroborate the authenticity of an individual's interpretation of reality. It is in this way that McLaren is properly labeled a phenomenological empiricist because he argues that an authentic connection to God should elicit a phenomenological experience of, or conform to, general human experiences. "This is why, for starters, I am a Christian: the image of God conveyed by Jesus as the Son of God, and the image of the universe that resonates with this image of God best fit my deepest experience, best resonate with my deepest intuition, best inspire my deepest hope" (*GO* §2, 76–77).[150] If a system's teachings about God conflict with what a person experientially and intuitively "knows" to be true, then that person must live with cognitive dissonance and be willing either to change or endure the costs of dissenting, or both (cf. *FOWA* §11, 107). Expectedly, McLaren classifies different types of spiritual experiences.

8.5.1.1 Types of Numinous Experiences

There exist numerous ways to experience the divine, such as through creation, ritual, and worship (*FFR* §1, 23–43; §2, 44–69; *GO* §11, 174–76).[151] For McLaren, the kind

---

an individual's already-established belief system. Known as the "feelings-as-evidence hypothesis," mysticism often signifies "empirical" evidence for the experiencer. For details, see Clore and Gasper, "Feeling is Believing," 10–44.

148. *AMP* §6, 107–9; *CIEC*, 248–49; *COOS1* §12a, 164; *FFS* §5, 124–25; *LWWAT* §6, 42. McLaren writes, "Through Jesus I have entered into a real, experiential relationship with God as Father, and I have received God's Spirit into my life. I have experienced the love of God through Jesus" (*GO* §2, 69). As Claude Geffré concludes, "We can only be sure of divine revelation within the experience of faith" (Geffré, *A New Age in Theology*, 18; emphasis in original).

149. Anderson, *A Church for the Twenty-First Century*, 21. For McLaren, the Pentecostal movement provided an invaluable service to Christianity by complementing rationality with the quest to experience God directly, which ultimately helps believers grasp their religion even deeper (*FOWA* §6, 53).

150. For McLaren, experiencing the Spirit is the best way to understand and follow Christ. Moreover, directly experiencing Jesus will make Christians want to "gush about him like a junior-high school girl with a new hunk of a boyfriend" (*GO* §2, 70–71).

151. McLaren tries not to answer precisely "how to experience God," insisting instead that these are the tactics of cavalier preachers (*AMP* §6, 100), though he does address different spiritual disciplines that can help people encounter the divine (*FFR* §1, 23–43; §2, 44–69; §3, 70–78). As a result of his early involvement with Pentecostalism, McLaren became sensitive to and expectant of encountering the living and powerful Christ in his personal life (*GO* §1, 51). He describes one such experience during a time of worship: "It was as if God were standing right beside me, or even closer . . . right inside me . . . or even bigger, so I was right inside God . . . and I felt embraced, contained, filled, saturated by God and God's love" (*FFR* §1, 39; ellipses in original).

of numinous experiences that people have may be determined by a person's character and disposition. "Perhaps the kind of person you are becoming determines how much of God you can experience—and maybe even which version of God you experience" (*FOWA* §2, 18). Nonetheless, there are two particular types that McLaren uses in his evaluative process. The first relates to his pivotal encounter as an adolescent (§2.2.4), which has since become his litmus test for evaluating Christian paradigms (*NS* §1, 10). In this first type, new phenomenologists describe the experience as a "divine excess" that overflows with such invested meaningfulness that it is inexplicable and uncontainable. The encounter is thought to be "genuine" if it has such a significant impact on experiencers that it forever changes their life (cf. *COOS1* §12b, 177).[152]

The second type of experience is far more mundane but no less essential: a sense of interconnectedness to creation and, therefore, to the Creator. Derived mostly from meditation and contemplation (§8.3.2.2), the goal of this type is to recognize the Holy Spirit's presence at every moment (*GO* §11, 175-76; *NS* §27, 234), particularly through acts of love (*FFR* §1, 40; §5, 115). McLaren labels this sense of divine intuitiveness as an "unknown knowledge" or, citing philosopher Michael Polanyi, "personal knowledge," which is something "one has and knows but doesn't even know one has and knows" (*GO* §3, 87).[153] He concludes,

> I'm convinced that what matters most—and is available to everyone—is daily, ordinary *spiritual experience*. With or without dramatic experiences, we can all find, expand, and hold a quiet, sacred space at the center of our lives, a space where we experience vital connection to the living God. We can all learn to tap into the quiet current of sacredness and love that runs the Creator through all creation. Dramatic experiences can awaken some of us to the reality of the spiritual life, but they are not sufficient to strengthen, sustain, and deepen us as truly spiritual people. (*NS* §1, 12; italics in original)

Thus, the rationale for prizing mystical experiences is because it contributes to the existential appropriation of Jesus' religio-ethics in a way that propositions and logic cannot.

---

152. Gadamer, *Truth and Method*, 350-86; Westphal, *Overcoming Onto-Theology*, 256-84. As Heidegger explained, the veracity of Christianity is, in fact, a ratification of religious phenomena. "The Christian is conscious that this facticity cannot be won out of his own strength, but rather originates from God—the phenomenon of the effects of grace" (Heidegger, *The Phenomenology of Religious Life*, 87)

153. Cf. McLaren, "Practicing Faith," 118 and Burson, *Brian McLaren in Focus*, 234-35. Hence, McLaren writes, "When [the disciples] were around Jesus, they felt—no, more than that, they somehow *knew* –they were experiencing God" (*GO* §2, 72; italics in original). Thus, the average person feels that what is most important to them is their "sense of God, their experiences of meaning or transcendence" (*MRTYR* §Intro, 14).

8.5.1.2 Experiential Rationale and Cautions

According to McLaren, "Postmodernism highly values subjective experience" (*COOS1* §12a, 164), being the "Holy Grail of the emerging culture" (*AIFA*, 119). He believes that the prevailing question among seekers today is, "Can your church help me experience God and experience personal transformation? By this question, they're telling us they don't just want to learn about. They want transformation."[154] In other words, intellectualizing Christianity often stifles personal intimacy with the divine (*AMP* §11, 171).[155]

Likewise, requiring phenomenological confirmation helps balance a reductionistic faith. In fact, spiritual experiences are often the only thing missing to convince someone of God's existence (cf. *AMP* §6, 107-8; *FFS* §5, 124-27). Theologically, McLaren sees a long history of people encountering the divine through dreams, visions, auditory or ocular apparitions, and in-the-flesh meetings (cf. *GO* §5, 108). The result, as Penner explains, is that proof of Christianity's validity relies on people's experience of Christ. "There is a vast difference in claiming something is true and claiming to be able to prove it. The only 'proofs' of resurrection ever offered in the New Testament is witness. This distinction between proof and claims to truth is an essential one to the logic of [postmodernity]."[156] Epistemically, the rationale is that experiences, combined with rationality, are more reliably accurate than those beliefs based solely on reason alone. It is Christianity's participatory nature that makes spiritual knowledge more authentic (*AIFA*, 119-23; 232-35; *AMP* §6, 102). "We're preaching and proclaiming an abundant life, and it doesn't speak well of our message if we don't experience the abundant life we're proclaiming."[157]

Nevertheless, McLaren cautions his readers that any and all experiences need rational testing so as not to be deceived by subjectivity (*FFR* §1, 26-27). He recognizes that numinous encounters are not proof of spiritual wisdom (*FOWA* §6, 53-54), and too many ignore the fact that these experiences are not the point of intersubjectivity (*AMP* §15, 234-38; *GO* §11, 175-76). For him, an authentic faith also involves

---

154. McLaren, "Informed, but Not Transformed."

155. McLaren explains, "Others of us, though, assume from the beginning that we will never 'fit God into our heads,' and so we set another goal—to try to get our heads, and hearts, 'into God.' In other words, it makes sense to us that we will experience our way into God before we think our way to God, if we are ever going to get connected to God at all. . . .The conclusion we usually make is that some sort of spiritual experience would be helpful in our quest" (*FFR* §1, 25). He writes elsewhere, "We have to find ways for people to simply encounter Christ—and God too!—without having to figure out two millennia of church history, controversy, and dogma" (*MRTYR* §2, 33).

156. Penner and Barnes, *A New Kind of Conversation*, 152-53. McLaren comments that he does not "see any value in that kind of miracles-as-proof argument" (*BMF*, 302).

157. McLaren, "TPC Interviews," 14. As he concludes, "God can be reliably experienced by ordinary people, and that the faith of Jesus is deeply distorted without this experiential principle at its heart (McLaren, foreword to *Solus Jesus*, xvii).

experiencing God's absence (*AIFA*, 121-22).[158] Likewise, he is cautious about allowing mysticism to dictate doctrine, as well. Though he encourages having a charitable attitude, he does not want "to condone every vision or dream proclaimed by an array of kooks, nuts, charlatans, and psychiatric patients" nor does he want "to ignore doctrinal nonsense promoted in the name of mystical experience" (*GO* §9, 156).[159] He is aware that spiritual experiences are psychological and, therefore, could be the manifestation of someone's disturbed psyche. He is also aware that people can simply reinterpret an experience in such a way that it conforms to their desired paradigm or belief system (*MRTYR* §13, 97; §14, 104-5). Thus, he writes, "Faith cannot be reduced to experience" (*AIFA*, 122). McLaren's second criteria supplements experience by stressing an internalized faith.

8.5.2 Internalized Appropriation

Kierkegaard once wrote, "Just as surely as the Savior of the world, our Lord Jesus Christ, did not bring any doctrine into the world and never delivered lectures, but as the *prototype* required *imitation*."[160] The result of these genuine numinous experiences is an internalized appropriation of Christ's religio-ethical teachings, meaning believers should now subjectively internalize and assimilate the values of Christ's ethics to the point that it becomes a part of their identity and character (*GO* §0, 33). McLaren explains, "This revolutionary plan of discipleship means that we must first and foremost be examples. We must embody the message and values of our movement" (*WMRBW*, 179). He continues, "I see the church as a community that teaches people to live in and for the kingdom, spiritually forming disciples who are agents of the kingdom in their daily lives, in their jobs, among their neighbors and even their enemies."[161]

What this criterion denotes is that McLaren evaluates the authenticity of a Christian belief system based on whether it produces an enriching quality that gives value and purpose to a believer's life. Rather than engage in theology as a detached scientist, intending never to interfere with or "contaminate" the data, McLaren views an intersubjective relationship with God as requiring personal involvement. Religious faith must be a personal passion, a spiritual quest, and a journey of discovery that affects each believer's emotions and desires. Otherwise, the belief system would be inconsequential due to a lack of excitement and veneration for the I-thou relationship

---

158. McLaren warns his readers, "In fact, 'experiencing God'—if by it we mean attaining a certain pleasant feeling—may become an idol, a narcotic, and a substitute for serving God, obeying God, or experiencing *obedience* to God" (*AIFA*, 122; italics in original).

159. Elsewhere, McLaren comments, "An open mind is like an open window . . . you need a screen to keep the bugs out" (*FFS* §8, 175; ellipses in original).

160. Kierkegaard, *For Self-Examination*, 209; italics in original.

161. Streett, "An Interview with Brian McLaren," 7.

(*AMP* §17, 257-69).¹⁶² "What we need is something lived, not just talked or written about" (*GO* §Intro, 19). Hence, one primary aim of McLaren's intersubjectivity is to internally appropriate religious knowledge; or, as Kierkegaard described, "The real action is not the external act, but an internal decision in which the individual puts an end to the mere possibility and identifies himself with the content of his thought in order to exist in it."¹⁶³

The type of Christian faith that McLaren discourages is the kind of "weak" and "nominal" religion that has "little practical significance to one's way of life" (*JMBM* §1, 10n15). For him, a valid Christian paradigm ought to foster a healthy existence that promotes honesty, forgiveness, love, unselfishness, and "aliveness." If the belief system is too embarrassing to share with others because of its intransigence, then it is neither plausible nor beautiful (*FFS* §8, 175-76). McLaren compares this criterion to the differences in Christian education:

> I don't want just to teach people about God, about the Bible, and so on. I want to drop the preposition in the same way the apostle Paul does in Ephesians 4:20 (NASB), when he speaks of the need for people to "learn Christ," not just learn about Christ. . . .This difference between learning and learning about parallels an important shift that is signaled by the change from "Christian education" to "spiritual formation." . . .the shift in language reveals a profound shift in values, from teaching about God to teaching people God, from teaching about the Christian life to teaching people to live it, enjoy it, practice it. At its best, the change in language signals a shift in priority from transferring information to training for transformation."¹⁶⁴

An intersubjective faith necessarily involves a sense of exigency in the pursuit of Truth by recognizing that people cannot remain objective about Christ. Here, Christians now view themselves as inhabiting God's storyline (cf. *TSS*, 44), being transformed by their experience with the divine.¹⁶⁵ McLaren concludes, "The kind of knowing that applies to God is not simply a matter of objective neutrality plus proper tools of research, plus the right text to be researched, plus due diligence. Knowledge of God involves being transformed into the kind of person . . . who is capable of knowing the holy"

---

162. McLaren writes, "We must see that analytical thinking without appropriate passion is as unbalanced as passion without consideration" (*AMP* §17, 269).

163. Kierkegaard, *Concluding Unscientific Postscript*, 302. Note, however, that McLaren does not minimize social action to the extent that Kierkegaard appears to do so in this quote (cf. §8.5.3).

164. McLaren, "Informed, but Not Transformed." See also, McLaren, "Spiritual Formation in a Postmodern Context," 183-89.

165. *LWWAT* §2, 16; *NKOC* §7, 77-85; *NKOCY* §9, 95-96. Kierkegaard once explained, "What would be the use of discovering so-called objective truth, of working through all the systems of philosophy and of being able, if required, to review them all and show up the inconsistencies within each system . . . what good would it do me to be able to explain the meaning of Christianity if it had *no* deeper significance *for me and for my life*?" (Kierkegaard, *The Soul of Kierkegaard*, 44; italics in original).

The Logic of Intersubjectivity

(*CIEC*, 158). The rationale that McLaren employs suggests that a belief system cannot be wholly valid if it does not, in fact, transform its adherents.

8.5.2.1 *Existential Rationale and Cautions*

McLaren's goal in stressing the existential implications of intersubjectivity is to replace the rigidness of dogmatism with a lifestyle that promotes solidarity and compassion (*GSM*, 43). The rationale for this second criterion is straightforward: if a belief system is not important enough to affect the way a Christian lives, then it cannot properly be labeled an actual "belief" *in* the system. For example, if people believe God exists but the belief does not stimulate them to seek and know God personally, then the idea is really no belief at all. It is merely a theoretical inkling with no existential import (*FFS* §1, 40). Ultimately, analyzing God's existence does nothing to change the planet for the better. "You don't argue about the fountain—you drink from it and experience its movement and flow within you" (*NS* §2, 17).

Underlying this argument is what McLaren calls being "a living parable" of Jesus' kingdom ideals. Intellectually assenting to Jesus' words without an internal appropriation would be to undercut Jesus' intended transformation of the world (*SMJ* §12, 102). "The focus for Jesus is not on the kinds of sophisticated arguments preferred by the religious scholar; for Jesus, the kingdom of God is about living life, and in particular, living a life of love for God and for neighbor" (*VL*, 80-81). As McLaren explains further, "Ultimately, one shows regard for Jesus not just by what he or she says or writes, but by how he or she lives life" (*GO* §2, 71n32). What is at issue is that far too many Christians *possess* doctrinal truth but *live* as though it were a lie:

> What people need first is not just information: they need a relationship with a caring, authentic, transparent Christian to see how that propositional message works. They need to see propositions incarnated in the biblical story, and in the lives of people who are living by that biblical story. . ..Postmoderns do care about truth but can't forget the fact that those proclaiming the truth have committed terrible injustices. So, to accept propositional arguments from Christians is morally abhorrent to them until they see the quality of our lives—as Jesus said, they need to see our light shining in good deeds before they're ready to glorify our God.[166]

From this exhortation, McLaren cautions his readers that internalizing Jesus' teachings is still only one means to an end. Believers need to turn God's desires into outward

---

166. Quoted in Frost, "A Snapshot of the Emergent Church," 21. McLaren approvingly cites one church's website as saying, "*We think the world is tired of religious people who claim to believe a list of ideas when those very ideas don't translate into any kind of personal transformation*" (*GSM*, 52; italics in original). For him, "Notable moral failures of religious leaders . . . [have] made claims of one religion's spiritual supremacy over others literally incredible and ethically reprehensible" (McLaren, "Conditions for the Great Religion Singularity," 41).

actions (*WMRBW*, 66). Referencing religious atrocities from the past, McLaren acknowledges the potential for heinous men to internalize a defunct belief system in order to commit unspeakable horrors. Belief systems are known, he suggests, by their fruits (*LWWAT* §6, 42; *SMJ* §1, 6).

8.5.3 Outward Actualization

McLaren's final criterion begins by asking, "If everyone on earth held this belief, would the results be good. . . .or would it lead to self-destruction and despair?. . . ..Does their belief produce good fruit in their lives as individuals and as a community?" (*FFS* §8, 176). For McLaren, the participatory nature of intersubjectivity indicates that a valid Christian belief system will express itself outwardly. "Human beings don't know the truth by abstract logic alone . . . but by experimenting with doing God's will (John 7:17; 8:31–32). . . .the proof comes in the practicing (Romans 12:2)" (*COOS1* §6, 80). Here, McLaren is rejecting "notional" belief systems where Christians hold to "notions, doctrines, or propositions about Christ, but again, [demonstrate] little fruit" (*GO* §13, 205). In his estimation, people's relationship with Christ should pervade the globe so much that it changes all world structures for the better (*FFR* §5, 115). He clarifies,

> If you listen to the Spirit, here is what will happen to you. You'll be in a voting booth or in a position of power. . . .But the Spirit will draw you to use your vote and your power for those who aren't at the table of privilege—the homeless, the sick or infirm in body or mind, the poor, the unemployed, those with special needs, the refugee, the immigrant, the alien, the minority, the different, the odd, the last, the least, the lonely, and the lost. The Spirit will invite you to hear their concerns, take them to heart, and join your heart with theirs. (*WMRBW*, 232)

Significantly, however, McLaren is not advocating for social or political revolt; rather, he advocates for a *spiritual* revolution that prioritizes charity, compassion, and peacemaking above all else (*FOWA* §1, 4; *GSM*, 198-99; *SMJ* §10, 86-89).[167] Here, being doctrinally correct is, in God's eyes, "something between boredom and nausea" without the pursuit of social justice, equality, and peace (*FOWA* §12, 120). The ultimate goal is to reverse the suicide machine by elevating society's vulnerable and alleviating global suffering (*EMC* §34, 295). "If our practices don't help us become people of this temper or flavor, Paul says, they're worth approximately—no, precisely—*zilch*. . . .God wants [people] to loose the bonds of injustice, break every yoke of oppression, share

---

167. See esp. Hawtrey and Lunn, "The Emergent Church," 65-74 and Reed, "Emerging Treason?," 74-78. McLaren writes, "I'm more concerned with whether the person is doing justice, loving mercy, and walking humbly with God" (McLaren, "Church Emerging," 143).

their bread with the hungry, invite the homeless poor into their own homes, clothe the naked, and see one another as family" (*FOWA* §12, 118, 120; italics in original).[168]

For McLaren, he wants a religion that empathizes with other humans and takes deliberate action to help them (*NS* §15, 133). The entire point of following Christ is to bless others (*SWFOI* §13, 94), but Christians have forgotten Jesus' revolutionary message to challenge the status quo and to confront injustice (*EMC* §9, 72). As a final criterion, McLaren argues that a valid Christian paradigm will combine firsthand experience and existential appropriation of Jesus' gospel message for the primary purpose of generating outward expressions of love. For him, a belief system is only acceptable if it emphasizes social action over abstractions (cf. *FOWA* §13, 125; *GSM*, 31). "*The more real God becomes to me, the more brilliant and revolutionary Jesus seems to me, the more precious life becomes to me, the more warmly I feel toward my neighbors*" (*GO* §13, 213; italics in original). McLaren maintains that Christians should promote God's kingdom by engendering a "fruitful way of life" (*EMC* §1, 5-6; *GO* §13, 199-209), which in turn upholds Christianity's experiential and existential elements (cf. *SMJ* §9, 72-80; §10, 81-89; *WMRBW*, 131-35). In this sense, McLaren follows the insights of Jamesian pragmatism.

8.5.3.1 *Jamesian Pragmaticism*

The epistemological pragmatist, William James (1842–1910), approached the formation of ideas with one central question in mind: What difference does something being "true" make in a person's life? For him, "truth" is something that *happens* when events surrounding the experience and the subsequent adoption of a viewpoint *make* the idea true (i.e., its pragmatic worth).[169] Reinhold Niebuhr later appropriated this "Jamesian pragmatism" for his own religious beliefs as he emphasized the consequential livability of religious truth-claims.[170] Here, both James and Niebuhr reflect a pragmatism that attempts to resolve real-world problems by reflecting on everyday experiences of human suffering.[171] In much the same way, McLaren's emphasis on actualizing God's kingdom conforms to Jamesian pragmatism by insisting Christians need to have a stronger concern for God's creation (cf. *GO* §0, 27-33; §13, 199-209).

---

168. Thus, when asked what makes his approach to faith different, McLaren responds, "The first is an understanding of the Gospel that centers on Jesus' teaching of the Kingdom of God. . . . The second thing would be an eschatology of engagement. . . . we're trying to have an eschatology that thrusts us into the world as agents of justice and peace and reconciliation and service" (McLaren, "10 Questions for Brian McLaren").

169. See for example, James, *Pragmatism and Other Writings*, 87-104, 135-41.

170. Fox, *Reinhold Niebuhr*, 84. Niebuhr himself admits, "I stand in the William James tradition" (quoted in Bingham, *Courage to Change*, 224).

171. Douglas, "Reinhold Niebuhr's Two Pragmatisms," 221-40. McLaren's pragmatism parallels these sentiments: "I'm less interested in how and when you were baptized than I am in why and whether you live the meaning of your baptism, whenever it happened and however much water was used to do it" (*GO* §13, 204).

In modernity, the priority was identifying correct doctrines and opinions. In McLaren's new paradigm, however, the focus is on whether faith-based assertions make the world better. "If we Christians would take all the energy we put into proving we're right and others are wrong and invested that energy in pursuing and doing good somehow I think that more people would believe we are right" (*NKOC* §8, 88). As McLaren's personal mentor, Dallas Willard, once remarked to him, "*In a pluralistic world, a religion is judged by the benefits it brings to its nonmembers*" (*JMBM* §5, 40; italics in original).[172] This reorientation from doctrine to behavior is the result of pursuing an "authentic" spirituality that betters its practitioners (cf. *AMP* §3, 57; *FFS* §1, 37).[173] Hence, McLaren supplements rationality by reminding Christians that logic is effective only when coupled with good deeds and loving relationships (*AMP* §6, 102-3).[174] In McLaren's schema, this emphasis on loving others ultimately manifests through social action.

8.5.3.2 Love and Social Action

Though Christ was capable of providing objective knowledge about ontological reality, he chose not to do so. The implication is that theological abstractions were not his primary concern; instead, Jesus' main function was to embody and actualize divine love (cf. *NKOCY* §11, 114). "Based on the priorities of many Christian leaders and institutions, we might conclude that Jesus said, 'By their beliefs you shall know them,' or 'This is my command, that you believe the right doctrines,' or 'Behold, a new systematic theology I give unto you'" (*GSM*, 19). For McLaren, however, faith adds another dimension to reality because it exists in the pragmatic realm of exercising love (cf. *AMP* §17, 262; *FFS* §2, 57-70; *NKOC* §16, 209). The rationale is a simple case of "transitive" identity: if transcendental Truth *is* God, and God *is* love (§6.2.4), then transcendental Truth *is* identical to love (cf. *GSM*, 42-48). Hence, to be an authentic Christian means to appropriate an "ethic of love" (*GSM*, 40-42), which then translates to a global perspective that cares about how certain actions affect humans in other parts of the world (*COOS1* §11, 148-49; *GO* §16, 241-42).[175] For McLaren, "the core Christian ethos" is to unify people under a shared goal of creating human solidarity (*GSM*, 3). The entire point of the incarnation was to found a new humanity

---

172. See also, McLaren, "A Conversation with Brian McLaren," and Burson, *Brian McLaren in Focus*, 186n135.

173. McLaren explains further, "Our job is not to defend the faith but to live the faith. That is the ultimate 'defense' anyway—a good offense. . . . The ultimate apologetic is *us* . . . believers!" (*AIFA*, 44; italics in original). Referencing Lesslie Newbigin, McLaren writes, "The greatest hermeneutic of the gospel, the greatest explanation of the gospel, is a community that lives by it. I think the importance of demonstrating the gospel at work in our lives becomes more and more important, because the gospel is no longer a disembodied message; it is a message embodied in a community" (*PTP*, 123).

174. Burson, *Brian McLaren in Focus*, 189-92.

175. See also, McLaren, "Religious Right or Wrong?," 10.

characterized by compassion and service toward others, being "more fully in solidarity with our neighbors everywhere" (*JMBM* §23, 219; cf. §16, 138n8).¹⁷⁶ It is here that McLaren's religio-philosophy parallels other "solidarity" theologies that criticize the church's institutional resistance against social and economic egalitarianism.¹⁷⁷

It is no surprise, then, that McLaren also focuses on how the poor and marginalized of society perceive and respond to God (*VL*, 8). "In a real way, Jesus is still here in the flesh, but now, instead of looking at the world through one pair of eyes, he sees through millions, and instead of touching and smiling . . . through two eyes and hands and ears, Jesus does so through one body composed of thousands and thousands of us" (*MRTYR* §18, 136). He explains that authentic Christ followers would choose to join God in his struggle for justice and peace in the world as they develop empathy for the plight of the oppressed (*FFR* §2, 47-50; (*FOWA* §18, 176; §20, 191-202). "Just as Jesus' incarnation bound him, not just to the Jewish people, but to all humanity, his incarnation links his followers to all people—*including . . . people of other religions*" (*GO* §17, 249; italics in original). Evangelism is no longer about converting people to a different religion; evangelism is now about inviting people to join God in changing the world. Consequently, a Christian belief system is evaluated by how well it undermines the status quo, not how many people adopt the label "Christian" (*CIEC*, 206, 211).¹⁷⁸ Here, McLaren's rationale for demanding the outward display of love and social action is simple: to not actualize Jesus' kingdom ethics would be to miss the point of Christian faith and the incarnation itself.

8.5.3.3 *Effectual Rationale*

There exists a deepening sense that Christians can and should unite together for more important causes. Instead of debating dogma, Christians should address global poverty. Instead of arguing about who is going to heaven, Christians should unite to stop sex trafficking and ecological destruction (cf. *GSM*, 154-63; *WMRBW*, 129).¹⁷⁹ McLaren explains further,

---

176. McLaren, "America the Exceptional," 18-19. Referencing Dietrich Bonhoeffer, McLaren wants a "religion-less Christianity" (McLaren, foreword to *The Way of Jesus*, xiii) where love, not humanity, is the real "protagonist" of God's story (*TSS*, 41-42).

177. See for example, Hessel, "Solidarity Ethics," 251-63 and Ortega, "The Gospel of Solidarity," 135-41.

178. Significantly, McLaren comments that his "main calling [in life] is evangelism" (McLaren, "An Interview with Brian McLaren," interview by Virgil Vaduva). See also, McLaren, "How to Evangelize Today" and "A Radical Rethinking of Our Evangelistic Strategy."

179. According to a July 2013 poll by The Public Religion Research Institute, there is an increase in moderate Christians who are rejecting conservative Christianity specifically because "younger Americans [are] seeking more action-oriented and less doctrinal expressions of faith" (Brumley, "Moderate Churches," 13). McLaren concurs, "Young people will increasingly see the church as a religious country club. They'll feel that if they morally want to make a difference in the world, the church isn't the place to go to find out how to do that" (McLaren, "TPC Interviews," 13). "To the degree they

> Word, deed, and example: it's important to keep these three integrated. After all, Jesus never said that the world would be convinced of the truth about him solely based on our logical words. Along with wise and true words, our good deeds, he said, would lead people to glorify God with us, and the living example of our loving relationships would be the ultimate evidence that he is real. Put good deeds and living examples of loving relationships together with clear and honest words, and you'll have the best apologetic of all. (*AMP* §6, 102-3)

In fact, according to McLaren, if Jesus were here today, he would expect his follower to speak out on behalf of the downtrodden, reminding them of the church's previously marginalized existence.[180] Not only does neglecting God's kingdom deride Jesus' teachings, but it also fails to prioritize what is truly important to God (*WMRBW*, 146), namely sacrificial service toward others (*VL*, 163-64). To McLaren, if Jesus is truly Lord and God, then Jesus' focus on producing good fruit in order to establish the kingdom ought to be every Christian's primary goal, as well (*GO* §3, 84; §15, 223; *JMBM* §16, 135). Hence, "[Jesus] shows us how to *be* the change we want to *see* in the world" (*WMRBW*, 136; italics in original).[181] Only then can Christians truly "win" in its pursuit for aliveness, but not at the expense of their global neighbors (cf. *TSS*, 40).

In paraphrasing Luke 3:8-9, McLaren writes, "Don't just talk of turning to God; you'd better bear the authentic fruit of a changed life. . . . *Face the facts, people! God is fed up with religious talk. God wants you to bear fruit!*" (*VL*, 23; italics in original). He further remarks, "A dream, an emotion, even an affirmation of a doctrine or creed—all of these fall short of what Jesus told us really mattered: 'By their fruit you shall know them,' or 'By this everyone will know you are my disciples . . . by your love for one another'" (*MRTYR* §13, 101; ellipses in original). In a joint statement with Tony Jones and others, McLaren declares:

> With millions suffering from hunger, disease, and injustice around the world, we hope that all of us—including our critics—can renew our commitment to "remember the poor" (Galatians 2:10) rather than invest excessive energy in "controversies about words." "They will know you are my disciples," Jesus said, not by our excessive disputation, but by our love. Words and ideas are essential, for they often set the course for thought and action, and constructive dialogue is needed and worthwhile, but we cannot let less productive internal debates preoccupy us at the expense of caring for those in need.[182]

---

preoccupy themselves with the question of who's right, to the exclusion of considering whether they are truly good (as in 'bearing good fruit'), they're destined to fade, wither, fail" (*GO* §8, 140).

180. McLaren, "Healing the Political Psyche," 36-37. Cf. Mackenzie, "Mission and the Inclusive Kingdom of Jesus," 258-69.

181. McLaren reminds Christians that Scripture does not say "God is a doctrine, and those who have the correct beliefs know God and abide in God" (cf. 1 John 4:8). Though doctrine is important, McLaren argues that it is not the essential or defining nature of Christian faith. Only love, expressed through sacrificial acts of service, is the undying essence of following Jesus (*GO* §12, 185; *GSM*, 21).

182. Jones et al., "Response to Recent Criticisms."

Therefore, only those who truly "get" Jesus are those who desire real-world solutions (*WMRBW*, 144-45); anything short of pragmatic love is not authentic Christianity (*AIFA*, 121-22). McLaren argues, "If you say you believe in [Jesus'] message, but you don't seek to practice it, your faith is a matter of words only; it's not substantial, not real. Faith that counts, then, is not the absence of doubt; it's the presence of action. . . .As Jesus' early disciple Paul put it, 'The only thing that counts is faith expressing itself through love'" (*SMJ* §13, 109; see also, *SMJ* §15, 137).

In other words, Christianity is only meaningful if it is linked to qualities that make better disciples who focus on bettering the world (*GSM*, 2). "Since real faith inspires action, if my faith produces no action, it cannot be good faith. If I cannot honestly say that my faith makes a difference—if I would behave just as I do without my faith—then my faith is bad faith or cheap faith, if it is faith at all" (*FFS* §1, 44). Citing Second Timothy (*GO* §10, 160-61), McLaren asserts that the goal ought to be equipping disciples for good works.[183] Hence, "If a professed belief is not sufficient to promote action, then it would be better called an opinion or an idea or concept," but not belief (*FFS* §1, 40). The implication is that a belief system must *become* real through embodied actions in order to *consider* it authentically real (*WMRBW*, 124).

8.6 CONCLUSION

For many, abandoning objectivity translates to a wholesale endorsement of subjectivity and, therefore, relativism; but for McLaren, this dichotomy is simply a false dilemma (*AIFA*, 163). Former notions of "truth" are giving way to new methods of inquiry and reflection (*NKOC* §8, 88). By embracing an existentially intersubjective relationship with God, McLaren is able to adopt a "conjunctive faith," which integrates intuitive convictions with a rational mindfulness. Here, people are able to accept dynamic tensions within their belief system while maintaining focus on ethical obligations.[184] His reason for constructing a new paradigm is because the absolutist nature of ontotheology has proliferated conflict, spiritual disillusionment, and church fragmentation all for the sake of doctrinal certainty (cf. *COOS1* §Intro, 14). Naturally, he recognizes his beliefs cannot be forced on anyone, and he expects many to reject it. "While I see this practice as a way of seeking and cherishing truth, some will interpret this approach as an abandonment of truth, doctrine, theology, etc. You are free to be among them" (*GO* §0, 30). In McLaren's estimation, however, proper religiosity should elevate the mystically intuitive aspects of faith (and their real-world implications) over propositional incorrigibility (*GO* §9, 147).

It is important to recognize that McLaren's religio-philosophy does not dispute Christian orthodoxy (*GO* §0, 30-33), though in some cases, "the 'body of historical Christian theologies' hangs on to plainly wrong beliefs" (*AMP* §2, 42). What McLaren

---

183. *AMP* §5, 75, 82-83; *GO* §10, 159, 163-66. Cf. Mayhue, "The Emerging Church," 191-205.
184. Fowler, *Stages of Faith*, 184-98.

challenges are those philosophies that endorse Enlightenment ideals as a basis for justification (cf. *AMP* §5, 76-79; *GO* §9, 152) while remaining irrelevant to those experiencing a spiritual paradigm shift (*COOS1* §6, 77; *GO* §10, 164; *NKOC* §7, 81-82).[185] His stratagem is to provide a witness to Christ that reduces arrogant self-assurance and generates interreligious cooperation. He wants a religion that reveals itself in "real-life stories about God" (*AMP* §6, 102) and how Christian faith has helped cure real-world problems (*COOS1* §6, 73). He takes into consideration divergent perspectives and religious traditions (*AMP* §6, 103-5) with the realization that Christ-like ortho*praxy* is the ultimate goal and purpose of Christian ortho*doxy*, not the other way around (*GO* §0, 31).

---

185. As McLaren commented during an in-person interview, "I see the romantic poets and Kierkegaard, and many others obviously, as saying we don't like where this is going. . . .We [have to] resist the Enlightenment, stand up for some kind of human values, and some kind of transcendent and deeper and ethical and aesthetic vision of the world because it's under assault" (McLaren, interviewed by Darren M. Slade, Denver, CO, May 14, 2015).

9

Conclusion

9.0 SUMMARY

The thesis of this book was that Brian McLaren is, in fact, a philosopher of Christian religion, being both an abductive rationalist and phenomenological empiricist, who employs provocative satire to induce a change in thinking among conventional religionists. The study revealed that McLaren's approach to faith is the result of a reflexive modelling practice, accumulated through years of experience, observation, and research. Possessing a rudimentary grasp of religious and philosophical semiology, McLaren constructed his new paradigm while considering experiential, theoretical, rational, scriptural, and historical principles. The goal of this investigation was to illuminate McLaren's reflexive method of discovery, which continues to develop in phases of ongoing observation and simplification.[1] By systematizing McLaren's philosophy of religion, future readers can now derive a more nuanced discernment of where they agree and disagree with his overall belief system.

At its core, McLaren argues that the essence of Christianity is a *lived* lifestyle of interdependent relationships, with both Creator and creation, rather than a system of propositional doctrines. As portrayed by Jesus, philosophy becomes the existential pursuit and embodiment of wisdom, not dogma (*SWFOI* §16, 114); and since Jesus' wisdom focused on living God's kingdom, his followers ought now to experience, internalize, and actualize the same example of love and self-sacrifice. In this sense,

---

1. Cf. Stark and Bainbridge, *A Theory of Religion*, 319-20. For a description of "reflexive" modelling, see Hofstadter, *Gödel, Escher, Bach*.

McLaren's religio-philosophy is the pursuit of a Christian faith that wisely interacts with and transforms the status quo of persons and power structures. Christianity is no longer about the acquisition of knowledge; it is about a way of life.[2] Nonetheless, these assertions have made McLaren a controversial figure among traditionalists; yet, for those who stumble over dogma, McLaren insists that what truly matters is embodying the kind of life that Jesus lived. Assenting to any particular group's doctrinal beliefs is simply not required in order to be a follower of Christ.[3] Even worse for his critics, McLaren's *semper reformanda* (§1.4.2) appears to suggest that the gospel's content should continually change over time. Only Christ-like behavior should remain unaffected. "You must enter a culture without judgment in order to understand it, and then you must incarnate the gospel in word and deed into that culture, so the gospel can be a liberating and transforming agent within it."[4]

The problem is that McLaren's critics often inflate these statements in order to portray him as an enemy of the church, incorrectly characterizing him as a relativistic liberal, an irrational postmodernist, or a manipulative antichrist who denies the divinity of Christ, Christian orthodoxy, and objective truth (see §1.4.1; §1.4.4; Appendix A). What this study has demonstrated, however, is that these are all *ad hominem* attacks resulting from a superficial, reactionary, and incomplete reading of his work. Simply stated, McLaren explicitly rejects theological and moral relativism (§8.3.3); he explicitly rejects theological and political liberalism (§3.4; §4.2.1); he explicitly believes in objective truth (§8.3.1); and he explicitly endorses a high Christology, as well as other orthodox doctrines (§6.1; §7.4). He neither wholly approves of postmodernity (§4.4.2) nor rebuffs the use of logic and reason (§5.3; §6.2.2; §8.5).

Rather than view McLaren as a subjectivist, this investigation has established that he simply disparages modernity's rejection of mysticism and intuition (§2.2.4; §6.2.2.3; §8.5.1). Rather than consider him a pagan, McLaren objects to the malicious culture-religion of American Christianity (§3.2; §7.1.2) and its un-Christlike apathy toward injustice and inequality (§3.4; §6.2.4.1; §7.4.2; §8.4.2). Rather than think he denies the gospel, McLaren merely contests the Greco-Roman reduction of Jesus' message to the abatement of God's wrath (§7.5) or a focus purely on the afterlife (§7.1.3; §7.2.1.1). In its place, McLaren is decidedly global in outlook by promoting a relationship with God (§6.2.2; §8.2; §8.5.1) through spiritual disciplines (§6.2.2.3; §8.5.2) and a prioritization of bettering the world (§6.2.4.1; §7.4; §8.1.1; §8.5.3). What separates McLaren's religio-philosophy from conventional paradigms is that he approaches faith

---

2. Hadot, *Philosophy as a Way of Life*, 265.

3. McLaren, "Q and R: Belief VERSUS Practice." McLaren also remarks, "Imagine what it would mean today for our churches to be known not as centers of indoctrination, but as schools of love; not as institutions interested in self-protection, but as outposts in a movement for personal and social transformation; not defenders of doctrine, but as *dojos* where beginners and saints together practice a way of life" (McLaren, "Everything Old Is New Again," 25; italics in original). See also, McLaren, "Best Outreach Opportunity *Ever*?," 96.

4. Quoted in Frost, "A Snapshot of the Emergent Church," 17.

from an *artistic* standpoint (§2.3.1; §7.3), emphasizing love (§6.2.4), beauty (§5.3.2), dialogue (§5.3.1; §8.4.1), collaboration (§6.2.4.1; §8.4.1.1), and practicality (§5.3.2; §8.5.3.1) more than Enlightenment rationalism (§4.2.2; §6.2.2.2) or propositional systematics (§4.4.1; §7.1.2). Ultimately, McLaren cherishes divine mystery (§6.2.2), relative certainty (§4.4; §5.1.1), and critical reflection (§4.4; §6.2.1.1) over absolutism (§4.2.2.2; §7.1.2; §8.2). Still, there is one aspect of McLaren's paradigm that generates the most backlash and, therefore, requires a closing explanation in light of this study's systematizing of his philosophy of religion.

9.1 MCLAREN AND *SEMPER REFORMANDA*

For McLaren, conventional Christianity is waning precisely because of its refusal to adapt to changing urgencies, having become domesticated by antiquated and trivial theological disputes (cf. *WMRBW*, xviii).[5] As a result, McLaren believes in reforming "Christian truth" to make it relevant to contemporary sensibilities (*CIEC*, 114). However, McLaren's critics misunderstand this premise by erroneously claiming he denies gospel orthodoxy (§6.1.1.1; §7.4). What this study has shown is that McLaren understands Christian truth (i.e., its "content") as the existentially intersubjective manifestation of Jesus' kingdom message (§8.2; 8.5). Thus, Christian truth is learning "how Jesus Christ wants to theologically incarnate himself for the postmodern world, just as he did for the post-Enlightenment world" (*COOS1* §5, 68).

What this "incarnation" entails is not a new religion but, rather, a new engagement with the twenty-first century (*AIFA*, 29). "Not a new Christ, but a new Christian. Not a new denomination, but a new kind of church in every denomination" (*COOS1* §Intro, 14).[6] Even so, how the church manifests Jesus' kingdom will necessarily change when divergent socio-historical contexts bring new challenges and new meanings to the foreground (*GO* §4, 191-93).[7] Hence, Christian truth revolves around two central questions: "What are our top global crises, and what does the message of Jesus have to say to these crises?"[8] It is in this sense that McLaren appears to view himself in the prophetic role of calling the church back to its kingdom priorities.

---

5. See McLaren, "The Church in America Today," 2-9 and "Conditions for the Great Religion Singularity," 40-49.

6. Cf. McLaren, "Overcoming Resistance," 19. He explains elsewhere, "What I've seen in hundreds of churches in dozens of denominations often causes me to wonder whether congregations as we know them can survive" (McLaren, review of *After the Baby Boomers*, 50). McLaren comments further, "Our aim is biblical integrity and cultural indigeneity: Not a first-century church reproduced in the 21st century, but a 21st-century church incarnating Jesus' presence and biblical values, leaning forward into God's gift of the future" (*AIFA*, 29).

7. See McLaren, "Brian McLaren Extended Interview"; "A Memo on the Arc of the Universe," 57; "A Postmodern View of Scripture," 14; and "TPC Interviews," 14.

8. McLaren, "This Changes Everything." He offers more precise questions elsewhere, "What does the gospel have to say about the global economy, about the growing gap between rich and poor, about stewardship of the environment, about the growing threat of violence?" (Streett, "An Interview

9.1.1 McLaren and Prophetic Action

McLaren highlights the fact that biblical prophets were not fortune tellers; they were sages intending to disrupt Israel's culture-religion and provoke controversy in order to elicit prioritizing God's kingdom. He characterizes their work as "bold and grand, artistic in a way that moved from gently evocative to stunningly provocative" (*CPA*, 112). Whereas priests were concerned with maintaining the institutional religion, the prophets articulated God's displeasure with an unjust status quo (*NKOCY* §10, 100). "Prophets in the Scriptures are actually focused on telling the truth about injustice in the present, often through stories about the past or warnings about the future" (*GSM*, 233n13). Significantly, McLaren describes the priests as having specialized credentials (something he lacks). Prophets, on the other hand, ascended almost entirely from a "self-authenticating passion and unavoidable moral substance" (see *SMJ* §3, 19-22), something McLaren does possess. From these descriptions, it is likely that he views his own activism as continuing in the same prophetic tradition, being a provocative poet who challenges today's religious and political establishment (*SWFOI* §16, 109-17).[9] "I believe that leaving religious status quo unquestioned is potentially ... destructive" (*LWWAT* §Intro, xvii).

McLaren's method of discourse is illustrative of other reform expressions in church history that attempt to challenge Christian complacency regarding social justice issues.[10] Rather than give new revelatory material, McLaren's writings simply remind the faithful of their obligation to represent God among the oppressed and marginalized in society, while also exposing the transgressions of current socio-economic and political loyalties. For McLaren, the alleviation of all forms of suffering ought to be a Christian's principal concern, whereby he summons believers to sacrifice their consumeristic and nationalistic comforts for the betterment of all people.[11] Not surprisingly, then, McLaren calls the church to repent of its participation in and enablement of global injustice (cf. *GSM*, xii, 6-11).[12] Like the remark of one of McLaren's fictional character, the poet Swifthorse, reveals about his activist role, "I travel the world seeking wisdom and beauty, and I share what I find in well-chosen words" (*CSS*, 27).

In recognizing that McLaren never proposes to construct a comprehensive academic treatise on any of his assertions, the failure to appreciate his provocative

---

with Brian McLaren," 11). See also, Riess, "Emerging Star," 52.

9. For examples of McLaren's activism, see McLaren, "A Prison of Cruelty."

10. See King, "Evangelical Confessions," esp. 79-87, 172-94.

11. As Amy King summarizes, "McLaren is characteristic of a new evangelical social ethic that is broader and more intellectually complex than what is currently expressed by the Christian Right. A large part of this is his emphasis on the politics of alleviating suffering" (King, "Evangelical Confessions," 11-12).

12. See McLaren, "Suicidal vs. Life-Giving," 64-67; foreword to *Healing the Gospel*, ix-xi; and Reed, "Emerging Treason?," 77.

Conclusion

disposition and "seeker" audience will likely result in over criticizing his philosophy of religion to the neglect of its corrective elements. He has a commendable goal of moving Christianity beyond the "us-them thinking and in-grouping and out-grouping that lead to prejudice, exclusion, and ultimately to religious wars" (*GO* §5, 109). While McLaren's religio-philosophy is innovative and undoubtedly liberationist, it is inappropriate to demand more from his literature than what is reasonably expected from a public theologian and philosopher. Readers must recall McLaren's deliberate incitements, prophetic objectives, and target audiences when reading his work; otherwise, they are liable to misconstrue his actual beliefs in relation to his stated intentions. As he relates, "Many things that are being confidently asserted as objective, absolute, propositional truth about 'Brian McLaren' are actually the truth about a fictional character, not about me."[13]

---

13. McLaren, "Becoming Convergent."

Appendix A

Extended Literature Review

The following is an extended literature review to supplement §1.4.4, which lists the more significant literary interactions with McLaren's work in rough chronological or thematic order:[1] To begin, Phil Johnson's 2004 article in *The Journal of Modern Ministry* was one of the first to interact with McLaren, treating his work under the heading of "cults." Here, Johnson argues that McLaren is no longer a Christian because he has syncretized with pagan philosophy (*§4.4.2*).[2] James King, in *The Journal of Ministry and Theology*, quickly identifies McLaren's provocative writing style (*§5.4*), which he explains is why McLaren is an easy target for conservative readers.[3] Likewise, Jonathan Wilson classifies McLaren as a pastoral practitioner rather than an academic (*§2.2.3.1*), who employs novel and imaginative methods for communicating with postmodernists (*§5.4*). While McLaren agrees that worldly cultures are often antithetical to Christianity (*§4.4.2*), he does not adequately account for apostolic tradition (*§7.4.2.2*) and appears to reject modernity out of a fear of being irrelevant to contemporary culture.[4]

---

1. Section numbers (*§*) *are also included* in this appendix to guide readers to those portions of the book that relate to or address the contentions of these literary interactions.

2. Johnson, "You Can't Handle the Truth," 219-45. This charge is echoed by Jere Phillips when he writes, "Like some cultists [McLaren] quickly moves to deconstruct elements of the creeds and reconstruct them to fit his own philosophical and theological constructs [*§4.4.2*]. McLaren seems to believe that meaning lies only in the mind of the listener or reader [*§7.3.2*]" (Phillips, "The Emerging Church Conversation," 35).

3. King, "Emerging Issues for the Emerging Church," 32-35.

4. Wilson, "Practicing Church," 69-70.

APPENDIX A

In *Reclaiming the Center*, Justin Taylor explains that McLaren believes the Christian message has routinely changed throughout church history to accommodate new socio-historical paradigms (§4.4.2) and that evangelicalism has uncritically conformed to the foundationalist standards of modernity (§4.3), which is itself antithetical to ancient Christianity.[5] Later, Andy Crouch clarified that for McLaren, the postmodern ethos means the reembrace of mystery over analytic philosophy (§4.4). Although McLaren is passionate about Christ (§6.1), his understanding of the gospel has evolved to include a "missional" orientation that concentrates on addressing global crises (§7.4.2).[6] However, D. A. Carson's book, *Becoming Conversant with the Emerging Church*, contends that McLaren is guilty of lacking nuance in his evaluation of conventional paradigms (§4.2.2.2), consigning discipleship to nothing more than social action, thereby implicitly denying the true gospel message itself (§7.4.2).[7]

In 2006, Mark Driscoll, a self-identified Emerging Church leader, reported that he had to separate himself from McLaren because the Emergent model has merely become the newest form of theological liberalism. Driscoll later created a taxonomy of Emergence Christianity, classifying McLaren as a liberal "revisionist," who disputes essential evangelical doctrines relating to Scripture, sin, salvation, and hell (§7.5).[8] Soon afterwards, Larry Dixon wrote a mock question-and-answer dialogue with McLaren as an extended book review, inappropriately placing words into McLaren's mouth. Here, Dixon expresses concern over McLaren's rejection of substitutionary atonement (§7.5.1), though he also agrees with McLaren that evangelicals have been too distracted with theological quarrels (§3.4.1). In 2010, Dixon published another article that refers to McLaren as the "friendly heretic," a derisive label characterizing him as aggressively attacking evangelicals. Dixon concludes that while McLaren appropriately asks crucial questions about contemporary Christianity, he ultimately provides unbiblical and heretical solutions, making him a pagan imposter advocating for rebellion against God (§6.1).[9]

In the journal *Themelios*, Jeffrey Jue describes McLaren's goal as eliminating the sectarian tribalism of evangelical culture (§3.2.2), and he contends that McLaren appears indebted to the study of church history and neoorthodoxy. Nevertheless, McLaren inaccurately portrays the Protestant Reformation as an Enlightenment-based entrance into modernity (§4.2.2), and his writings are so miserably perplexing

---

5. Taylor, "An Introduction to Postconservative Evangelicalism," 22-24.

6. Crouch, "The Emergent Mystique," 36-41.

7. See Carson, *Becoming Conversant*, esp. 74, 127-30, 133-42, 157-82.

8. See Driscoll, *Confessions of a Reformission*, 21-23 and "A Pastoral Perspective," 87-93. For McLaren, of course, the old liberal-conservative dichotomy is simply no longer relevant: "The older generations of the evangelical world have lived in a cold war situation for a long time. . ..in a cold war situation, anything that's not 'us' is 'them.' So for many older evangelicals, 'them' means 'liberal'" (McLaren, "A Postmodern View of Scripture," 7).

9. See Dixon, "'Five by McLaren,'" 217-71 and "Whatever Happened to Heresy?," 219-20.

(§5.4) that it has the potential of isolating him from mainstream Christianity.[10] Similarly, R. Scott Smith argues that McLaren has a deficient understanding of modernity and foundationalist epistemology (§4.2.2). While he agrees with McLaren that younger generations are suspicious of Christianity (§3.1), particularly when evangelicals appear legalistic, judgmental, and arrogant, McLaren does not fully consider the merits of a moderate form of foundationalist epistemology (§8.2.1.3). Thus, if left unchecked, McLaren's brand of postmodern Christianity will eventually destroy the church.[11] Larry Pettegrew further articulates McLaren's rejection of epistemological certainty (§8.3) and theological exclusivism (§8.4), comparing him to a type of liberalism by seeking to eliminate all denominational distinctives (8.4.2).[12] Trevor Craigen continues the alarmism by referring to McLaren's soteriology as a wicked display of double-speak, abandoning the Christian gospel in the process (§7.4.2).[13] Relatedly, Richard Mayhue's article in *The Master's Seminary Journal* offered a fundamentalist review of McLaren, concluding that McLaren's understanding of "orthodoxy" is a deceitful invention devoid of spiritual guidance (cf. §8.6).[14]

Also, in 2006, John Hammett attempted an ecclesiological assessment, acknowledging that McLaren does reject radical postmodernism (§4.4.2) and relativism (§8.3.3). While McLaren views conventional paradigms as untenable (§4.4), Hammett reiterates the general criticism that McLaren is willing to discard objective or biblical truth (§8.3.1) for the sake of reaching postmodernists.[15] In the *Conspectus* journal, Noel Woodbridge follows Driscoll in labeling McLaren a "revisionist" for believing that conventional paradigms are antithetical to Jesus' message (§7.4). Woodbridge denounces McLaren's stance on homosexuality (§3.2.4.1), believing the Bible is clear on the subject, yet praises him for contextualizing the gospel (§4.4.2).[16] John Pless explains that McLaren considers himself "missional," meaning he seeks to connect people to an authentic faith community that is historically rooted, inclusive, and relevant to global society (§7.4.2). As a result, McLaren's paradigm endorses a mystical-contemplative spirituality that accentuates imagination, intuition, poetry, and experiential encounters with the divine (§6.2.2.3).[17] Similar to earlier criticisms, Malcolm Yarnell strenuously objects to McLaren's openness to learning from other religions (§8.4.1.1) and renounces any suggestion that Scripture is not clear or consistent

---

10. Jue, "What's Emerging in the Church?," 20-39.

11. See Smith, *Truth and the New Kind of Christian*, esp. 50-66, 108-34; "Some Suggestions for Brian McLaren," 67-85; and "Reflections on McLaren," 227-41.

12. Pettegrew, "Evangelicalism," 159-75.

13. Craigen, "Emergent Soteriology," 177-90.

14. Mayhue, "The Emerging Church," 191-205.

15. Hammett, "An Ecclesiological Assessment," 29-49.

16. Woodbridge, "Understanding the Emerging Church," 97-113.

17. Pless, "Contemporary Spirituality," 347-63.

in its theological proclamations (§8.4.1).¹⁸ David Hesselgrave follows suit by asserting that McLaren's contextualization of the gospel is a form of hyper enculturation (§4.4.2) and, therefore, will eventually fail as a viable paradigm.¹⁹

Elsewhere, Michael Haykin addresses McLaren's recovery of medieval mysticism, which reflects the rising fascination of many to move beyond evangelical spirituality (§6.2.2.3). Haykin quickly scorns McLaren's work for having a positive stance toward Islam (§8.4.2), believing that spiritual disciplines ought to focus on the cross, instead (§7.5). Haykin insinuates that McLaren is thoroughly unchristian since his spiritual disciplines lack Christocentricity.²⁰ Continuing the same pattern, J. B. Hixson devotes an entire chapter to condemning McLaren's "puzzling" and "false" gospel message (§7.4), arguing he is inconsistent, inaccurate, and imprecise (§5.4). For Hixson, enemies of true Christianity either minimize or redefine the nature of sin (§7.1.3.1), thereby supplanting soteriological issues with an extreme focus on living profitably (§8.5.3). He concludes that society has embraced philosophical pluralism to such an extent that even pagan beliefs are now falsely called "orthodox" (§8.3.3).²¹

In the *Christian Apologetics Journal*, Ron Rhodes believes McLaren represents the kind of inclusive spirituality that profanely appropriates Eastern mysticism (§6.2.2.3).²² In the same issue, Derwin Gray categorizes McLaren's beliefs as a combination of neo-liberalism and neo-orthodoxy, which has wholly abandoned evangelicalism (§4.3.1).²³ Elsewhere, Tony Jones chronicled McLaren's rise to fame, calling it the "*New Kind of Christian* effect" where McLaren has become the voice of a previously unknown subculture of disenchanted Christians, who secretly bemoan the religious establishment. As a call for revolution, McLaren's work is indicative of the church's current paradigm shift away from conventional Christianity.²⁴ In *Evangelicals Engaging Emergent*, Douglas Blount argues that McLaren's crisis of faith (§3.1) resulted in appropriating a faulty future-oriented reading of Scripture instead of a precritical apostolic hermeneutic (§7.3).²⁵ Michael Horton's book, *Christless Christianity*, also implies a level of deception when he comments that leaders like McLaren express theological ambiguity (§5.4), masked as humility, and do not require actual faith in Christ (§6.2.1). Horton compares McLaren's message to the prosperity gospel of Joel Osteen, who (like McLaren) simply focuses on good actions and good attitudes (§8.5.3).²⁶

18. Yarnell, "Shall We," 203-204.
19. Hesselgrave, "Brian McLaren's Contextualization," 92-100.
20. Haykin, "Recovering Ancient Church Practices," 62-66.
21. Hixson, *Getting the Gospel Wrong*, 223-251.
22. Rhodes, "The Maze of Mysticism," 6-8.
23. Gray, "The Emergence of The Emerging Church," 27-62.
24. See Jones, *The New Christians*, 49-51 and "Post-Evangelicalism," 32.
25. Blount, "A New Kind of Interpretation," 109-28.
26. Horton, *Christless Christianity*, 64-66. Significantly, McLaren explicitly denounces the

Likewise, Jeffrey Straub argues that Emergence Christianity is inducing a neo-liberal resurgence within the church (§4.3.1), denouncing McLaren's affinity for imprecise and illusory theological pronouncements (§5.4), as well as his penchant for re-imagining the kingdom of God to conform to liberal agendas (§7.4.2).[27] R. Scott Clark's chapter in the book, *Reforming or Conforming?*, discusses the need for creedal restrictions on McLaren's supposed "catholic" theology (§6.1). Clark concludes that Christianity is inherently absolutist and exclusivistic but also opposed to Enlightenment foundationalism (§8.2.1.3). Intriguingly, Clark argues that McLaren is not, in fact, a postmodernist but, rather, a fully committed modernist (§4.4.2).[28] In the same book, Guy Waters addresses N. T. Wright's influence on McLaren's soteriology (§7.5.2), which has resulted in an emphasis on narrative theology (§7.3.2) and the recovery of a kingdom-oriented gospel message (§7.4.2). However, Waters contends that McLaren's ambiguous pronouncements on particular doctrines make it difficult to identify his actual beliefs on many issues (§5.4).[29] Greg Gilbert's chapter similarly expresses concern over McLaren's lack of attention to the cross (§7.5). According to Gilbert, McLaren has rejected all historic understandings of the atonement and eternal damnation in favor of his own innovations (§7.4.2). He acknowledges that McLaren's "disarming" and "irenic" approach to Christianity is beneficial for evangelizing postmodernists, but his approach compromises too much when it jettisons anything deemed offensive to the postmodern milieu (§4.4.2).[30]

Next, in *Christianity Today*, Scot McKnight details McLaren's sociopolitical emphasis in relation to God's kingdom and its implications for discipleship (§3.4.1). McKnight clarifies that McLaren's beliefs are still "works in progress" where he does not pretend to possess a completed system (§5.1.1). Instead, McLaren is publicly working on his theology as an open dialogue, though he has a penchant for attacking evangelicalism, which has become McLaren's demonized out-group with whom he chastises in typical straw man style (§5.4). According to McKnight, McLaren's understanding of the cross strongly resembles René Girard, who theorized that Christ's death intended to identify with the marginalized and oppressed of society (§7.5.2).[31] For McKnight, McLaren's emphasis is incomplete because it lacks a discussion on the forgiveness of sins. Moreover, when discussing McLaren's "Greco-Roman narrative" (§7.1.3), McKnight argues that no theologian actually adheres to this supposed storyline, finding McLaren's assertions laughably absurd and historically discredited. With McLaren's

---

prosperity gospel, labeling it "a financial scam, a form of theft," though elsewhere he does praise Joel Osteen's approach to the Bible (*GSM*, 4, 248n7).

27. Straub, "The Emerging Church," 69–91.
28. Clark, "Whosoever Will Be Saved," 112–28.
29. Waters, "It's 'Wright,' but Is It Right?," 188–210.
30. Gilbert, "Saved from the Wrath of God," 245–68.
31. Interestingly, Tony Jones made a similar observation, recounting how McLaren has immersed himself in Girard's literature for several years (Jones, "The McLaren Lectionary").

evolutionary understanding of revelation (§8.4.1), he reminds McLaren that the Bible does not present a coherent evolutionary model as portrayed in his books.[32]

In 2009, John Bohannon's work on homiletics identifies McLaren as a purposely provocative and ambiguous writer (§5.4) whose fictional novels complicate the reader's ability to detect his theological agreements (see §1.6.2). Bohannon recognizes the astonishment-driven intent of McLaren's abductive provocations, but he concludes that McLaren is just another liberal "revisionist" and a denier of objective religious truth (§8.3.1).[33] Also in 2009, Amy King discussed the internal struggles within evangelicalism over political identities (§3.1), using McLaren in one chapter as an example of the more compassionate trajectory among certain believers (§2.3). Rightly acknowledging McLaren's politically progressive viewpoints *(§3.2.1), Amy King explains that McLaren refuses to use his religious beliefs to fight the kind of culture wars that could stigmatize and harm* other human beings (§3.2.4). Using what she labels "prophetic rhetoric" (§5.4), McLaren would rather devote his energies to combatting economic, racial, ecological, religious, and other communal injustices (§7.4) that he feels conservatives too often ridicule or ignore (§9.1.1).[34]

Similarly, Jim Belcher characterizes McLaren's paradigm as a "rebooting" of Christianity that intends to "debug" contemporary faith and eradicate those viruses that were acquired during the Enlightenment (§4.3). Belcher also describes McLaren as a revisionist whose notoriety is a result of his provocative writing style, which Belcher agrees is for the sake of generating dialogue (§5.4.2).[35] In the book, *Holy Mavericks*, authors Shayne Lee and Phillip Sinitiere introduce McLaren as one of five Christian icons likely to replace Billy Graham as American's next top preacher (cf. *§1.2*). Offering alternative theological, spiritual, and political viewpoints for an otherwise Republican-dominated monopoly, McLaren has been most influential among younger generations in their distaste for impersonal megachurches and the neoconservative nationalism of conventional evangelicalism (§3.2.1).[36] Later, Brian Robertson completed his dissertation on the evangelistic strategies of the Emergent Church, arguing that many within the association have a deficient understanding of hamartiology (§7.1.3.1), eschatology (§6.3), and Christ's atoning death (§7.5). Suggesting that McLaren rejects objective truth (§8.3.1) and adheres to an inclusivistic universalism (§7.5.3), Robertson compares McLaren to the ancient heresy of

---

32. See McKnight, "The Ironic Faith of Emergents," 62-63; "McLaren Emerging," 58-66; and "Rebuilding the Faith from Scratch," 59-66.

33. See Bohannon, "Preaching and the Emerging Church," 55-69 and "Preaching and the Emerging Church (PhD diss.), esp. 40-44, 61-69, 191-268.

34. See King, "Evangelical Confessions," esp. 11-12, 79-87, 92-102, 109-11, 147-48, 172-94, 204-5. As Amy King summarizes, "McLaren is characteristic of a new evangelical social ethic that is broader and more intellectually complex than what is currently expressed by the Christian Right. A large part of this is his emphasis on the politics of alleviating suffering" (pp. 11-12).

35. See Belcher, *Deep Church*, esp. 38, 46-49, 74-76, 107-19.

36. Lee and Sinitiere, *Holy Mavericks*, 77-105.

Gnosticism, particularly in his dismissal of original sin, and concludes that McLaren denies the existence of hell or any focus on the afterlife (§7.2.1.1).[37]

Similarly, *The Gospel Coalition* released numerous web-based articles criticizing McLaren, often charging him of being unorthodox and misinformed about the true gospel. For instance, Justin Taylor commented that McLaren's work is a significant attack on Christian orthodoxy (cf. §8.6).[38] Likewise, Kevin DeYoung denounces McLaren's understanding of the gospel (§7.4), arguing that he is merely a liberal (§4.3.1) with affinities for open theism (§6.2.3.1).[39] Denny Burk then published two journal articles elsewhere on why evangelicals ought to rebuff McLaren's "five-year moratorium" on condemning homosexuality. For McLaren, not only are there disagreements about how to interpret Scripture on the subject, but ferociously attacking homosexuals makes the church appear intolerant and draconian. For Burk, however, McLaren's call for theologians to show due diligence, deference, and thoughtfulness on the homosexual question is blindly anti-Christian. As guardians of morality, evangelicals must not remain silent on the evils of homosexuality (§3.2.4.1). Going so far as to claim McLaren disdains the apostles by focusing only on Jesus' teachings (§7.2), Burk also suggests McLaren is deliberately rejecting Jesus' counter-cultural endorsement of heterosexual monogamy (§7.4).[40]

In a socioeconomic study, economists Kim Hawtrey and John Lunn explain that McLaren intends a revolutionary reconsideration of Christian mission with a social consciousness that targets contemporary economics (§7.4.2). For McLaren, Jesus' kingdom message specifically addressed worldwide income inequality and commercial oppression that is the result of overconsumption, usurpation of resources, exploitation, and corporate greed (§3.3.2). The difficulty is in McLaren's tendency toward extreme language and over generalizations (§5.4), which are then moderated in other parts of his writings. Hawtrey and Lunn conclude that McLaren's insights are helpful, but there are much more complex matters of practicality that would make implementing his socialist-leaning marketplace far from simple.[41] Gary Shogren also published an article on McLaren, warning readers to avoid his liberationist interpretation of the Apostle Paul (§7.4.2.2). Here, Shogren is concerned that McLaren will affect people's salvation, contending that Paul's gospel did not include social or economic dimensions (§7.4).[42]

In 2011, John Duncan wrote a second dissertation on McLaren's homiletics, arguing that McLaren has been too focused on ecological and social discussions (§7.4) to the neglect of saving souls (§7.2.1.1). Duncan views McLaren as minimizing (if

---

37. See Robertson, "A Critical Analysis," esp. 93-102, 121-24, 133-39, 170-90.
38. Taylor, "Christianity and McLarenism."
39. DeYoung, "Christianity and McLarenism."
40. See Burk, "Why Evangelicals Should Ignore," 212-26 and "Editorial," 2-4.
41. Hawtrey and Lunn, "The Emergent Church," 65-74.
42. Shogren, "'The Wicked Will Not,'" 95-113.

Appendix A

not entirely abandoning) orthodoxy (§6.1.1) and doctrinal correctness for the sake of exhorting Christians to live better lives (§4.4.1), which firmly places McLaren in the "revisionist" camp of Christianity. Duncan also contends that McLaren denies the divine origin of Scripture (§7.3) and rejects Paul's understanding of the gospel message (§7.4.2.2), replacing Jesus' redemptive mission with universalist pluralism and a liberationist agenda (§8.3.3). As a result, McLaren forsakes all notions of objective truth and divine authority in order to reconstruct a more agreeable religion (§8.3.1).[43] Christopher Peppler likewise argues that McLaren is presenting a new liberalism (§4.3.1) and rejects his proposal that Christians interpret Scripture retrospectively (§7.3.2).[44] HeeDuck Yoo's 2014 dissertation likewise examines McLaren's preaching methods, simply reiterating the same conclusions as his predecessors. For example, Yoo concludes that McLaren rejects objective truth (§8.3.1) and the divine authority of Scripture (§7.3.1). Yoo even refers to McLaren as a typical liberal who denies the Trinity and the divinity of Christ (§6.1.1).[45]

In 2012, Eldon Woodcock devoted an entire chapter to McLaren's beliefs on hell. For Woodcock, McLaren's overemphasis on building relationships neglects clear biblical teachings about God, humanity, atonement, and damnation (§7.5). McLaren seeks to reconceptualize God as wholly loving without any hint of indignation toward individual sinfulness (§6.2.4), which eliminates the need for Christ's death (§7.5). Woodcock concludes that McLaren denies objective and absolute truth (§8.3.1) for a relativistic-subjectivistic religion (§8.2) concomitant with old liberalism (§4.3.1).[46] Woo Kim likewise completed a dissertation that addressed McLaren's hermeneutical methodology. He argues that McLaren's interpretation of Scripture is opposed, in both theory and practice, to a genuinely biblical hermeneutic (§7.3), asserting that McLaren simply rejects objective truth (§8.3.1) and embraces universalism (§7.5.3). Because spiritual conversion takes place in a communal context, McLaren's hermeneutic must necessarily downplay the extraction of propositional information from Scripture (§4.4.1).[47]

In 2013, Jeremy Bouma released two self-published books providing interactions with McLaren's work. In *Reimagining the Kingdom*, Bouma contends that McLaren's kingdom terminology is merely a façade for liberal ideologies (§4.3.1) that locate the problem of sin to power structures (§7.4) rather than human nature (§7.1.3.1). In *The Gospel According to Brian McLaren*, Bouma takes specific issue with McLaren's theology of religions (§8.4.1.1), arguing that an emphasis on the universal brotherhood of humanity (§6.2.3) is a perversion of Christian identity and the mission of the

---

43. See Duncan, "A Critical Analysis," esp. 5–6, 31, 45, 59–60, 63–73, 85–113, 116–18, 134–47.
44. Peppler, "A New Kind of Liberalism," 187–201.
45. See Yoo, "A Critical Analysis," esp. 27–53, 81–84, 97–101, 188–90.
46. Woodcock, *Hell*, 489–518.
47. See Kim, "An Evangelical Critique."

church (§6.2.4.1).⁴⁸ Randall Reed later explored the relationship between Emergence Christianity and politics where he explains that evangelicalism is in a state of destabilization and crisis, especially among younger generations (cf. §1.2.1). Reed comments that McLaren focuses more on the overall narrative of Scripture (§7.3.2), which increasingly displays a trajectory toward inclusion and social action on behalf of the oppressed (§6.2.3.1). Reed notes that McLaren's political and philosophical polemics, though generalized and hyperbolized (§5.4), are far more nuanced than simply being anti-corporation and anti-capitalism (§3.3.2). Instead, McLaren intends to correct the destructive ideological belief systems underlying many of the failed social and political institutions today (§3.2.1).⁴⁹

Ed Mackenzie likewise wrote an article on McLaren's missiological inclusiveness as it relates to reaching a postmodern and pluralistic society. He focused on three primary aspects of McLaren's approach to Christian missions: his view of Jesus as the quintessential paradigm (§6.1), the establishment of the kingdom of God as the purpose of mission (§7.4.2), and a revision of theological doctrines in the interest of evangelism (§9.1). Mackenzie concludes that McLaren's missiology provides a much-needed corrective in terms of working with other religions for the betterment of the world (§8.4.1.1). However, McLaren is far too willing to compromise biblical truth and orthodoxy for the sake of achieving social action (§8.5.3).⁵⁰

Finally, in a 2017 dissertation on the historical origins of Emergence Christianity, Michael Clawson reconstructs the philosophical and institutional roots of the movement. Clawson argues that it arose specifically out of other evangelical detractors in the latter half of the twentieth century, which then fused together in the 1990s. Historically, there were three primary influences that shaped the movement: 1) the Jesus People Movement and similar paradigms (§2.2.1.1) that emphasized church growth through experimental practices; 2) the missional emphases of ecclesial and theological scholars, such as Lesslie Newbigin and N. T. Wright (§7.5.2); and 3) the continued existence of socially and politically progressive remnants from the 1960s and Latin American liberationism (§7.6). Providing only an historical examination of the movement's origins, impact, and evolution, Clawson utilizes McLaren's writings solely to chronicle his influence on contemporary evangelical Christianity. Implied throughout, however, is McLaren's notorious tendency to create controversy with his writings (§5.4), signifying that Emergence Christianity would not have had a significant effect on church history without McLaren appearing as one of the movement's most outspoken representatives.⁵¹

---

48. See Bouma, *Reimagining the Kingdom*, 143–68 and *The Gospel of Brian McLaren*.
49. See Reed, "Emerging Treason?," esp. 74–78.
50. Mackenzie, "Mission and the Inclusive Kingdom," 258–69.
51. Clawson, "Emerging from What?"

Bibliography

Adida, Claire L., David D. Laitin, and Marie-Anne Valfort. "Religious Homophily in a Secular Country: Evidence from a Voting Game in France." *Economic Inquiry* 53, no. 2 (April 2015) 1187-1206.
Agostinone-Wilson, Faith. *Marxism and Education Beyond Identity: Sexuality and Schooling.* New York: Palgrave, 2010.
Aldwinckle, R. F. "Is There a Christian Philosophy?" *Religious Studies* 2, no. 2 (April 1967) 233-42.
Alessi, Adriano. "L'essere e la crose. Dibattito sul' 'onto-teologia.'" *Salesianum* 52, no. 1 (1990) 53-111.
Aliseda, Atocha. *Abductive Reasoning: Logical Investigations into Discovery and Explanation.* Synthese Library 330. Dordrecht, Netherlands: Springer, 2006.
Allen, Paul L. *Theological Method: A Guide for the Perplexed.* New York: T&T Clark, 2012.
Allison, Dale C. Jr. "Jesus was an Apocalyptic Prophet." In *The Apocalyptic Jesus: A Debate*, edited by Robert J. Miller, 17-29. Santa Rosa, CA: Polebridge, 2001.
———. *The New Moses: A Matthean Typology.* Minneapolis, MN: Fortress, 1993.
Amstutz, Mark R. *Evangelicals and American Foreign Policy.* New York: Oxford University Press, 2014.
Anderson, Leith. *A Church for the Twenty-First Century: Bringing Change to Your Church to Meet the Challenges of a Changing Society.* Minneapolis, MN: Bethany House, 1992.
Aronowitz, Stanley. "Considerations on the Origins of Neoconservatism: Looking Backward." In *Confronting the New Conservatism: The Rise of the Right in America*, edited by Michael J. Thompson, 56-70. New York: New York University Press, 2007.
Aronson, Elliot. *The Social Animal.* 7th ed. New York: Freeman, 1995.
Ashley, David. "Postmodernism and Antifoundationalism." In *Postmodernism and Social Inquiry.* 1994, edited by David R. Dickens and Andrea Fontana. Reprint, 53-75. New York: Routledge, 2015.
Auerbach, Erich. *Mimesis: The Representation of Reality in Western Thought.* 1953. Translated by Willard R. Trask. Reprint, Princeton, NJ: Princeton University Press, 2003.
Aulén, Gustaf. *Christus Victor: An Historical Study of the Three Main Types of the Idea of the Atonement.* Translated by Arthur Gabriel Hebert. London: SPCK, 1931.
Babinski, Edward T. *Leaving the Fold: Testimonies of Former Fundamentalists.* Amherst, NY: Prometheus, 1995.

Baker, Keith Michael, and Peter Hanns Reill, eds. *What's Left of Enlightenment? A Postmodern Question*. Stanford, CA: Stanford University Press, 2001.

Balmer, Randall Herbert. "Critical Junctures in American Evangelicalism (I-IV)." *Ashland Theological Journal* 38 (2006) 43-75.

Barad, Judith, and Ed Robertson. *The Ethics of Star Trek*. New York: HarperCollins, 2000.

Barbour, John D. *Versions of Deconversion: Autobiography and the Loss of Faith*. Charlottesville, VA: University Press of Virginia, 1994.

Barnett, Timothy J. "Enlightened Economics and Free Markets." In *Is the Good Book Good Enough? Evangelical Perspectives on Public Policy*, edited by David K. Ryden, 75-94. Lanham, MD: Lexington, 2011.

Barnhart, Melissa. "Nearly 200 Evangelical Leaders Slam Christianity Today for Questioning Their Christian Witness." *The Christian Post*, December 22, 2019. https://www.christianpost.com/news/nearly-200-evangelical-leaders-slam-christianity-today-for-questioning-their-christian-witness.html.

Baron, Craig A. "The Theology of Gerald O'Collins and Postmodernism." *American Theological Inquiry* 2, no. 1 (January 2009) 11-26.

Barr, James. "Abbā Isn't 'daddy.'" *Journal of Theological Studies* 39, no. 1 (April 1988): 28-47.

———. *Fundamentalism*. 2nd ed. London: SCM, 1981.

Barry, Carolyn, Laura Padilla-Walker, and Larry Nelson. "The Role of Mothers and Media on Emerging Adults' Religious Faith and Practices by Way of Internalization of Prosocial Values." *Journal of Adult Development* 19, no. 2 (June 2012) 66-78.

Barstow, David. "McCain Denounces Political Tactics of Christian Right." *New York Times*, February 29, 2000.

Barth, Karl. *Church Dogmatics*. 2nd ed. Edited by Geoffrey W. Bromiley and Thomas F. Torrance. Translated by Geoffrey W. Bromiley. Vol. 1, *The Doctrine of the Word of God: Part 1*. New York: T&T Clark, 2004.

Bass, Diana Butler. *Christianity After Religion: The End of Church and the Birth of a New Spiritual Awakening*. New York: HarperCollins, 2012.

Bastit, Michel. "Le Thomisme est-il un Aristotelianism?" *Revue Thomiste* 101, no. 1 (2001) 101-16.

Batson, C. Daniel. "Rational Processing or Rationalization? The Effect of Disconfirming Information on a Stated Religious Belief." *Journal of Personality and Social Psychology* 32, no. 1 (July 1975) 176-84.

Batto, Bernard F. *In the Beginning: Essays on Creation Motifs in the Ancient Near East and the Bible*. Siphrut: Literature and Theology of the Hebrew Scriptures 9. Winona Lake, IN: Eisenbrauns, 2013.

Baudrillard, Jean. "Modernity." *Canadian Journal of Political and Social Theory* 11, no. 3 (1987) 63-72.

———. *Selected Writings*. 2nd ed. Edited by Mark Poster. Stanford, CA: Stanford University Press, 2001.

Bebbington, David W. *Evangelicalism in Modern Britain: A History from the 1730s to the 1980s*. 1989. Reprint, London: Routledge, 2002.

Belcher, Jim. *Deep Church: A Third Way Beyond Emerging and Traditional*. Downers Grove, IL: InterVarsity, 2009.

Bell, Daniel. *The Winding Passage: Sociological Essays and Journeys*. Rev. ed. New Brunswick, NJ: Transaction, 1991.

Bendroth, Margaret L. "The Search for 'Women's Role' in American Evangelicalism, 1930-1980." In *Evangelicalism and Modern America*, edited by George M. Marsden, 122-34. Grand Rapids, MI: Eerdmans, 1984.

Benovenli, Liza, Elizabeth Fuller, Jan Sinnott, and Sarah Waterman. "Three Applications of Postformal Thought: Wisdom, Concepts of God, and Success in College." *Research in the Social Scientific Study of Religion* 20 (2011) 141-54.

Benson, Bruce Ellis. *Graven Ideologies: Nietzsche, Derrida and Marion on Modern Idolatry*. Downers Grove, IL: InterVarsity, 2002.

———. "Theology and (Non)(Post)Foundationalism." In *A New Kind of Conversation: Blogging Toward a Postmodern Faith*, edited by Myron Bradley Penner and Hunter Barnes, 65-69. Colorado Springs, CO: Authentic, 2007.

———. "What Is 'Postmodernism'?" In *A New Kind of Conversation: Blogging Toward a Postmodern Faith*, edited by Myron Bradley Penner and Hunter Barnes, 5-10. Colorado Springs, CO: Authentic, 2007.

Benson, Bruce Ellis, and Peter Goodwin Heltzel, eds. *Evangelicals and Empire: Christian Alternatives to the Political Status Quo*. Grand Rapids, MI: Brazos, 2008.

Bentley, Philip J. "Uncertainty and Unity: Paradox and Truth." *Judaism* 33, no. 2 (March 1984) 191-201.

Berger, Kathleen Stassen. *The Developing Person Through the Life Span*. 9th ed. New York: Worth, 2014.

Berger, Peter L., and Thomas Luckmann. *The Social Construction of Reality: A Treatise in the Sociology of Knowledge*. 1966. Reprint, New York: Anchor, 1967.

Berlet, Chip, and Matthew N. Lyons. *Right-Wing Populism in America: Too Close for Comfort*. New York: Guilford, 2000.

Bernstein, Alan E. *The Formation of Hell: Death and Retribution in the Ancient and Early Christian Worlds*. Pbk. ed. Ithaca, NY: Cornell University Press, 1996.

Best, Steven, and Douglas Kellner. *Postmodern Theory: Critical Interrogations*. New York: Guilford, 1991.

———. *The Postmodern Turn*. Critical Perspectives. New York: Guilford, 1997.

The Bible Rules (Season 1). Commentary by Brian D. McLaren. History Channel 2: A&E Television Networks, 2014.

Bingham, June. *Courage to Change: An Introduction to the Life and Thought of Reinhold Niebuhr*. 1961. Reprint, Lanham, MD: University Press of America, 1993.

Bivins, Jason C. *Religion of Fear: The Politics of Horror in Conservative Evangelicalism*. New York: Oxford University Press, 2008.

Blackwell, Gary E. "Return or Rereading: The Spirituality of Brian D. McLaren." PhD diss., New Orleans Baptist Theological Seminary, 2015.

Blount, Douglas K. "A New Kind of Interpretation: Brian McLaren and the Hermeneutics of Taste." In *Evangelicals Engaging Emergent: A Discussion of the Emergent Church Movement*, edited by William D. Henard and Adam W. Greenway, 109-28. Nashville, TN: B&H, 2009.

Blythe, Rick. "Missouri Synod and the Changing Definitions of Fundamentalism." *Concordia Historical Institute Quarterly* 82, no. 1 (Spring 2009) 31-51.

Boa, Kenneth D., and Robert M. Bowman Jr. *Faith Has Its Reasons: Integrative Approaches to Defending the Christian Faith*. 2nd ed. Downers Grove, IL: InterVarsity, 2005.

Bohannon, John S. "Preaching and the Emerging Church." *Faith and Mission* 23, no. 2 (Spring 2006) 55-69.

———. "Preaching and the Emerging Church: A Homiletical Analysis and Critique of a Select Number of Emerging Church Pastors—Mark Driscoll, Dan Kimball, Brian McLaren, and Doug Pagitt—with Contemporary Implications for Evangelical (Expository) Preaching." PhD diss., Southeastern Baptist Theological Seminary, 2009.

Boisvert, Raymond. "Walker Percy's Postmodern Existentialism." *Soundings* 71, no. 4 (Winter 1988) 639-55.

Booth, Wayne C. *The Company We Keep: An Ethics of Fiction*. Berkeley, CA: University of California Press, 1988.

———. *Critical Understanding: The Powers and Limits of Pluralism*. Chicago: University of Chicago Press, 1979.

———. *The Rhetoric of Fiction*. 2nd ed. Chicago: University of Chicago Press, 1983.

Bosserman, B. A. *The Trinity and the Vindication of Christian Paradox: An Interpretation and Refinement of the Theological Apologetic of Cornelius Van Til*. Eugene, OR: Pickwick, 2014.

Bouma, Jeremy. *The Gospel of Brian McLaren: A New Kind of Christianity for a Multi-Faith World*. Grand Rapids, MI: Theoklesia, 2012.

———. *Reimagining the Kingdom: The Generational Development of Liberal Kingdom Grammar from Schleiermacher to McLaren*. Grand Rapids, MI: Theoklesia, 2012.

Bouma-Prediger, Steven. "Yearning for Home: The Christian Doctrine of Creation in a Postmodern Age." In *Postmodern Philosophy and Christian Thought*, edited by Merold Westphal, 169-201. Bloomington, IN: Indiana University Press, 1999.

Boyd, Gregory A. "Christus Victor View." In *The Nature of the Atonement: Four Views*, edited by James Beilby and Paul R. Eddy, 23-46. Downers Grove, IL: InterVarsity, 2006.

Bradley, James E., and Richard A. Muller. *Church History: An Introduction to Research Methods and Resources*. 2nd ed. Grand Rapids, MI: Eerdmans, 2016.

Braverman, Mark. Endorsement to *Why Did Jesus, Moses, the Buddha, and Mohammed Cross the Road? Christian Identity in a Multi-Faith World*, Pbk. ed., by Brian D. McLaren, iii. New York: Jericho, 2012.

Bray, Gerald L. "Evangelicals: Are They the Real Catholics and Orthodox?" In *Evangelicals and the Early Church: Recovery, Reform, Renewal*, edited by George Kalantzis and Andrew Tooley, 214-36. Eugene, OR: Cascade, 2012.

Brockenbrough, Martha. *Unpresidented: A Biography of Donald Trump*. New York: Feiwel and Friends, 2018.

Bromiley, Geoffrey W., ed., trans. *The Encyclopedia of Christianity*. 5 vols. Grand Rapids, MI: Eerdmans, 1999-2008.

Brow, Robert. "Evangelical Megashift." *Christianity Today* 34, no. 3 (February 19, 1990) 12-14.

Brownson, James V. *Bible, Gender, Sexuality: Reframing the Church's Debate on Same-Sex Relationships*. Grand Rapids, MI: Eerdmans, 2013.

Brumley, Jeff. "Moderate Churches Face a Particular Challenge." *The Christian Century*, August 21, 2013.

Buchler, Justus. *Charles Peirce's Empiricism*. 1939. The International Library of Philosophy. Reprint, New York: Routledge, 2001.

Bultmann, Rudolph. "Introduction" to *What Is Christianity?*, by Adolf von Harnack, vii-xviii. New York: Harper & Brothers, 1957.

Burk, Denny. "Editorial: Brian McLaren, Homosexuality, and Apostolic Loathing." *The Journal for Biblical Manhood and Womanhood* 15, no. 1 (Spring 2010) 2-4.

———. "Why Evangelicals Should Ignore Brian McLaren: How the New Testament Requires Evangelicals to Render a Judgment on the Moral Status of Homosexuality." *Themelios* 35, no. 2 (July 2010) 212-26.

Burson, Scott Robert. "Apologetics and the New Kind of Christian: An Arminian Analysis of Brian D. McLaren's Emergent Reconstruction of the Faith." PhD diss., London School of Theology, 2014.

———. *Brian McLaren in Focus: A New Kind of Apologetics*. Abilene, TX: Abilene Christian University Press, 2016.

Byassee, Jason. "An Emergent Voice: New Kind of Christian." *The Christian Century*, November 30, 2004.

Cady, Linell E. "A Model for a Public Theology." *Harvard Theological Review* 80, no. 2 (April 1987) 193-212.

Callaway, H. G. "Abduction, Competing Models and the Virtues of Hypotheses." In *Model-Based Reasoning in Science and Technology: Theoretical and Cognitive Issues*, edited by Lorenzo Magnani. Studies in Applied Philosophy, Epistemology and Rational Ethics, 263-80. New York: Springer, 2014.

Calo, Zachary R. "'The New Internationals': Human Rights and American Evangelicalism." In *Is the Good Book Good Enough? Evangelical Perspectives on Public Policy*, edited by David K. Ryden, 149-64. Lanham, MD: Lexington, 2011.

Campolo, Tony. *Is Jesus a Republican or a Democrat? And 14 Other Polarizing Issues*. Dallas, TX: World Publishing Group, 1995.

Campos, Daniel. "On the Distinction between Peirce's Abduction and Lipton's Inference to the Best Explanation." *Synthese* 180, no. 3 (June 2011) 419-42.

Cannon, Mae Elise, Lisa Sharon Harper, Troy Jackson, and Soong-Chan Rah. *Forgive Us: Confessions of a Compromised Faith*. Grand Rapids, MI: Zondervan, 2014.

Caputo, John D. "Methodological Postmodernism: On Merold Westphal's Overcoming Onto-theology." *Faith and Philosophy* 20, no. 3 (July 2005) 284-96.

———. *Philosophy and Theology*. Horizons in Theology. Nashville, TN: Abingdon, 2006.

———. "Who Comes After the God of Metaphysics?" In *The Religious*, 1-19. Malden, MA: Blackwell, 2002.

Carmody, Denise Lardner, and John Carmody. *Catholic Spirituality and the History of Religions*. New York: Paulist, 1991.

Carolan, Patrick and Brian D. McLaren. "It's Time to Change the Abortion Debate in America." *National Catholic Reporter*, January 9, 2020. https://www.ncronline.org/news/opinion/its-time-change-abortion-debate-america/.

Carson, D. A. *Becoming Conversant with the Emerging Church: Understanding a Movement and Its Implications*. Grand Rapids, MI: Zondervan, 2005.

———. *The Gagging of God: Christianity Confronts Pluralism*. Grand Rapids, MI: Zondervan, 1996.

Catherwood, Christopher. *The Evangelicals: What They Believe, Where They Are, and Their Politics*. Wheaton, IL: Crossway, 2010.

Chalke, Steve, and Alan Mann. *The Lost Message of Jesus*. Grand Rapids, MI: Zondervan, 2003.

Christian Century. McLaren Talk Canceled by Kentucky Baptists. March 22, 2005.

Christy, Mark Wayne. "Neoorthopraxy and Brian D. McLaren: A Postmodern Reconstruction of Kingdom of God Theology." PhD diss., Southwestern Baptist Theological Seminary, 2011.

Claiborne, Shane, and Tony Campolo. *Red Letter Revolution: What If Jesus Really Meant What He Said?* Nashville, TN: Thomas Nelson, 2012.

Clark, David K. *To Know and Love God: Method for Theology.* 2003. Foundations of Evangelical Theology. Reprint, Wheaton, IL: Crossway, 2010.

Clark, Kelly James. "Reformed Epistemology Apologetics." In *Five Views on Apologetics*, edited by Stanley N. Gundry and Steven B. Cowan. Counterpoints: Bible and Theology, 266-84. Grand Rapids, MI: Zondervan, 2000.

Clark, R. Scott. "Whosoever Will Be Saved: Emerging Church, Meet Christian Dogma." In *Reforming or Conforming: Post-Conservative Evangelicals and the Emerging Church*, edited by Gary L. W. Johnson and Ronald N. Gleason, 112-28. Wheaton, IL: Crossway, 2008.

Clawson, Michael. "A Brief History of the Emerging Church Movement in the United States." In *Crossing Boundaries, Redefining Faith: Interdisciplinary Perspectives on the Emerging Church Movement*, edited by Michael Clawson and April Stace, 17-44. Eugene, OR: Pickwick, 2016.

———. "Emerging from What? The Historical Roots of the Emerging Church Movement." PhD diss., Baylor University, 2017.

Clinchy, Blythe McVicker. "Beyond Subjectivism." *Tradition and Discovery: The Polanyi Society Periodical* 34, no. 1 (2007-2008) 15-30.

Clore, Gerald L., and Karen Gasper. "Feeling is Believing: Some Affective Influences on Belief." In *Emotions and Beliefs: How Feelings Influence Thoughts*. Pbk. ed, edited by Nico H. Frijda, Antony S. R. Manstead, and Sacha Bem. Studies in Emotion and Social Interaction: Second Series, 10-44. New York: Cambridge University Press, 2000.

Clowney, Edmund P. "A Critical Estimate of Søren Kierkegaard's Notion of The Individual." *Westminster Theological Journal* 5, no. 1 (November 1942) 29-61.

Coleman, James S. "Social Capital in the Creation of Human Capital." *American Journal of Sociology* (Supplement) 94 (1989) 95-120.

Collins, Kenneth J. *Power, Politics and the Fragmentation of Evangelicalism: From the Scopes Trial to the Obama Administration.* Downers Grove, IL: InterVarsity, 2012.

Come, Arnold B. *Kierkegaard as Theologian: Recovering My Self.* McGill-Queen's Studies in the History of Ideas 24. Buffalo, NY: McGill-Queen's University Press, 1997.

Conway, Flo, and Jim Siegelman. *Holy Terror: The Fundamentalist War on America's Freedoms in Religion, Politics, and Our Private Lives.* Garden City, NY: Doubleday, 1982.

Cooke, Gillian, and Alan Sheard. "Understanding Homosexuality in the 21st Century." *Modern Believing* 48, no. 1 (January 2007) 7-14.

Coontz, Stephanie. *Marriage, A History: From Obedience to Intimacy or How Love Conquered Marriage.* New York: Viking, 2005.

Cooper-White, Pamela. "Intersubjectivity." In *Encyclopedia of Psychology and Religion*, edited by David A. Leeming. Berlin, Heidelberg: Springer, 2017. http://dx.doi.org/10.1007/978-3-642-27771-9_9182-2.

Cooperman, Alan, Greg Smith, Allison Pond, Neha Sahgal, Jacqueline Wenger, Brian J. Grim, Conrad Hackett, and Scott Clement. *Global Survey of Evangelical Protestant Leaders.* Washington, DC: Pew Research Center, June 22, 2011. Accessed March 31, 2018. http://assets.pewresearch.org/wp-content/uploads/sites/11/2011/06/Global-Survey-of-Evan.-Prot.-Leaders.pdf.

Cotter, Wendy J. "Greco-Roman Apotheosis Traditions and the Resurrection Appearances in Matthew." In *The Gospel of Matthew in Current Study: Studies in Memory of William G. Thompson, S.J.*, edited by David E. Aune, 127-53. Grand Rapids, MI: Eerdmans, 2001.

Cottingham, John. *Philosophy of Religion: Towards a More Humane Approach*. New York: Cambridge University Press, 2014.

Cox, Harvey. *The Future of Faith*. New York: HarperOne, 2009.

Craig, William Lane. *Reasonable Faith: Christian Truth and Apologetics*. 3rd ed. Wheaton, IL: Crossway, 2008.

Craigen, Trevor P. "Emergent Soteriology: The Dark Side." *Master's Seminary Journal* 17, no. 2 (Fall 2006) 177-90.

Crossan, John Dominic. "Jesus and the Challenge of Collaborative Eschatology." In *The Historical Jesus: Five Views*, edited by James K. Beilby and Paul Rhodes Eddy. Spectrum Multiview Books, 105-52. Downers Grove, IL: InterVarsity, 2009.

Crouch, Andy. "The Emergent Mystique." *Christianity Today*, November 2004.

Csikszentmihalyi, Mihaly. *Creativity: The Psychology of Discovery and Invention*. 1996. Modern Classics. Reprint, New York: Harper, 2013.

Csinos, David M., and Brian D. McLaren. "Breaking the Bubble Wrap." *Sojourners Magazine*, July 2012.

Cunningham, Robert. "In Love with Donald Trump." Tates Creek Presbyterian Church. March 17, 2016. Accessed December 29, 2018. https://tcpca.org/blog/2016/3/17/in-love-with-donald-trump.

Dahl, Ronald E. "Adolescent Brain Development: A Period of Vulnerabilities and Opportunities; Keynote Address." *Annals of The New York Academy of Sciences* 1021 (June 2004) 1-22.

Danto, Arthur C. *The Transfiguration of the Commonplace: A Philosophy of Art*. Cambridge, MA: Harvard University Press, 1981.

———. *What Art Is*. New Haven, CT: Yale University Press, 2013.

Darnell, Alfred, and Darren E. Sherkat. "The Impact of Protestant Fundamentalism on Educational Attainment." *American Sociological Review* 62 (April 1997) 306-15.

Daston, Lorraine. "Enlightenment Fears, Fears of Enlightenment." In *What's Left of Enlightenment? A Postmodern Question*, edited by Keith Michael Baker and Peter Hanns Reill, 115-28. Stanford, CA: Stanford University Press, 2001.

Davis, Charles. *What Is Living, What Is Dead in Christianity Today? Breaking the Liberal-Conservative Deadlock*. San Francisco, CA: Harper & Row, 1986.

Dawe, Donald G. *The Form of a Servant: A Historical Analysis of the Kenotic Motif*. Philadelphia, PA: Westminster Press, 1963.

Daws, Richard E., and Adam Hampshire. "The Negative Relationship between Reasoning and Religiosity Is Underpinned by a Bias for Intuitive Responses Specifically When Intuition and Logic Are in Conflict." *Frontiers in Psychology* 8 (December 2017). http://dx.doi.org/10.3389/fpsyg.2017.02191.

Decker, Kevin S., and Jason T. Eberl, eds. *The Ultimate Star Trek and Philosophy: The Search for Socrates*. Malden, MA: Wiley, 2016.

Derrida, Jacques. *Deconstruction in a Nutshell: A Conversation with Jacques Derrida*. 1997. Edited by John D. Caputo. Perspectives in Continental Philosophy 1. Reprint, New York: Fordham University Press, 2013.

———. *Of Grammatology*. 1976. Translated by Gayatri Chakravorty Spivak. Reprint, Baltimore, MD: Johns Hopkins University Press, 2016.

DeYoung, Kevin. "Christianity and McLarenism: Ten Questions and Ten Problems." The Gospel Coalition. Accessed January 29, 2019. https://media.thegospelcoalition.org/static-blogs/kevin-deyoung/files/2010/02/Christianity-and-McLarenism1.pdf.

Diamond, Sara. *Not by Politics Alone: The Enduring Influence of the Christian Right*. New York: Guilford, 1998.

———. *Spiritual Warfare: The Politics of the Christian Right*. Cheektowaga, NY: Black Rose, 1990.

Dickens, David R., and Andrea Fontana, eds. *Postmodernism and Social Inquiry*. 1994. Reprint, New York: Routledge, 2015.

Dillon, John. "Logos and Trinity: Patterns of Platonist Influence on Early Christianity." In *The Philosophy in Christianity*, edited by Godfrey Vesey. Royal Institute of Philosophy Lecture Series 25, 1-13. New York: Cambridge University Press, 1989.

Dishion, Thomas J., François Poulin, and Bert Burraston. "Peer Group Dynamics Associated with Iatrogenic Effects in Group Interventions with High-Risk Young Adolescents." In *The Role of Friendship in Psychological Adjustment*, edited by Douglas W. Nangle and Cynthia A. Erdley. New Directions for Child and Adolescent Development 91, 79-92. San Francisco, CA: Jossey-Bass, Inc., 2001.

Dixon, Larry. "'Five by McLaren: A Narrative Review Article of Five Books by Brian McLaren." *Emmaus Journal* 14, no. 2 (Winter 2005) 217-71.

———. "Whatever Happened to Heresy? Examples of Heresy Today (Part Four)." *Emmaus Journal* 19, no. 2 (Summer 2010) 211-22.

Dobson, James C. "Dedicated to the Preservation of the Home." Dr. Dobson's Study. Accessed January 13, 2019. http://ontology.buffalo.edu/smith/clinton/character.html.

———. *Marriage Under Fire: Why We Must Win This Battle*. Sisters, OR: Multnomah, 2004.

Dorrien, Gary J. *The Remaking of Evangelical Theology*. Louisville, KY: John Knox, 1998.

Douglas, Mark. "Reinhold Niebuhr's Two Pragmatisms." *American Journal of Theology and Philosophy* 22, no. 3 (September 2001) 221-40.

Driscoll, Mark. *Confessions of a Reformission Rev.: Hard Lessons from an Emerging Missional Church*. Leadership Network Innovation Series. Grand Rapids, MI: Zondervan, 2006.

———. "A Pastoral Perspective on the Emergent Church." *Criswell Theological Review* 3, no. 2 (Spring 2006) 87-93.

Dulles, Avery Cardinal. *A History of Apologetics*. 2nd ed. Modern Apologetics Library. San Francisco, CA: Ignatius, 2005.

———. *Models of Revelation*. 2nd ed. Maryknoll, NY: Orbis, 1992.

Duncan, John Alan. "A Critical Analysis of Preaching in the Emerging Church." PhD diss., Southern Baptist Theological Seminary, 2011.

Durkheim, Émile. *The Elementary Forms of Religious Life*. Translated by Carol Cosman. Oxford World's Classics. New York: Oxford University Press, 2001.

Eagleton, Terry. *Literary Theory: An Introduction*. 3rd ed. Malden, MA: Blackwell, 2008.

Eberl, Jason T., and Kevin S. Decker, eds. *Star Trek and Philosophy: The Wrath of Kant*. Popular Culture and Philosophy 35. Chicago, IL: Open Court, 2008.

Eddy, Paul Rhodes, and James K. Beilby. "The Quest for the Historical Jesus: An Introduction." In *The Historical Jesus: Five Views*, edited by James K. Beilby and Paul Rhodes Eddy. Spectrum Multiview Books, 9-54. Downers Grove, IL: InterVarsity, 2009.

Eller, Jack David. "Agnomancy: Conjuring Ignorance, Sustaining Belief." *Socio-Historical Examination of Religion and Ministry* 2, no. 1 (Spring 2020): 150-80. https://doi.org/10.33929/sherm.2020.vol2.no1.07.

Elrod, John W. *Kierkegaard and Christendom*. Princeton, NJ: Princeton University Press, 1981.

Elwell, Walter A., ed. *Baker Encyclopedia of the Bible*. Grand Rapids, MI: Baker, 1988.

Emerson, Michael O., and Christian Smith. *Divided by Faith: Evangelical Religion and the Problem of Race in America*. 2000. Pbk. ed. New York: Oxford University Press, 2001.

Enns, Peter. "Apostolic Hermeneutics and an Evangelical Doctrine of Scripture: Moving Beyond A Modernist Impasse." *Westminster Theological Journal* 65, no. 2 (Fall 2003) 263–87.

———. "Biblicism: What is it and Why Does it Make Baby Jesus Cry?" *Pete's Blog*, 2017. https://peteenns.com/biblicism-make-baby-jesus-cry/.

———. "Fuller Meaning, Single Goal: A Christotelic Approach to the New Testament Use of the Old in Its First-Century Interpretive Environment." In *Three Views on the New Testament Use of the Old Testament*, edited by Kenneth Berding and Jonathan Lunde. Counterpoints: Bible and Theology, 165–217. Grand Rapids, MI: Zondervan, 2008.

———. "My Interview with Brian McLaren." Interview by Brian D. McLaren. *Pete's Blog*, 2014. https://peteenns.com/my-interview-with-brian-mclaren-part-1/.

Erickson, Millard J. *Postmodernizing the Faith: Evangelical Responses to the Challenge of Postmodernism*. 1998. Reprint, Grand Rapids, MI: Baker, 2002.

Eskridge, William N. Jr. *Dishonorable Passions: Sodomy Laws in America (1861–2003)*. New York: Viking, 2008.

Evans, C. Stephen. *Kierkegaard's "Fragments" and "Postscript": The Religious Philosophy of Johannes Climacus*. Atlantic Highlands, NJ: Humanities, 1983.

Fairbairn, Donald. "Patristic Exegesis and Theology: The Cart and the Horse." *Westminster Theological Journal* 69, no. 1 (Spring 2007) 1–19.

Falk, Darrel R. *Coming to Peace with Science: Bridging the Worlds Between Faith and Biology*. Downers Grove, IL: InterVarsity, 2004.

Falwell, Jerry Sr. *Listen, America!* Garden City, NY: Doubleday, 1980.

Fann, K. T. *Peirce's Theory of Abduction*. The Hague: Martinus, 1970.

Featherstone, Mike. "In Pursuit of the Postmodern: An Introduction." *Theory, Culture and Society* 5, no. 2/3 (June 1988) 195–215.

Festinger, Leon. *A Theory of Cognitive Dissonance*. Stanford, CA: Stanford University Press, 1957.

Festinger, Leon, Henry W. Riecken, and Stanley Schachter. "When Prophecy Fails." In *Extending Psychological Frontiers: Selected Works of Leon Festinger*, edited by Stanley Schachter and Michael Gazzaniga, 258–69. New York: Russell Sage, 1989.

Fiedler, Klaus, and Herbert Bless. "The Formation of Beliefs at the Interface of Affective and Cognitive Processes." In *Emotions and Beliefs: How Feelings Influence Thoughts*. Pbk. ed, edited by Nico H. Frijda, Antony S. R. Manstead, and Sacha Bem. Studies in Emotion and Social Interaction: Second Series, 144–70. New York: Cambridge University Press, 2000.

Fields, Bruce L. *Introducing Black Theology: Three Crucial Questions for the Evangelical Church*. Grand Rapids, MI: Baker, 2001.

Fish, Stanley E. "Interpreting the *Variorum*." In *Reader-Response Criticism: From Formalism to Post-Structuralism*, edited by Jane P. Tompkins, 164–84. Baltimore, MD: Johns Hopkins University Press, 1980.

Fitch, David E. *The End of Evangelicalism? Discerning a New Faithfulness for Mission: Towards an Evangelical Political Theology*. Theopolitical Visions 9. Eugene, OR: Cascade, 2011.

Fitzgerald, Frances. *The Evangelicals: The Struggle to Shape America.* New York: Simon & Schuster, 2017.

Foucault, Michael. *Archaeology of Knowledge.* 1969. Translated by A. M. Sheridan Smith. Reprint, New York: Routledge, 2002.

———. "What Is an Author?" In *Textual Strategies: Perspectives in Post-Structuralist Criticism,* edited by Josué V. Harari, 141-60. Ithaca, NY: Cornell University Press, 1979.

Fowler, James W. *Stages of Faith: The Psychology of Human Development and the Quest for Meaning.* 1981. Pbk. ed. Reprint, New York: HarperCollins, 1995.

Fox, Richard Wightman. *Reinhold Niebuhr: A Biography.* San Francisco, CA: Harper & Row, 1985.

Frame, John M. *The Doctrine of the Knowledge of God: A Theology of Lordship.* Phillipsburg, NJ: Presbyterian and Reformed, 1987.

———. "Presuppositional Apologetics." In *Five Views on Apologetics,* edited by Stanley N. Gundry and Steven B. Cowan. Counterpoints: Bible and Theology, 208-31. Grand Rapids, MI: Zondervan, 2000.

Frank, Doug. *Less Than Conquerors: The Evangelical Quest for Power in the Early Twentieth Century.* Eugene, OR: Wipf and Stock, 2009.

Franke, John R. *The Character of Theology: An Introduction to Its Nature, Task, and Purpose.* Grand Rapids, MI: Baker, 2005.

———. Foreword to *A Generous Orthodoxy,* by Brian D. McLaren, 9-14. Grand Rapids, MI: Youth Specialties, 2004.

Frankfurt, Harry G. "Peirce's Notion of Abduction." *Journal of Philosophy* 55 (July 1958) 593-96.

Fredriksen, Paula. *Jesus of Nazareth, King of the Jews: A Jewish Life and the Emergence of Christianity.* 1999. Reprint, New York: Vintage Books, 2000.

Frei, Hans W. *The Eclipse of Biblical Narrative: A Study in Eighteenth and Nineteenth Century Hermeneutics.* New Haven, CT: Yale University Press, 1974.

Frijda, Nico H., Antony S. R. Manstead, and Sacha Bem. "The Influence of Emotions on Beliefs." In *Emotions and Beliefs: How Feelings Influence Thoughts.* Pbk. ed. Studies in Emotion and Social Interaction: Second Series, 1-9. New York: Cambridge University Press, 2000.

Froehlich, Karlfried, ed., trans. *Biblical Interpretation in the Early Church.* Sources of Early Christian Thought. Philadelphia, PA: Fortress, 1984.

Froese, Paul, Jeremy Uecker, Kenneth Vaughan, Jerry Park, James Davidson, Andrew Whitehead, and Bob Thomson. *American Values, Mental Health, and Using Technology in the Age of Trump: Findings from the Baylor Religion Survey, Wave 5.* Waco, TX: Baylor University, September 2017. https://www.baylor.edu/baylorreligionsurvey/doc.php/292546.pdf.

Frost, Elton Toby. "A Snapshot of the Emergent Church with Interviews of Brian McLaren, Doug Pagitt, and Ed Stetzer." *Midwestern Journal of Theology* 5, no. 2 (Spring 2007) 3-25.

Gadamer, Hans-Georg. *Truth and Method.* 1975. 2nd rev. ed. Translated by Joel Weinsheimer and Donald G. Marshall. New York: Bloomsbury, 2013.

Gaebelein, Frank E. "Evangelicals and Social Concern." *Journal of the Evangelical Theological Society* 25, no. 1 (March 1982) 17-22.

Gallagher, Sally K. *Evangelical Identity and Gendered Family Life.* New Brunswick, NJ: Rutgers University Press, 2003.

Galli, Mark. "Trump Should Be Removed from Office." *Christianity Today*, December 19, 2019. https://www.christianitytoday.com/ct/2019/december-web-only/trump-should-be-removed-from-office.html.

Gardner, Sebastian. "Sartre, Schelling, and Onto-Theology." *Religious Studies: An International Journal for the Philosophy of Religion* 42, no. 3 (September 2006) 247-71.

Garff, Joakim. *Søren Kierkegaard: A Biography*. 2005. Translated by Bruce H. Kirmmse. Reprint, Princeton, NJ: Princeton University Press, 2007.

Gaston, Thomas E. "The Influence of Platonism on the Early Apologists." *Heythrop Journal: A Bimonthly Review of Philosophy and Theology* 50, no. 4 (July 2009) 573-80.

Geffré, Claude. *A New Age in Theology*. New York: Paulist, 1974.

Geisler, Norman L., ed. *Baker Encyclopedia of Christian Apologetics*. Grand Rapids, MI: Baker, 1999.

———. *Christian Apologetics*. Grand Rapids, MI: Baker, 1976.

Geisler, Norman L., and Paul D. Feinberg. *Introduction to Philosophy: A Christian Perspective*. Grand Rapids, MI: Baker, 1980.

Geisler, Norman L., and Ronald M. Brooks. *Come, Let Us Reason: An Introduction to Logical Thinking*. Grand Rapids, MI: Baker, 1990.

Geisler, Norman L., and Thomas A. Howe. "A Postmodern View of Scripture." *Christian Apologetics Journal* 7, no. 1 (Spring 2008) 63-79.

———. "A Postmodern View of Scripture." In *Evangelicals Engaging Emergent: A Discussion of the Emergent Church Movement*, edited by William D. Henard and Adam W. Greenway, 92-108. Nashville, TN: B&H, 2009.

Gerber, Alan S., Gregory A. Huber, David Doherty, and Conor M. Dowling. "The Big Five Personality Traits in the Political Arena." *Annual Review of Political Science* 14, no. 1 (2011) 265-87.

Gergen, Kenneth J. "Relativism, Religion, and Relational Being." *Common Knowledge* 13, no. 2/3 (Spring/Fall 2007) 362-78.

Gibbs, Eddie, and Ryan K. Bolger. *Emerging Churches: Creating Christian Community in Postmodern Cultures*. Grand Rapids, MI: Baker, 2005.

Gilbert, Greg D. "Saved from the Wrath of God: An Examination of Brian McLaren's Approach to the Doctrine of Hell." In *Reforming or Conforming: Post-Conservative Evangelicals and the Emerging Church*, edited by Gary L. W. Johnson and Ronald N. Gleason, 245-68. Wheaton, IL: Crossway, 2008.

Gleason, John P. "How St. Mary's College Offers Religious Education Through a Program of Christian Culture." *Religious Education* 55 (1960) 257-60.

Global Center for Religious Research. "An Open Letter to Evangelicals of Moral Conscience." January 18, 2020. https://www.gcrr.org/evangelicals-and-trump.

Gnanakan, Ken. "Evangelicals and Environmental Stewardship." In *Evangelicals Around the World: A Global Handbook for the 21st Century*, edited by Brian C. Stiller et al, 188-93. Nashville, TN: Thomas Nelson, 2015.

Gordon, Daniel, ed. *Postmodernism and the Enlightenment: New Perspectives in Eighteenth-Century French Intellectual History*. New York: Routledge, 2001.

Granovetter, Mark S. "The Strength of Weak Ties." *American Journal of Sociology* 78, no. 6 (1973) 1360-80.

Gray, Derwin L. "The Emergence of The Emerging Church." *Christian Apologetics Journal* 7, no. 1 (Spring 2008) 27-62.

Green, Joel B. "Heaven and Hell." In *Dictionary of Jesus and the Gospels*. 2nd ed, edited by Joel B. Green, Jeannine K. Brown, and Nicholas Perrin, 370-76. Downers Grove, IL: InterVarsity, 2013.

Grenz, Stanley J. *A Primer on Postmodernism*. Grand Rapids, MI: Eerdmans, 1996.

———. "Star Trek and the Next Generation: Postmodernism and the Future of Evangelical Theology." *Crux* 30, no. 1 (March 1994) 24-32.

Grenz, Stanley J., and John R. Franke. *Beyond Foundationalism: Shaping Theology in a Postmodern Context*. Louisville, KY: John Knox, 2001.

Grenz, Stanley J., and Roger E. Olson. *Twentieth-Century Theology: God and the World in a Transitional Age*. Downers Grove, IL: InterVarsity, 1992.

Griffin, David Ray, ed. *The Reenchantment of Science: Postmodern Proposals*. Albany, NY: State University of New York Press, 1988.

Griffin, James, Sarah Gooding, Michael Semesky, Brittany Farmer, Garrett Mannchen, and Jan Sinnott. "Four Brief Studies of Relations between Postformal Thought and Non-Cognitive Factors: Personality, Concepts of God, Political Opinions, and Social Attitudes." *Journal of Adult Development* 16, no. 3 (August 2009) 173-82.

Grillmeier, Aloys. *Christ in Christian Tradition: From the Apostolic Age to Chalcedon (451)*. 2nd ed. Translated by John Bowden. Vol. 1. Atlanta, GA: John Knox, 1975.

Groothuis, Douglas R. "The Postmodernist Challenge to Theology." *Themelios* 25, no. 1 (November 1999) 4-22.

Grudem, Wayne. *Evangelical Feminism: A New Path to Liberalism?* Wheaton, IL: Crossway, 2006.

Gschwandtner, Christina M. *Postmodern Apologetics? Arguments for God in Contemporary Philosophy*. Perspectives in Continental Philosophy. New York: Fordham University Press, 2013.

Guarino, Thomas G. "Contemporary Theology and Scientific Rationality." *Studies in Religion* 22, no. 3 (1993) 311-22.

Gushee, David P. *The Future of Faith in American Politics: The Public Witness of the Evangelical Center*. Waco, TX: Baylor University Press, 2008.

Gushee, David P., and Justin Phillips. "Moral Formation and the Evangelical Voter: A Report from the Red States." *Journal of the Society of Christian Ethics* 26, no. 2 (2006) 23-60.

Hadot, Pierre. *Philosophy as a Way of Life: Spiritual Exercises from Socrates to Foucault*. Edited by Arnold I. Davidson. Translated by Michael Chase. Malden, MA: Blackwell, 1995.

Hagerty, Barbara Bradley. "Jesus, Reconsidered: Book Sparks Evangelical Debate" (NPR Podcast). March 26, 2010. Accessed January 19, 2019. https://www.npr.org/templates/story/story.php?storyId=125165061.

Hall, Douglas John. *Why Christian? For Those on the Edge of Faith*. Minneapolis, MN: Fortress, 1998.

Hammett, John S. "An Ecclesiological Assessment of the Emerging Church." *Criswell Theological Review* 3, no. 2 (Spring 2006) 29-49.

Hanley, Richard. *The Metaphysics of Star Trek*. New York: BasicBooks, 1997.

Hanna, Mark M. *Crucial Questions in Apologetics*. Grand Rapids, MI: Baker, 1981.

Harding, Susan. *The Book of Jerry Falwell: Fundamentalist Language and Politics*. Princeton, NJ: Princeton University Press, 2000.

Harman, Gilbert H. "The Inference to the Best Explanation." *Philosophical Review* 74 (January 1965) 88-95.

Harmon-Jones, Eddie. "A Cognitive Dissonance Theory Perspective on the Role of Emotion in the Maintenance and Change of Beliefs and Attitudes." In *Emotions and Beliefs: How Feelings Influence Thoughts*. Pbk. ed, edited by Nico H. Frijda, Antony S. R. Manstead, and Sacha Bem. Studies in Emotion and Social Interaction: Second Series, 185-211. New York: Cambridge University Press, 2000.

Haroutunian, Ellen. "Postmodern Ministry: In Search of a Living Orthodoxy." In *A New Kind of Conversation: Blogging Toward a Postmodern Faith*, edited by Myron Bradley Penner and Hunter Barnes, 163-71. Colorado Springs, CO: Authentic, 2007.

Hartman, Andrew. *A War for the Soul of America: A History of the Culture Wars*. Chicago, IL: The University of Chicago Press, 2015.

Hatch, John. "Hearing God Amid Many Voices: Brian McLaren's (Polyphonically) Novel Approach to the Bible." *Journal of Communication and Religion* 38, no. 1 (Spring 2015) 23-47.

Hawtrey, Kim, and John Lunn. "The Emergent Church, Socio-Economics and Christian Mission." *Transformation* 27, no. 2 (April 2010) 65-74.

Haykin, Michael A. G. "Recovering Ancient Church Practices: A Review of Brian McLaren, *Finding Our Way Again: The Return of the Ancient Practices*." *The Southern Baptist Journal of Theology* 12, no. 2 (Summer 2008) 62-66.

Hebblethwaite, Brian. "The Nature and Limits of Metaphysical Understanding." In *The Nature and Limits of Human Understanding*, edited by Anthony Sanford. The 2001 Gifford Lectures at the University of Glasgow, 210-36. New York: T&T Clark, 2003.

Heidegger, Martin. *Identity and Difference*. 1969. Translated by Joan Stambaugh. Reprint, Chicago, IL: University of Chicago Press, 2002.

———. *Pathmarks*. 1967. Edited by William McNeill. Reprint, New York: Cambridge University Press, 1999.

———. *The Phenomenology of Religious Life*. 2004. Translated by Matthias Fritsch and Jennifer Anna Gosetti-Ferencei. Reprint, Bloomington, IN: Indiana University Press, 2010.

Heim, Joe. "Jerry Falwell Jr. Can't Imagine Trump 'Doing Anything That's Not Good for the Country.'" *Washington Post*, January 1, 2019. Accessed January 3, 2019. www.washingtonpost.com/lifestyle/magazine/jerry-falwell-jr-cant-imagine-trump-doing-anything-thats-not-good-for-the-country/2018/12/21/6affc4c4-f19e-11e8-80d0-f7e1948d55f4_story.html.

Heltzel, Peter G. *Jesus and Justice: Evangelicals, Race, and American Politics*. New Haven, CT: Yale University Press, 2009.

Hemming, Laurence Paul. "Nihilism: Heidegger and the Grounds of Redemption." In *Radical Orthodoxy: A New Theology*, edited by John Milbank, Catherine Pickstock, and Graham Ward, 91-108. New York: Routledge, 1999.

Hempton, David. *Evangelical Disenchantment: Nine Portraits of Faith and Doubt*. New Haven, CT: Yale University Press, 2008.

Hengel, Martin. *The "Hellenization" of Judaea in the First Century after Christ*. Translated by John Bowden. Philadelphia, PA: Trinity, 1989.

———. *Judaism and Hellenism: Studies in Their Encounter in Palestine during the Early Hellenistic Period*. Translated by John Bowden. 2 vols. Philadelphia, PA: Fortress, 1974.

Henry, Carl F. H. "Who are the Evangelicals." In *Evangelical Affirmations*, edited by Kenneth S. Kantzer and Carl F. H. Henry, 69-94. Grand Rapids, MI: Academie, 1990.

Henry, Michel. *I am the Truth: Toward a Philosophy of Christianity*. Translated by Susan Emanuel. Cultural Memory in the Present. Stanford, CA: Stanford University Press, 2003.

Hessel, Dieter T. "Solidarity Ethics: A Public Focus for the Church." *Review of Religious Research* 20, no. 3 (Summer 1979) 251-63.

Hesselgrave, David. "Brian McLaren's Contextualization of the Gospel." *Evangelical Missions Quarterly* 43, no. 1 (January 2007) 92-100.

Hiebert, Paul G. *Transforming Worldviews: An Anthropological Understanding of How People Change*. Grand Rapids, MI: Baker, 2008.

Hill, Robert J. "Troubling Adult Learning in the Present Time." In *Third Update on Adult Learning Theory*, edited by Sharan B. Merriam. New Directions for Adult and Continuing Education 119, 83-92. Hoboken, NJ: Wiley, 2008.

Hill, William J. *The Three-Personed God: The Trinity as a Mystery of Salvation*. 1982. Reprint, Washington, DC: The Catholic University of America Press, 1988.

Hinkson, Craig Q. "Luther and Kierkegaard: Theologians of the Cross." *International Journal of Systematic Theology* 3, no. 1 (March 2001) 27-45.

Hintikka, Jaakko. "What: Is Abduction? The Fundamental Problem of Contemporary Epistemology." *Transactions of the Charles S. Peirce Society* 34, no. 3 (Summer 1998) 503-33.

Hixson, J. B. *Getting the Gospel Wrong: The Evangelical Crisis No One Is Talking About*. Maitland, FL: Xulon, 2008.

Hobbes, Thomas. *Leviathan*. 1651. Penguin Classics. Reprint, New York: Penguin, 1985.

Hodge, Charles. *Systematic Theology*. 1872. Vol. 1. Reprint, Bellingham, WA: Lexham, 1997.

Hödl, Ludwig. "Das scholastische Verständnis von Kirchenamt und Kirchengewalt unter dem frühen Einfluss der aristotelischen Philosophie." *Scholastik* 36 (1961) 1-22.

Hoeveler, J. David Jr. *The Postmodernist Turn: American Thought and Culture in the 1970s*. 1996. Reprint, Lanham, MD: Rowman & Littlefield Publishers, 2004.

Hofstadter, Douglas R. *Gödel, Escher, Bach: An Eternal Golden Braid*. 1979. Reprint, New York: Basic Books, 1999.

Homer, Paul L. *On Kierkegaard and the Truth*. Edited by David J. Gouwens and Lee C. Barrett III. Cambridge, England: James Clarke, 2012.

Hong, Howard V., and Edna H. Hong, trans. *Søren Kierkegaard's Journals and Papers*. 7 vols. Bloomington, IN: Indiana University Press, 1967-1978.

Horkheimer, Max, and Theodor W. Adorno. *Dialectic of Enlightenment: Philosophical Fragments*. 1987. Edited by Gunzelin Schmid Noerr. Translated by Edmund Jephcott. Reprint, Stanford, CA: Stanford University Press, 2002.

Horsley, Richard A. *Jesus and Empire: The Kingdom of God and the New World Disorder*. Minneapolis, MN: Fortress, 2003.

Horton, Michael. *Christless Christianity: The Alternative Gospel of the American Church*. Grand Rapids, MI: Baker, 2008.

Howard, Ken. *Paradoxy: Creating Christian Community Beyond Us and Them*. Brewster, MA: Paraclete, 2010.

———. "The Religion Singularity: A Demographic Crisis Destabilizing and Transforming Institutional Christianity." *International Journal of Religion and Spirituality in Society* 7, no. 2 (2017) 77-93.

Howe, Thomas A. "A Review of *A Generous Orthodoxy* By Brian D. McLaren." *Christian Apologetics Journal* 7, no. 1 (Spring 2008) 81-102.

Hubbard, Thomas K., ed. *A Companion to Greek and Roman Sexualities*. Malden, MA: Wiley, 2014.

Hubery, Douglas S. "Jesus Movement." *The Expository Times* 84, no. 7 (April 1973) 212-14.

Huntington, Samuel P. "Robust Nationalism." *National Interest*, Winter 1999/2000.

Hurley, Patrick J., and Lori Watson. *A Concise Introduction to Logic*. 13th ed. Boston, MA: Cengage, 2018.

Husserl, Edmund. *Cartesian Meditations: An Introduction to Phenomenology*. Translated by Dorion Cairns. The Hague, Netherlands: Martinus, 1960.

———. *Ideas Pertaining to a Pure Phenomenology and to a Phenomenological Philosophy: First Book; General Introduction to a Pure Phenomenology*. Translated by F. Kersten. Boston, MA: Martinus, 1982.

———. *Logical Investigations*. 1970. Pbk. ed. Edited by Dermot Moran. Translated by J. N. Findlay. Vol. 2, *On the Theory of Wholes and Parts*. Reprint, New York: Routledge, 2001.

———. *The Paris Lectures*. Translated by Peter Koestenbaum. The Hague, Netherlands: Martinus, 1975.

Ingraffia, Brian D. *Postmodern Theory and Biblical Theology: Vanquishing God's Shadow*. New York: Cambridge University Press, 1995.

Insole, Christopher J. "Against Radical Orthodoxy: The Dangers of Overcoming Political Liberalism." *Modern Theology* 20, no. 2 (April 2004) 213-41.

Irwin, William. *Intentionalist Interpretation: A Philosophical Explanation and Defense*. Contributions in Philosophy 73. Westport, CT: Greenwood, 1999.

Isaak, Jon M. *New Testament Theology: Extending the Table*. Eugene, OR: Cascade, 2011.

James, William. *Pragmatism and Other Writings*. 1907. Edited by Giles Gunn. Reprint, New York: Penguin, 2000.

Janicaud, Dominique. "The Theological Turn of French Phenomenology." In *Phenomenology and the "Theological Turn": The French Debate*, by Dominique Janicaud et al. Translated by Bernard G. Prusak, 16-103. New York: Fordham University Press, 2000.

Jenkins, Philip. *The Next Christendom: The Coming of Global Christianity*. New York: Oxford University Press, 2002.

Johnson, Phil. "You Can't Handle the Truth: The Sinful Tolerance of Postmodernism." *The Journal of Modern Ministry* 1, no. 2 (Fall 2004) 219-45.

Johnston, Robert K. *Evangelicals at an Impasse: Biblical Authority in Practice*. Atlanta, GA: John Knox, 1979.

Jones, Edward E., and Harold B. Gerard. *Foundations of Social Psychology*. New York: Wiley, 1967.

Jones, Robert P., and Daniel Cox. *America's Changing Religious Identity: Findings from the 2016 American Values Atlas*. Washington, DC: PRRI, 2017. www.prri.org/research/american-religious-landscape-christian-religiously-unaffiliated/.

Jones, Robert P., Daniel Cox, and Rachel Lienesch. *Who Sees Discrimination? Attitudes on Sexual Orientation, Gender Identity, Race, and Immigration Status: Findings from PRRI's American Values Atlas*. Washington, DC: PRRI, 2017. Accessed April 5, 2018. https://www.prri.org/research/americans-views-discrimination-immigrants-blacks-lgbt-sex-marriage-immigration-reform/.

Jones, Tony. "The McLaren Lectionary." Patheos. June 10, 2014. https://www.patheos.com/blogs/tonyjones/2014/06/10/the-mclaren-lectionary/.

———. *The New Christians: Dispatches from the Emergent Frontier*. San Francisco, CA: Jossey-Bass, 2008.

———. "Post-Evangelicalism: Last in a Series of Responses to Brian McLaren's Book, *A New Kind of Christian*." *Books and Culture* 8 (May 2002) 32.
Jones, Tony, Doug Pagitt, Spencer Burke, Brian D. McLaren, Dan Kimball, Andrew Jones, and Chris Seay. "Response to Recent Criticisms." www.theooze.com. June 2, 2005. patheos.com/blogs/tonyjones/2005/06/02/official-response-to-critics-of-emergent/.
Jonkers, Peter. "God in France: Heidegger's Legacy." In *God in France: Eight Contemporary French Thinkers on God*, edited by Peter Jonkers and Ruud Welton. Vol. 28, *Studies in Philosophical Theology*, 1-42. Leuven, Belgium: Peeters, 2005.
Jordahl, Leigh D. "The American Evangelical Tradition and Culture-religion." *Dialog* 4, no. 3 (Summer 1965) 188-93.
Jue, Jeffrey K. "What's Emerging in the Church? Postmodernity, The Emergent Church, and The Reformation." *Themelios* 31, no. 2 (January 2006) 20-39.
Kahneman, Daniel. "A Perspective on Judgment and Choice: Mapping Bounded Rationality." *American Psychologist* 58, no. 9 (September 2003) 697-720.
Kallio, Eeva. "Integrative Thinking Is the Key: An Evaluation of Current Research into the Development of Adult Thinking." *Theory and Psychology* 21, no. 6 (December 2011) 785-801.
Kandiah, Krish. *Paradoxology: Why Christianity was Never Meant to be Simple*. 2014. Reprint, Downers Grove, IL: InterVarsity, 2017.
Kantzer, Kenneth S., and Carl F. H. Henry, eds. *Evangelical Affirmations*. Grand Rapids, MI: Academie Books, 1990.
Kearney, Richard. *Anatheism: Returning to God After God*. 2010. Pbk. ed. Reprint, New York: Columbia University Press, 2011.
Kearns, Laurel. "Green Evangelicals." In *The New Evangelical Social Engagement*, edited by Brian Steensland and Philip Goff, 157-77. New York: Oxford University Press, 2014.
Kee, Howard Clark. *Christian Origins in Sociological Perspective: Methods and Resources*. Philadelphia, PA: Westminster, 1980.
Kellner, Douglas. "Postmodernism as Social Theory: Some Challenges and Problems." *Theory, Culture and Society* 5, no. 2/3 (June 1988) 239-69.
Kelly, Michael A. "Solidarity: A Foundational Educational Concern." *Religious Education* 93, no. 1 (Winter 1998) 44-64.
Kenneson, Philip D. "There's No Such Thing as Objective Truth, and It's a Good Thing, Too." In *Christian Apologetics in a Postmodern World*, edited by Timothy R. Phillips and Dennis L. Okholm, 155-70. Downers Grove: InterVarsity, 1995.
Kierkegaard, Søren. *Concluding Unscientific Postscript*. Translated by David F. Swenson and Walter Lowrie. Princeton, NJ: Princeton University Press, 1941.
———. *Concluding Unscientific Postscript to the Philosophical Crumbs*. 2009. Edited and translated by Alastair Hannay. Cambridge Texts in the History of Philosophy. New York: Cambridge University Press, 2013.
———. *Concluding Unscientific Postscript to "Philosophical Fragments."* Edited and Translated by Howard V. Hong and Edna H. Hong. 2 vols. Princeton, NJ: Princeton University Press, 1992.
———. *Edifying Discourses*. Translated by David F. Swenson and Lillian Swenson. 4 vols. Minneapolis, MN: Augsburg, 1943-1946.
———. *For Self-Examination* and *Judge for Yourself!* 1990. Edited and translated by Howard V. Hong and Edna H. Hong. Reprint, Princeton, NJ: Princeton University Press, 1991.

———. *Philosophical Fragments: Johannes Climacus*. Translated by Howard V. Hong and Edna H. Hong. Princeton, NJ: Princeton University Press, 1985.

———. *Practice in Christianity*. Edited and translated by Howard V. Hong and Edna H. Hong. Princeton, NJ: Princeton University Press, 1991.

———. *The Soul of Kierkegaard: Selections from His Journal*. 1959. Edited by Alexander Dru. Reprint, Mineola, NY: Dover, 2003.

———. *Training in Christianity and the Edifying Discourse which 'Accompanied' It*. Translated by Walter Lowrie. Princeton, NJ: Princeton University Press, 1941.

Kim, Hana. "'Sojourners' Magazine, 1971–2005: Peace and Justice, a Voice of American Progressive Evangelicals." PhD diss., Drew University, 2011.

Kim, Woo Joon. "An Evangelical Critique of the Emergent Church's Hermeneutics and Its Effects on Theology, Message, and Method of Evangelism." PhD diss., Southwestern Baptist Theological Seminary, 2012.

Kim-Spoon, Jungmeen, Gregory Longo, and Michael McCullough. "Parent-Adolescent Relationship Quality as a Moderator for the Influences of Parents' Religiousness on Adolescents' Religiousness and Adjustment." *Journal of Youth and Adolescence* 41, no. 12 (December 2012) 1576–87.

Kimball, Dan. *The Emerging Church: Vintage Christianity for New Generations*. Grand Rapids, MI: Zondervan, 2003.

King, Amy Laine. "Evangelical Confessions: An Ideological Struggle Over Evangelical Political Identity." PhD diss., University of North Carolina at Chapel Hill, 2009.

King, James. "Emerging Issues for the Emerging Church." *The Journal of Ministry and Theology* 9, no. 2 (Fall 2005) 24–62.

King, Pamela Ebstyne, and Robert W. Roeser. "Religion and Spirituality in Adolescent Development." In *Handbook of Adolescent Psychology*. 3rd ed, edited by Richard M. Lerner and Laurence Steinberg. Vol. 1, *Individual Bases of Adolescent Development*, 435–78. Hoboken, NJ: Wiley, 2009.

Kinnaman, David, and Gabe Lyons. *Unchristian: What a New Generation Really Thinks About Christianity . . . And Why It Matters*. Grand Rapids, MI: Baker, 2007.

Koestler, Arthur. *Janus: A Summing Up*. New York: Random House, 1978.

Kohut, Andrew, Scott Keeter, Carroll Doherty, and Michael Dimock. *Some Social Conservative Disillusionment: More Americans Question Religion's Role in Politics* (Results from the 2008 Annual Religion and Public Life Survey). Washington, DC: Pew Research Center, August 21, 2008. Accessed April 5, 2018. http://assets.pewresearch.org/wp-content/uploads/sites/5/legacy-pdf/445.pdf.

Krattenmaker, Tom. *The Evangelicals You Don't Know: Introducing the Next Generation of Christians*. Lanham, MD: Rowman & Littlefield, 2013.

Kristof, Nicholas. "What Religion Would Jesus Belong To?" *New York Times*, September 3, 2016. Accessed April 3, 2020. www.nytimes.com/2016/09/04/opinion/sunday/what-religion-would-jesus-belong-to.html/.

Kruse, Kevin M. *One Nation under God: How Corporate America Invented Christian America*. 2015. Pbk. ed. Reprint, New York: Basic Books, 2016.

Kugel, James L. *Traditions of the Bible: A Guide to the Bible as It Was at the Start of the Common Era*. Rev. ed. Cambridge, MA: Harvard University Press, 1998.

Kuhn, Deanna. "Reasoning." In *The Oxford Handbook of Developmental Psychology*, edited by Philip David Zelazo. Vol. 1, *Body and Mind*. Oxford Library of Psychology, 744–64. New York: Oxford University Press, 2013.

Kuhn, Thomas S. *The Structure of Scientific Revolutions*. 1962. 4th ed. Chicago, IL: The University of Chicago Press, 2012.

Küng, Hans. *On Being a Christian*. Translated by Edward Quinn. Garden City, NY: Doubleday, 1976.

Kyle, Richard G. *Evangelicalism: An Americanized Christianity*. New Brunswick, NJ: Transaction, 2006.

Laats, Alar. "Luther's Idea of *Deus Absconditus* and the Apophatic Theology." *Trames: A Journal of the Humanities and Social Sciences* 3, no. 3 (1999) 170-84.

Labberton, Mark. "Introduction: Still Evangelical?" In *Still Evangelical? Insiders Reconsider Political, Social, and Theological Meaning*, edited by Mark Labberton, 1-17. Downers Grove, IL: InterVarsity, 2018.

Lancaster, Roger N. *Sex Panic and the Punitive State*. Berkeley, CA: University of California Press, 2011.

Larson, Marion H., and Sara L. H. Shady. "Love My (Religious) Neighbor: A Pietist Approach to Christian Responsibility in a Pluralistic World." In *The Pietist Vision of Christian Higher Education: Forming Whole and Holy Persons*, edited by Christopher Gehrz, 134-48. Downers Grove, IL: InterVarsity, 2014.

Law, David R. *Kierkegaard's Kenotic Christology*. New York: Oxford University Press, 2013.

Lazarsfeld, Paul F., and Robert K. Merton. "Friendship as a Social Process: A Substantive and Methodological Analysis." In *Freedom and Control in Modern Society*, edited by Morroe Berger, Theodore Abel, and Charles Page, 18-66. New York: Van Nostrand, 1954.

Lee, Bandy, ed. *The Dangerous Case of Donald Trump: 37 Psychiatrists and Mental Health Experts Assess a President*. 2nd ed. New York: Thomas Dunne, 2019.

Lee, Shayne, and Phillip Luke Sinitiere. *Holy Mavericks: Evangelical Innovators and the Spiritual Marketplace*. New York: New York University Press, 2009.

Lemieux, André "Post-Formal Thought in Gerontagogy or Beyond Piaget." *Journal of Behavioral and Brain Science* 2, no. 3 (August 2012) 399-406.

Letham, Robert. *The Holy Trinity: In Scripture, History, Theology, and Worship*. Phillipsburg, NJ: P&R, 2004.

Levine, Michael P. "Contemporary Christian Analytic Philosophy of Religion: Biblical Fundamentalism, Terrible Solutions to a Horrible Problem, and Hearing God." *International Journal for Philosophy of Religion* 48, no. 2 (October 2000) 89-119.

Lewis, Andrew R. *The Rights Turn in Conservative Christian Politics: How Abortion Transformed the Culture Wars*. 2017. Pbk. ed. Reprint, New York: Cambridge University Press, 2018.

Lewis, Gordon R. "Faith and History in St. Augustine." *Trinity Journal* 3, no. 1 (Spring 1982) 39-50.

———. *Testing Christianity's Truth Claims: Approaches to Christian Apologetics*. 1976. Pbk. ed. Reprint, Chicago, IL: Moody, 1980.

Lienesch, Michael. *Redeeming America: Piety and Politics in the New Christian Right*. Chapel Hill, NC: The University of North Carolina Press, 1993.

Lindbeck, George A. *The Nature of Doctrine: Religion and Theology in a Postliberal Age*. Louisville, KY: John Knox, 1984.

Lindsay, D. Michael. *Faith in the Halls of Power: How Evangelicals Joined the American Elite*. New York: Oxford University Press, 2007.

Lipka, Michael, and Claire Gecewicz. *More Americans Now Say They're Spiritual but Not Religious*. Washington: Pew Research Center, September 6, 2017. pewresearch.org/fact-tank/2017/09/06/more-americans-now-say-theyre-spiritual-but-not-religious/.

Lipset, Seymour Martin. *American Exceptionalism: A Double-Edged Sword*. 1996. Reprint, New York: Norton, 1997.

Lipton, Peter. *Inference to the Best Explanation*. 2nd ed. New York: Routledge, 2004.

Livingston, Paisley. *Art and Intention: A Philosophical Study*. 2005. Pbk. ed. Reprint, New York: Oxford University Press, 2007.

Lohse, Bernhard. "Reason and Revelation in Luther." *Scottish Journal of Theology* 13, no. 4 (December 1960) 337–65.

Longman, Temper III. "What I Mean by Historical-Grammatical Exegesis: Why I Am Not a Literalist." *Grace Theological Journal* 11, no. 2 (Fall 1990) 137–55.

Lyon, William S. "The Necessity to Rethink Magic." *Journal for the Study of Religion, Nature and Culture* 10, no. 2 (2016) 208–27.

Lyotard, Jean-François. *The Postmodern Condition: A Report on Knowledge*. 1979. Translated by Geoff Bennington and Brian Massumi. Reprint, Minneapolis, MN: University of Minnesota Press, 1984.

———. "Rules and Paradoxes and Svelte Appendix." *Cultural Critique* 5, no. 2 (Winter 1986–1987) 209–19.

Lyra, Synesio Jr. "Rise and Development of the Jesus Movement." *Calvin Theological Journal* 8, no. 1 (April 1973) 40–61.

Luntz, Frank I. *What Americans Really Want. . .Really: The Truth About Our Hopes, Dreams, and Fears*. New York: Hyperion, 2009.

MacArthur, John F. Jr. "Perspicuity of Scripture: The Emergent Approach." *Master's Seminary Journal* 17, no. 2 (Fall 2006) 141–58.

———. *The Truth War: Fighting for Certainty in an Age of Deception*. Nashville, TN: Thomas Nelson, 2007.

MacCulloch, Diarmaid. *Christianity: The First Three Thousand Years*. 2009. Reprint, New York: Viking, 2010.

Mackenzie, Ed. "Mission and the Inclusive Kingdom of Jesus: Assessing the Missiological Approach of Brian McLaren." *Missiology: An International Review* 43, no. 3 (2015) 258–69.

Madsen, Deborah L. *American Exceptionalism*. Jackson, MS: University Press of Mississippi, 1998.

Maier, Johann. *Zwischen den Testamenten: Geschichte und Religion in der Zeit des zweiten Tempels*. Die Neue Echter Bibel Ergänzungsband zum Alten testament 3. Würzburg, Germany: Verlag, 1990.

Mannucci, Valerio. "Il teo-finalismo nel quarto vangelo." *Vivens Homo* 1 (1990) 15–30.

Marsden, George M. *Fundamentalism and American Culture*. 2nd ed. New York: Oxford University Press, 2006.

———. "Fundamentalism and American Evangelicalism." In *The Variety of American Evangelicalism*. 1991. Reprint, 22–35. Knoxville, TN: The University of Tennessee Press, 2001.

Marti, Gerardo, and Gladys Ganiel. *The Deconstructed Church: Understanding Emerging Christianity*. New York: Oxford University Press, 2014.

Markofski, Wes. *New Monasticism and the Transformation of American Evangelicalism*. New York: Oxford University Press, 2015.

Markos, Louis. *Apologetics for the Twenty-First Century*. Wheaton, IL: Crossway, 2010.

Martin, William. *With God on Our Side: The Rise of the Religious Right in America*. Rev. ed. New York: Broadway, 2005.

Marty, Martin E. "Reinhold Niebuhr: Public Theology and the American Experience." *The Journal of Religion* 54, no. 4 (October 1974) 332-59.

Mattingly, Terry. "Time to Pin New Label on Brian McLaren?" Patheos. September 26, 2012. www.patheos.com/blogs/getreligion/2012/09/time-to-pin-new-label-on-brian-mclaren/.

Mayhue, Richard L. "The Emerging Church: Generous Orthodoxy or General Obfuscation?" *Master's Seminary Journal* 17, no. 2 (Fall 2006) 191-205.

McAuliffe, William H. B. "How Did Abduction Get Confused with Inference to the Best Explanation?" *Transactions of the Charles S. Peirce Society: A Quarterly Journal in American Philosophy* 51, no. 3 (Summer 2015) 300-19.

McBrien, Richard P. *Catholicism*. Rev. ed. San Francisco, CA: HarperSanFrancisco, 1994.

McCasland, Selby Vernon. "Matthew Twists the Scriptures." *Journal of Biblical Literature* 80, no. 2 (June 1961) 143-48.

McCune, Rolland D. "The Self-Identity of Fundamentalism." *Detroit Baptist Seminary Journal* 1, no. 1 (Spring 1996) 9-34.

McKnight, Scot. "Five Streams of the Emerging Church: Key Elements of the Most Controversial and Misunderstood Movement in the Church Today." *Christianity Today*, February 2007.

———. "The Ironic Faith of Emergents." *Christianity Today*, September 2008.

———. "McLaren Emerging." *Christianity Today*, September 2008.

———. "Rebuilding the Faith from Scratch." *Christianity Today*, March 2010.

McLaren, Brian D. "5 Books for Ministry." *The Christian Century*, May 4, 2010.

———. "10 Questions for Brian McLaren." Interview by Terry L. Heaton. *Terry Heaton's Pomo Blog*, May 24, 2005. http://www.thepomoblog.com/papers/10Q7.htm.

———. "12 Ounce Interview W/ Brian McLaren: A Christian Response to People of Other Faiths" (video). Accessed October 8, 2018. www.youtube.com/watch?v=hbAwGoMJ-II&feature=youtu.be.

———. Afterword to *A Faith Embracing All Creatures*, by Tripp York and Andy Alexis-Baker, eds., 181-83. Eugene, OR: Cascade, 2012.

———. "America the Exceptional." *Sojourners Magazine*, January 2012.

———. "America's Most Influential Evangelicals." Interview by Larry King. *CNN Larry King Live*, February 1, 2005. http://transcripts.cnn.com/TRANSCRIPTS/0502/01/lkl.01.html.

———. "Ask Brian McLaren. . ." Interview by Rachel Held Evans. *Rachel Held Evans Blog*, June 6, 2014. https://rachelheldevans.com/blog/ask-brian-mclaren-response.

———. "Author Brian McLaren Wants Churches to Move Beyond Charity." Interview by Rachel Zoll. *Canadian Press*, May 07, 2008.

———. "Becoming Convergent." *Emergent-Us* (message board), August 12, 2005. https://emergent-us.typepad.com/emergentus/files/becoming_emergent.pdf.

———. "Best Outreach Opportunity *Ever*?" *Leadership* 25, no. 2 (Spring 2004) 96.

———. "Between Mixed Martial Arts and the 'L' Word: An Interview with Brian McLaren." Interview by Tom Ryan. *The Other Journal*, September 11, 2010. theotherjournal.com/2010/09/11/between-mixed-martial-arts-and-the-l-word-an-interview-with-brian-mclaren/.

———. "Beyond Business-as-Usual Christianity." Interview by Sherry Huang. *Beliefnet*, May 2005. www.beliefnet.com/faiths/christianity/2005/05/beyond-business-as-usual-christianity.aspx?.

———. "Beyond Fire and Brimstone." *Sojourners Magazine*, February 2014.

———. "Bless This House?" *Leadership* 25, no. 3 (Summer 2004) 96.

———. "Brian McLaren Extended Interview." Interview. *Religion and Ethics Newsweekly*, July 15, 2005. https://www.pbs.org/wnet/religionandethics/2005/07/15/july-15-2005-brian-mclaren-extended-interview/11774/.

———. "Brian McLaren: It's Time to Re-Write Pro-War Hymns." Interview by Jeff Brumley. *Baptist News Global*, February 18, 2016. https://baptistnews.com/article/brian-mclaren-time-to-re-write-pro-war-hymns/#.XFB9E89KjzK.

———. "Brian McLaren on How to Build the NSP." *Tikkun Magazine*, September/October 2010.

———. "Brian McLaren on Outreach." Interview by Lynne Marian. *Outreach*, July/August 2005.

———. "Brian McLaren on Walter Brueggemann." *Walter Brueggemann* (blog), June 3, 2013. https://www.walterbrueggemann.com/2013/06/03/brian-mclaren-on-walter-brueggemann/.

———. "Brian McLaren Rebuilds Spirituality." Interview by Josh Lujan Loveless. *Relevant Magazine*, May 16, 2011. https://relevantmagazine.com/god/church/features/25621-brian-mclaren-rebuilds-spirituality.

———. "Brian McLaren Reflects on 25 Years of Emergence." Interview by Jonathan Merritt. *Religion News Service*, August 7, 2014. https://religionnews.com/2014/08/07/brian-mclaren-reflects-25-years-emergence/.

———. "Brian McLaren Reflects on 'Seizing An Alternative' Conference" (YouTube video). June 7, 2015. Accessed September 24, 2018. https://www.youtube.com/watch?v=-0g6hOPu_-E&feature=youtu.be.

———. "Brian McLaren Responds to Everything Must Change Concerns." Interview by Andrew Jones. *Tall Skinny Kiwi: Religious Conversations*, March 26, 2008. https://tallskinnykiwi.typepad.com/tallskinnykiwi/2008/03/brian-mclaren-r.html.

———. "Brian McLaren: The Equation of Change." Interview by Krista Tippett. *On Being*, March 23, 2014. https://onbeing.org/programs/brian-mclaren-the-equation-of-change/.

———. "Brian McLaren's Post." *Dwight Friesen Blog*, March 9, 2005. http://www.authorviews.com/authors/mclaren/public/screenshots/dwightfriesen2.pdf.

———. "Brian's Annotation to 'The Emergent Mystique'—CT Article." *Brian McLaren Blog*, January 20, 2005. brianmclaren.net/brians-annotation-to-the-emergent-mystique-ct-article/.

———. "A Bridge Far Enough?" *Sojourners Magazine*, September/October 2005.

———. "A Brief History of the 21st Century." *Sojourners Magazine*, August 2006.

———. "Can We Talk?" *Sojourners Magazine*, March 2010.

———. "Changing Faith, Staying Faithful." Interview by Stephen Tomkins. *Reform Magazine*, December 2014/January 2015.

———. "Chosen for What?" *Tikkun Magazine*, May/June 2008.

———. "Christian Conference Says 'Everything Must Change.'" Interview by Michelle Bearden. *Tampa Tribune*, February 28, 2008.

———. "Church Emerging: Or Why I Still Use the Word *Postmodern* but with Mixed Feelings." In *An Emergent Manifesto of Hope*, edited by Doug Pagitt and Tony Jones, 141-51. Grand Rapids, MI: Baker, 2007.

———. "The Church in America Today." In *A New Evangelical Manifesto: A Kingdom Vision for the Common Good*, edited by David P. Gushee, 2-9. Atlanta, GA: Chalice, 2012.

———. "Church Leaders Wonder: Will Preaching Survive a Post Modern World?." Baylor University Hearn Symposium, Waco, TX, October 7, 2004. https://www.baylor.edu/mediacommunications/news.php?action=story&story=21277.

———. *The Church on the Other Side: Doing Ministry in the Postmodern Matrix*. Rev. ed. Grand Rapids, MI: Zondervan, 2000.

———. *The Church on the Other Side: Exploring the Radical Future of the Local Congregation*. Rev. ed. Grand Rapids, MI: Zondervan, 2006.

———. "Conditions for the Great Religion Singularity." *Socio-Historical Examination of Religion and Ministry* 1, no. 1 (2019) 40-49. doi.org/10.33929/sherm.2019.vol1.no1.05.

———. "A Conversation with Brian McLaren." Interview. *Kolbe Times*, June 7, 2018. http://www.kolbetimes.com/brian-mclaren/.

———. "Conversations." Interview. *Missiology: An International Review*, July 2005.

———. "The Cross as Prophetic Action." In *Proclaiming the Scandal of the Cross: Contemporary Images of the Atonement*, edited by Mark D. Baker, 110-21. Grand Rapids, MI: Baker, 2006.

———. "Dallas Morning News—Interview with Brian McLaren." Interview by Lesa Engelthaler. *reposted on Brian McLaren Blog*, September 17, 2005. https://brianmclaren.net/dallas-morning-news-interview-with-brian-mclaren/.

———. "Darkwood Brew Interview of Brian McLaren" (YouTube video). May 15, 2011. Accessed January 1, 2019. https://youtu.be/RMYQ7xyxe6c.

———. "Dear White Evangelical Christians . . .." *Brian McLaren Blog*, May 19, 2018. https://brianmclaren.net/dear-white-evangelical-christians/.

———. "Dorothy on Leadership." *Rev. Magazine* (reposted on Brian McLaren Blog), November/December 2000. https://brianmclaren.net/dorothy-on-leadership/.

———. "The Emerging Church, Part Two." Interview. *Religion and Ethics Newsweekly*, July 15, 2005. https://www.pbs.org/wnet/religionandethics/2005/07/15/july-15-2005-the-emerging-church-part-two/11767/.

———. "Emerging Values: The Next Generation Is Redefining Spiritual Formation, Community, and Mission." *Leadership* 24, no. 3 (Summer 2003) 34-39.

———. "Entering without Knocking." In *My Neighbor's Faith: Stories of Interreligious Encounter, Growth, and Transformation*. 2012, edited by Jennifer Howe Peace, Or N. Rose, and Gregory Mobley. Reprint, 3-6. Maryknoll, NY: Orbis, 2014.

———. *Everything Must Change: Jesus, Global Crises, and a Revolution of Hope*. Nashville, TN: Thomas Nelson, 2007.

———. "Everything Old Is New Again." *Sojourners Magazine*, July 2009.

———. "Faith Beyond All Answers: A Response to John Piper's Theodicy." *The Other Journal* (March 23, 2011). https://theotherjournal.com/2011/03/23/faith-beyond-all-answers-a-response-to-john-pipers-theodicy/.

———. "Faithfully Dangerous Christians in Postmodern Times." *Books and Culture* 8, no. 3 (May/June 2002) 33. www.booksandculture.com/articles/2002/mayjun/17.33.html.

———. *Finding Faith: A Search for What Is Real*. Grand Rapids, MI: Zondervan, 2007.

———. *Finding Faith: A Search for What Makes Sense*. Grand Rapids, MI: Zondervan, 2007.

———. *Finding Our Way Again: The Return of the Ancient Practices*. The Ancient Practices Series. Nashville, TN: Thomas Nelson, 2008.

———. "Finding the Seventh Story." In *2010Boston: The Changing Contours of World Mission and Christianity*, edited by Todd M. Johnson et al, 124-31. Eugene, OR: Pickwick, 2012.

———. "Fire Without Brimstone." Interview by Abigail Tucker. *Baltimore Sun*, April 27, 2005. https://www.baltimoresun.com/news/bs-xpm-2005-04-27-0504270049-story.html.

———. "Florida, Recognize My Gay Son's Vows." *Tampa Bay Times*, December 19, 2014.

———. Foreword to *Anabaptist Preaching: A Conversation Between Pulpit, Pew and Bible*, edited by David B. Greiser and Michael A. King, 7-9. Telford, PA: Cascadia, 2003.

———. Foreword to *Brief Christian Histories: Getting a Sense of Our Long Story*, by James W. White, xiii-xv. Eugene, OR: Wipf and Stock, 2014.

———. Foreword to *Changing Our Mind*, by David P. Gushee, xviii-xx. Canton, MI: Read the Spirit, 2017.

———. Foreword to *Christian America and the Kingdom of God*, by Richard T. Hughes, xi-xiii. Chicago, IL: University of Illinois Press, 2009.

———. Foreword to *Compassion or Apocalypse? A Comprehensible Guide to the Thought of René Girard*, by James Warren, 1-3. Alresford, UK: Christian Alternative, 2013.

———. Foreword to *Disarming Scripture*, by Derek Flood, xvii-xxi. San Francisco, CA: Metanoia, 2014.

———. Foreword to *An Emergent Theology for Emerging Churches*, by Ray S. Anderson, 3-6. Downers Grove, IL: InterVarsity, 2006.

———. Foreword to *The Emerging Church: Vintage Christianity for New Generations*, by Dan Kimball, 9-10. Grand Rapids, MI: Zondervan, 2003.

———. Foreword to *A Generous Community: Being the Church in a New Missionary Age*, by C. Andrew Doyle, vii-ix. New York: Morehouse, 2015.

———. Foreword to *Generous Orthodoxies: Essays on the History and Future of Ecumenical Theology*, edited by Paul Silas Peterson, xiii-xvi. Eugene, OR: Pickwick, 2020.

———. Foreword to *The Gospel in Christian Traditions*, by Ted A. Campbell, vii-ix. New York: Oxford University Press, 2009.

———. Foreword to *Healing the Gospel: A Radical Vision for Grace, Justice, and the Cross*, by Derek Flood, ix-xi. Eugene, OR: Cascade, 2012.

———. Foreword to *A Heretic's Guide to Eternity*, by Spencer Burke and Barry Taylor, vii-x. San Francisco, CA: Jossey-Bass, 2006.

———. Foreword to *The Hidden Power of Electronic Culture: How Media Shapes Faith, the Gospel, and Church*, by Shane A. Hipps, 9-11. Grand Rapids, MI: Zondervan, 2005.

———. Foreword to *The Holy No: Worship as a Subversive Act*, by Adam Hearlson, ix-x. Grand Rapids, MI: Eerdmans, 2018.

———. Foreword to *How (Not) to Speak of God*, by Peter Rollins, ix-xii. Brewster, MA: Paraclete, 2006.

———. Foreword to *Intelligent Church*, by Steve Chalke and Anthony Watkis, 9-11. Grand Rapids, MI: Zondervan, 2006.

———. Foreword to *The Jesus Driven Life: Reconnecting Humanity with Jesus*, by Michael Hardin, xiii-xiv. Lancaster, PA: JDL, 2013.

———. Foreword to *Life at the End of Us Versus Them: Cross Culture Stories*, by Marcus Peter Rempel, xxi-xxii. Victoria, BC: Friesen, 2017.

———. Foreword to *Love Is an Orientation: Elevating the Conversation with the Gay Community*, by Andrew Marin, 9-14. Downers Grove, IL: InterVarsity, 2009.

———. Foreword to *Manifold Witness: The Plurality of Truth*, by John R. Franke, xi-xiii. Nashville, TN: Abingdon, 2009.

———. Foreword to *The Missionary Letters of Vincent Donovan: 1957-1973*, by John P. Bowen, ed., ix-xiii. Eugene, OR: Pickwick, 2011.

———. Foreword to *A New Kind of Youth Ministry*, by Chris Folmsbee, 6-8. Grand Rapids, MI: Youth Specialties, 2007.

———. Foreword to *Paradoxy: Creating Christian Community Beyond Us and Them*, by Kenneth W. Howard, ix-xi. Brewster, MA: Paraclete, 2010.

———. Foreword to *Picturing the Gospel: Tapping the Power of the Bible's Imagery*, by Neil Livingstone, 7-8. Downers Grove, IL: InterVarsity, 2007.

———. Foreword to *Poacher's Pilgrimage: An Island Journey*, by Alastair McIntosh, xvii-xxii. Eugene, OR: Cascade, 2005.

———. Foreword to *Reimagining Evangelism: Inviting Friends on a Spiritual Journey*, by Rick Richardson, 7-9. Downers Grove, IL: InterVarsity, 2006.

———. Foreword to *Renewing the Center: Evangelical Theology in a Post-Theological Era*, by Stanley J. Grenz, 7-14. Grand Rapids, MI: Baker, 2006.

———. Foreword to *Secrets in the Dark: A Life in Sermons*, by Frederick Buechner, ix-xii. San Francisco, CA: HarperSanFrancisco, 2006.

———. Foreword to *Solus Jesus: A Theology of Resistance*, by Emily Swan and Ken Wilson, xv-xvii. Canton, MI: Read the Spirit, 2018.

———. Foreword to *The Way of Jesus: A Journey of Freedom for Pilgrims and Wanderers*, by Jonathan S. Campbell and Jennifer Campbell, xi-xiv. San Francisco, CA: Jossey-Bass, 2005.

———. Foreword to *What Would Jesus Deconstruct? The Good News of Postmodernity for the Church*, by John D. Caputo, 9-12. Grand Rapids, MI: Baker, 2007.

———. "Found in Translation." *Sojourners Magazine*, March 2006.

———. "From Organized Religion to Organizing Religion: Brian D. McLaren Wants Christians to Be Better." Interview by Peter Laarman. *Religion Dispatches*, September 11, 2016. http://religiondispatches.org/from-organized-religion-to-organizing-religion-brian-d-mclaren-wants-christians-to-be-better/.

———. "A Generous, Not Suspicious, Orthodoxy." Interview. *Homiletics Online*, 2011. http://www.homileticsonline.com/subscriber/interviews/mclaren.asp.

———. *A Generous Orthodoxy*. Grand Rapids, MI: Youth Specialties, 2004.

———. *The Girl with the Dove Tattoo*. Brentwood, TN: Creative Trust Digital, 2012. Kindle.

———. "Go Deeper." *Tikkun Magazine*, January/February 2009. http://www.tikkun.org/article.php/jan09_mclaren.

———. *The Great Spiritual Migration: How the World's Largest Religion Is Seeking a Better Way to Be Christian*. New York: Convergent, 2016.

———. "Healing the Political Psyche." Review of *The Left Hand of God: Taking Back Our Country from the Religious Right*, by Michael Lerner. *The Christian Century*, March 21, 2006.

———. "Honey, I Woke Up in a Different Universe! Confessions of a Postmodern Pastor." *Mars Hill Review* 15 (Fall 1999) 35-46.

———. "How I Got Here." *Progressing Spirit* (blog), April 11, 2019. https://progressingspirit.com/2019/04/11/how-i-got-here/.

———. "How to Evangelize Today: Reaching People Who Think Negatively About Christianity." Interview. *Christianity Today*, August 1, 2001. https://www.christianitytoday.com/pastors/2001/august-online-only/cln10801.html.

———. "Hurtful Stereotypes." *Sojourners Magazine*, April 2014.

———. "Informed, but Not Transformed: Too Many 'Educated' Christians Have Gotten Lots of Information but Are the Least Christ-like." *Leadership Journal* (August 15, 2005). http://www.besidestillwaters.net/informed_but_not_transformed.html.

———. "'Instead of Ruling'—Prayers." In *Buffalo Shout, Salmon Cry: Conversations on Creation, Land Justice, and Life Together*, edited by Steve Heinrichs, 225-28. Harrisonburg, VA: Herald, 2013.

———. "Interview: Brian McLaren on Anglicans, Mission and Reconciliation." Interview by Maria Mackay. *Christian Post*, July 28, 2008. christianpost.com/news/interview-brian-mclaren-on-anglicans-mission-and-reconciliation.html.

———. "An Interview on Christian Publishing and Postmodernity." Interview by Sara Long. reposted on *Brian McLaren Blog*, December 10, 2003. https://brianmclaren.net/an-interview-on-christian-publishing-and-postmodernity/.

———. "An Interview with Brian McLaren: Conversation Partners." *Modern Reformation* 14, no. 4 (July/August 2005) 49-52.

———. "An Interview with Brian McLaren." Interview by Joshua Graves. *Wineskins*, July-October 2008. http://archives.wineskins.org/article/an-interview-with-brian-mclaren-jul-oct-2008/.

———. "An Interview with Brian McLaren." Interview by Rachel Held Evans. *Progressive Christianity*, n.d. https://progressivechristianity.org/resources/an-interview-with-brian-mclaren/.

———. "Interview with Brian McLaren." Interview by Stephen Roach Knight. *Charlotte Observer*, January 26, 2008.

———. "An Interview with Brian McLaren." Interview by Virgil Vaduva. *Planet Preterist*, January 30, 2006. http://planetpreterist.com/news-2774.html.

———. "An Interview with Brian McLaren on Faith, Doubt, and Atheism." Interview by Kile Jones. *Progressive Christian*, May 1, 2014. https://www.patheos.com/blogs/emergentvillage/2014/05/an-interview-with-brian-mcclaren-on-faith-doubt-and-atheism/.

———. Introduction to *Not Religion But Love: Practicing a Radical Spirituality of Compassion*, by Dave Andrews, iii-vi. 1999. Reprint, Eugene, OR: Wipf and Stock, 2012.

———. "Is God Violent?" *Sojourners Magazine*, January 2011.

———. "Is It Christian or Illegal to Aid Migrants? A Hung Tucson Jury, a Fork in the Road of Faith." *USA Today*, June 16, 2019. https://www.usatoday.com/story/opinion/2019/06/16/scott-warren-tucson-trial-deepens-religious-freedom-divides-column/1435497001/.

———. *Is Jesus the Only Way? A Reading of John 14:6*. N.p.: 2006. PDF.

———. *The Last Word and the Word After That: A Tale of Faith, Doubt, and a New Kind of Christianity*. Book 3. San Francisco, CA: Jossey-Bass, 2005.

———. "'Lord, Have Mercy.'" *Sojourners Magazine*, January 2007.

———. "Making Eschatology Personal." *Presence*, May 8, 2015. http://www.presence.tv/making-eschatology-personal-brian-mclaren/.

———. "Making Waves." Interview by Gerald Gauthier. *New Internationalist*, June 2008.

———. "A Memo on the Arc of the Universe." *Tikkun Magazine*, Winter 2011.

———. "The Method, the Message, and the Ongoing Story." In *The Church in Emerging Culture: Five Perspectives*, edited by Leonard Sweet, 191-230. Grand Rapids, MI: emergentYS, 2003.

———. "More Important Than Being Right?" *Leadership* 27, no. 1 (Winter 2006) 128.

———. *More Ready Than You Realize: Evangelism as Dance in the Postmodern Matrix*. Grand Rapids, MI: Zondervan, 2002.

———. *Naked Spirituality: A Life with God in 12 Simple Words*. New York: HarperOne, 2011.

———. "A New Kind of Bible Reading." *Unpublished Book Chapter*, 2011. http://gracespace.org.uk/wp-content/uploads/2011/08/Brian-McLaren-A-New-Kind-of-Bible-Reading.pdf.

———. *A New Kind of Christian: A Tale of Two Friends on a Spiritual Journey*. Pbk. ed. Book 1. San Francisco, CA: Jossey-Bass, 2001.

———. *A New Kind of Christianity: Ten Questions That Are Transforming the Faith*. Pbk. ed. New York: HarperCollins, 2011.

———. "A New Kind of Old Christian." *Leadership* 26, no. 1 (Winter 2005) 112.

———. "A New Quest for Christianity: Author Says It's Time for Sequel to Luther's 95 Theses." Interview by David Yonke. *The Blade*, February 27, 2010.

———. "An Open Letter to Chuck Colson from Brian McLaren." Youth Specialties. October 5, 2009. youthspecialties.com/blog/an-open-letter-to-chuck-colson-from-brian-mclaren/.

———. "An Open Letter to Jerry Falwell Jr, Students and Faculty of Liberty University." *HuffPost*. December 7, 2015. https://www.huffingtonpost.com/brian-d-mclaren/an-open-letter-to-jerry-falwell-jr_b_8735674.html.

———. "Our Allergic Reactions." *Christianity Today*, March 1, 2007. https://www.christianitytoday.com/pastors/2007/spring/11.121.html.

———. "Out of the Echo Chamber." *Leadership* 28, no. 1 (Winter 2007) 110.

———. "Overcoming Resistance." *Sojourners Magazine*, May 2010.

———. "The Politics of Joy." *Sojourners: God's Politics* (blog), December 15, 2006. https://sojo.net/articles/brian-mclaren-politics-joy.

———. "A Postmodern View of Scripture." Interview by Gary W. Moon. *Conversations*, Spring 2005.

———. "Practicing and Loving Diversity: An Interview with Brian McLaren." Interview by Kevin D. Hendricks. *PRISM Magazine*, January/February 2005.

———. "Practicing Faith, or Faithing Our Practices?" *Leadership* 27, no. 3 (Summer 2006) 118.

———. "Preaching to Postmoderns." In *Preaching with Power: Dynamic Insights from Twenty Top Communicators*, edited by Michael Duduit, 125. Grand Rapids, MI: Baker, 2006.

———. Preface to *Blue Ocean Faith*, by Dave Schmelzer, xiii-xv. Canton, MI: Front Edge, 2017.

———. "Presence Means Everything." In *Cancer and Theology*, edited by Jake Bouma and Erik Ullestad, 19-22. Des Moines, IA: Elbow, 2013.

———. "A Prison of Cruelty: End Injustice in Criminal Justice System." Justice Not Jails. September 2, 2013. Accessed January 20, 2019. justicenotjails.org/prison-of-cruelty/.

———. "The Problem Isn't the Bible." *Patheos*, June 18, 2014. https://www.patheos.com/topics/2014-religious-trends/progressive-christian/the-problem-isnt-the-bible-brian-mclaren-06182014.

———. "Public Theology." In *Theologians and Philosophers Using Social Media: Advice, Tips, and Testimonials*, edited by Thomas Jay Oord, 289-91. San Diego, CA: SacraSage, 2017.

———. "*PW* Talks with Brian McLaren: Jesus's Mysterious Kingdom." Interview by Lori Smith. *Publishers Weekly*, January 30, 2006.

———. "Q and R: Belief VERSUS Practice, or Belief AND Practice?." *Brian McLaren Blog*, September 7, 2018. brianmclaren.net/q-r-belief-versus-practice-or-belief-and-practice/.

———. "Q and R: Discernment of Spirits?." *Brian McLaren Blog*, May 30, 2018. https://brianmclaren.net/q-r-discernment-of-spirits/.

———. "Q and R: Hints of Kierkegaard. What about Chalcedon?." *Brian McLaren Blog*, February 17, 2015. brianmclaren.net/q-r-hints-of-kierkegaard-what-about-chalcedon/.

———. "Q and R: Should I go with the Republican moral agenda?." *Brian McLaren Blog*, October 1, 2018. brianmclaren.net/q-r-should-i-go-with-the-republican-moral-agenda/.

———. "Q and R: Sorry, I'm not going to answer this, and here's why . . ." *Brian McLaren Blog*, June 22, 2018. brianmclaren.net/q-r-sorry-im-not-going-to-answer-this-and-heres-why/.

———. "Q and R: What about the cross? (A Good Friday meditation)." *Brian McLaren Blog*, March 30, 2018. brianmclaren.net/q-r-what-about-the-cross-a-good-friday-meditation/.

———. "Q and R: When Do I Leave My Evangelical Church?." *Brian McLaren Blog*, June 1, 2018. https://brianmclaren.net/q-r-when-do-i-leave-my-evangelical-church/.

———. "A Radical Rethinking of Our Evangelistic Strategy." *Fuller Youth Institute* (post), August 22, 2005. https://fulleryouthinstitute.org/articles/a-radical-rethinking-of-our-evangelistic-strategy.

———. "Red State, Purple Church." *The Christian Century*, June 21, 2017.

———. "Reflection on Postcolonial Friendship." In *Evangelical Postcolonial Conversations: Global Awakenings in Theology and Praxis*, edited by Kay Higuera Smith, Jayachitra Lalitha, and L. Daniel Hawk, 13-15. Downers Grove, IL: InterVarsity, 2014.

———. *Reinventing Your Church*. Softcover ed. Grand Rapids, MI: Zondervan, 1998.

———. "Religious Right or Wrong?" Interview. *Christian Network Journal*, Winter 2004.

———. "The Report Back to Mars." *Leadership* 25, no. 4 (Fall 2004) 112.

———. "Rethinking the Doctrines of the Trinity and the Holy Spirit." *Tikkun Magazine*, Summer 2012.

———. Review of *After the Baby Boomers: How Twenty- and Thirty-Somethings Are Shaping the Future of American Religion*, by Robert Wuthnow. *The Christian Century*, October 16, 2007.

———. Review of *Who Speaks for Islam? What a Billion Muslims Really Think*, by John L. Esposito and Dalia Mogahed. *The Christian Century*, October 7, 2008.

———. "Rewriting Brethren Distinctives." *The Journal of the Christian Brethren Research Fellowship* 125 (August 1991) 39-42.

———. "Risky Business." *Sojourners Magazine*, September 2004.

———. "Ruining Your Ministry for Good: Seeing the 'Missed' Beyond Church Walls." In *Seeing Beyond Church Walls: Action Plans for Touching Your Community*, edited by Steve Sjogren, 49-63. Loveland, CO: Group Publishing, 2002.

———. "The Secret Message of Jesus." *Tikkun Magazine*, January/February 2006.

———. *The Secret Message of Jesus: Uncovering the Truth that Could Change Everything*. Nashville, TN: Thomas Nelson, 2006.

———. *Seeking Aliveness: Daily Reflections on a New Way to Experience and Practice the Christian Faith*. New York: Faith Words, 2017.

———. "Seeking to Do One Thing Well: A Response to Three Helpful Reviews." *Reformation and Revival* 14, no. 3 (2005) 121-40.

———., vocalist. *Songs for a Revolution of Hope "Everything Must Change."* Vol. 1. The Restoration Project. Digital Album. 2007 (brianmclaren.bandcamp.com/album/songs-for-a-revolution-of-hope).

———. "Spiritual Formation in a Postmodern Context." In *A New Kind of Conversation: Blogging Toward a Postmodern Faith*, edited by Myron Bradley Penner and Hunter Barnes, 183-89. Colorado Springs, CO: Authentic Publishing, 2007.

———. "Spiritual Formation in Unexpected and Dangerous Places." Youth Specialties. October 2, 2009. https://youthspecialties.com/blog/spiritual-formation-in-unexpected-and-dangerous-places/.

———. "The Stories We Tell Ourselves." *Sojourners Magazine*, November 2007.

———. *The Story We Find Ourselves In: Further Adventures of a New Kind of Christian*. Pbk. ed. Book 2. San Francisco, CA: Jossey-Bass, 2003.

———. "Suicidal vs. Life-Giving Religious Narratives." *Tikkun Magazine*, September/October 2010.

———. "Take Time to Breathe." *Sojourners Magazine* 38, no. 1 (January 2009) 21-23.

———. "Targeted Medicine: Resident Aliens at 25." *The Christian Century*, September 15, 2014. https://www.christiancentury.org/article/2014-09/targeted-medicine.

———. "There's A Bigger Story: Brian McLaren." Interview. *Relevant Magazine*, April 25, 2003. relevantmagazine.com/god/church/blog/436-theres-a-bigger-story-brian-mclaren.

———. "This Changes Everything: An Interview with Brian McLaren." Interview by Melvin Bray. *Braytown*, February 6, 2008. http://melvinbray.com/2008/02/06/this-changes-everything-an-interview-with-brian-mclaren/.

———. "This Good Earth." In *Holy Ground: A Gathering of Voices on Caring for Creation*, edited by Lyndsay Moseley, 166-69. San Francisco, CA: Sierra Club, 2008.

———. "This is not normal." Twitter, January 21, 2019. https://twitter.com/brianmclaren/status/1087339095561592835.

———. "TPC Interviews." Interview. *The Progressive Christian*, January/February 2008.

———. "Underneath the Cosmetics." *Christianity Today*, September 1, 2005. https://www.christianitytoday.com/pastors/2005/fall/21.136.html.

———. "Unterror Cells." *Leadership* 27, no. 2 (Spring 2006) 114.

———. "Virtual Virtue and Real Presence." *Leadership* 28, no. 3 (Summer 2007) 110.

———. *(The Voice of Acts) The Dust Off Their Feet: Lessons from the First Church*. The Voice: A Scripture Project to Rediscover the Story of the Bible. Nashville, TN: Thomas Nelson, 2006.

———. *The Voice of Luke: Not Even Sandals*. The Voice: A Scripture Project to Rediscover the Story of the Bible. Nashville, TN: Thomas Nelson, 2007.

———. "Walker Percy: The Point of View for His Work as an Author." Master's thesis, University of Maryland, 1980.

———. *We Make the Road by Walking: A Year-Long Quest for Spiritual Formation, Reorientation, and Activation*. New York: Jericho, 2014.

———. "What I'm Reading." *Sojourners Magazine*, December 2004.

———. *Why Did Jesus, Moses, the Buddha, and Mohammed Cross the Road? Christian Identity in a Multi-Faith World*. Pbk. ed. New York: Jericho, 2012.

———. *Why Don't They Get It? Overcoming Bias in Others (and yourself)*. N.p.: 2019.

———. "Why Everything Must Change: A Conversation with Brian McLaren." Interview by Jon Stanley. *The Other Journal*, October 15, 2007. theotherjournal.com/2007/10/15/why-everything-must-change-a-conversation-with-brian-mclaren/.

———. "Why I'll Be in Charlottesville this Weekend." *Brian McLaren Blog*, August 11, 2017. https://brianmclaren.net/why-ill-be-in-charlottesville-this-weekend/.

———. "'Women on the Edge': Brian McLaren Sermon" (YouTube video). December 7, 2014. Accessed September 24, 2018. youtube.com/watch?v=vLyIluvpSf4&feature=youtu.be.

———. *The Word of the Lord to Democrats*. Brentwood, TN: Creative Trust Digital, 2012. Kindle.

———. *The Word of the Lord to Evangelicals*. Brentwood, TN: Creative Trust Digital, 2012. Kindle.

———. *The Word of the Lord to Republicans: A Tale for an Election Year*. Brentwood, TN: Creative Trust Digital, 2012. Kindle.

McLaren, Brian D., and Duane Litfin. "Emergent Evangelism." *Christianity Today*, November 2004.

McLaren, Brian D., and Frank Schaeffer. "Brian McLaren Talks with Frank Schaeffer" (YouTube video). July 12, 2014. Accessed September 23, 2018. https://www.youtube.com/watch?v=AY1b9cc08jo&feature=youtu.be.

McLaren, Brian D., and Gareth Higgins. *Cory and the Seventh Story*. N.p.: 2018.

———. *The Seventh Story: Us, Them, and the End of Violence*. N.p.: 2018.

McLaren, Brian D., and Scot McKnight "Conversations on Being a Heretic" (YouTube video). April 2010. Accessed November 2, 2018. https://youtu.be/LnKqkp5Tfh4.

McLaren, Brian D., and Tony Campolo. *Adventures in Missing the Point: How the Culture-Controlled Church Neutered the Gospel*. Grand Rapids, MI: Zondervan, 2003.

McLaren, Brian D., Elisa Padilla, and Ashley Bunting Seeber, eds. *The Justice Project*. Grand Rapids, MI: Baker, 2009.

McMullen, Horace. "Institutional Church as House Church: A Vision and a Reality." *Chicago Theological Seminary Register* 64, no. 1 (1973) 1-18.

Meacham, Jon, and Eliza Gray. "The End of Christian America." *Newsweek*, April 13, 2009.

Mead, Richard T. "A Dissenting Opinion About Respect for Context in Old Testament Quotations." *New Testament Studies* 10, no. 2 (January 1964) 279-89.

Merritt, Carol Howard. "The Church's New Foundation." *Christian Century*, November 12, 2014.

Metzger, Greg. "Brian McLaren Responds to Terry Mattingly's Scurrilous Question." *Faith and the Common Good* (blog), September 27, 2012. debatingobama.blogspot.com/2012/09/brian-mclaren-responds-to-mattinglys.html.

Meynell, Hugo Anthony. "Two Traditions and the Philosophy of Religion." *Religious Studies* 17, no. 2 (June 1981) 267-74.

Micklethwait, John, and Adrian Wooldridge. *The Right Nation: Conservative Power in America*. New York: Penguin, 2004.

Middleton, J. Richard, and Brian J. Walsh. *Truth is Stranger Than It Used to Be: Biblical Faith in a Postmodern Age*. Downers Grove, IL: InterVarsity, 1995.

Milkman, Katherine L., Dolly Chugh, and Max H. Bazerman. "How Can Decision Making Be Improved?" *Perspectives on Psychological Science* 4, no. 4 (July 2009) 379-83.

Bibliography

Miller, Emily McFarlan. "Brian McLaren, Others Apologize to Native Americans in Video Series." *Religion News Service*, January 31, 2017. religionnews.com/2017/01/31/brian-mclaren-others-apologize-to-native-americans-in-video-series/.

Mohler, R. Albert Jr. *The Disappearance of God: Dangerous Beliefs in the New Spiritual Openness.* Colorado Springs, CO: Multnomah, 2009.

———. "Mohler, Jr. Discusses Evangelical Support for Trump" (YouTube video). October 11, 2016. Accessed December 30, 2018. https://www.youtube.com/watch?v=s6hsLyodimA&feature=youtu.be.

Moltmann, Jürgen. *The Coming of God: Christian Eschatology.* Translated by Margaret Kohl. Minneapolis, MN: Fortress, 1996.

———. *God in Creation: A New Theology of Creation and the Spirit of God.* Translated by Margaret Kohl. Gifford Lectures 1984–1985. Minneapolis, MN: Fortress, 1993.

———. *The Trinity and the Kingdom: The Doctrine of God.* Translated by Margaret Kohl. Minneapolis, MN: Fortress, 1993.

———. *The Way of Jesus Christ: Christology in Messianic Dimensions.* Translated by Margaret Kohl. Minneapolis, MN: Fortress, 1993.

Monsma, Stephen V. "Evangelicals and Poverty." In *Is the Good Book Good Enough? Evangelical Perspectives on Public Policy*, edited by David K. Ryden, 41-55. Lanham, MD: Lexington, 2011.

Montgomery, John Warwick. "The Theologian's Craft: A Discussion of Theory Formation and Theory Testing in Theology." *Concordia Theological Monthly* 37 (1966) 67-98.

Moon, Young Bin. "God as a Communicative System *Sui Generis*: Beyond the Psychic, Social, Process Models of the Trinity." *Zygon* 45, no. 1 (March 2010) 105-26.

Moore, Russell. "Have Evangelicals Who Support Trump Lost Their Values?" *New York Times*, September 17, 2015. Accessed December 30, 2018. https://www.nytimes.com/2015/09/17/opinion/have-evangelicals-who-support-trump-lost-their-values.html?_r=0.

Moreland, J. P. "Truth, Contemporary Philosophy, and the Postmodern Turn." *Journal of the Evangelical Theological Society* 48, no. 1 (March 2005) 77-88.

Moreland, J. P., and William Lane Craig. *Philosophical Foundations for a Christian Worldview.* 2nd ed. Downers Grove, IL: InterVarsity, 2017.

Morris, Thomas V. *Our Idea of God: An Introduction to Philosophical Theology.* 2nd ed. Vancouver, British Columbia: Regent College Publishing, 2002.

Moseley, Lyndsay "Just Ecology: What Demands of Justice Does the Planet Make upon Followers of Christ?" In *The Justice Project*, edited by Brian D. McLaren, Elisa Padilla, and Ashley Bunting Seeber, 166-71. Grand Rapids, MI: Baker, 2009.

Moss, Otis III. *Blue Note Preaching in a Post-Soul World: Finding Hope in an Age of Despair.* Louisville, KY: John Knox, 2015.

Mukan, Hauwa. "Some evangelicals taking leap of faith to Obama." *New York Amsterdam News*, July 31-August 6, 2008.

Muller, Richard A. *Dictionary of Latin and Greek Theological Terms: Drawn Principally from Protestant Scholastic Theology.* 1985. Pbk. ed. Reprint, Grand Rapids, MI: Baker, 1995.

Murphy, Caryle. "Evangelical Author Puts Progressive Spin on Traditional Faith." *Washington Post*, September 10, 2006.

Musgrave, Alan. "Strict Empiricism Versus Explanation in Science." In *Varieties of Scientific Realism: Objectivity and Truth in Science*, edited by Evandro Agazzi, 71-93. Cham, Switzerland: Springer, 2017.

Nash, Ronald H. "Nietzsche, Kierkegaard, and the Death of God." *Bridges* 3 (Spring–Summer 1991) 1–8.

"The Nation's Best Bible College Gets Low Grades on Racial Diversity." *The Journal of Blacks in Higher Education* 31 (Spring 2001) 43–45.

Neece, Kevin C. *The Gospel According to Star Trek: The Original Crew*. Eugene, OR: Cascade, 2016.

Neff, David. "Has God Been Held Hostage by Philosophy? A Forum on Free-Will Theism, a New Paradigm for Understanding God." *Christianity Today* 39, no. 1 (January 9, 1995) 30–34.

Newbigin, Lesslie. *The Gospel in a Pluralist Society*. Grand Rapids, MI: Eerdmans, 1989.

Nicole, Roger. "Biblical Egalitarianism and the Inerrancy of Scripture." *Priscilla Papers* 20, no. 2 (Spring 2006) 4–9.

Nie, Norman H., Jane Junn, and Kenneth Stehlik-Barry. *Education and Democratic Citizenship in America*. Chicago, IL: The University of Chicago Press, 1996.

Niebuhr, H. Richard. *The Kingdom of God in America*. 1937. Reprint, Middletown, CT: Wesleyan University Press, 1988.

Nietzsche, Friedrich. *The Gay Science: With a Prelude in Rhymes and an Appendix of Songs*. 1887. Translated by Walter Kaufmann. Reprint, New York: Vintage, 1974.

———. *Thus Spoke Zarathustra: A Book for Everyone and Nobody*. 1883. Translated by Graham Parkes. Oxford World's Classics. Reprint, New York: Oxford University Press, 2005.

———. *The Will to Power*. 1901. Translated by Walter Kaufmann and R. J. Hollingdale. Reprint, New York: Random, 1967.

Noll, Mark A. *The Rise of Evangelicalism: The Age of Edwards, Whitefield and the Wesleys*. Vol. 1. A History of Evangelicalism: People, Movements and Ideas in the English-Speaking World. Downers Grove, IL: InterVarsity, 2003.

———. *The Scandal of the Evangelical Mind*. Grand Rapids, MI: Eerdmans, 1994.

Nunn, Clyde, Henry Crockett, and J. Allen Williams. *Tolerance for Conformity: A National Survey of Americans' Changing Commitment to Civil Liberties*. San Francisco, CA: Jossey-Bass, 1978.

Olson, Roger E. "An Open Letter to My Fellow Evangelicals About Trump." Patheos. January 18, 2018. https://www.patheos.com/blogs/rogereolson/2018/01/open-letter-fellow-evangelicals-trump/.

———. *Reformed and Always Reforming: The Postconservative Approach to Evangelical Theology*. Grand Rapids, MI: Baker, 2007.

———. *The Story of Christian Theology: Twenty Centuries of Tradition and Reform*. Downers Grove, IL: InterVarsity, 1999.

"On the Danger of a Single Story . . . from a White South African: In Response to Brian McLaren's *A New Kind of Christianity*." *Catholic New Times*, July 5, 2010.

Ortega, Ofelia. "The Gospel of Solidarity." *Ecumenical Review* 46, no. 2 (April 1994) 135–41.

Packard, Jerrold M. *American Nightmare: The History of Jim Crow*. 2002. Reprint, New York: St. Martin's Griffin, 2003.

Paloutzian, Raymond F., Sebastian Murken, Heinz Streib, and Sussan Rößler-Namini. "Conversion, Deconversion, and Spiritual Transformation: A Multilevel Interdisciplinary View." In *Handbook of the Psychology of Religion and Spirituality*. 2nd ed, edited by Raymond F. Paloutzian and Crystal L. Park, 399–421. New York: Guilford, 2013.

Pattison, George. *God and Being: An Enquiry*. New York: Oxford University Press, 2011.

Pattyn, Bart. "The Emotional Boundaries of Our Solidarity." *Ethical Perspectives* 3, no. 2 (July 1996) 101-8.

Payne, William P. "Discerning an Integral Latino Pentecostal Theology of Liberation." *Ashland Theological Journal* 45 (2013) 87-100.

Pêcheux, Michel. *Language, Semantics and Ideology: Stating the Obvious*. 1982. Edited by Stephen Heath and Colin MacCabe. Translated by Harbans Nagpal. Reprint, New York: Macmillan, 1983.

Peirce, Charles Sanders. *Collected Papers of Charles Sanders Peirce*. 1935. Edited by Charles Hartshorne and Paul Weiss. Vol. 5, *Pragmatism and Pragmaticism*. Reprint, Cambridge, MA: Belknap, 1974.

Pelikan, Jaroslav. *Credo: Historical and Theological Guide to Creeds and Confessions of Faith in the Christian Tradition*. New Haven, CT: Yale University Press, 2003.

———. *From Luther to Kierkegaard: A Study in the History of Theology*. 2nd ed. St. Louis, MO: Concordia, 1963.

Penner, Myron Bradley. *The End of Apologetics: Christian Witness in a Postmodern Context*. Grand Rapids, MI: Baker, 2013.

———. "Postmodern Apologetics." In *A New Kind of Conversation: Blogging Toward a Postmodern Faith*, edited by Myron Bradley Penner and Hunter Barnes, 137-42. Colorado Springs, CO: Authentic Publishing, 2007.

Penner, Myron Bradley, and Hunter Barnes, eds. *A New Kind of Conversation: Blogging Toward a Postmodern Faith*. Colorado Springs, CO: Authentic Publishing, 2007.

Peppler, Christopher C. "A New Kind of Liberalism: Review of Brian McLaren, *A New Kind of Christianity*." *Conspectus: The Journal of the South African Theological Seminary* 11 (March 2011) 187-201.

Peterson, Michael, William Hasker, Bruce Reichenbach, and David Basinger. *Reason and Religious Belief: An Introduction to the Philosophy Religion*. 5th ed. New York: Oxford University Press, 2013.

Pettegrew, Larry D. "Evangelicalism, Paradigms, and The Emerging Church." *Master's Seminary Journal* 17, no. 2 (Fall 2006) 159-75.

Phillips, Gary A. "Exegesis as Critical Praxis: Reclaiming History and Text from a Postmodern Perspective." *Semeia* 51 (1990) 7-49.

Phillips, Jere. "The Emerging Church Conversation: A Study of the Emerging Church Movement in Its Theological Adolescence." *Theology for Ministry* 3, no. 1 (May 2008) 27-45.

Plantinga, Cornelius Jr. "The Threeness/Oneness Problem of the Trinity." *Calvin Theological Journal* 23, no. 1 (April 1988) 37-53.

Pless, John T. "Contemporary Spirituality and the Emerging Church." *Concordia Theological Quarterly* 71 (2007) 347-63.

Pojman, Louis P. "Kierkegaard, Subjectivity and Paradox: A Response to Gregory Schufreider." *International Journal for Philosophy of Religion* 12, no. 3 (1981) 165-69.

———. *The Logic of Subjectivity: Kierkegaard's Philosophy of Religion*. Tuscaloosa, AL: The University of Alabama Press, 1984.

Poling, Alan, Laura L. Methot, and Mark G. LeSage. *Fundamentals of Behavior Analytic Research*. Applied Clinical Psychology. New York: Plenum, 1995.

Poythress, Vern S. *Symphonic Theology: The Validity of Multiple Perspectives in Theology*. Grand Rapids, MI: Zondervan, 1987.

Prickett, Stephen. *Words and The Word: Language, Poetics and Biblical Interpretation*. 1986. Reprint, New York: Cambridge University Press, 1989.

Putnam, Robert D., and David E. Campbell. *American Grace: How Religion Divides and Unites Us*. New York: Simon & Schuster, 2010.

Quebedeaux, Richard. *The Young Evangelicals: Revolution in Orthodoxy*. New York: Harper & Row, 1974.

Rah, Soong-Chan. *The Next Evangelicalism: Releasing the Church from Western Cultural Captivity*. Downers Grove, IL: InterVarsity, 2009.

Raja, Masood Ashraf. *The Religious Right and the Talibanization of America*. New York: Palgrave, 2016.

Rambo, Lewis R. *Understanding Religious Conversion*. New Have, CT: Yale University Press, 1993.

Rand, Ayn. *Capitalism: The Unknown Ideal*. New York: Signet, 1966.

———. *The Virtue of Selfishness: A New Concept of Egoism*. New York: Signet, 1964.

Raschke, Carl. *The Next Reformation: Why Evangelicals Must Embrace Postmodernity*. Grand Rapids, MI: Baker, 2004.

Rasmussen, Larry L. "Reinhold Niebuhr: Public Theologian." *Cross Currents* 38, no. 2 (Summer 1988) 198-210.

Reed, Randall W. "Emerging Treason? Politics and Identity in the Emerging Church Movement." *Critical Research on Religion* 2, no. 1 (2014) 66-85.

Reimer, Samuel H., and Jerry Z. Park. "Tolerant (In)civility? A Longitudinal Analysis of White Conservative Protestants' Willingness to Grant Civil Liberties." *Journal for the Scientific Study of Religion* 40, no. 4 (December 2001) 735-45.

Religion. Gallup, 2018. https://news.gallup.com/poll/1690/religion.aspx.

Rengstorf, Karl Heinrich. "Jesus Christ, Nazarene, Christian." In *New International Dictionary of New Testament Theology*, edited by Colin Brown. Vol. 2, 330-43. Grand Rapids, MI: Zondervan, 1986.

Rescher, Nicholas. *Plausible Reasoning: An Introduction to the Theory and Practice of Plausibilistic Inference*. Assen, Netherlands: Van Gorcum, 1976.

Reynolds, Amy, and Stephen Offutt. "Global Poverty and Evangelical Action." In *The New Evangelical Social Engagement*, edited by Brian Steensland and Philip Goff, 242-61. New York: Oxford University Press, 2014.

Rhodes, Ron. "The Maze of Mysticism in The Emerging Church Movement." *Christian Apologetics Journal* 7, no. 1 (Spring 2008) 1-26.

Richardson, James T., and Mary Stewart. "Conversion Process Models and the Jesus Movement." *American Behavioral Scientist* 20, no. 6 (July/August 1977) 819-38.

Ricoeur, Paul. *Essays on Biblical Interpretation*. Edited by Lewis Seymour Mudge. Philadelphia, PA: Fortress, 1980.

———. *Figuring the Sacred: Religion, Narrative, and Imagination*. Edited by Mark I. Wallace. Translated by David Pellauer. Minneapolis, MN: Fortress, 1995.

———. *Hermeneutics and the Human Sciences: Essays on Language, Action and Interpretation*. 1981. Edited and translated by John B. Thompson. Cambridge Philosophy Classics. Reprint, New York: Cambridge University Press, 2016.

———. *Interpretation Theory: Discourse and the Surplus of Meaning*. Fort Worth, TX: Texas Christian University Press, 1976.

Riess, Jana. "Emerging Star." *Publishers Weekly* 254, no. 32 (August 13, 2007) 52.

Bibliography

Rimmon-Kenan, Shlomith. *Narrative Fiction: Contemporary Poetics.* New York: Methuen, 1983.

Roberts, Kyle A. *Emerging Prophet: Kierkegaard and the Postmodern People of God.* Eugene, OR: Cascade, 2013.

Robertson, Brian. "A Critical Analysis of Selected Evangelistic Strategies within the Emerging Church Movement." PhD diss., Southwestern Baptist Theological Seminary, 2010.

Rockmore, Tom. *On Foundationalism: A Strategy for Metaphysical Realism.* Lanham, MD: Rowman & Littlefield, 2004.

Rodes, Robert E. "Last Days of Erastianism: Forms in the American Church-State Nexus." *Harvard Theological Review* 62, no. 3 (July 1969) 301-48.

Rogers, Jack. *Confessions of a Conservative Evangelical.* 2nd ed. Louisville, KY: Geneva, 2001.

Rogers, Tim B. "Nature of the Third Kind: Toward an Explicitly Relational Constructionism." *Environmental Ethics* 31, no. 4 (Winter 2009) 393-412.

Rorty, Richard. *Objectivity, Relativism, and Truth.* 1991. Vol. 1. Philosophical Papers. Reprint, New York: Cambridge University Press, 1999.

Roukema-Koning, Barbara. "Het sociaal constructionisme en zijn meta-theoretische betekenis voor de theologie." *Nederlands theologisch tijdschrift* 56, no. 1 (January 2002) 48-64.

Rowe, William L. *Philosophy of Religion: An Introduction.* 2nd ed. Belmont, CA: Wadsworth, 1993.

Ruf, Henry L., ed. *Religion, Ontotheology and Deconstruction.* New York: Paragon, 1989.

Ryden, David K. "Evangelicals and the Elusive Goal of Racial Reconciliation: The Role of Culture, Politics, and Public Policy." In *Is the Good Book Good Enough? Evangelical Perspectives on Public Policy*, edited by David K. Ryden, 205-24. Lanham, MD: Lexington, 2011.

———. "Introduction: The Evolving Policy Agenda of Evangelical Christians." In *Is the Good Book Good Enough? Evangelical Perspectives on Public Policy*, edited by David K. Ryden, 1-19. Lanham, MD: Lexington, 2011.

Saewyc, Elizabeth M. "Research on Adolescent Sexual Orientation: Development, Health Disparities, Stigma, and Resilience." *Journal of Research on Adolescence* 21, no. 1 (2011) 256-72.

Scheitle, Christopher P., and Amy Adamczyk. "It Takes Two: The Interplay of Individual and Group Theology on Social Embeddedness." *Journal for the Scientific Study of Religion* 48, no. 1 (2009) 16-29.

Schmitz, Kenneth L. "The Authority of Institutions: Meddling or Middling?" *Communio: International Catholic Review* 12, no. 1 (Spring 1985) 6-24.

Schürmann, Heinz. *Gottes Reich—Jesu Geschick. Jesu Ureigener Tod Im Licht Seiner Basileia Verkündigung.* Freiburg, Germany: Herder, 1983.

Schurz, G. "Patterns of Abduction." *Synthese* 164, no. 2 (September 2008) 201-34.

Schwandel, Philip. "Individual, Congregational, and Denominational Effects on Church Members' Civic Participation." *Journal for the Scientific Study of Religion* 40, no. 2 (2005) 159-71.

Schwartz, Sanford. "Cosmic Anthropology: Race and Reason in *Out of the Silent Planet*." *Christianity and Literature* 52, no. 4 (2003) 523-56.

Schwartz, Werner. "Antinomy." In *The Encyclopedia of Christianity*, edited and translated by Geoffrey W. Bromiley. Vol. 1, 81. Grand Rapids, MI: Eerdmans, 1999.

Schwarz, Hans. *Eschatology.* Pbk. ed. Grand Rapids, MI: Eerdmans, 2000.

Schwarz, Norbert, and Gerald L. Clore. "How Do I Feel About It? Informative Functions of Affective States." In *Affect, Cognition, and Social Behavior: New Evidence and Integrative Attempts*, edited by Klaus Fiedler and Joseph P. Forgas, 44–62. Toronto, Canada: Hogrefe, 1988.

———. "Mood, Misattribution, and Judgments of Well-Being: Informative and Directive Functions of Affective States." *Journal of Personality and Social Psychology* 45, no. 3 (September 1983) 513–23.

Schwarz, Robert C. "What the Thunder Said: The Desert Fathers and Mothers on Compassion." *Sewanee Theological Review* 35, no. 2 (1992) 139–57.

Seel, John. "Nostalgia for the Lost Empire." In *No God but God: Breaking with the Idols of Our Age*, edited by Os Guinness and John Seel, 66–80. Chicago, IL: Moody, 1992.

Segers, Mary C., and Timothy A. Byrnes, eds. *Abortion Politics in American States*. 1995. Reprint, New York: Routledge, 2015.

Shakespeare, Steven. "The New Romantics: A Critique of Radical Orthodoxy." *Theology* 103, no. 813 (May–June 2000) 163–77.

Sharp, Douglas R. "Evangelicals, Racism, and the Limits of Social Science Research." *Christian Scholar's Review* 33, no. 2 (Winter 2004) 237–61.

Shogren, Gary Steven. "'The Wicked Will Not Inherit the Kingdom of God': A Pauline Warning and the Hermeneutics of Liberation Theology and of Brian McLaren." *The Trinity Journal* 31, no. 1 (Spring 2010) 95–113.

Shults, F. LeRon. *Christology and Science*. Ashgate Science and Religion Series. Burlington, VT: Ashgate, 2008.

Sider, Ronald J. "Evangelicals and Social Justice." In *Evangelicals Around the World: A Global Handbook for the 21st Century*, edited by Brian C. Stiller et al, 128–33. Nashville, TN: Thomas Nelson, 2015.

———. "McCain or Obama?" *PRISM Magazine*, September/October 2008. https://issuu.com/prismmagazine/docs/mccain_or_obama/1?e=2263645/66649533.

———. *Rich Christians in an Age of Hunger: Moving from Affluence to Generosity*. 6th ed. Nashville, TN: W Publishing, 2015.

———. *The Scandal of the Evangelical Conscience: Why Are Christians Living Just Like the Rest of the World?* Grand Rapids, MI: Baker, 2005.

Silvia, Paul J., and Camilla E. Sanders. "Why are Smart People Curious? Fluid Intelligence, Openness to Experience, and Interest." *Learning and Individual Differences* 20, no. 3 (June 2010) 242–45.

Simmons, Ernest. "Quantum Perichoresis: Quantum Field Theory and the Trinity." *Theology and Science* 4, no. 2 (July 2006) 137–50.

Simmons, J. Aaron, and Bruce Ellis Benson. *The New Phenomenology: A Philosophical Introduction*. Pbk. ed. New York: Bloomsbury, 2013.

Siniscalchi, Glenn B. "Knowing that God Exists: Retrieving the Teaching of *Dei Filius*." *American Theological Inquiry* 3, no. 2 (July 2010) 45–68.

Sinitiere, Phillip Luke. "Embracing the Early Church: Reflections on Evangelicals, Patristics, Ecclesiology, and Ecumenism." *Reformation and Revival* 13, no. 4 (Fall 2004) 13–38.

Sinnott, Jan D. *The Development of Logic in Adulthood: Postformal Thought and Its Applications*. New York: Plenum, 1998.

Skinner, Marilyn B. *Sexuality in Greek and Roman Culture*. 2nd ed. Malden, MA: Wiley, 2014.

Slade, Darren M. "*Hagioprepēs*: The Rationalizing of Saintly Sin and Atrocities." In *Sacred Troubling Topics in Hebrew Bible, New Testament, and Qur'an*, edited by Roberta Sabbath, forthcoming. Boston, MA: De Gruyter, 2021.

———. "Religious Homophily and Biblicism: A Theory of Conservative Church Fragmentation." *The International Journal of Religion and Spirituality in Society* 9, no. 1 (2019) 13-28.

———. "What is the Socio-Historical Method in the Study of Religion?" *Socio-Historical Examination of Religion and Ministry* 2, no. 1 (Spring 2020) 1-15. https://doi.org/10.33929/sherm.2020.vol2.no1.01.

Smidt, Corwin E. *American Evangelicals Today*. 2013. Pbk. ed. Reprint, Lanham, MD: Rowman & Littlefield, 2015.

Smith, Christian. *The Bible Made Impossible: Why Biblicism Is Not a Truly Evangelical Reading of Scripture*. Grand Rapids, MI: Brazos, 2011.

———. *Christian America? What Evangelicals Really Want*. Berkeley, CA: University of California Press, 2000.

———. "Evangelicals Behaving Badly with Statistics." *Books and Culture* 13 (January/February 2007) 11.

Smith, Don. "The Work of the Holy Spirit in Revival and Renewal." *Foundations* 47 (2001) 20-31.

Smith, Gerald Birney. "Systematic Theology and Ministerial Efficiency." *The American Journal of Theology* 16, no. 4 (October 1912) 589-613.

Smith, James K. A. "Continental Philosophy of Religion: Prescriptions for a Healthy Subdiscipline." *Faith and Philosophy* 26, no. 4 (October 2009) 440-48.

Smith, R. Scott. "Reflections on McLaren and the Emerging Church." In *Passionate Conviction: Contemporary Discourses on Christian Apologetics*, edited by Paul Copan and William Lane Craig, 227-41. Nashville, TN: B&H, 2007.

———. "Some Suggestions for Brian McLaren (and His Critics)." *Criswell Theological Review* 3, no. 2 (Spring 2006) 67-85.

———. *Truth and the New Kind of Christian: The Emerging Effects of Postmodernism in the Church*. Wheaton, IL: Crossway, 2005.

Snodgrass, Klyne "The Use of the Old Testament in the New." In *The Right Doctrine from the Wrong Texts? Essays on the Use of the Old Testament in the New*, edited by G. K. Beale, 29-51. Grand Rapids, MI: Baker, 1994.

Snyman, Gerrie. "Homoseksualiteit en tydgerigtheid: 'n etiek van Bybellees?" [Homosexuality and Time-Orientedness: An Ethic of Reading the Bible?] *Die Skriflig* 40, no. 4 (2006) 715-44.

Soskice, Janet Martin. "The Truth Looks Different from Here." In *Christ and Context: The Confrontation between Gospel and Culture*. 1993, edited by Hilary Regan and Alan J. Torrance. Religious Studies: Christianity and Society. Reprint, 43-59. New York: Bloomsbury, 2016.

Sperber, Dan. "Intuitive and Reflective Beliefs." *Mind and Language* 12, no. 1 (March 1997) 67-83.

Stanovich, Keith E., and Richard F. West. "Individual Differences in Reasoning: Implications for the Rationality Debate." *Behavioral and Brain Sciences* 23, no. 5 (October 2000) 645-65.

Star Trek: First Contact. Directed by Jonathan Frakes. Paramount Pictures, 1996.

Stark, Rodney. *The Rise of Christianity*. 1996. Pbk. ed. Reprint, San Francisco, CA: HarperSanFrancisco, 1997.

———. *What Americans Really Believe: New Findings from the Baylor Surveys of Religion.* Waco, TX: Baylor University Press, 2008.

Stark, Rodney, and William Sims Bainbridge. *A Theory of Religion.* 1987. Pbk. ed. Reprint, New Brunswick, NJ: Rutgers University Press, 1996.

The State of the Church 2016. Barna Group, September 15, 2016. barna.com/research/state-church-2016/.

Sternberg, Meir. *The Poetics of Biblical Narrative: Ideological Literature and the Drama of Reading.* Bloomington, IN: Indiana University Press, 1985.

Stewart, Joe Randell. "The Influence of Newbigin's Missiology on Selected Innovators and Early Adopters of the Emerging Church Paradigm." EdD diss., Southern Baptist Theological Seminary, 2013.

Stewart, Kenneth J. *In Search of Ancient Roots: The Christian Past and the Evangelical Identity Crisis.* Downers Grove, IL: InterVarsity, 2017.

Straub, Jeffrey P. "The Emerging Church: A Fundamentalist Assessment." *Detroit Baptist Seminary Journal* 13 (2008) 69-91.

Streett, R. Alan. "An Interview with Brian McLaren." *Criswell Theological Review* 3, no. 2 (Spring 2006) 5-14.

Streib, Heinz, Ralph W. Hood, and Constantin Klein. "The Religious Schema Scale: Construction and Initial Validation of a Quantitative Measure for Religious Styles." *The International Journal for the Psychology of Religion* 20, no. 3 (July-September 2010) 151-72.

Suk, John. *Not Sure: A Pastor's Journey from Faith to Doubt.* Grand Rapids, MI: Eerdmans, 2011.

Suleiman, Susan. *The Reader in the Text: Essays on Audience and Interpretation.* Princeton, NJ: Princeton University Press, 1980.

Susen, Simon. *The 'Postmodern Turn' in the Social Sciences.* New York: Palgrave, 2015.

Suskind, Ron. "Without a Doubt." *New York Times Magazine*, October 17, 2004.

Sutton, Matthew Avery. *American Apocalypse: A History of Modern Evangelicalism.* Cambridge, MA: Belknap, 2014.

Swanson, Dennis M. "Bibliography of Works on the Emerging Church." *Master's Seminary Journal* 17, no. 2 (Fall 2006) 223-29.

Sweeney, Douglas A. *The American Evangelical Story: A History of the Movement.* Grand Rapids, MI: Baker, 2005.

Sweet, Leonard, Brian D. McLaren, and Jerry Haselmayer. *A is for Abductive: The Language of the Emerging Church.* Grand Rapids, MI: Zondervan, 2003.

Szesnat, Holger. "Human Sexuality, History, and Culture: The Essentialist/Social Constructionist Controversy and the Methodological Problem of Studying 'Sexuality' in the New Testament and Its World." *Scriptura* 62 (1997) 335-61.

Tallman, Ruth. "Was It All a Dream? Why Nolan's Answer Doesn't Matter." In *Inception and Philosophy: Because It's Never Just a Dream*, edited by David Kyle Johnson and William Irwin. The Blackwell Philosophy and Pop Culture, 17-30. Hoboken, NJ: Wiley, 2012.

Taylor, Daniel. *The Myth of Certainty: The Reflective Christian and the Risk of Commitment.* 1986. Reprint, Downers Grove, IL: InterVarsity, 1992.

Taylor, Justin. "Christianity and McLarenism." The Gospel Coalition. February 18, 2010. https://www.thegospelcoalition.org/blogs/justin-taylor/christianity-and-mclarenism/.

———. "An Introduction to Postconservative Evangelicalism and the Rest of This Book." In *Reclaiming the Center: Confronting Evangelical Accommodation in Postmodern Times*, edited by Millard J. Erickson, Paul Kjoss Helseth, and Justin Taylor, 17-32. Wheaton, IL: Crossway, 2004.

Taylor, Lewis Jerome. "Walker Percy's Knights of the Hidden Inwardness." *Anglican Theological Review* 56, no. 2 (April 1974) 125-51.

Taylor, Mark C. *Erring: A Postmodern A/theology*. 1984. Pbk. ed. Reprint, Chicago: University of Chicago Press, 1987.

Thiselton, Anthony C. *New Horizons in Hermeneutics: The Theory and Practice of Transforming Biblical Reading*. Grand Rapids, MI: Zondervan, 1992.

Thomas, Cal, and Ed Dobson. *Blinded by Might: Why the Religious Right Can't Save America*. Grand Rapids, MI: Zondervan, 1999.

Tomlinson, Dave. *The Post Evangelical*. 1995. SPCK Classics. Reprint, London: SPCK, 2014.

Thompson, Evan. *Mind in Life: Biology, Phenomenology and the Sciences of Mind*. Cambridge, MA: Belknap, 2007.

Tickle, Phyllis. *Emergence Christianity: What It Is, Where It Is Going, and Why It Matters*. Grand Rapids, MI: Baker, 2012.

———. *The Great Emergence: How Christianity is Changing and Why*. Grand Rapids, MI: Baker, 2008.

Tilley, Terrence W. *Story Theology*. Theology and Life Series 12. Wilmington, DE: Michael Glazier, 1985.

Toly, Noah J. "Evangelicals and the Environment: From Political Realism to a Politics of Freedom." In *Is the Good Book Good Enough? Evangelical Perspectives on Public Policy*, edited by David K. Ryden, 23-40. Lanham, MD: Lexington, 2011.

Trabbic, Joseph G. "Aquinas and Continental Philosophy of Religion: Finding a Way Out of Ontotheology." *Proceedings of the American Catholic Philosophical Association* 76 (2002) 210-28.

"Trump Supporter Admits He Believes Trump Over Jesus" (YouTube video). 2017. Accessed December 29, 2018. https://youtu.be/OVSMzqgou7U.

Turcotte, Paul-Andre. "Sociologie et historie des religions. Les jeux et enjeux d'une pratique." *Eglise et Theologie* 24, no. 1 (1993) 43-73.

Turner, William C. Jr. "Black Evangelicalism: Theology, Politics, and Race." *The Journal of Religious Thought* 45, no. 2 (Winter-Spring 1989) 40-56.

Utter, Glenn H., and John W. Storey. *The Religious Right: A Reference Handbook*. 3rd ed. Millerton, NY: Grey House, 2007.

Van Biema, David, Cathy Booth-Thomas, Massimo Calabresi, John F. Dickerson, John Cloud, Rebecca Winters, Sonja Steptoe, Bower, Rita Healey, Sean Scully, and Elaine Shannon. "The 25 Most Influential Evangelicals in America." *Time*, February 7, 2005.

van den Toren, Benno. *Christian Apologetics as Cross-Cultural Dialogue*. New York: T&T Clark, 2011.

van Fraassen, Bas C. *The Scientific Image*. Clarendon Library of Logic and Philosophy. New York: Oxford University Press, 1980.

VandenBos, Gary R., ed. *APA Dictionary of Psychology*. Washington, DC: American Psychological Association, 2007.

Vanhoozer, Kevin J. *Is There a Meaning in This Text? The Bible, The Reader, and the Morality of Literary Knowledge*. 1988. Reprint, Grand Rapids, MI: Zondervan, 1998.

Vardy, Peter. *The SPCK Introduction to Kierkegaard*. Rev. ed. London: Society for Promoting Christian Knowledge, 2008.

Verduin, Leonard. *The Reformers and Their Stepchildren.* Dissent and Nonconformity Series 14. Reprint, Paris, AR: Baptist Standard Bearer, 1964.

Via, Dan O. "The Bible, the Church, and Homosexuality." In *Homosexuality and the Bible: Two Views*, 1-39. Minneapolis, MN: Fortress, 2003.

Volz, Carl. "Lex Orandi Lex Credendi." *Response* 14, no. 2 (1974): 17-22.

Waldstein, Michael. "Covenant and the Union of Love in M. J. Scheeben's Theology of Marriage." In "The Hermeneutic of Continuity: Christ, Kingdom, and Creation," ed. Scott W. Hahn. *Letter and Spirit: A Journal of Catholic Biblical Theology* 3 (2007) 139-52.

Walker, Evan Harris. *The Physics of Consciousness: The Quantum Mind and the Meaning of Life.* Cambridge, MA: Basic Books, 2000.

Wallis, Jim. *God's Politics: Why the Right Gets It Wrong and the Left Doesn't Get It.* New York: HarperSanFrancisco, 2005.

———. *Who Speaks for God? An Alternative to the Religious Right; A New Politics of Compassion, Community and Civility.* New York: Delacorte, 1996.

Walsh, Sylvia. *Kierkegaard: Thinking Christianly in an Existential Mode.* Christian Theology in Context. New York: Oxford University Press, 2009.

Walton, Douglas. *Abductive Reasoning.* Tuscaloosa, AL: University of Alabama Press, 2014.

———. "Rules for Plausible Reasoning." *Informal Logic* 14, no. 1 (Winter 1992) 33-51.

Walton, John H. *Genesis 1 as Ancient Cosmology.* Winona Lake, IN: Eisenbrauns, 2011.

———. *The Lost World of Genesis One: Ancient Cosmology and the Origins Debate.* Downers Grove, IL: InterVarsity, 2009.

Warfield, Benjamin Breckinridge. *The Works of Benjamin B. Warfield.* 1932. Vol. 9, *Studies in Theology.* Reprint, Grand Rapids, MI: Baker, 2000.

Waters, Guy Prentiss. "It's 'Wright,' but Is It Right? An Assessment and Engagement of an 'Emerging' Rereading of the Ministry of Jesus." In *Reforming or Conforming: Post-Conservative Evangelicals and the Emerging Church*, edited by Gary L. W. Johnson and Ronald N. Gleason, 188-210. Wheaton, IL: Crossway, 2008.

Watkin, Julia. *The A to Z of Kierkegaard's Philosophy.* The A to Z Guide Series 157. Lanham, MD: Scarecrow, 2010.

Weaver, J. Denny. *The Nonviolent Atonement.* 2nd ed., Greatly Rev. and Expanded. Grand Rapid, MI: Eerdmans, 2011.

Webber, Robert E. *Ancient-Future Faith: Rethinking Evangelicalism for a Postmodern World.* Grand Rapids, MI: Baker, 1999.

———. *The Younger Evangelicals: Facing the Challenges of the New World.* Grand Rapids, MI: Baker, 2002.

Wells, David F. *The Courage to Be Protestant: Truth-Lovers, Marketers, and Emergents in the Postmodern World.* Grand Rapids, MI: Eerdmans, 2008.

Welz, Claudia. "God – A Phenomenon? Theology as Semiotic Phenomenology of the Invisible." *Studia theologica* 62, no. 1 (2008) 4-24.

Westphal, Merold. "Inverted Intentionality: On Being Seen and Being Addressed." *Faith and Philosophy* 26, no. 3 (July 2009) 233-52.

———. "Onto-theology, Metanarrative, Perspectivism, and the Gospel." In *Christianity and the Postmodern Turn: Six Views.* 2005, edited by Myron B. Penner. Reprint, 141-53. Grand Rapids, MI: Brazos, 2006.

———. *Overcoming Onto-Theology: Toward a Postmodern Christian Faith.* New York: Fordham University Press, 2001.

———. *Transcendence and Self-Transcendence: On God and the Soul.* Bloomington, IN: Indiana University Press, 2004.

Wilcox, Clyde, and Ted Jelen. "Evangelicals and Political Tolerance." *American Politics Quarterly* 18, no. 1 (January 1990) 25-46.

Willard, Dallas. *The Divine Conspiracy: Rediscovering Our Hidden Life in God.* New York: HarperCollins, 1998.

Williams, Daniel K. *God's Own Party: The Making of the Christian Right.* New York: Oxford University Press, 2010.

———. "Prolifers of the Left: Progressive Evangelicals' Campaign against Abortion." In *The New Evangelical Social Engagement*, edited by Brian Steensland and Philip Goff, 200-20. New York: Oxford University Press, 2014.

Wilson, Jonathan R. "Practicing Church: Evangelical Ecclesiologies at the End of Modernity." In *The Community of the Word: Toward an Evangelical Ecclesiology*, edited by Mark Husbands and Daniel J. Treier, 63-72. Downers Grove, IL: InterVarsity, 2005.

Wink, Walter. *The Powers That Be: Theology for a New Millennium.* New York: Galilee, 1998.

Winner, Lauren. "Houses of Worship: Burnt Offerings." *Wall Street Journal*, Eastern edition, November 6, 2009.

Woodberry, Robert D., and Christian Smith. "Fundamentalism et al: Conservative Protestants in America." *Annual Review of Sociology* 24 (1998) 25-56.

Woodbridge, Noel B. "Evaluating the Changing Face of Worship in the Emerging Church in terms of the ECLECTIC Model: Revival or a Return to Ancient Traditions?" *Conspectus: The Journal of the South African Theological Seminary* 5 (2008) 185-205.

———. "Understanding the Emerging Church Movement: An Overview of Its Strengths, Areas of Concern and Implications for Today's Evangelicals." *Conspectus: The Journal of the South African Theological Seminary* 4 (2007) 97-113.

Woodcock, Eldon. *Hell: An Exhaustive Look at a Burning Issue.* Bloomington, IN: WestBow, 2012.

Woods, Tim. *Beginning Postmodernism.* New York: Manchester University Press, 1999.

Woodward, Bob. *Fear: Trump in the White House.* New York: Simon & Schuster, 2018.

Wright, Bradley R. E. *Christians Are Hate-Filled Hypocrites. . .and Other Lies You've Been Told.* Minneapolis, MN: Bethany, 2010.

Wright, N. T. *Jesus and the Victory of God.* Vol. 2. Christian Origins and the Question of God. Minneapolis, MN: Fortress, 1996.

———. *Surprised by Hope: Rethinking Heaven, the Resurrection, and the Mission of the Church.* New York: HarperCollins, 2008.

Wuthnow, Robert. *After the Baby Boomers: How Twenty- and Thirty-Somethings Are Shaping the Future of American Religion.* Princeton, NJ: Princeton University Press, 2007.

Yarnell, Malcolm B. III. "Shall We 'Build Bridges' or 'Pull Down Strongholds'?" *Southwestern Journal of Theology* 49, no. 2 (Spring 2007) 200-19.

Yoo, HeeDuck. "A Critical Analysis of the Preaching Methodology of Prominent Emergent Preachers in the Light of 2 Timothy 3:14-4:2." PhD diss., Mid-America Baptist Theological Seminary, 2014.

Zimmermann, Jens. *Incarnational Humanism: A Philosophy of Culture for the Church in the World.* Strategic Initiatives in Evangelical Theology. Downers Grove, IL: InterVarsity, 2012.

Zovkic, Mato. "Dhelovanje Duha Bozjega u nekscanskim religijama i kulturama." *Vrhbosnensia* 2, no. 1 (1998) 55-83.

www.ingramcontent.com/pod-product-compliance
Lightning Source LLC
Chambersburg PA
CBHW081145230426
43664CB00018B/2811